C++

For Beginners...... Masters

C++

For Beginners...... Masters

Ankit Asthana
Department of Electrical and Computer Engineering
McMaster University
Ontario, Canada

RGS Asthana ***(Editor)***
IT Consultant
Max Healthcare
New Delhi

PUBLISHING FOR ONE WORLD

NEW AGE INTERNATIONAL (P) LIMITED, PUBLISHERS
(formerly Wiley Eastern Limited)
New Delhi • Bangalore • Chennai • Cochin • Guwahati • Hyderabad
Jalandhar • Kolkata • Lucknow • Mumbai • Ranchi
Visit us at **www.newagepublishers.com**

Published by New Age International (P) Ltd., Publishers
First Edition: 2007

ISBN : 81-224-2024-9

Rs. 375.00

C-07-01-1257

Printed in India at Sanjeev Press, Delhi.
Typeset in-house.

PUBLISHING FOR ONE WORLD

NEW AGE INTERNATIONAL (P) LIMITED, PUBLISHERS
(formerly Wiley Eastern Limited)
4835/24, Ansari Road, Daryaganj, New Delhi - 110002
Visit us at **www.newagepublishers.com**

PREFACE

C++ is a general-purpose object oriented programming language with features, such as, economy of expression, modern flow control and data structures, and a rich set of operators. C++ is not tied to any particular hardware or system and it is easy to write programs that will run without change on any machine that supports C++.

The purpose of this book is to provide an introductory text for understanding the C++ language and to empower the reader to write C++ programs. The book also introduces reader to the paradigm of object oriented programming. The main strength and USP of this book is that it is written by a student for students but will be equally useful for intermediate level programmers, and software development professional. The author is in the best position to identify and address issues and areas where a student needs maximum help in understanding the C++ concepts and developing programming skills.

The book is written in an easy to comprehend format and includes inline programs, illustrations, number of well chosen completely solved and tested examples to explain difficult concepts associated with OOP and unsolved exercises to ensure that reader understands both C++ language and underneath algorithms.

The book also covers database concepts including SQL, data structures and explains how to interface C++ programs with any database using Open database connectivity (ODBC); basic windows graphics programming and a write up on Standard Template Library (STL) which is now part of standard C++.

One salient feature of this book is not to fathom the depths of topics such as the Databases, SQL, ODBC, Windows API, the Windows Graphics Device Interface GDI, STL, or any other hardcore technical syntax. Instead, we endeavor to show you how to speedily build real-world applications with only basic knowledge of the Windows architecture. We do know that these are sticky subjects that take many pages to cover appropriately. However, an interested reader can always refer to many other volumes dedicated to such topics.

Author

ACKNOWLEDGEMENTS

I would like to deeply thank the various people who, during the several months in which this endeavor lasted, provided me with useful and helpful assistance. Without their care and consideration, this book would not be possible.

First, I would like to thank my teachers and professors 'Dr T.E. Doyle' 'Lecturer for department of Electrical and Computer Engineering, Mc Master University', 'Mrs. Romi Sharma', Delhi Public School, New Delhi and 'Dr. Peter Smith' 'Associate Dean of Engineering', McMaster University for introducing me to the world of computers and should I say a world of 'C++'.

Second, I would like to give a very special thanks to Susan Visser (IBM DB2 Publishing Manager, Toronto, On, Canada) for the help, encouragement and guidance in completion of the book.

Third, on a personal level I would like to commend the interest, encouragement provided by my mother ('Dr. Geeta Asthana') and sister ('Deepti Asthana') whose support, patience and understanding made this possible.

Forth, I would really like to thank all my friends Chris, Avi, Fahad, Rohan, Jaimy, Helen, Neha and Samina.

Most important, to my dad 'Dr R.G.S. Asthana' who put up his weekends, working hours and his patience throughout the editing and cross-reviewing process which constitutes a rather difficult balancing act.

Author

CONTENTS

PART I

INTRODUCTION TO C++

Part I

CHAPTER 1

INTRODUCTION

AIM

- To enlighten the origin of computers and programming languages
- To elucidate the development of programming languages
- To discuss Object-oriented Languages.
- To explain purpose and plan of the book

OUTLINE

1.1 Evolution of Computers and Programming Languages
1.2 Chronology of Development of Programming Languages
1.3 Object - Oriented Programming
1.4 C++ Programming Language
1.5 Structure of the book

1.1Evolution Of Computers and Programming Languages

We've come a long way since the invention of Charles Babbage's 'difference engine' in 1822 and the period when computers used wires and punch cards for programming purposes. The evolution in the history of computers though began in the early 50's of the nineteenth century. Since then both computers and programming languages written to work on them have expanded manifolds both due to development of new languages and also due to the slow death of older, outdated ones. Computer languages were first composed only of a series of steps to wire a particular program. These resulted into a series of steps keyed into the computer which were then executed one by one. With time, these languages attained many additional features and capabilities, such as, logical branching and objects orientation and this is how we know these languages today.

In the beginning, Charles Babbage's difference engine was made to execute tasks by changing the gears which executed the calculations. Thus, we can say that the earliest form of a computer language was described by physical motion. The next major development occurred when the US Government built the 'ENIAC' in 1942 which used electrical signals instead of physical motion. In 1945, John Von Neumann developed two important concepts:

1. The first was known as the "shared-program technique" stating that the actual computer hardware should be simple and need not be hand-wired for each program, instead, complex instructions should be used to control the simple hardware, allowing it to be reprogrammed much faster.
2. The second concept was referred to as "Conditional control transfer" which defined the concept of 'subroutines'. 'Subroutines' are small blocks of code that can be jumped to in any order, instead of a single set of instructions for the computer to take.

Subroutines were used to branch from one instruction to another in a program based on logical statements such as the 'IF (expression) THEN', and FOR looping construct. This was also one of the major milestone paving the way for the development of 'libraries' of functions commonly used in variety of programming applications. Libraries are used in almost every programming language today.

The first computing language though was developed in 1949 and was called 'Short Code'. It was used for electronic devices and it required the programmer to change its statements into 0's and 1's by hand. This concept gave birth to machine language. Machine language, in fact, is a system of codes directly understandable by a computer's CPU. Machine code is composed only of the two binary digits 0 and 1.

Every CPU has its own machine language and programming in it was the only way to work on these machines. It was time taking and cumbersome experience to program in machine language, therefore, development efforts were put to find ways to enable working on these computers without knowing the machine language. This showed the way for development of 'assembly languages'. Assembly languages are nothing but a human-readable notation for the machine language that specific computer architecture uses. Machine language, a pattern of bits encoding machine operations, is made readable by replacing the raw values with symbols called mnemonics. This process of conversion of machine to assembly language is made possible with the help of an 'assembler'.

The next milestone was achieved in programming history with the development of 'compilers' in 1951. A compiler is a program that converts another program from some source language (or a programming language) to machine language (object code). The compiler allowed automatic conversion to machine language, i.e., 0's and 1's so that statements could be interpreted and executed by the computer. This resulted in faster programming as the programmer no longer had to work by hand for converting statements into 0's and 1's. A compiler is distinguished from an assembler by the fact that each input statement does not, in general, correspond to a single machine instruction. A compiler may support such features as automatic allocation of variables, arbitrary arithmetic expressions, control structures such as FOR and WHILE loops, variable scope, input/ouput operations, higher-order functions and portability of source code.

With the advances in technology it became viable to introduce computers in business and scientific application, thereby, enhancing importance and power of both computers and programming languages. The following section outlines the salient events in history in chronological order which lead to the development of various programming languages.

1.2 Chronology of Development of Programming Languages

This section outlines the salient events in history in chronological order which lead to the development of various programming languages.

1.2.1 FORTRAN

Fortran also known 'FORTRAN' is one of the oldest programming language. The language was originally developed in the 1950s and is still seriously used, particularly in parallel programming applications. The language derives its name from the words 'Formula Translator/Translation'. Today, this language is considered outdated as it only included the 'IF', 'DO', and 'GOTO' statements, but at the time, these commands were a huge step forward. The basic types of data types used today were derived from FORTRAN, which included logical variables, integer, real, and double-precision numbers.

1.2.2 COBOL

Though FORTRAN was good at manipulating numbers, it was not so good at handling input and output requirements, an aspect important to business computing. This lead to the development of 'COBOL' in 1959. 'COBOL's name is an acronym, for 'Common Business Oriented Language', defining its primary domain in business, finance, and administrative systems for companies and governments. COBOL statements had very English-like grammar making it quite easy to learn. These features made it easier to program the business applications and COBOL became the most popular language for the businessmen.

1.2.3 LISP

In 1958, John McCarthy of Massachusetts Institute of Technology (MIT) created the List Processing (or LISP) language. It was primarily designed for Artificial Intelligence (AI) research. The main difference between LISP and other languages was that the basic and only type of data supported was the list, denoted by a sequence of items enclosed in parentheses. LISP is in use even today in certain specialized applications due to its highly specialized and abstract nature.

1.2.4 Algol

Algol was created for scientific use in 1958. In fact, Algol is the root of the tree that not only guided but resulted in the development of languages such as Pascal & C/C++. It was also the first language with a formal grammar, known as 'Backus-Naar Form' or BNF. Algol was first language to introduce recursive calling of functions but its next version called 'Algol 68' was packed with too many features and thus became difficult to use. These limitations of 'Algol' lead to the development of simple and compact languages like Pascal.

1.2.5 APL

APL is acronym for "A Programming Language" or "Array Processing Language". It was invented in 1962 by Kenneth E. Iverson. Iverson received the Turing Award in 1979 for his work. APL has evolved over time and has changed significantly from the original language described by Iverson in his book.

1.2.6 Simula

In 1962, Simula introduced the object-oriented programming paradigm and thus can be considered the first and true object-oriented programming language and a predecessor to Smalltalk, C++, Java, and all modern class-based object-oriented languages. As its name implies Simula was, primarily, designed for facilitating development of application program for carrying out simulations, and had the framework for many of the features of object oriented languages present today.

1.2.7 Basic

Kurtz and John Kemeny co-developed BASIC in 1964. BASIC belongs to a family of high-level programming languages. Originally devised as an easy-to-use tool, it became very popular on home microcomputers in the 1980s, and remains popular to this day. BASIC's acronym stands for Beginner's All-purpose Symbolic Instruction.

1.2.8 PL/I

In 1968, PL/I ("Programming Language One", pronounced "pee el one") emerged in the market. It was designed for scientific, engineering, and business applications. The language syntax was English-like and hence suited for describing complex data formats, with a wide set of functions available to verify and manipulate them. The principal domain of PL/1 was data processing. PL/I supported both recursion and structured programming.

1.2.9 Pascal

Development of Pascal began in 1968 by Niklaus Wirth. Pascal derived best features of the languages in use at the time, viz., COBOL, Fortran, and Algol. Pascal also improved the "pointer" data type, a very powerful feature of any language that implements it. It also added a '**Case**' statement that allowed instructions to branch like a tree in such a manner:

```
Case expression of
    expression-value-1:
        statements to execute...
    expression-value-2:
        statements to execute...
End
```

Pascal also supported dynamic variables, which could be created while a program was being run through the NEW and DISPOSE commands. The combination of features, input/output and solid mathematical features made Pascal a highly successful language. Pascal did not implement dynamic arrays, or groups of variables, which proved to be needed and led to its downfall. Niklaus Wirth tried to bridge the gap and created Modula-2 - a successor to Pascal, but by the time it appeared, C had already gaining popularity and had become a established language.

1.2.10 Ada

'Ada' is a structured and statically typed programming language. It was designed by Jean Ichbiah of 'Cii Honeywell Bull' in the 1970s. It is similar to C or C++. 'Ada' was named after 'Ada, Lady Lovelace', often thought to be the first computer programmer. 'Ada' targeted at embedded and real-time systems. In

1983, the Department of Defense, U.S.A. directs that all new "mission-critical" applications be written in Ada. The Ada 95 revision included better support for systems, numerical, and financial programming.

1.2.11 SQL

Structured Query Language (SQL) is the most popular computer language used to create, modify and query databases. Technically, SQL is a declarative computer language for use with "quasi-relational databases".

1.2.12 C

The C programming language was developed in the early 1970s by Ken Thompson and Dennis Ritchie. C was originally developed for and implemented on the UNIX operating system, on a PDP-11 computer. Ritchie restructured the language and rewrote the compiler and gave his new language the name "C" in 1972. In fact, 90% of UNIX was then written in C. C uses pointers extensively and was built to be fast and powerful but in the process it became cryptic and hard to read.

C code is portable, i.e., it is not tied to any particular hardware/computer or operating system. C combines the elements of high-level languages with the functionality of assembly language. C makes it easy to adapt software for one type of computer to another. C was a direct descendant of the language B. The language B was developed by Ken Thompson in 1970 for the new UNIX OS. By the mid 90's, the Internet had become part of our society. With the start of the new millennium, the Internet is as common as the television, and with it comes new languages designed specifically for its use.

1.2.13 Java

In the early 1990's, interactive TV was believed to be the technology of the future. Sun Microsystems decided to develop a new language for the interactive TV which should be portable (i.e., it can run on many types of machines). This language led to the development of Java. In 1995, Netscape licensed Java for use in their internet browser. This development became a milestone in Java attaining the status of the language of the future. Java was easy-to-learn and use, therefore, it easily became popular among faculty members, students, and everyone else.

1.2.14 Visual Basic

Even with all the new languages introduced, use of BASIC continues to grow. Visual Basic is often taught as a first programming language today as it is based on the BASIC language developed in 1964. Microsoft has extended BASIC in its Visual Basic (VB) product. The heart of VB is the form, or blank window on which you drag and drop components such as menus, pictures, and slider bars.

These items are known as "widgets." Widgets have properties (such as its color) and events (such as clicks and double-clicks) and are central to building any user interface today in any language.

1.2.15 Perl

Perl has often been described as the "duct tape of the Internet," because it is most often used as the engine for a web interface or in scripts that modify configuration files. It has very strong text matching functions which make it ideal for these tasks. Perl was developed by Larry Wall in 1987.

1.2.16 C#

An object-oriented and type-safe programming language supported by Microsoft for use with the .NET Framework. C# (pronounced "see-sharp") was created specifically for building enterprise-scale applications using the .NET Framework. It is similar in syntax to both C++ and Java and is considered by Microsoft as the natural evolution of the C and C++ languages.

Programming languages have been under development for years and this process will continue for many years to come. They got their start with a list of steps to wire a computer to perform a task. These steps eventually found their way into software and began to acquire newer and better features. The first major languages were intended for special purposes while the languages of today are differentiated by the way they are programmed in, as they can be used for almost any purpose and perhaps the languages of tomorrow will be more natural with the invention of quantum and biological computers. The entire evolution of programming languages is also shown in table 1.1 in chronological order.

Table 1.1: Evolution of Programming Languages

Year	Name of the Language	Brief Description
1957	FORTRAN	Mathematical FORmula TRANslating system developed by John Backus and his team.
1958	FORTRAN II	Upgraded to handle subroutines and links to assembly language.
1959	LISP 1.5 COBOL	Created by the Conference on Data Systems and Languages (CODASYL).
1960	ALGOL 60	It was First block-structured language.
1960 - 1962	APL	Kenneth Iverson begins work on APL (A Programming Language). It uses a specialized character set that, for proper use, requires APL-compatible I/O devices.
1964	APL\360	Implemented
	BASIC	BASIC was invented by Prof. John G. Kemeny and Thomas E. Kurtz at Dartmouth College in 1964 to

		give students a simple programming language that was easy-to-learn.
1966	FORTRAN 66	Comes in Market
	LOGO	LOGO is best known for its "turtle graphics."
1968	ALGOL 68	ALGOL 68 proves difficult to implement.
1970	SMALLTALK	Work on Prolog and SMALLTALK begins.
1972	C	Dennis Ritchie produces C.
1975	Tiny BASIC	Bob Albrecht and Dennis Allison (implementation by Dick Whipple and John Arnold) runs on a microcomputer in 2 KB of RAM. Bill Gates and Paul Allen write a version of BASIC that they license to Micro Instrumentation and Telemetry Systems on a per-copy royalty basis.
	RATFOR--RATional FORTRAN	It is a preprocessor that allows C-like control structures in FORTRAN. RATFOR is used in Kernighan and Plauger's "Software Tools," which appears in 1976.
1978	AWK	A text-processing language named after the designers, Aho, Weinberger, and Kernighan.
	UCSD Pascal	Kenneth Bowles makes Pascal available on PDP-11 and Z80-based computers.
	FORTRAN 77	The ANSI standard appears.
1980	Smalltalk- and Modula-2	Emerge
	C++	Bjarne Stroustrup develops a set of languages -- collectively referred to as "C With Classes" -- that serve as the breeding ground for C++.
1982	ISO Pascal & PostScript	Emerge
1983	Smalltalk-80	Goldberg et al publish its implementation.
	Ada	Its name comes from Lady Augusta Ada Byron, the first computer Programmer because of her work on Charles Babbage's analytical engine.
1983-1984	C	Microsoft and Digital Research release the first C compilers for microcomputers.
	C++	The name C++ is coined by Rick Mascitti and its implementation emerges.
	Borland's Turbo Pascal	Comes in the market and becomes extremely popular.
1986	Turbo Prolog	Borland releases Turbo Prolog.
1986	Smalltalk/V	The first widely available version of Smalltalk for microcomputers
	Object Pascal	Apple releases it for the Mac.
1987	Perl	Perl was developed by Larry Wall and has very

		strong text matching functions.
1989	ANSI C	The specification is published.
	C++ 2.0	The 2.0 version adds features such as multiple inheritance and pointers to members.
1990	C++ 2.1	An Annotated C++ Reference Manual by B. Stroustrup et al, is published. This adds templates and exception-handling features.
1991	Java	Java is an object-oriented programming language developed primarily by James Gosling and colleagues at Sun Microsystems. The language, initially called Oak (named after the oak trees outside Gosling's office), was intended to replace C++, although the feature set better resembles that of Objective C
1993	Object-oriented COBOL	ANSI releases the first-draft proposal.
1998	C++	The C++ programming language standard was ratified in 1998 as ISO/IEC 14882:1998, the current version of which is the 2003 version, ISO/IEC 14882:2003.
2000	C#	C# (pronounced "See-Sharp" was developed by Microsoft fo ruse with its .net platform.

1.3 Object-Oriented Programming

In the late 1970's, a new programming paradigm known as 'Object Oriented Programming', or OOP was developed. Objects are pieces of data that can be packaged and manipulated by the programmer. Bjarne Stroustrup liked this method and developed extensions to C known as "C with Classes." This set of extensions developed into the full-featured language C++, which was released in 1983.

OOP languages are the natural choice for implementation of an Object-Oriented Design because they directly support the object notions of classes, inheritance, information hiding, and dynamic binding. An object-oriented system programmed with an OOP language results in least complexity in the system design and implementation, which can lead to an increase in maintainability.

Object-oriented applications can be written in conventional languages but they are much easier to write in languages especially designed for OO programming. OOP language can

be divided into two categories: hybrid languages and pure OO languages. Hybrid languages are based on some non-OO model that has been enhanced with OO concepts.

C++ (a superset of C), Ada 95, and CLOS (an object-enhanced version of LISP) are sometimes referred to as hybrid languages. Pure OO languages are based entirely on OO principles; Smalltalk, Eiffel, Java, and Simula are pure OO languages. The emergence of high level languages and their relationship with the hardware is shown in figure 1.1.

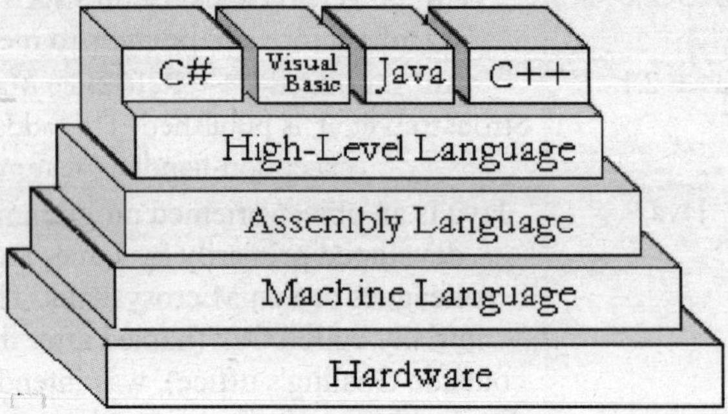

Figure 1.1: Emergence of high level languages

1.4 C++ Programming Language

C++ (pronounced "see plus plus") is a general-purpose computer programming language. It supports procedural programming, data abstraction, object-oriented and generic programming. Prior to 1983, Bjarne Stroustrup added features to C and formed what he called "C with Classes". He combined the Simula's use of classes and object-oriented features with the power and efficiency of C. Further, enhancements started with the addition of classes, followed by, among many features, virtual functions, operator overloading, multiple inheritance, information hiding, polymorphism, dynamic binding, templates and exception handling.

During the 1990s, C++ became one of the most popular commercial programming languages. In particular, "ARM C++" added exceptions and templates, and ISO C++ added RTTI, namespaces, and a standard library. C++ was originally designed for the UNIX system environment. With C++, programmers could improve the quality of code they produced and reusable code was easier to write. The C++ programming language standard was ratified in 1998 as ISO/IEC 14882:1998, the current version of which is the 2003 version, ISO/IEC 14882:2003.

C++ was designed to organize the raw power of C using OOP, but maintain the speed of C and be able to run on many different types of computers. In terms of number of applications, the most popular OO language in use is C++. One advantage of C++ for commercial use is its syntactical familiarity to C, which many programmers already know and use; this lowers training costs. One disadvantage of C++ is that it lacks the level of polymorphism and dynamics most OO programmers expect.

1.5 Structure of the book

The book has been divided into four parts. Part I includes seven chapters which introduce the basics of procedural programming in C++. Part II of the book comprises of two chapters which introduce the concept of object oriented programming and its applications. Part III covers 'Data structures' and 'Files' in C++ and Part IV of the book comprises of basic concepts of databases; SQL also known as 'Structured Query Language' - A database sublanguage used in querying, updating, and managing relational databases; SQL also known as 'Structured Query Language'. The book includes appendices, viz., ASCII table which is a standard code used for information interchange and communication between data processing systems; the Standard Template Library (STL) - a general-purpose C++ library of algorithms and data structures, container classes, and iterators; the list of recommended compilers to be used when dealing with C++, graphics programming in C++ and number systems.

To enable beginners to grasp and master complex concepts in topics, such as, Pointers and data structure, we have provided step by step pictorial representation of the logic. The unsolved exercises at the end of each chapter have been created from a set of very common and unique questions to test how much you have learned from the chapter. These are followed by the 'Programming Projects' and the 'Let us revise' sections to enhance the books usefulness in the class room environment.

The book is also accompanied with electronic C.D. which consists of source code of all solved examples and an animated tutorial to facilitate reader to understand data structures better.

Notes

Part I

CHAPTER 2

FUNDAMENTALS OF C++

AIM

- Introduce the fundamentals of C++.
- Learn about types of expressions and operations used in programming languages.
- Learn the concept of program creation and optimization.

OUTLINE

2.1 Introduction
2.2 Our first C++ program
2.3 Comments
2.4 Tokens in C++
2.5 Escape Sequences
2.6 The cin statement
2.7 Mathematical expressions in C++
2.8 Relational Operators
2.9 Logical Operators
2.10 Types of operators
2.11 Output Manipulators
2.12 The 'conio.h' header file
2.13 Errors
2.14 Type Conversion & Type Casting
2.15 Unsigned Datatypes
2.16 Postfix and Prefix Operators
2.17 What is an algorithm?
2.18 Flow-charts
2.19 Building your own programs.
2.20 Review Exercise
2.21 Programming Project
2.22 Let us revise!

2.1 Introduction

As we already know, C++ was developed by Bjarne Stroustrup of AT&T Bell Laboratories in the early 1980's, and was based on the C language. The name is a pun - "++" is a syntactic construct used in C (to increment a variable). The language 'C' is a subset of C++ written before C++ came into being. In this chapter, we will introduce the fundamental concepts of C++ and then slowly move towards creating our own C++ programs.

2.2 Our first C++ program

Look at the program 2.1. This program prints the message 'My first C++ program' on the screen.

Program 2.1

```
# include<iostream.h>

void main()
{
 cout<<" My first C++ Program";
}
```

Let us observe this piece of code carefully. This program consists of a function called 'main'. Functions are one of the fundamental building blocks of C++. We will learn more about them in later chapters but for now all we need to know is that every C++ program has a 'main' function. It is from this function where the execution of the program starts. The round brackets '()' after the word 'main' are known as 'parenthesis' and they tell the compiler that this is a function and not a variable. They are followed by '{}' curly braces. The first curly bracket '{'begins the function and its counterpart '}' is used to delimit the function. They can be compared to the BEGIN and the END keywords in some other programming languages.

Functions have the following general syntax.

Syntax:

```
return_type main()
{
.............
 body of the function
 ............
}
```

As of now, we will always be using the key word 'void' as the return type when referring to function 'main'. Now let us come to the piece of code inside the function or to the function body. In the body of the function, we have used the program statement 'cout<<" My first C++ Program";'. Program statements instruct the computer to execute a desired operation. Both these statements tell the compiler to display the quoted text on the screen. So when this program is executed we will observe the following footage on the screen:

OUTPUT SCREEN

```
My first C++ Program
```

The semicolon after every program statement marks the end of the program statement. Forgetting the semi colon will result in a syntax error. So we should always remember to use them.

Now let us look at the first line of the program '# include<iostream.h>'. This statement is a preprocessor directive. A preprocessor directive is an instruction to the compiler. A part of the compiler known as the 'preprocessor' deals with these directives before the actual compilation process of the program begins. The preprocessor directive '#' include tells the compiler to insert another file into the source file. As a result of this the compiler replaces the '# include' directive with the contents of the file indicated. There exist many such preprocessor directives; all preprocessor directives begin with the '#' sign.

The type of file included by '#include' is defined as a header file, 'iostream' is an example of a header file and deals with the basic input/output operations and contains information about 'cout' that is necessary for our program. Header files usually have the '.h' extension. They are predefined in the compiler but we can also create our own header files.

2.3 Comments

Comments make programming simple. They not only help us to understand a piece of code written by some one else better but also help in writing ones own program specially in large programs where one needs to keep track of what's going on. Comments help in increasing the program readability and increase program's maintainability. In C++ comments can be given in two ways:

a) Single line comments: They start with // (double slash) symbol and terminate at the end of the line.

E.g.:

int a ; // declares the variable 'a' of integer type

b) Multi line comments: Start with a /* symbol and terminate with a */ symbol. For example,

```
/* This is a multi line
comment */
```

2.4 Tokens in C++

A Token is a group of characters that logically belong together. It is the smallest individual unit in a program. For example, look at the following statement:

```
int y=10;
```

The statement declares 'y' to be an integer variable and assigns a value '10' to it. Here 'int', 'y', '=', '10' and semicolon (;) are all referred to as tokens. C++ supports the following types of tokens.

2.4.1 Identifiers

It is the symbolic name given by a programmer for any data item or function. The identifier is a sequence of characters taken from the C++ character set. The rules for the formation of an identifier are:

- Can consist of alphabets, digits and only one special character i.e. underscore " _ ".
- Can start with an alphabet or underscore, but not with a digit.
- C++ is case sensitive language

Variables are also a kind of identifiers. They are the most fundamental part of any language. A variable is a location in the computer memory which can store data and is given a symbolic name for easy reference. Its value can change during the program execution. The syntax for declaring a variable is given below:

```
< data type >< variable name >;
```

In the syntax given above, the 'data type' parameter has to be any one of the data types present in C++. The basic data types available in C++ are given in Table 2.1.

Table 2.1: Basic Data Types in C++

Data Type	Range	Bytes required	Bits (8 bits = 1 byte) Required	Usage
int	-32768 to 32767	2	16	For storing numbers without decimal
long	-2,147,483,648 to 2,147,4836,47	4	32	For storing integers. Has higher range than 'int'.
char	0 to 255	1	8	For storing characters
float	$-3.4 * 10^{38}$ to $3.4 * 10^{38}$	4	32	For storing floating point numbers. Its has seven digits of precision
double	1.7e + / - 308 (15 digits)	8	64	It is used to store double precision floating point numbers.

The size acquired by a variable in the computer memory depends upon whether we are storing it as an integer, a character or a decimal. In other words, a variables size depends upon its data type.

The computer memory is organized in the form of 'bytes'. Each 'byte' is further a collection of even smaller units called 'bits'. We will now discuss the fundamental data types available in C++.

2.4.1.1 Integer variables

An integer variable exists in variable sizes. In Microsoft DOS also known as MSDOS it is 16 bits or 2 bytes long whereas in operating systems like Windows 2000/NT it is found to be 32 bits (4 bytes) long. Integer variables represent integers like 1, 2 and -100. Integer variables as the name suggests do not represent decimals or have a fractional part. They were built to express the idea of '1' using integers and not '1.5'.

Program 2.2 given below declares two integer variables and prints them on the screen.

Program 2.2: To declare two integer variables

```
# include <iostream.h>

void main()
{
  int var1=10;
  int var2=20;
  cout<<" Var 1:"<<var1;
  cout<<" Var 2:"<<var2;
}
```

This is the output one will observe on the screen when this program is executed. All C++ programs run in such MSDOS windows.

Output Screen

Let us now try to understand how this program actually works. We again begin with the header file 'iostream.h' as it contains the necessary definition for using the basic I/O operations in the language. Then we enter the 'main' function from where the actual execution of the program begins. If we notice carefully we have declared two integer variables 'var1=10' and 'var2=20'. As variables are also identifiers, we have to keep in mind to use the guidelines given earlier when declaring variables. To declare variables one uses the basic syntax given below:

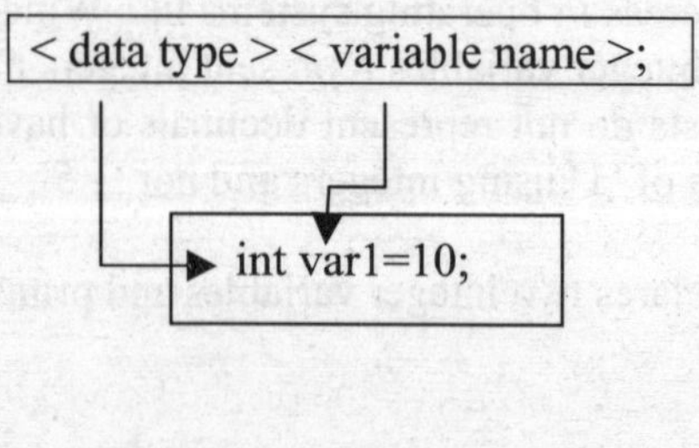

Then we have used 'cout' to display these variables on the screen. The important thing to note is that 'cout' knows how to handle integers and characters. So if an integer is fed into it than it prints the integer as a number and if an alphabet is fed into it, it prints it like a character.

For example,

```
cout << "The total of 7 and 10 is " << (7 + 10);
```

This statement sends the 'string' and 'value' to cout

<u>String:</u> "The total of 7 and 10 is"
<u>Value:</u> value of the expression 7 + 10
<u>Display produced:</u> The total of 7 and 10 is 17

PROGRAMMING TIPS

- Using commas, decimal points, and special signs with integer entries is not allowed and will result in syntax errors.
  For example,
  - <u>Valid</u>: 15 -110 +235 243 -643 +16
  - <u>Invalid</u>: $255.62 23,521 6,282 14.89
- The 'cout' program statement is defined under the 'iostream.h' header file and it is used to display data fed into it using the standard output device

2.4.1.2 Character Variables

Character variables are used to store integers from the range of (-128 to 127) they are also used to store ASCII characters. ASCII which stands for 'American Standard for Information Interchange' is the numerical representation of a character such as 'a' or '@' or an action of some sort. These numbers range from 0 to 127. ASCII character set includes every key present on a keyboard of a computer in numerical form so that it can be read by the computer. For example, the alphabet 'a' is represented by the number '97' in ASCII format. When the C++ compiler encounters a character it translates to the corresponding ASCII code. The entire ASCII table is given in the appendix A of the book. Character variables are stored as character constants and it occupies a byte of the computers memory. Which means a character variable storing the character '1' and an integer variable '1' are not equivalent. Figure 2.1 given below shows how character variables are stored in the computers memory.

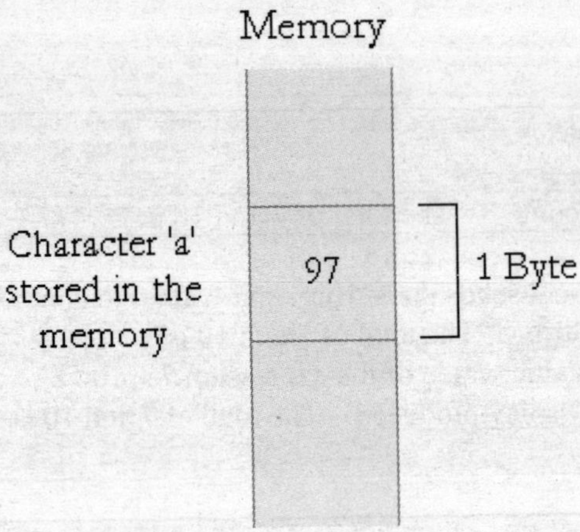

Figure 2.1: Character 'a' stored in the computers memory

Character variables are also declared using the syntax used for declaring integer variables the only difference being that this time the 'data type' changes to 'char'. Program 2.3 given below declares two character variables and prints them on the screen.

Program 2.3: To declare two character variables

```
// Header Files
# include <iostream.h>

// Function 'main'
void main()
{

 // Declaring variables
  char var1='10';
  char var2='20';

 cout<<" Var 1:"<<var1;

  cout<<" Var 2:"<<var2;
 }
```

In program 2.3, we have declared two character variables 'var1' and 'var2' and assigned them the characters '10' and '20' using the assignment statement. If we observe carefully we have used single codes (' ') when assigning characters to 'var1' and 'var2', this is done so that the compiler can differentiate between character constants and integer values.

2.4.1.3 Floating Point Variables

We have already learnt about how the compiler stores integers and characters using the 'int' and the 'char' data types. In this section, we will learn about floating point variables and understand how they are stored in the computers memory. Floating points represent numbers with decimals or they represent those numbers which have a fractional part attached to them for example, 10.2, -10.2 or 2.10. Floating point variables occupy 4 bytes of the computers memory and have a range of about $3.4 * 10^{38}$ to $3.4 * 10^{38}$. Figure 2.2 given below shows how floating variables are stored in the computers memory.

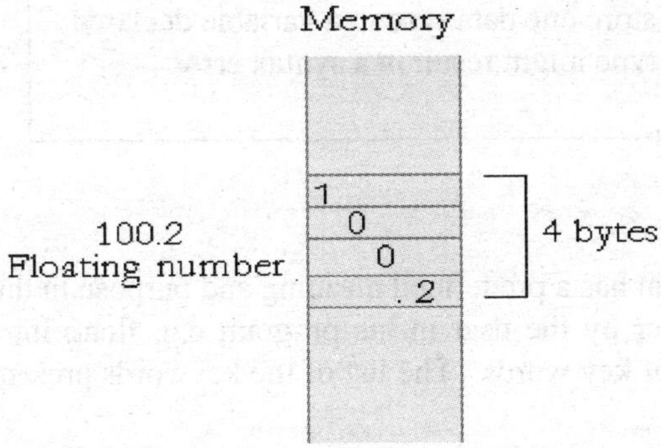

Figure 2.2: Storing floating variables

Program 2.4 given below declares two floating variables 'var1' and 'var2' and displays them on the screen.

Program 2.4: To declare two floating variables

```
// Header File
# include <iostream.h>

// Main Function
void main()
{
 // Floating variables
 float var1=-10.2;
 float var2=10.2;

 // Printing Variables
 cout<<" Var 1:"<<var1;
 cout<<" Var 2:"<<var2;
}
```

COMMON PROGRAMMING ERRORS

- Not declaring all variables used in a program will lead to a syntax error.
- Attempting to store one data type in a variable declared for a different type might result in a syntax error.

2.4.2 Keywords in C++

A keyword is a reserved word that has a predefined meaning and purpose in the language. It cannot be used as an identifier by the user in his program e.g. float, int and so on. Every language has its own set of key words. The list of the keywords present in C++ is given in Table 2.2.

Table 2.2: Keywords in C++

asm	float	register
auto	for	return
break	friend	short
case	goto	signed
catch	huge	sizeof
cdecl	If	static
char	inline	struct

class	int	switch
const	interrupt	template
continue	long	this
default	near	typedef
do	new	union
double	operator	unsigned
else	pascal	virtual
enum	private	void
extern	protected	volatile
far	public	while

2.4.3 Constants in C++

A constant is an expression whose value doesn't change during program execution. A constant can be declared as an integer, floating point or character. Constants can be declared in C++ using any of the following procedures. One can define a constant identifier by using the ' #define' preprocessor directive. It has the following syntax.

Syntax: **#define** *identifier value*

For example,

```
#define PI 3.14159265
#define length 100
```

Once these constants are declared they can be used in the rest of the program as shown in program 2.5.

Program 2.5: Calculating circumference of a circle

```
// Header File
# include <iostream.h>

// Declaring constant PI
# define PI 3.14

// Main Function
void main()
{
 // Declaring Variables
 float circle_circumference;
 float radius=3.0;

 circle_circumference=(2*PI*radius); // Calculating circumference

  cout<<" The circumference of the circle is "<<circle_circumference;
}
```

There is yet another method of declaring constants using the 'access modifier'. It has the following syntax:

Syntax: const <data type of the constant > < name of the constant identifier >;

For example,

```
const float pi = 3.14;
const int length=100;
```

Once a constant is declared any attempt to alter the value of the constant variable will elicit an error message from the compiler. We can use either of the two methods describe above to declare and use constant variables.

2.5 Escape Sequences

Escape sequences are a combination of characters preceded by a code-extension character (also called as escape character). The code-extension character indicates that the succeeding characters are interpreted differently.
Escape sequences are normally used to control printed or displayed output. Some of them will be used very regularly when we start writing programs. The list of various common escape sequences is given in table 2.3.

Table 2.3: Escape sequences in C++

Escape Sequence	Meaning
\a	Alarm
\b	Back space
\f	Form feed (for the printer)
\n	New line
\r	Carriage return
\t	Tab
\v	Vertical tab
\\	Backslash
\?	Question mark

The most commonly used escape sequences are the '\n' and the '\t' sequences. The '\n' escape sequence is used to shift the cursor to the next line where as the '\t' sequence is used to shift the cursor by eight spaces when printing lines of text. It acts like the 'tab' key on our keyboard.

PROGRAMMING TIPS

- Variables with the same data type can be grouped together and declared in one statement
  Format: *dataType variableList;*
  For example,
  ```
  int A1, A2, A3;
  ```
- A good programming practice is to declare each initialized variable on a line by itself.
- C++ also allows us to create same named variables, functions belonging to different data types. We will learn how to do that in later chapters.

2.6 The cin Statement

Just as we have the 'cout' statement to display data on the screen, the 'cin' statement is used to extract data from the user or insert data into a variable. The statement is used with the insertion operators (<<). It is also defined under the <iostream.h> header file and has the following syntax:

```
Syntax: cin>>variable1>>variable2……………;
```

You may observe that we have used the insertion operator repeatedly '>>' in the syntax. This is perfectly valid and is known as cascading of operators.

For example,

```
cin>>variable1>>variable2;
```

Cascading the insertion operators allow us to input multiple variables using a single 'cin' statement. This is the same as using the 'cin' statement twice.

```
cin>>variable1;
cin>>variable2;
```

Cascading can also be done with the extraction operators (<<) used with output statement 'cout'.

To understand how the 'cin' statement works let us create a program which enters two integers from the user and displays their sum on the screen.

Program 2.6: To find the sum of two integers

```
// Header File
# include <iostream.h>

// Main Function
void main()
{

 int a,b;
```

```
cout<<" Enter the two integers";

// Entering the integers
cin>>a>>b;

// Displaying the sum of the integers
cout<<" The sum of the two integers "<<a<<" and "<<b<<" is "<<a+b;
}
```


Note: Both 'cin' and 'cout' refer to the basic input/output devices usually keyboards and monitors.

2.7 Mathematical expressions in C++

A mathematical expression is any expression containing arithmetic operators. The arithmetic operators available in C++ are given in the table 2.4.

Table 2.4: Arithmetic operators in C++

Operator	Usage
+	Used for addition
-	Used for subtraction
*	Used for multiplication
/	Used for division
%	This operator is called the remainder or the modulus operator. It is used to find the remainder when the integer value/variable is divided by another value/variable. This operator cannot be used with floating type variables.

The piece of code given below illustrates use of arithmetic operators:

```
int a = 10, b=3;
cout << " Sum  = " << a + b << endl;
cout << " Difference = "<< a – b << endl;
cout << " Product = "<<a *  b <<endl;
cout << "Quotient = "<<a /b << endl;
cout << " Remainder = "<< a %b << endl;
```

Output Screen

```
Sum=13
Difference=7
Product=30
Quotient=3
Remainder=1
```

COMMON PROGRAMMING ERRORS

- Not using the multiplication operator (*) when required results in an error. For Example, (x+2)(x) this statement is illegal.
- Using the '%' operator with float variables will result in a syntax error.

2.7.1 Precedence of operators

The multiplication (*), division (/) and the remainder operation (%) are given precedence over addition (+) and subtraction (-) operations. All operations of the same precedence are performed from left to right. Parentheses have the highest precedence among all the operators. Table 2.5 further enlightens the concept of precedence of operators.

Table 2.5: Precedence of Mathematical Pperators

S.NO	OPERATOR	PRECEDENCE
1.	( )	Highest precedence given to parentheses. In case of several pairs of parentheses without nesting, they are evaluated from left to right.
2.	*, /, %	Multiplication, division and remainder operators are evaluated after the parentheses. In case of several such operators, they are evaluated from left to right
3.	+, -	Plus and minus are evaluated last. If there are several such operators then they are evaluated from left to right

Let us look at the following examples to understand how we use the precedence of operators.

2.7.1.1 Solved Examples

Example 2.7.1.1.1

Assuming the following declaration, evaluate the value stored in the variable 'result' using precedence of operators.

```
int a=5,b=20,c=10,d=5,e=7;
int result=0;
```

(a) result= a * b + c – d % e;

(b) result= (a * b) + c – d % e;

(c) result= a * b + (c – d) % e;

(d) result= a * (b + c) – d % e;

Solution of 2.7.1.1.1

(a) The value '105' is stored in variable 'result' after the first statement is executed. Figure 2.3 illustrates how this expression is evaluated by the compiler.

result = a * b + c – d % e;

Step1: The first operator we encounter is the multiplication (*) operator with 'a=5' and 'b=20' as its operands. By looking at table 2.5, we see that the (*) operator has higher precedence than the addition operator (+) which happens to be the next operator in the expression. Hence the expression (a*b) is evaluated to obtain '100' as the result.

result = 100 + c – d % e;

Step 2: Now if we again look at table 2.5 we can see that addition and subtraction operators have the same precedence but as the addition operator comes first in the expression the expression '100+c' is calculated and replaced in the overall expression.

result = 110 – d % e;

Step 3: So now we are left with the statement '110 - d % e'. As the (%) operator has higher precedence over the subtraction operator (-). Hence the modulus operator with 'd' and 'e' as operands is executed even though the subtraction operator comes first in the expression.

Step 4: As a result of the preceding steps the value of '105' is stored in the variable 'result'.

result = 105

Figure 2.3: Solution of 2.7.1.1.1(a)

Now solve the remaining parts of the example to obtain the following results:

(b) result = 105

(c) result = 105

(d) result = 145

COMMON PROGRAMMING ERRORS

- Using a variable in an expression before the variable is assigned a value will lead to unexpected result as unintialized variables may have junk value.
- Dividing a variable with zero will lead to an over flow error.
- Forgetting to separate individual data streams passed to 'cout' with an insertion ("put to") symbol will result in a syntax error.

2.8 Relational Operators

An operator is a symbol or letter used to indicate a specific operation on variables or values in a program. In order to carry out a comparison between two expressions (values/variables) one needs to use the relational operators. ANSI C++ standards specify that the result of a relational expression is binary. That means that the result of a comparison operation is either 'True' or 'False'. Relational Operators are generally used in control structures and loops which we will study in later chapters. A list of relational operators supported in C++ is given in table 2.6.

Table 2.6: Relational operators in C++

Operator	Usage	Example	Explanation
<	Less than	A<B	A is less than B
>	Greater than	A.>B	A is greater than B
<=	Less than or equal to	A<=B	A is less than or equal to B
>=	Greater than or equal to	A>=B	A is greater than or equal to B
!=	Not equal to	A != B	A is not equal to B
==	Equality	A == B	Compares the two variables 'A' and 'B' and checks for equality between these variables. If the variables seem to have equal values stored in them then the expression returns the integer value '1' otherwise it returns the integer value '0'. Note: The values '1' and '0' are not any random values but are 'Boolean digits' where '1' corresponds to the expression being true and '0' corresponds to the expression being false.

For Example,

Relational Expression	Result
(2 == 4)	The expression would check for the equality of the two integers '2' and '4'. As they are not equal the expression would return 'false' as the result of the statement.

(1 > 4)	As the integer '1' is not greater than '4' the expression would return 'false' as the result of the expression.
(3 != 0)	As the two operands '3' and '0' are not equal the expression would return 'true' as the result of the statement.

2.9 Logical Operators

The logical operators are used to combine multiple conditions formed using relational or equality expressions. Table 2.7 describes the logical operators present in the language.

Table 2.7: Logical operators in C++

Operator		Usage	Example
&&	AND	The compound condition evaluates to true, if both the conditions in the compound condition evaluate to true	((a>b) && (a>c))
||	OR	The compound statement evaluates to true, if any or both the conditions in the compound condition evaluate to true	((a>b) || (a>c))
!	NOT	It negates the condition That is: • If the condition evaluates to true, it makes it false • If the condition evaluates to false, it makes to true	!(a>b)

For Example,

Logical Expression	Result
((2 == 4) && (7>5))	The expression would evaluate to false as we are using the 'and' operator. For which both the conditions have to evaluate to true but the relational expression (2==4) is not true.

!(1 > 4)	The expression would evaluate to true as '1' is not greater than '4' hence the condition in the parentheses will evaluate to 'false' but as we are using the not operator (!) the resultant condition will evaluate to true. (!(False) = true)
((2 > 0) | | (5<0))	The result of this statement is true. As in this statement we are using the 'or' operator and if any of the two relational conditions evaluate to true so will the resultant expression.

2.10 Types of Operators

Besides the logical and relational operators, we can also divide operators into different groups depending upon the number of operands applicable with an operator. In C++, there exist mainly three data types when divided using this criteria.

2.10.1 Unary Operators

They are the operators which operate on a single operand. Examples of the Unary operators are the 'increment' and the 'decrement' operators or the logical 'not' operator as shown below:

```
X++; // Increases the value stored in X by '1' (Increment operator)

Y--; // Decreases the value stored in Y by '1' (Decrement operator)
```

2.10.2 Binary Operators

They are the operators which operate on two operands. For example, all arithmetic operators and all relational operators AND (&&) and OR (||) are the binary operators as shown below:

```
((X>Y) && (X>Z))  // Binary 'and' operator

((X>Y) || (X>Z)) // Binary 'or' operator
```

2.10.3 Ternary operators

As the name suggests, they are the operators which are applicable on three operands. C and C++ both have only one conditional ternary operator. It is commonly known as short hand if-else statement (?:). It is generally used where conditional looping is required. The syntax for this operator is as follows:

Syntax:

Expression3 = ((condition)? Expression1: Expression2);

If the 'condition' is true than 'Expression3' is assigned the value stored in 'Expression1'. On the other hand, if the condition evaluated is false then 'Expression3' is assigned the value of 'Expression2'.

Example,

```
int y = 3;
int x;
x = ((y > 10) ? 1 : 0);  // Since y is lesser than 10, x is assigned a value of 0
```

2.11 Output Manipulators

Output manipulators are operators used with the insertion operators (<<) to control or manipulate how data is displayed. Manipulators are the most common way to control output formating. They are used to make the printed data look appealing and make programs user friendly. All the ouput manipulators in C++ are defined under the '**iomanip.h**' header file. We will discuss some of the most commonly used output manipulators in the follwing sub-sections.

2.11.1 The 'setw' manipulator

The 'setw 'manipulator is used to set the field width for the next insertion operator. It applies only to the next element inserted in the output. We can use either the left or the right direction to justify the data appropriately in the field. Output is right justified by default. The default field width is just wide enough to hold the expression. The 'setw' operator overcomes this problem by allowing a fixed field width. Let us look at program 2.7 to understand how 'setw' overcomes the problems posed by default field widths.

Program 2.7: Default Field width

```
// Header Files
# include<iostream.h>
# include<iomanip.h>

// Main Function
```

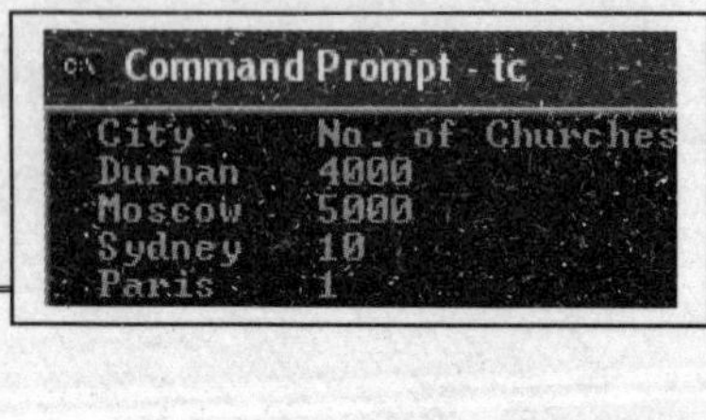

```
void main()
{
 int Durban=4000, Moscow=5000, Sydney=10, Paris=1;
 cout<<"  City "<<"\t No. of Churches";
 cout<<"\n  Durban \t"<<Durban;
 cout<<"\n  Moscow \t"<<Moscow;
 cout<<"\n  Sydney \t"<<Sydney;
 cout<<"\n  Paris  \t"<<Paris;
}
```

The output window of this program is shown along with the program. As one might observe, it is hard to read and compare these numbers. It would be better if they are right justified. Program 2.8 uses the 'setw' manipulator to eliminate the problem by specifying field widths to the respective columns.

Program 2.8: Setting field widths using the 'setw' manipulator

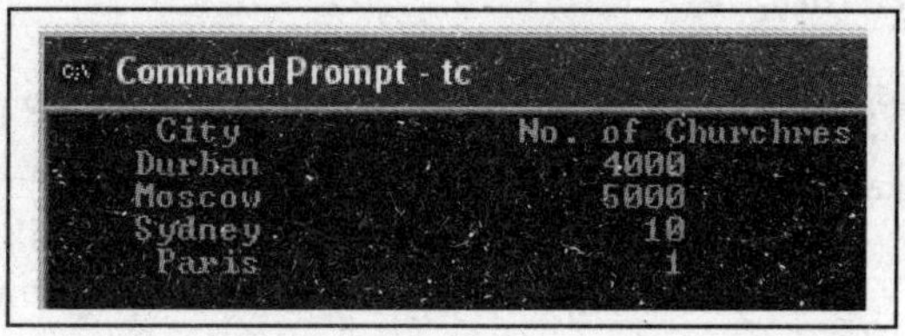


```
// Header Files
# include<iostream.h>
# include<iomanip.h>

// Main Function
void main()
{
 int Durban=4000, Moscow=5000, Sydney=10, Paris=1;
  // Using 'setw' manipulator
 cout<<setw(10)<<"  City "<<setw(30)<<" No. of Churches \n";
 cout<<setw(10)<<"  Durban"<<setw(20)<<Durban<<"\n";
 cout<<setw(10)<<"  Moscow"<<setw(20)<<Moscow<<"\n";
 cout<<setw(10)<<"  Sydney"<<setw(20)<<Sydney<<"\n";
 cout<<setw(10)<<"  Paris"<<setw(20)<<Paris<<"\n";
}
```

2.11.2 The 'endl' Manipulator

The 'endl' operator works exactly like the "\n" escape sequence. The only difference being that we do not use quotes (" ") while using this operator, Just like 'setw', it is also defined under the **'iomanip.h'** header file. When this operator is used, it shifts the cursor to the next line so that lines of text are displayed from the new line.

2.12 The 'conio.h' Header File

The conio.h header file contains a large set of functions that are used to perform input and output operations. Functions defined under this header file can directly access the standard input or output devices. Table 2.8 describes some of the commonly used functions defined under the 'conio.h' header files.

Table 2.8: Functions under 'conio.h'

Functions	Purpose
clrscr()	Clears the screen
getch()	Extracts a character from the user. Can also be used to pause programs.

2.13 Errors

There are three types of errors encountered in any programming language.

a) <u>Syntax Errors</u>
The errors which are traced by the compiler during compilation, due to wrong grammar of the language used in the program, are called as syntax errors.
For Example,

```
cin<<a; // instead of extraction operator the insertion operator is used
```

b) <u>Run–Time Errors</u>: The errors encountered during the execution of the program due to unexpected calculation or input or output, are called as runtime errors.
For Example,

```
a=n/0; // Division by zero
```

c) <u>Logical Errors</u>: These errors are encountered when the program does not give the desired output, due to wrong logic of the program.
For Example,

```
a = b + c;     // The programmer used addition operator though
               // intended to use multiplication operator
```

2.14 Type Conversion & Type Casting

In program 2.9, we have calculated the value of the 'double' variable 'c' using an integer variable 'a' and a float variable 'b'. One might wonder, whether this program compiles successfully or not, as in this program we are using variables of different data types in a single prorgam statement.

Program 2.9: Automatic Type Conversion

```
# include <iostream.h>
# include <conio.h>

void main()
{
  clrscr();
  int a=10;
  float b=4.23;
  double c;
  c=a*b;
  cout<<" c: "<<c;
}
```

C++ is very flexible when treating mixed datatypes. In C++, it is perfectly normal to perform any arithmetic operations on variables of different data types. This is achieved by a process called 'Automatic Type Conversion'. Such a conversion takes place when two operands of different data types are encountered in the same expression. In such a case the variable of lower data type is automatically converted to the variable with the higher data type. Table 2.9, gives the order of data types in C++ according to which type conversions take place.

Table 2.9: Order of data types in C++

Data Type	Priority
long double	Highest
double	↓
float	↓
long	↓
int	↓
char	Lowest

Look at the following program to understand how type casting really works.

Program 2.10: Automatic Type Conversion

```
# include <iostream.h>
# include <conio.h>

void main()
{
clrscr();
int A=10;
float B=4.2;
float C=A/B;
cout<<"C:"<<C;
}
```

So what happens when this program is executed. As we have already learnt that when the compiler confronts with such mixed expressions in same statement it converts the variable belonging to the lower data type to the variable belonging to the higer data type. That is in our program the variable 'A' is converted to a float variable and then divided by the float variable 'B' so that the it can be assigned to the float variable 'C.' If suppose variable 'C' was of type 'double' then both these variables 'A' and 'B' would get converted to type 'double'. The entire process is also explained in figure 2.4.

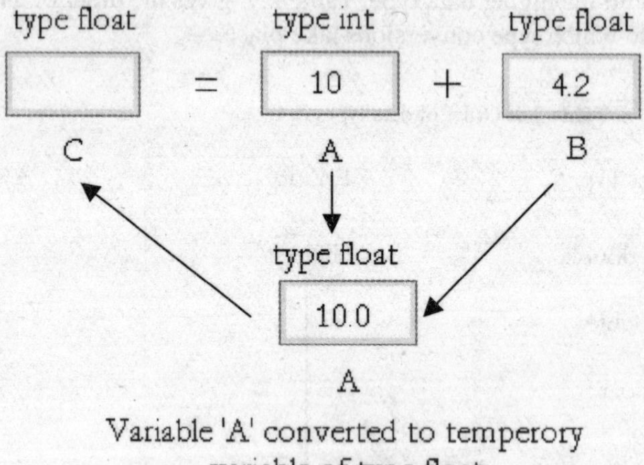

Figure 2.4: Automatic Type Conversion

These conversions are automatically done by the compiler but it is also possible to exercise data conversion manually as opposed to automatic type conversion provided by the compiler. This process of exercising data conversion manually is known as 'type casting'. We will learn about this process in the next section.

2.14.1 Type Casting

Type casting is required as while programming occasionly we might want to convert a value from one data type to another. If in such a case the compiler doesnot do it automatically or without warnings it might be handy if we can perfrom the process manually. A cast, is special programming instuction which specifies what data type to treat a variable as in a given expression. Type casting can be done using the any of the following syntax.

> **Syntax**:
>
> type(expression);
>
> Where 'type' refers to the data type to which the variable/value needs to be casted

To understand how type casting is useful study program 2.11.

Program 2.11: Type casting vs. Type conversion

Type Casting

```
// Header Files
# include <iostream.h>
# include <conio.h>

// Main Function
void main()
{
clrscr();
// Variable Declarations
int A=10;
int B=4;
float C;
// Type Casting
C = (float (A))/B;
// Printing C on the screen
cout<<"C:"<<C;
}
```

OUTPUT SCREEN

Automatic Type Conversion

```
//Header Files
# include <iostream.h>
# include <conio.h>

void main()
{

clrscr();

// Variable Declarations
int A=10;
int B=4;
float C;
C = A/B;
cout<<"C:"<<C;
}
```

OUTPUT SCREEN

As we can observe both these programs give different outputs. The compiler in this case does not automattically type cast the following expression and one need to type cast it manually.

```
C = A/B;
```

2.14.2 Solved Examples

Example 2.14.2.1

Find the value stored in the variables using the declaration given below:

```
int var1, var2, var3;

double var4, var5, var6;

var1 = 120; var2 = 14; var3 = 12.9; var4 = 10.1;
```

(a) var1= var2+ var3; // Find the value stored in var1
(b) var3 = var3/var4; // Find the value stored in var3
(c) var2=var1/var3; // Find the value stored in var2
(d) var6=var1/var3; // Find the value stored in var6
(e) var6=var4*(var2/var1); // Find the value stored in var6
(f) var3=(int)((double)var1*(int) var3 + 1.0)/var4; // Find the value stored in var3

Solution of 2.14.2.1

(a) var1 = 26

(b) var3 = 1

(c) var2 = 10

(d) var6 = 10

(e) var6 = 0

(f) var3 = 142

2.15 Unsigned Data Types

Unsigned data types store non negative (0 and positive) data entries. Unsigned data types provide us with a range of positive values double that of unsigned counterparts. Table 2.9 given below depicts the unsigned versions of the data types as we explained in Table 2.1.

Table 2.9: Unsigned data types

Keyword	Range	Bytes Occupied	Bits Occupied
unsigned int	0 to 65,535	2	16
unsigned long	0 to 4,294,967,295	4	32
unsigned char	0 to 255	1	8

Unsigned data types are used when ever quantities represented by variables are non negative, e.g., when representing day, months or years of a particular date.

2.16 Postfix and Prefix Operators

One unique feature of unary operators, such as, increment/decrement operators is that these operators can be used either as 'prefix' or as 'postfix' operators. In the 'prefix' notation as the word 'pre' suggests, the operator precedes the variable (++ sample_variable;) where as in 'postfix' notation the variable comes after the operator (sample_variable++;). So how does it matter whether we use the prefix operator with a variable or the postfix operator? Program 2.12 explains the difference.

Program 2.12: Prefix, Postfix Notations

Prefix Notation	Postfix Notation

int a= 10;
int b= 11;
int c;
c = a + ++b;
	int a= 10;
	int b= 11;
	int c;
	c = a + b++;

What is the value stored in 'C' in each case? When using the prefix notation the variable is first incremented and then this incremented value is used in the rest of the expression. Where as when we are using the postfix expression the variable is first used in the expression it is in and then it is incremented. Looking at the program we created, when we are using the 'prefix notation' with variable 'b', the variable is first incremented to '12' and then this incremented value '12' is used in the expression 'c = a + ++b' the result is '22'. On the other hand when variable 'b' is incremented using the postfix operator, the variable is first used in the program statement it is in and then its value is incremented by 1 as a result of which a different value for variable 'c' (21) is obtained. Figure 2.5 also explains how postfix and prefix operators differ from each other.

FUNDAMENTALS OF C++

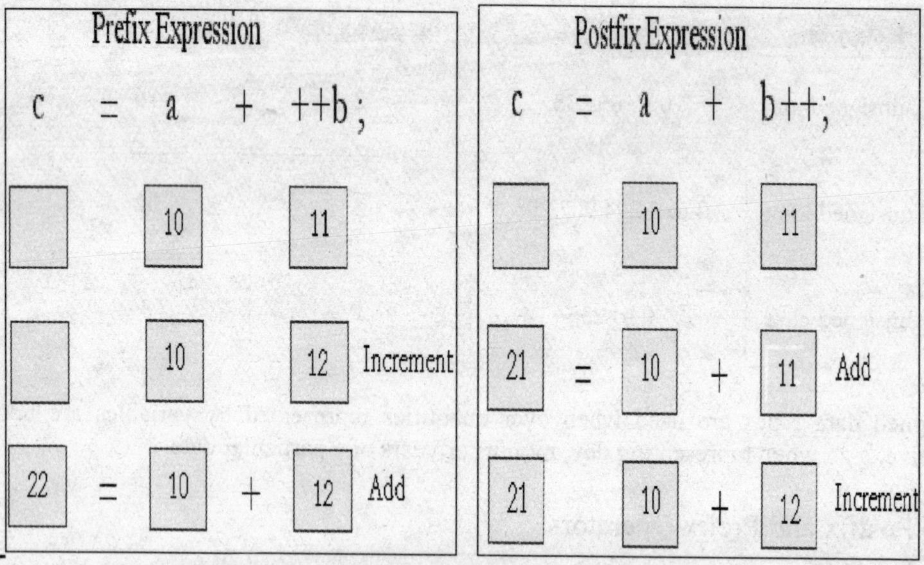

Figure 2.5: The increment operator

2.14.1 Solved Examples

Example 2.14.1 .1

Determine the output for the following piece of code:

```
// Header Files
# include<iostream.h>
# include<conio.h>

void main()
{
// Clears the screen
clrscr();

// Variable Declarations
 int a =10, b=4, c=0;
 c = a % b;
 cout<<" a "<<++a;
 cout<<"\n a "<<( ++a + (a++) + b);
 cout<<"\n a "<<( a++ + (a++) + (b++ * c));
}
```

Solution of 2.14.1.1

OUTPUT SCREEN

This is the output we will observe on our screen when this program is executed. Let us see how we arrive at this output. We begin with ‘a=10’, ‘b=4’ and ‘c=0’. We can refer to these variables as rectangular boxes shown below:

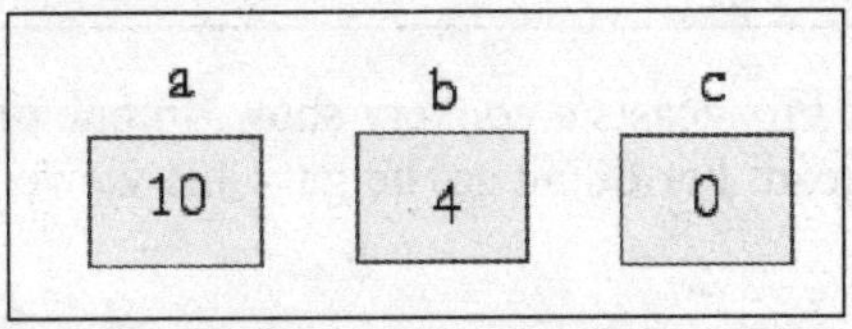

Then we assign ‘c’ the value obtained by the expression ‘a%b’. In this expression ‘a%b’ one might observe that we are using the ‘remainder of operator’. As ’10/4’ leaves ‘2’ as the remainder, so ‘2’ is the value assigned to variable ‘c’.

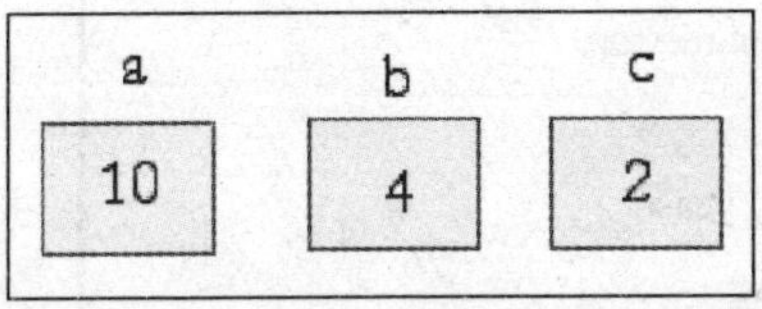

Next, the compiler reads the statement ‘cout<<" a "<<++a;’. As we are using the prefix operator with variable ‘a’, so ‘a’ will first be incremented to ‘11’ and then displayed on the screen.

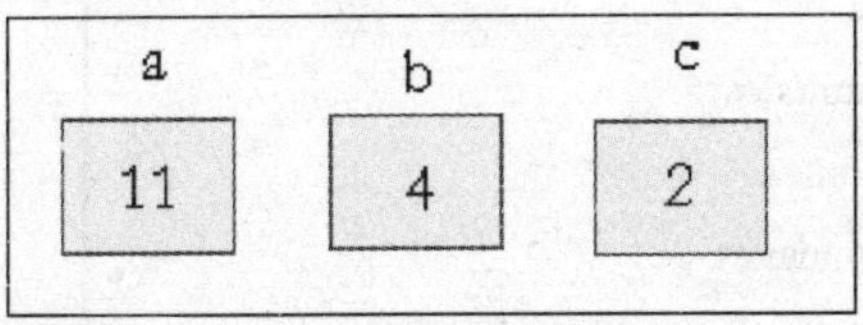

Similarly, the compiler then reaches the second ‘cout’ statement “(++a + (a++) + b);”. Remember that the compiler reads the program statement from right to left as a result of which the compiler will evaluate this expression to ‘28’.

Once this is done, the compiler would then encounter the last ‘cout’ statement ‘cout<<"\n a "<< (a++ + (a++) + (b++ * c)); ’. The compiler will first read the expression ‘(b++ *c).

The result of this expression would be the value we get by multiplying b and c, i.e., '4 * 2 = 8' after which variable 'b' will be incremented to '5'.

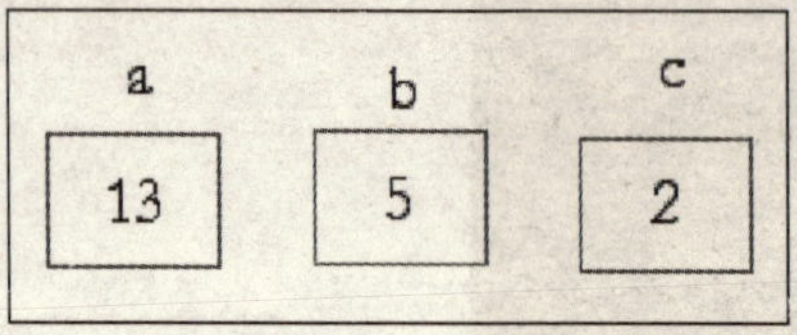

The remaining expression would then look like 'a++ + (a++) + 8;. Next in this expression, we are using the postfix increment operator with variable 'a' twice as a result of which the expression would then evaluate to '35'.

2.17 What is an Algorithm?

A popular television network broadcasts a cookery show. In one of the episodes the host demonstrated how to bake bread. For doing so, he gave his viewers a list of instructions (called 'recipe').

Algorithm Example: Recipe for baking bread

- Preparing mixture of ingredients
    - 1/2 cups sugar
    - 2 cups of dry yeast mixture
    - 1 tablespoon salt
    - 2 packages of dry yeast
    - 1/4 cup shortening
    - 3 cups warm water
    - Knead 5 minutes.
- Final Preparations
    - Punch down.
    - Let rise 30 minutes.
    - Knead 2 minutes.
    - Shape into 4 loaves.
    - Place loaves into greased bread pans.
    - Let rise until doubled.
    - Bake at 350 degrees F for 30 minutes.

In the process, what the host has just demonstrated is an interesting metaphor to understand the concept of algorithm design. An algorithm is basically a set of instructions to solve a given problem or in other words, an algorithm is any well-defined computational procedure that takes some value, or set of values, as input and produces some value, or set of values as output. For example, in our analogy, 'packets of dry yeast', 'sugar', 'water' and 'flour' serve as a part of our inputs where as the 'baked bread' is the manufactured output when the definite procedure is followed.

Let us take a simpler example, say we wish to calculate the area of a circle given the radius of the circle. For doing so, we would follow the following algorithm:

1. Get a value for *r*, the radius of the circle
2. Set the value of *area* to (pi * r^2)
3. Print the value of *area*

So again, in this example, 'r: radius of the circle' serves as an input and the 'area: area of the circle' turns out to be the output for our algorithm. As it might be evident by now, algorithms act as a road map for accomplishing a given, well-defined tasks. Algorithms are usually written in easy to understand language and are independent of any programming languages. Now, let us learn about another important concept required for quality control before we get started with building our own programs.

2.18 Flow-charts

In simple words, flow-charts can be defined as maps or pictorial representations of a well defined process where the various steps in a process are depicted with symbolic shapes and the flow of the process is indicated with arrows connecting these symbolic shapes.

Flow-charts are important as they provide a pictorial view of the program flow and hence provide a better understanding of the complete process or algorithm. While implementing a complex algorithm, different people may have different interpretation of how a process/algorithm is implemented. A flow-chart helps in gaining an agreement about the sequence of steps and how they are implemented.

Let us take a simple example to understand the concept of flow-charts. Figure 2.6 shows the flow chart for calculating the area of the circle.

Each symbol in flow-chart signifies a different operation (see Figure 2.6). The 'terminal' symbol '1: flow-chart key' is used to mark the starting or the ending point of a program, symbol '4' is used to represent any input/output operations taking place for example in the flow chart given in Figure 2.6 the first input/output symbol is used to read the radius of the circle 'r', where as the latter is used to output the area of the circle. A process in a flow-chart is represented by a rectangle (symbol '2':flow-chart key). This symbol usually indicates a process such as a mathematical computation or a variable assignment, e.g., calculation of the area of the circle in our ecample.

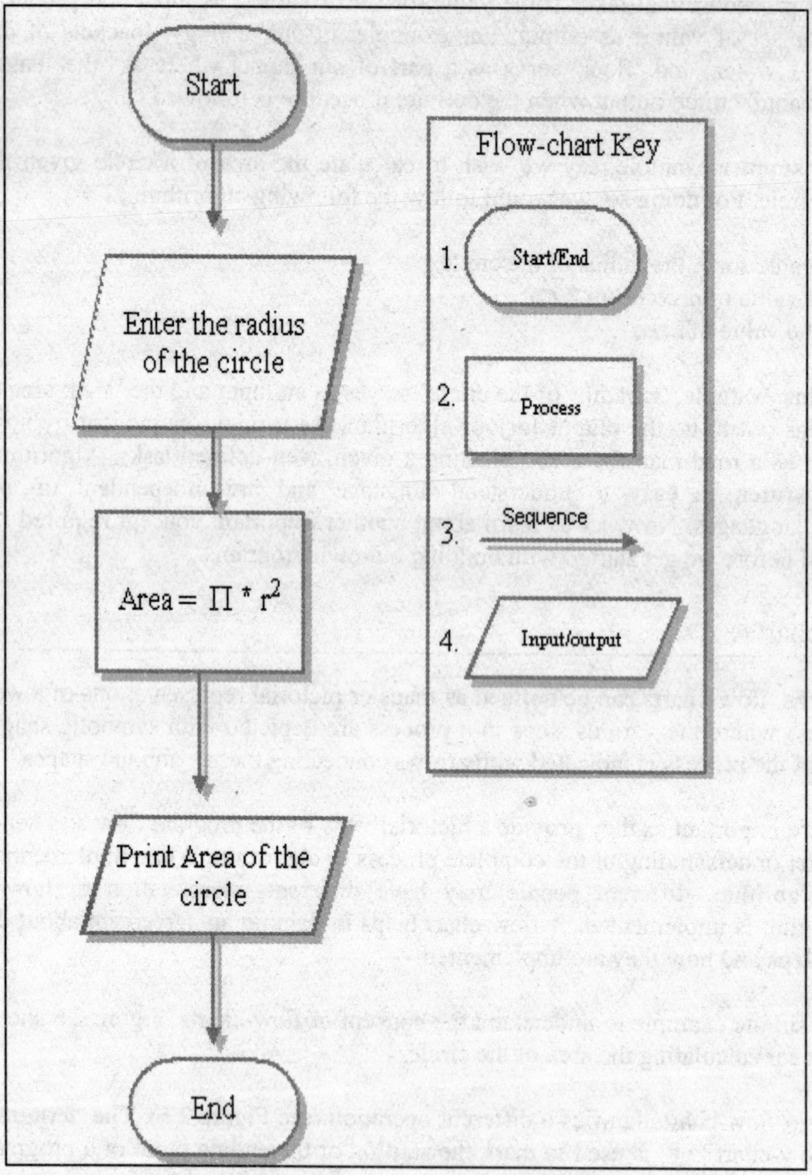

Figure 2.6: Flow-chart: Calculating area of a circle

The entire list of the design elements used to generate a flow-chart along with their pictorial representation and description is given in table 2.10.

Table 2.10 Elements of a Flow-chart

FLOW-CHART DESIGN ELEMENTS

Symbol	Description
	This symbol is used for the beginning and the end of a program or of a module of a program. The words START (alternatively BEGIN) or STOP (END) would typically be entered in this symbol.
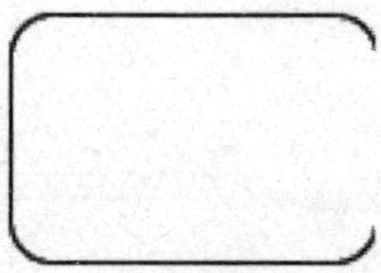	This symbol is used for all processes in a program. A process is generally used for arithmetic/computational operations.
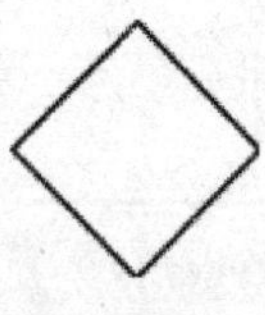	Used to test for a given condition. Testing whether one quantity is larger than another is one example of a testing/decision operation. Similarly, testing whether a specific quantity is positive or zero is another typical test. 'IF...THEN...ELSE statements would typically characterize this test operation
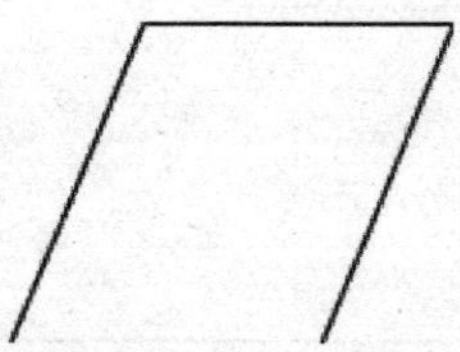	This symbol is used for input or output operations. For example, if we want to input the radius of a circle or output the calculated area of the circle.

2.18.1 Types of Structured Flow-charts

We described sequence flow-chart in the previous section, in this section we will learn about the other two types of widely used structured flow-charts.

Let us start with decision structured flow-charts. The decision structured flow-charts are implemented when the flow of the program depends upon the inputs to the program. Let us take a simple example, say we want to determine whether the integer(X) entered by a user is a positive or a negative integer. The solution to this problem is shown in the flow-chart given in figure 2.7.

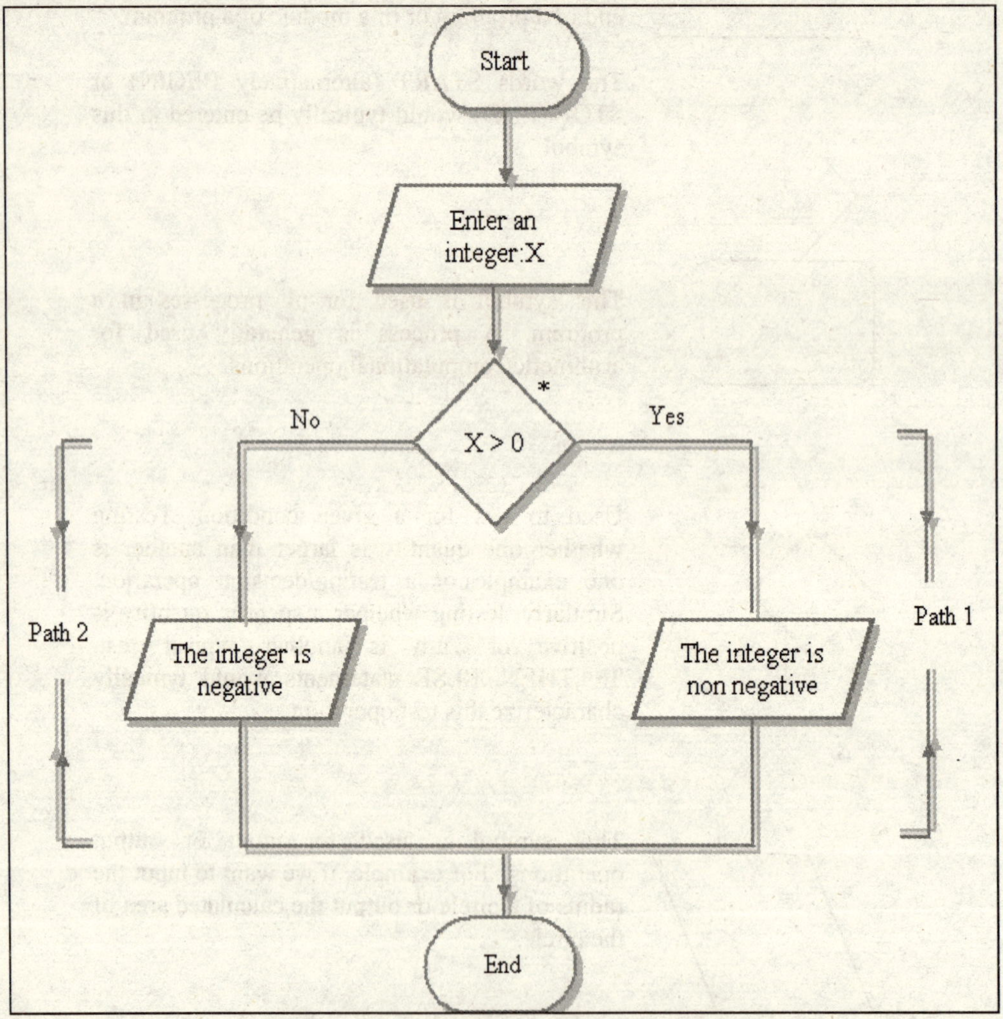

Figure 2.7: Decision structured flow-chart

Note the use of the decision structure '*' in figure 2.7. The flow of the program depends upon the value of the integer 'X' read into the program. If the value of the integer 'X' happens to be greater than zero, then the program follows 'path 1' of the flow-chart where as if the value of the integer 'X' is negative the program follows 'path 2' until it reaches the terminal 'End' symbol. The general form of this type of flow-chart is given in figure 2.8.

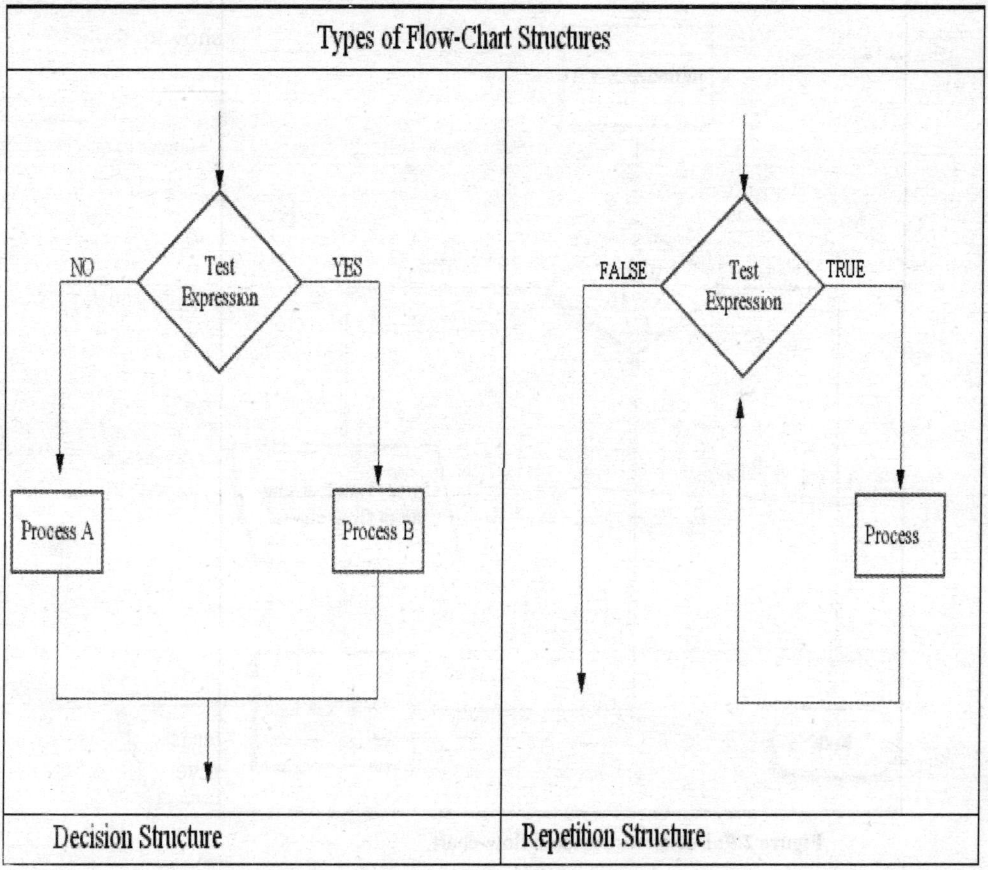

Figure 2.8: Type of structured flow-charts

Let us now look at the structured flow-chart, known as the 'repetitive structured flow-chart'. We take an example involving these flow-chart to understand the concept behind it. Say, we want to display the string, "I am learning about flow-charts" ten times on the screen. For doing so, we would require a repetitive structured flow-chart, the general structure for this type of flow-chart is given in figure 2.8. Customizing this structure we can now form a solution to our problem as illustrated in figure 2.9.

A repetitive structure repeats itself until the test expression evaluates to a true value.

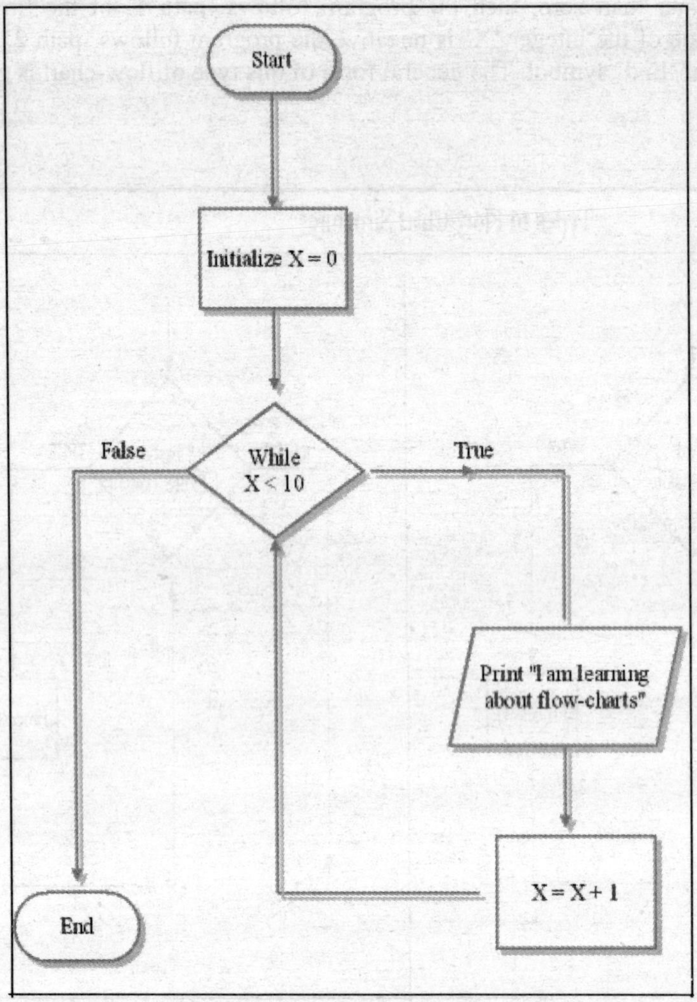

Figure 2.9: Decision structured flow-chart

As shown in figure 2.9, the program written using this flow-chart will print "We are learning flow-charts" until the counter X is less than '10' once this condition evaluates to false the program will terminate.

2.19 Building Your Own Programs

Till now we have learnt the basics of the language. In this section, we will learn how to create and write C++ programs. We will take a few programs in this section to teach you to think like computer scientists. Let's begin with the following example:

Example 2.19.1

Write a program to enter marks of 5 subjects of a student and print the '%' marks scored by the student on the screen.

Solution of 2.19.1

Before writing a program it is very helpful if we can make an outline of how the program would look like in our head. Once we have the outline of the program ready we can use it to create our program. Let us begin our job in a step wise manner.

Step 1: We need to enter the marks of a student in 5 subjects.

Things to do

- Declare 5 integer variables say Mark1, Mark2. . . Mark5.
- Use the 'cin' function defined under 'iostream.h' header file to enter these 5 variables

Step 2: Add all the five variables to find the total marks secured by the student.

Things to do

- Declare a variable 'Total' of type *int*.
- Initialize it to 'zero' to get rid of junk values.
- Assign the value of (Mark1+Mark2…+Mark5) to 'Total'.

Step 3: Find the percentage of marks scored by the student and display it on the screen.

Things to do

- Declare a variable percentage of type *float*.
- Assign the value obtained by (Total/5).
- Display this using the 'cout' function defined under the header file 'iostream.h'.

These are the steps which we need to perform in order to create our program. By noting down these steps (things to do not included) what we have done is that we have developed a 'pseudo code' for our program. A 'pseudo code' is an outline of a program, written in a form that can easily be converted into real programming statements. Pseudo code can neither be compiled nor executed, and there is no real formatting or syntax rules. The benefit of pseudo code is that it enables the programmer to concentrate on the algorithms without worrying about all the syntactic details of a particular programming language. In fact, you can write pseudo code without even knowing what programming language you will use for the final implementation. Getting back to our example, let us now create our program using the pseudo code we developed.

```
// Header Files
# include<iostream.h>
# include<conio.h>

// Main Function
void main()
{

    /* Function clrscr(), to clear the screen */
    clrscr(); // To clear the screen

    /* Variable Declrations */
    int Mark1, Mark2, Mark3, Mark4, Mark5;
    int Total=0;
    float Percentage=0;

    cout<<" Enter the marks scored in five subjects"<<endl;
    cin>>Mark1>>Mark2>>Mark3>>Mark4>>Mark5;

    /* To calculate the percentage*/
    Total = Mark1 + Mark2 + Mark3 + Mark4 + Mark5;
    Percentage = (Total/5);

    cout<<"    The    percentage    scored    by    the    student    is
        "<<Percentage<<"%";
}
```

Example 2.19.2

Write a program which asks the user for the radius of a circle and then uses it to find the area of the circle?

Solution of 2.19.2

Let us begin the program by writing the pseudo code.

Pseudo code

Step 1: Define a constant PI .

Things to do

- Using the '# define' preprocessor directive declare a constant PI = 3.1426

Step 2: Enter the radius of the circle from the user.

Things to do

- Declare a variable 'radius' of type *int.*
- Using the 'cin' statement to input 'radius' from the user.

Step 3: Calculate the area of the circle and display it on the screen.

Things to do

- Declare a *float* variable 'area'
- Assign the value obtained by the formula (PI * $(\text{radius})^2$) to the variable 'area'.
- Display the variable 'area' on the screen with the help of the 'cout' statement.

Program

```
# include<iostream.h>
# include<conio.h>

# define PI 3.1426

//main function
void main()
{
int radius=0;
float area=0;
cout<<" Enter the radius of the circle\n";
cin>>radius;
area= PI * (radius * radius);
cout<<"\n The area of the circle is"<<area;
getch();
}
```

Example 2.19.3

Write a program to calculate the perimeter of a triangle. The length of all the three sides of the triangle will be fed by the user through the keyboard.

Solution of 2.19.3

Again, let us begin with the pseudo code of the program.

Pseudo code

Step 1: Obtain the length of the three sides from the user

Things to do

- Declare three integer variables 'length', 'breadth' and 'width'.
- Using the 'cin' statement obtain values for the 'length', 'breadth' and 'width' of the triangle.

Step 2: Calculate the perimeter of the triangle and display it on the screen

Things to do

- Declare a variable 'perimeter' of type *float* to store the perimeter of the triangle.
- Assign the value obtained by the expression (length + breadth + height) to the variable 'perimeter'
- Using the 'cout' statement display the 'perimeter' on the screen.

Program

```
// Header Files
# include<iostream.h>
# include<conio.h>

// Main Function
void main()
{
 clrscr();

 int length, breadth, height;

 int perimeter=0;

 cout<<" Enter the three sides of the triangle";
 cin>>length>>breadth>>height;

 perimeter = length + breadth + height;
 cout<<" The perimeter of the triangle is "<<perimeter<<" Units";
}
```

If you notice that our pseudo codes are shrinking in size as we move on. Just as while learning how to ride a bicycle we take help of the support wheels and leave them when we know how to ride one. Similar logic applies to pseudo codes. Now that we can solve simple programs let us try a tricky one.

Example 2.19.4

Suppose we have three fractions (a/b), (c/d) and (e/f). Their sum can be obtained by using the formula given below.

$$\frac{a}{b} + \frac{c}{d} + \frac{e}{f} = \frac{adf + bcf + ebd}{bdf}$$

For example,

$$\frac{1}{4} + \frac{1}{8} + \frac{1}{16} = \frac{7}{16}$$

Formula to add three fractions

Write a program which asks the user to enter three fractions. Using the three fractions inputted by the user and the formula given above, find the resultant sum in fractional form and display it on the screen as shown in the example given above.
Hint: Use cascading of operators to simplify program.

Solution of 2.19.4

This problem is slightly more complicated than the previous ones that we have encountered. So how does one approach such a problem? We again begin with writing the pseudo code for the problem.

Pseudo code

Step 1: Obtain the three fractions from the user.

Things to do

- Declare six integer variables 'numerator1', 'numerator2', 'numerator3','denominator1','denominator2' ,'denominator3'.
- Using the 'cin' statement obtain the values for the these six variables from the user.

Step 2: Obtain the sum of the three fraction using the given formula..

Things to do

- Declare two integer variables 'numerator_sum' and 'denominator_sum'.
- Assign the variable 'numerator_sum' the value obtained by

```
((numerator1)*(denominator2)*(denominator3) +
((numerator2)*(denominator1)*(denominator3)  +
((numerator3)*(denominator1)*(denominator2))  +
```

- Assign the variable 'denominator_sum' the value obtained by

```
(denominator1*denominator2*denominator3)
```

Step 3: Display the fraction ((a/b) form) obtained after adding the three fractions.

Things to do

- Display the variables numerator1 and denominator1 on the screen using the 'cout' statement.

Program

```
// Header Files
# include<iostream.h>
# include<conio.h>

void main()
{
clrscr();

// Declaring Numerators (Step I: Pseudo code)
int numerator1, numerator2, numerator3, numerator_sum=0;

// Declaring Denominators
int denominator1, denominator2, denominator3,denominator_sum=0;

// entering the fractions from the user
cout<<" Enter the fractions:"<<endl;

// entering the numerator
```

```
cout<<" Enter the three numerators";
cin>>numerator1>>numerator2>>numerator3;

// entering the denominator
cout<<" Enter the three denominators";
cin>>denominator1>>denominator2>>denominator3;

/* Finding sum using the given formula
   Calculating the resultant numerator (Step 2: Pseudo code) */

numerator_sum = ((numerator1*denominator2*denominator3)+
     (numerator2*denominator1*denominator3)+
     (numerator3*denominator1*denominator2));

// Finding the resultant denominator

denominator_sum = (denominator1 * denominator2 * denominator3);

// Displaying the resultant fraction (Step 3: Pseudo code)
cout<<" So the resultant fraction is"<<numerator_sum<<"/"<<denominator_sum;
}
```


Example 2.19.5

Find the error(s) in the following piece of code:

```
// Program to calculate the product of three integers entered by the user
// Header Files
# include <"iostream.h">

Void main
{
clrscr();
int a;
int b;
int c;
cout>>" Enter the variables whose product has to be calculated /n";
cin <<a<<b<<c;
d = a * b * c;
cout>>" The sum of three integers entered is ">> d;
getch();
}
```

Solution of 2.19.5

When ever we program, errors will take place. So it becomes important that a programmer can understand and be able to remove errors. The common programming errors described in the chapter should help you in developing skills to be able to create efficient programs. This example is a specially designed to include some of the most common errors.

As we know that errors are mainly of three types, i.e., 'syntax', 'logical' and 'runtime' errors. In these errors, syntax and logical are the most common errors. Let us learn how to identify errors using the piece of code given above.

The first error in the piece of code occurs in the statement '# include <"iostream.h">'. This is a syntax error as it is not allowed to use codes (" ") as well as (< >) together when calling header files. The next error occurs in the function header of the main function 'Void main'. This has two errors both being syntax errors. The first error that will occur is that C++ is a 'case sensitive' language and there is a difference between 'void' and 'Void'. Hence the compiler doesn't recognize 'Void' as a keyword. The second error in the statement is that the function header are always followed by parentheses () which are missing in this case. The next few errors occur in function 'main'. They are shown in the table given below.

Statement	Type of Error	Error
clrscr();	Syntax	The function is defined under the header file 'conio.h' but this header file is not included in this program as a result it would result in an error.
Void main	Syntax	C++ is a case sensitive language and the compiler doesn't recognize 'Void' as a valid return type. Also the function header is always followed by parentheses '( )' which define the number of parameters that can be passed to the function.
cout>>" Enter the variables whose product has to be calculated /n";	Syntax	Use of extraction operators (>>) is not allowed with the 'cout'

		statement. Instead we use the insertion operators (<<)
Cin <<a<<b<<c;	Syntax	Insertion operators (<<) are not used with 'cin' statements. Instead we use the extraction operators (>>)
D = a * b * c;	Syntax	Variable'd' has not been declared in function main.
cout>>" The sum of three integers entered is ">> d;	Syntax	Usage of extraction operators (>>).
getch();	Syntax	The function is defined under the header file 'conio.h' but this header file is not included in this program as a result it would result in an error

These are some of the most typical errors one observes while programming. Using a step wise approach is a viable solution to reduce errors while programming.

2.20 Review Exercise

<u>1 Mark/2 Mark Questions</u>

Q1) Header files usually have the following extension
 a) '.h'
 b) '.head'
 c) '.dat'
 d) '.mpeg'
 e) None of the above

Q2) Preprocessor directives are:
 a) instructions to the compiler.
 b) instructions to the preprocessor.
 c) instructions to the operating system.
 d) Both 'a' and 'b' are correct.
 e) None of the above.

Q3) A key word is
a) an example of an identifier
b) a reserved word that has a predefined meaning and purpose in the language.
c) a preprocessor directive.
d) both 'a' and 'b' are correct
e) None of the above

Q4) _____ is/are (an) example(s) of a ternary operator.
a) The conditional operator (?:)
b) The increment/decrement operators
c) All relational operators
d) All relational and logical operators
e) None of the above.

Q5) The logical not operator (!) is an example of
a) an unary operator.
b) a binary operator
c) a ternary operator
d) a relational operator
e) both a and d are correct

Q6) State whether the following statements are true or false:
i) Preprocessor is a part of the compiler and it is from here that all preprocessor directives are assessed.
ii) Header files always have '.h' extension.
iii) A variable of type 'double' occupies '8' bytes and '63' bits of the computers memory
iv) It is not possible to use the 'modulus' operator (%) with float and double variables.
v) ASCII which stands for 'American Standard for Internet Information'

Q7) Find the error(s) in the following piece of code?

```
// Program to calculate the sum of two integers entered by the user
\\ Header Files
# include <"iostream.h">

Void main
{
 clrscr();
// Variable Declrations
```

```
int a;
int b;

cout>>" Enter the variables whose sum has to be calculated /n";
cin <<a<<b;
c = a + b;

cout>>" The sum of two integers entered is ">> c;
getch();
}
```

Q8) Determine the output of the following piece of code:

(a)

```
// Header Files
# include <iostream.h>
# include <conio.h>

void main()
{
 clrscr();
 int var1 = 10.5;
 float var2 = 10.7;
 float var3;
 var3 = (float)var1 + var2;
 cout<<(int)var3<<"\t"<<var3;
 getch();
}
```

(b)

```
// Header Files
# include<iostream.h>
# include<conio.h>

void main()
{
 clrscr();
 int a =2, b=2, c=4;
 c = a % b + c;
 cout<<" a "<<a%3;
 cout<<"\n a "<<++a<<"\t"<<a++;
 cout<<"\n a "<<(c++ + (a-b)/4);
}
```

Q9) Fill the missing blanks (___) to complete the following C++ program:

```
# include <iostream.h>
# include <_____>

/* A program to calculate the length of each side of triangle given
   the perimeter of an equilateral triangle */

___ main()
{
  clrscr();

  float perimeter = 0;

  ___ length = 0;

  cout<<" Enter the perimeter of the triangle";

  cin>> ___;

  length = perimeter/3;

  cout<<" The length of each side is"<<length;

  cout<<" The length of each side is"<<___;

  getch();
}
```

3/4 Mark Questions

Q10) Write a program to calculate the area of the circle using the circumference of the circle provided by the user. **Hint:** Area of a circle = ^ R^2, Circumferance of the circle = 2 ^ R.

Q11) Write a program to enter the currency of five countries from the user. The program should then display the 'currency' and the respective country in the format given below:

Country	Currency
India	Rupee
Canada	Dollar
Nepal	Rupee
England	Pound
Singapore	Dollar

Q12) Write a program to display the following format given below using only 'cout' and output manipulators:

City	Population
New Delhi	10,00,220
London	90,000
California	100,000
Hamilton	9,200

2.21 Programming Project

Hero's formula is used to calculate the area of triangle provided all the sides of a triangle are given. Our programming project is to use the 'Hero's' formula to calculate the area of a triangle. The sides of the triangle 'a', 'b' and 'c' will be inputted by the user. The Hero's formula for calculating the area of a triangle is given below:

Hero's formula: A formula for calculating the area of a triangle:

A = *s*(*s* a formula for the area of a triangle:

$$\mathbf{A = \sqrt{(s(s - a)(s - b)(s - c))}}$$

where *a, b*, and *c* are the lengths of the sides of the triangle,

's' is the half perimeter (*s = (Perimeter of triangle)/2)*.

2.22 Let us revise!

- ✓ There are three basic types of data recognized by C++: 'integer', 'floating-point' and 'character' data types.
- ✓ Every variable in a C++ program must be declared to inform compiler to allocate suitable space based on the type of variable.
- ✓ A simple C++ program containing declaration statements has the following format:

```
// Header Files
# include <iostream.h>

// Main function
void main()
{
    ....
    declaration statements;
    ....
    ....
    other program statements;
}
```

- ✓ A preprocessor directive is an instruction to the compiler. A part of the compiler known as the 'preprocessor' deals with these directives before the actual compilation process of the program begins.
- ✓ The type of file included by '#include' is defined as a header file. Header files usually have the '.h' extension. They are predefined in the compiler but we can also create our own header files.
- ✓ Comments help in increasing the program readability and increase program's maintainability. In C++, comments can be given in two ways:

  (i) Single Line Comments: They start with // (double slash) symbol and terminate at the end of the line.

  (ii) Multi Line Comments: Start with a /* symbol and terminate with a */ symbol.

- ✓ A Token is a group of characters that logically belong together. It is the smallest individual unit in a program

- ✓ A variable is a location in the computer memory which can store data and is given a symbolic name for easy reference. Its value can change during the program execution.

- ✓ There are three fundamental data types recognized by C++. There are the 'integer', 'floating-point' and the character data types.

- ✓ Integer variables represent integers like 1, 2 and -100.

- ✓ Character variables are used to store integers from the range of (-128 to 127) they are also used to store ASCII characters.

- ✓ ASCII which stands for 'American Standard for Information Interchange' is the numerical representation of a character such as 'a' or '@' or an action of some sort.

- ✓ Floating points represent numbers with decimals or they represent those numbers which have a fractional part attached to them for example, 10.2, -10.2 or 2.10.

- ✓ A keyword is a reserved word that has a predefined meaning and purpose in the language.

- ✓ A constant is an expression whose value doesn't change during program execution. It can be declared using any of the following two methods:

  (i) The '#define' preprocessor directive:
  One can define a constant identifier by using the ' #define' preprocessor directive it has the following syntax:
  Syntax: **#define** *identifier value*

  (ii) The 'const' access modifier:
  The 'const' access modifier can also be used to declare constant identifiers. It is done using the following syntax.
  Syntax: const <data type of the constant > < name of the constant identifier >;

- ✓ Escape sequences are a combination of characters preceded by a code-extension character (also called as escape character)

- ✓ Output manipulators are operators used with the insertion operators (<<) to control or manipulate how data is displayed

✓ When the compiler confronts mixed expressions in same statement it converts the variable belonging to the lower data type to the variable belonging to the higer data type. This process is known as automatic type conversion. It is also possible to type cast a variable manually for special program needs.

Notes

Part I

CHAPTER 3

CONTROL STRUCTURES

AIM

- To introduce the concept of control structures.
- To be able to use the conditional structure: if then else.
- To understand and use looping constructs for, while loop.
- Learn about 'multiple selection' using the switch selection statement.

OUTLINE

3.1 Introduction
3.2 Conditional structure: if then else
3.3 Repetitive structures or loops
3.4 Bifurcation of control loops
3.5 The Selective Structure: *switch*
3.6 Review Examples
3.7 Review Exercise

3.1 Introduction

A program control flow is usually not limited to execute a linear sequence of instructions. During execution of a program the programmer might want to use a set of code repeatedly or may want to jump or branch to another set of instructions based on certain conditions. Let us take up an example, suppose you want to display your name 5 times on the screen then based upon your current knowledge you would generate the following piece of code.

```
// Header Files
# include <iostream.h>
# include <conio.h>

void main ()
{
 clrscr();
 cout<< "My name is Ankit Asthana"<<endl;
 cout<< "My name is Ankit Asthana"<<endl;
 cout<< "My name is Ankit Asthana"<<endl;
 cout<< "My name is Ankit Asthana"<<endl;
 cout<< "My name is Ankit Asthana"<<endl;
 getch();
}
```

It might acceptable if we have to do this 5 times but what happens if we want to display out name a hundred times on the screen. Then in order to achieve this we would have to repeat this statement 'cout<< "My name is Ankit Asthana"<<endl;' a hundred times. This would result in wastage of a lot of time and resources. To overcome this problem C++ provides us with control structures which not only allow us to repeat such block of instructions but also allow the programmer to respond to changing circumstances during execution of a program.

C++ allows the following types of control structures:
(a) 'If' then else
(b) The 'while' loop and do while loop
(c) The 'for' loop
(d) The 'switch' case construct

3.2 Conditional structure: *if* then *else*

The 'if' statement allows you to execute an instruction or block of instructions only if the specified condition is true. It has the following syntax:

Syntax:

if (***condition***) ***statement***

If the statements to be executed in the conditional structure are more than one then the set of statements also referred to as block of instructions to be executed are enclosed in curly braces ({}).

```
if (condition)
{
  block of instructions
}
```

Where '*condition*' is the expression that is being evaluated. If this expression evaluates to 'true', then the ***statement(s)*** are executed. On the other hand if the 'condition' provided in the 'if' statement evaluates to 'false', then the *statement(s)* are ignored and the program jumps to the next instruction after the conditional structure. Let us take up an example,

The following pieces of code are executed if x has an even value assigned to it.

```
if (x %2==0)
  cout << "x is even";
```

Case 1

```
if (x %2==0)
{
 cout << "x is even";
 cout << x;
}
```

Case 2

As one might observe in the second case we have used curly brackets to execute the block of instructions. Now let me ask you a very interesting question. What happens if we want to execute a set of statements if the condition is true and another set of statements if the condition is false?

This is where the 'if...else' structure comes in. It consists of the 'if' statement followed by a set of instructions, followed by the keyword 'else', followed by another set of instructions which is executed if the specified condition evaluates to false. The syntax for the 'if...else' structure is given below:

Syntax:

if (*condition***)**

```
{
  // statements executed if specified condition is true
  statement(s);
}
else
{
  // statements executed if the specified condition is false
  statement(s);
}
```

For example,

```
if (x %2== 0)
  {
    cout << "x is even";
  }
else
  {
   cout << "x is odd";
  }
```

When the piece of code given above is executed then the program evaluates the expression ‘x%2==0’. If the expression evaluates to true, the program prints ‘x is even’ on the screen. On the other hand if this expression evaluates to false the message ‘x is not even’ is printed on the screen. The figure 3.1 explains the same concept with the help of a flow chart.

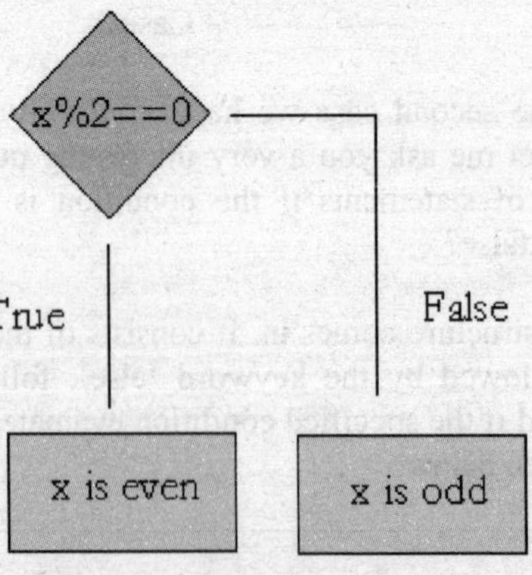

Figure 3.1: The 'if...else' statement

The *if...else* structure can also be nested or concatenated in order to verify a range of values. For example, list of grades achieved by a group of students in their final exams (program 3.1).

Program 3.1: Nested if...else structure

```
// Header Files
# include <iostream.h>
# include <conio.h>

// Main Function
void main ()
{
 clrscr();

 int grade;
 cout<<" Enter the grade achieved by the student (0 to 100)";
 cin>>grade;

 if (grade<=50)
 {
  cout<<" Grade achieved by the student F:Fail ";
 }

 else if (grade>50 && grade <=70)
 {
 cout<<" Grade achieved by the student is B";
 }

 else if (grade>70 && grade <=100)
 {
 cout<<" Grade achieved by the student is A";
 }

}
```

3.3 Repetitive structures or loops

Loops allow us to repeat instructions or a block of instructions while the specified condition to initiate the loop remains true. Loops have an objective to repeat a statement (or a set of statements) a certain number of times or till the moment the required condition is fulfilled.

3.3.1 The *while* loop

The while loop, is one of the most commonly used loops in most programming language. This loop is generally used when we are not sure how many number of times do we want to execute a loop. It has the following syntax:

Syntax:

```
while (expression)
    {

    statement(s)

    }
```

Its function is to simply repeat *statement(s)* while *expression* provided is true. Program 3.2 shows the use a *while* loop.

Program 3.2: The 'while' loop

```
// Header Files
# include <iostream.h>
# include <conio.h>

// Main Function
void main ()
{
 clrscr();
 // Variable declaration
 int i;
 cout << " Enter the starting number > ";
 cin >> i;
 // Entering the while loop
 while (i>0)
  {
   cout << i << " ";
   i--;
  }
 cout << " BANG! BANG!";
 getch();
 // End of program
}
```

```
Command Prompt - tc
Enter the starting number > 8
8 7 6 5 4 3 2 1  BANG! BANG!_
```

When the program is executed the user is prompted to insert a starting number for the countdown. Assuming that the user enters the starting number as greater than zero the program then enters the 'while' loop. As a result of which the instructions provided in the loop are executed. This process is repeated till the point 'i' is no longer greater than zero and the condition provided evaluates to false. A brief step by step description of what happens in program 3.2 is given below.

Program 3.2

1. User enter the starting number 'i'.

2. The while instruction checks for the expression '(i > 0)' resulting in two possibilities.
   - **True:** The program follows to step 3.
   - **False:** The program jumps the while loop and follows in to step **5.**.

3. Executes the block of instructions provided in the while loop.
   - Print the value stored in 'i'.
   - Decrement 'i' by 1.

4. End of block. Return to 'step 2'.

5. Print 'BANG! BANG!' on the screen.

Figure 3.2 also illustrates how the while loop operates.

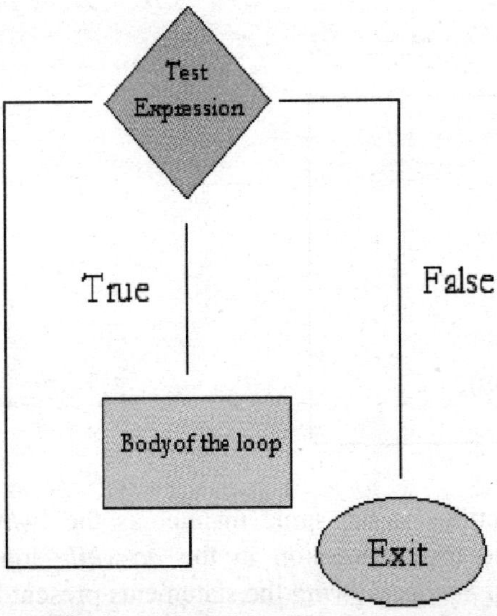

Figure 3.2: The 'while' loop

COMMON PROGRAMMING ERROR

- Missing curly brackets {} for opening and closing the loops will lead to a compilation/logical error.
- When using the do while loop not using semicolon **(;)** at the end of the while condition will lead to a compilation error.
- Remember that in case we want more than a single instruction to be executed, we must group them in a *block of instructions* by using curly brackets { }.

3.3.2 The *do-while* loop.

The do-while loop as the name suggests is similar to the while loop. As we have already studied in the while loop the condition or the text expression is evaluated at the starting of the loop. If this expression evaluates to false then the program statements are not executed at all but in some cases we actually might want to execute a set of instructions at least once. This is made possible with the help of the do-while loop. It has the following syntax:

Syntax:

```
do
{
    statement
}
while (condition);
```

The do-while loop functions is the same manner as the '*while*' loop except that the *condition* containing the test expression in the *do-while* loop is evaluated after the execution of *statement(s) hence allowing* the statements present in the block to execute at least once. Program 3.3 illustrates how the do-while loop is used in C++

Program 3.3: Do while loop

```
// Header Files
# include <iostream.h>
# include <conio.h>

// Main Function
void  main ()
{
 clrscr();
 int i;
 do
  {
   cout << "Enter number (0 to end) (sentinel Value): ";
   cin >> i;
   cout << "Number entered: " << i << "\n";
  }
 while (i != 0);

 getch();
}
```

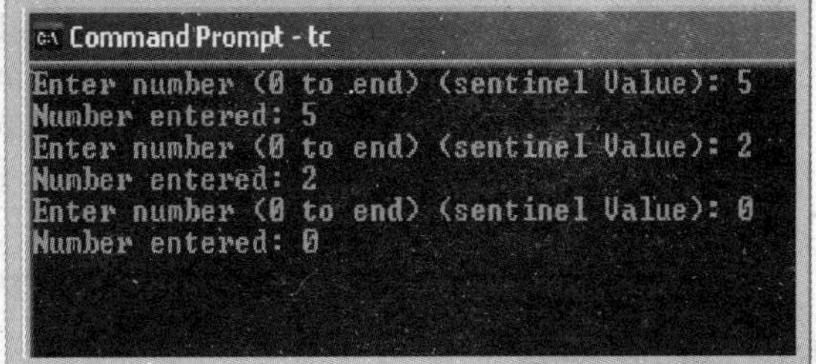

The working of the 'do while' is also shown in figure 3.3.

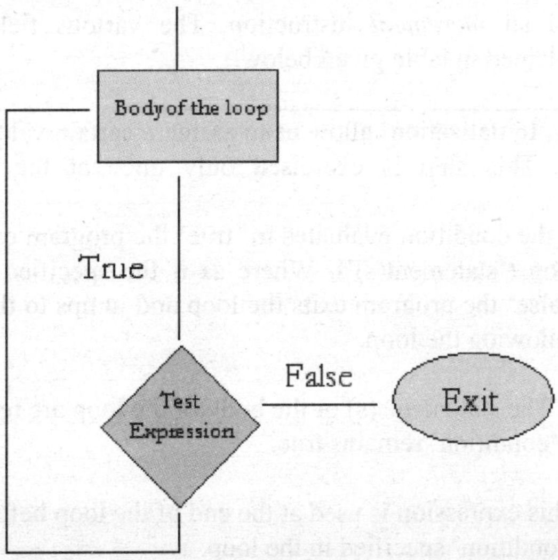

Figure 3.3: 'do while' loop

PROGRAMING TIPS

- The while loop is an entry controlled loop that is used when the condition given is clearly defined.
- The do while loop is an exit controlled loop. That is a do while loop is executed once even if the specified condition is not true.

3.3.3 The *for* loop.

The for loop executes a given section of code a given number of times. A for loop is generally used when it is previously known from before how many times a loop has to be executed. To be truthful the 'for' loop works exactly like the 'while' loop having space for variable initialization and incrementation in its expression. It has the following syntax:

Syntax:

```
for (initialization; condition; increment)
{

 statement(s);

}
```

As one might observe the syntax for the '*for*' loop provides space to specify an *initialization* and an *increment* instruction. The various fields in the 'for' looping construct are explained in table given below.

1. **Initialization:** 'Initialization' allow us to assign a certain value to the counter variable. This step is exercised only once at the beginning of the loop.

2. **Condition:** If the condition evaluates to 'true' the program enters into the body of the loop ('statement(s)'). Where as if the specified 'condition' evaluates to 'false' the program exits the loop and jumps to the statement immediately following the loop.

3. **Statement(s):** The statements(s) or the body of the loop are repeated till the 'condition' remains true.

4. **Increment:** This expression is used at the end of the loop before checking for the 'condition' specified in the loop.

Let us take up an example to understand how the 'for' loop actually works.

```
for (int i = 1; i <3; i++)
{
cout<<"\n Value of i:"<<i;
}
```

Let us begin with the 'for' statement. 'for(int i=1; i<3; i++)'. Now when the compiler reads this statement. It firsts declares a variable 'i' and assigns it a value of '1'. Once this is done it then checks for the condition 'i<3' provided in the for expression. As 'i=0' at this stage the program enters the body of the 'for' loop displaying the value of 'i' on the screen. As now we have reached the end of the loop the incrementation step is exercised and the counter variable 'i' is incremented by a single value. After this the 'condition' for loop continuation is again checked for and as the condition is satisfied '2<3' the loop is again repeated. This process is repeated till this condition is satisfied. The working of the 'for' loop is also explained in figure 3.4.

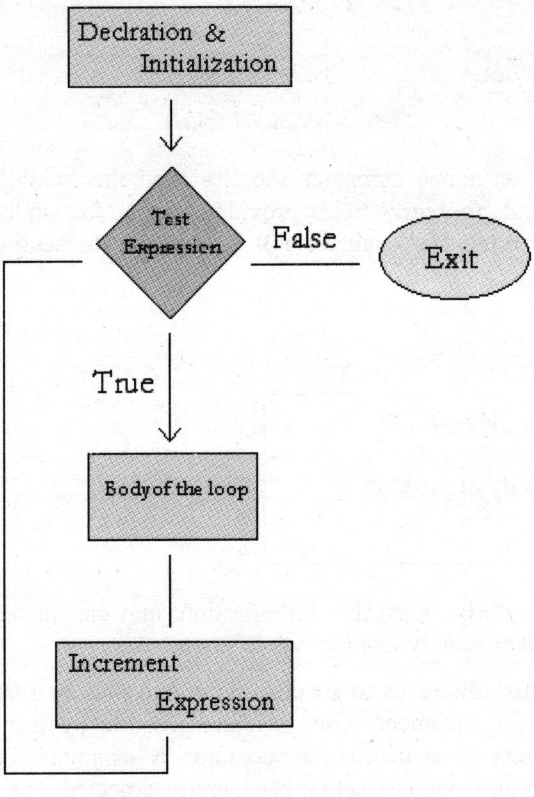

Figure 3.4: The for loop

Now that we understand how the 'for' loop works we are now at a stage where we can compare the 'for' and the 'while' looping constructs. So let us now create program 3.1 again using for loop.

Program 3.4: The 'for' loop

```
// Header Files
# include <iostream.h>
# include <conio.h>

// Main Function
void main ()
{
 clrscr();
 for (int i=10; i>0; i--)
 {
  cout << i << " ";
 }
 cout << " BANG!
BANG!";
 getch();
}
```

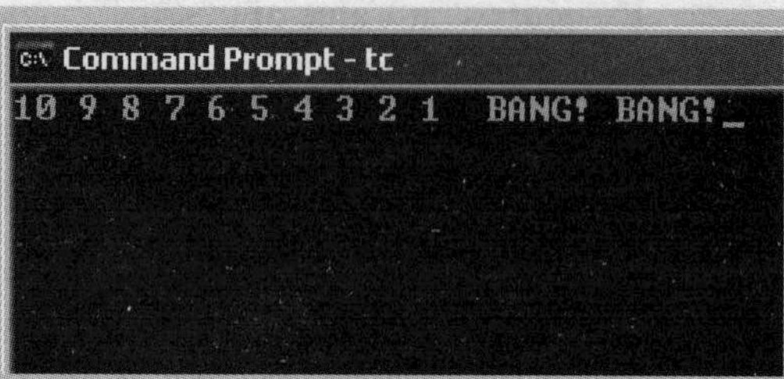

The program given above compares the 'for' and the 'while' looping construct. The '***initialization***' and '***increase***' fields provided in the 'for' statement are optional hence these fields can be left blank but we still have to use the semi colons(;) provided at the end of these fields.

For example,

```
for ( ; i<5 ; )
{
   Body of the loop
}
```

If we observe carefully, when the 'initialization' and the 'increase' fields are left blank the for loop behaves exactly like the 'while' loop.

The 'for' loop also allows us to specify more than one instruction in any of the fields included in the for statement. This is made possible by the use of the 'comma (,)' operator which acts as an instruction separator, it separates and allows more than one instruction where only one instruction is generally expected. For example,

```
for ( e=0, i=80 ; e!=i ; e++, i-- )
{
 // Body of the loop.
```

```
}
```

This loop will execute 40 times provided neither ‘e’ nor ‘i’ are modified within the for loop.

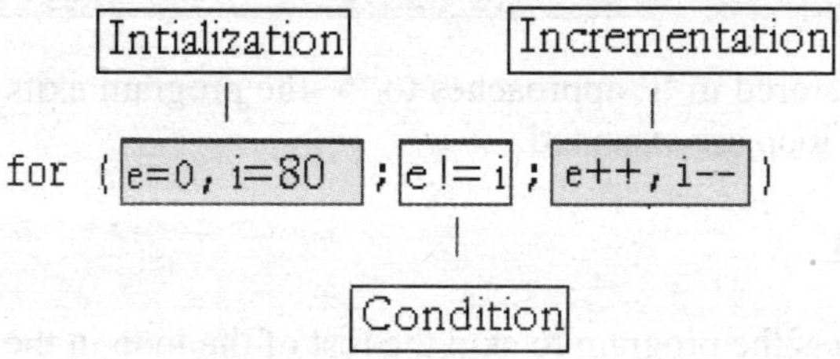

3.4 Bifurcation of control loops

In this section, we will discuss the statements that are used to alter the flow of control. This can be done by the usage of the following statements. In C++ this is termed as bifurcation of control loops.

3.4.1 The *break* instruction

The ‘*break’* instruction is used to exit a given loop even if the condition specified evaluates to true. It is generally used to end an infinite loop. Program 3.5 explains how the ‘break’ instruction is used in C++.

Program 3.5: The break instruction

```
// Header Files
# include <iostream.h>
# include <conio.h>

// Main Function
void main ()
{
 clrscr();
 int i;
 for (i=10; i>0; i--)
 {
  cout << i << " ";
  if (i==5)
  {
   cout << " Stop BANG! BANG!";
```

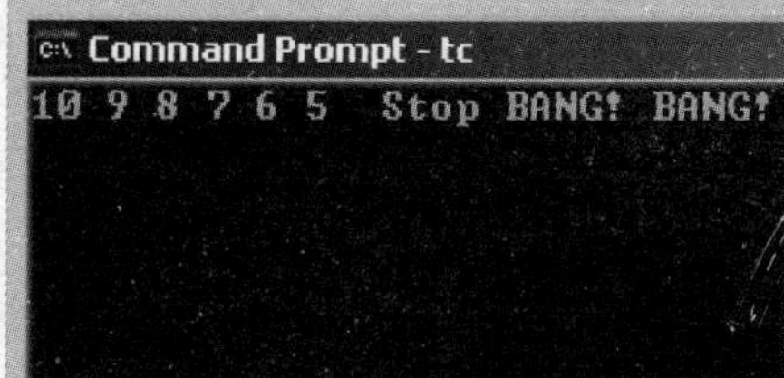

```
        break;
      }
    }
    getch();
}
```

In this program as the value stored in 'i' approaches to '5' the program exits the loop and the statements following the loop are executed.

3.4.2 The 'continue' expression

The '*continue*' expression instructs the program to skip the rest of the loop in the ongoing iteration as if the program has reached the end of *statement(s)* block. This causes the program to jump to the next iteration. Program 3.6 given below explains how this expression is used in C++.

Program 3.6: The 'continue' expression

```
// Header Files
# include <iostream.h>
# include <conio.h>

// Main Function
void main ()
{

 clrscr();

 for (int i=10; i>0; i--)
 {
  if (i==3)continue;

  cout << i << " ";
 }
 cout << " BANG! BANG!";

 getch();
}
```

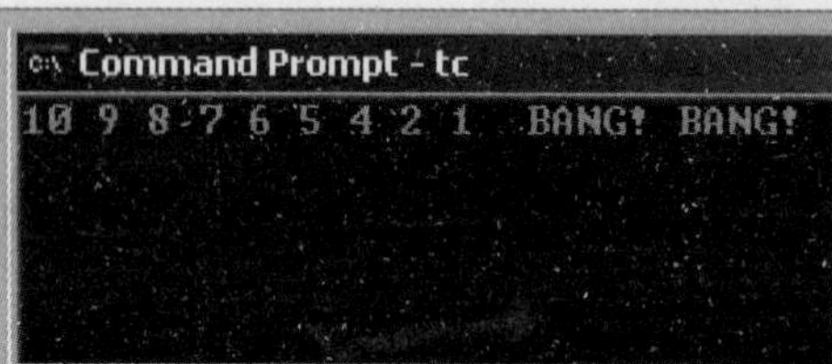

In this program as 'i' approaches the value '3' the program skips the statements following this instruction to reach the end of the loop and then begins the next iteration. As it is also evident from the output of the program.

3.4.3 The *goto* instruction

The 'goto' instruction allows the programmer to make a jump from one point in the program to another point in the program. Program 3.7 explains how this instruction is used in C++. Although the statement might seem very handy it is not advisory to use it.

Program 3.7: The goto instruction

```
# include <iostream.h>
# include <conio.h>

void main ()
{
 clrscr();
 int i=10;
 restart:
 cout << i << " ";
 i--;
 if (i>0) goto restart;
 cout << " BANG! BANG!";
 getch();
}
```

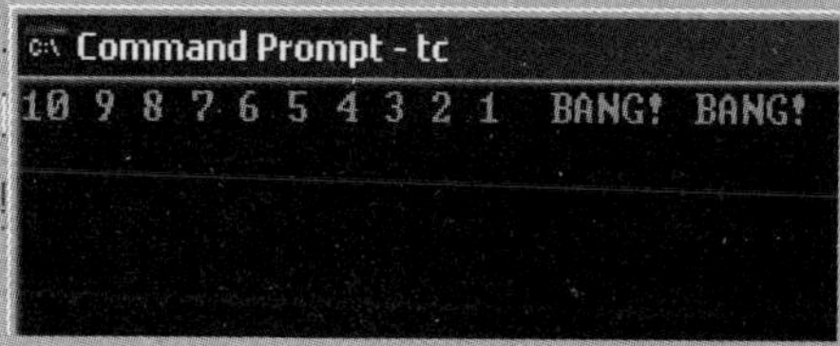

3.5 The Selective Structure: *switch*.

The selective structure: switch is a multiple selection statement structure to handle decision making. The switch-case statement is a multi-way decision statement. Unlike the multiple decision statement that can be created using the 'if-else' structure, the switch statement evaluates the conditional expression and tests it against a list of constant values. The branch corresponding to the value that the expression matches is taken during execution. The switch statement along with a series of case labels also contains an optional default case statement. The only draw back of using the 'switch' structure is that one cannot use the 'float' or the 'double' data types. We can also think about switch case statements as a substitute for long if statements that compare a variable to several "integral" values. They have the following syntax:

```
switch (expression)
{
 case constant1:
             statement(s) 1
             break;
case constant2:
             statement(s) 2
             break;
```

```
default:
statement(s)
}
```

So how does the 'switch' statement work?

The switch selection statement begins by evaluating the expression passed to it as a parameter. It then checks for this evaluated value to be equivalent to 'constant1'. If it comes out to be equal then it executes the block of instructions provided under the case constant until it reaches the optional 'break' keyword. This tells the compiler that it has reached the end of the block of instruction as a result of which the compiler jumps to the end of the selective switch structure. On the other hand if the evaluated expression does not equal the 1st case constant then the structure checks the evaluated expression to the second case constant. If it comes out to be equal, it then executes the second *block of instructions* until it approaches the **break** keyword. Finally, if the value of the evaluated expression does not match any of the previously specified constants the program executes the block of instructions under the 'default:' keyword. Let us take up an example to understand how the switch case operates (Program 3.8).

Program 3.8: 'Switch Case' statement

```
// Header Files
# include<iostream.h>
# include <conio.h>

void main()
{
clrscr();
int day;
cout<<" Enter the week day (1-5)";
cin>>day;

// Switch Case statement
switch(day)
{
 case 1:
        cout<<" The day is Monday";
        break;
 case 2:
        cout<<" The day is Tuesday";
        break;
```

```
case 3:
        cout<<" The day is Wednesday";
        break;
case 4:
        cout<<" The day is Thursday";
        break;
case 5:
        cout<<" The day is Friday";
        break;
default:
        cout<<" Not a valid Entry";
}
getch();
}
```


The following output is observed when this piece of code is executed.

Now that we understand how the switch operation works we can now compare the 'switch' and the 'if-else' conditional structures.

***switch* example**

```
switch (z) {
 case 5:
  cout << "z is 5";
  break;
 case 10:
  cout << "z is 10";
  break;
 default:
  cout << "value of z is not known";
}
```

if-else

```
If (z == 5) {
 cout << "z is 5";
 }
else if (z == 10) {
 cout << "z is 2";
 }
else {
 cout << "value of z is not known";
 }
```

At this point let me ask you a very interesting question. What happens if we do not include the optional 'break' keyword?

If we do not include the optional 'break' keyword at the end of every block of instructions then the program would not jump to the end of the block of instructions instead it would enter the blocks of other case constants and keep on executing them until it approaches the **'break'** instruction or reaches the end of the switch selective block. An example of such a case is given below.

```
// Header Files
# include<iostream.h>
# include <conio.h>

void main()
{
 clrscr();
 int day;
 cout<<" Enter the week day (1-5)";
 cin>>day;

 // Switch Case statement
 switch(day)
 {
  case 1:
         cout<<"\n The day is Monday";

  case 2:
         cout<<"\n The day is Tuesday";

  case 3:
         cout<<"\n The day is Wednesday";

  case 4:
         cout<<"\n The day is Thursday";

  case 5:
         cout<<"\n The day is Friday";
         break;
  default:
          cout<<" Not a valid Entry";
 }
 getch();
}
```

As you might observe the piece of code given above is quite similar to program 3.7 the only difference being that in this program we are missing the optional break statements in this 'switch' structure. As a result of this the following output is observed which is quite different from the one we observed with program 3.7.

Output Screen

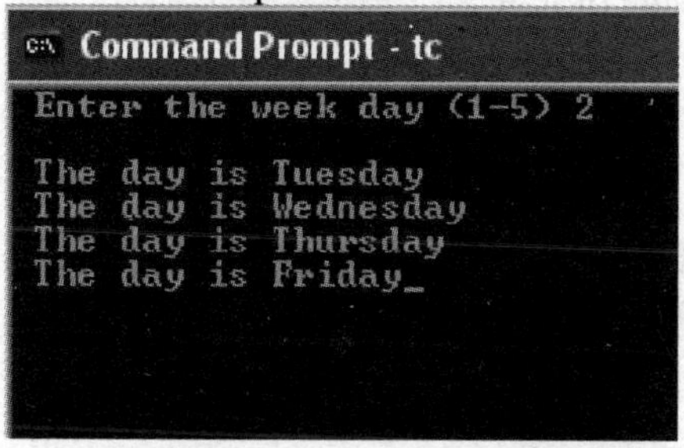

COMMON PROGRAMMING ERROR

- Missing the break statements may result in a logical error.
- Switch case statements can only be used for integral values and usage of switch case with decimal index values with result in a compilation error.
- Switch case can be only be used to compare an expression with different constants therefore using the following expressions will result in a compilation error.

'case (i*2)':, 'case (a+b*c)': ...

3.6 Review Examples

Example 3.6.1

Write a program to find the sum of the series 1 + 3 + 5 + 7……n terms. The value of 'n' is given by the user during program execution?

Solution of 3.6.1

```
// Header Files
# include <iostream.h>
# include <conio.h>
```

```
// Main Function
void main()
{
  int i=1,sum=0,n;
  cout<<"Enter the value of n \n";
  cin>>n;

  while (i<= n*2)
     {
       cout<<i<<endl;
       sum = sum + i;
       i = i + 2;
     }
  cout<<"Sum="<<sum<<endl;
}
```

Output Screen

```
Enter the value of n
5
1
3
5
7
9
Sum = 25
```

Example 3.6.2

Write a program to find the sum of the series $1^3 + 3^3 + 5^3 + 7^3 + \ldots$ n terms. Assume that the value of n is given by the user during program execution?

Solution of 3.6.2

```
// Header Files
# include <iostream.h>
# include <conio.h>

// Main Function
void main()
{
```

```
  int i =1, sum=0,n;

  cout<<" Enter the value of n \n";
  cin>>n;

  while ( i<=n+2)
  {
   sum = sum + (i * i * i ) ;
   i = i + 2 ;
  }

  cout<<" The sum of the series = "<<sum<<endl;
}
```

Output Screen

```
Enter the value of n
3
The sum of the series = 153
```


Example 3.6.3

Write a program to find the sum of the following series:

1 + ½! + 1/3! + … n terms.

Assume that the value of n is given by the user?

Solution of 3.6.3

```
 // Header Files
# include <iostream.h>
# include <conio.h>

// Main Function
void main()
{
 int i,j,n;
 float fact;
 float sum=0;

 cout<<" Enter the value of n \n";
 cin>>n;
```

```
for (i=1;i<=n;i++)
{
        fact=1;

        for (j=1;j<=i;j++)
                {
                        fact = fact * j;
                }

        sum += (float)  1/fact;

}

cout<< " The sum of the series "<< sum;
getch();
}
```

Output Screen

```
Enter the value of n
2
The sum of the series is 1.5
```

Example 3.6.4

Write a program to print the following pattern:

```
1      1
12    21
123  321
1234321
```

Solution of 3.6.4

```
 // Header Files
# include<iostream.h>
# include<conio.h>

void main ()
{
```

```
int a,b,c,d,e,f=1,r=2; //Variable Declarations
for ( a=1;a<=4;a++)
  {
    for ( b=1;b<=a;b++)
                cout<<b;

            for (d=5; d>=f ; d=d-1)
                cout<<" ";

            for (e=1;e<r;e++)
                cout<<a;

            for ( c=1;c<a;c++)
                cout<<a-c;

            cout<<endl;
    f=f +2;

            if ( a==3)
    {
                r=0;
    }
                else
                        r =2;
  }
 getch();
}
```

Example 3.6.5

Write a program to ask the user to input two integers and an operator. Based on the operator (+,-,/,*,%) perform the desired operation and print the result (use switch case) ?

Solution of 3.6.5

```
# include <iostream.h>
# include <conio.h>
  void main()
{
  clrscr();
```

```
int n1,n2,res;
char ch;
cout<<" Enter 2 numbers \n";
cin>>n1>>n2;
cout<<" Enter an operator (+,-,/,*,%) \n";
cin>>ch;
switch(ch)
{
 case '+' : res = n1+n2;
             cout<<" The result is  "<<res;
             break;

 case '-' : res = n1- n2;
             cout<<" The result is  "<<res;
             break;

  case '*' : res = n1* n2;
             cout<<" The result is  "<<res;
             break;

  case '/' : res = n1/n2;
             cout<<" The result is  "<<res;
             break;

  case '%' : res = n1%n2;
             cout<<" The result is  "<<res;
             break;
  default: cout<<" Invalid choice";
  }
getch();
}
```

Output Screen

```
Enter 2 numbers
81
9
Enter an operator (+,-,/,*,%)
%
The result is 0
```

Example 3.6.6

Write a program to ask the user to input a number between 1 to 12 and print the corresponding month
(Use switch case)

Solution of 3.6.6

```
# include <iostream.h>
# include <conio.h>
void main()
{
 clrscr();
 int month;
 cout<<" Enter any number between 1-12\n";
 cin>>month;
 switch(month)
        {
                case 1: cout <<"Jan";
                        break;
                case 2: cout <<"Feb";
                        break;
                case 3: cout<<"Mar";
                        break;
                case 4: cout<<"Apr";
                        break;
                case 5: cout<<"May";
                        break;
                case 6: cout<<"June";
                        break;
                case 7: cout<<"July";
                        break;
                case 8: cout<<"Aug";
                        break;
                case 9: cout<<"Sept";
                        break;
                case 10: cout<<"Sept";
                        break;
                case 11: cout<<"Nov";
                        break;
                case 12: cout<<"Dec";
                        break;
                default: cout<<"Invalid choice";
        }
    getch();
```

```
}
```

Output Screen

```
Enter any number between 1-12
4
Apr
```

Example 3.6.7

Write a program to ask the user to input three numbers. The program should then print the largest number on the screen.

Solution of 3.6.7

```
// Header Files
# include <iostream.h>
# include <conio.h>

// Main Function
void main()
{
  int n1,n2,n3;
  cout<<"Enter three numbers \n";
  cin>>n1>>n2>>n3;

  if (n1>n2&&n1>n3)
      {
       cout<<"The largest number is "<<n1;
      }
            else if (n2>n1&&n2>n3)
            {
                    cout<<"The largest number is "<<n2;
            }
                    else if (n3>n1&&n3>n2)
                    {
                            cout<<"The largest number is "<<n3;
                    }

 getch();
}
```

Output Screen

```
Enter three numbers
3
5
6
The largest number is 6
```

Example 3.6.8

Write a program to ask the user to input a number and find out whether it is a palindrome or not?

Solution of 3.6.8

```
// Header Files
# include <iostream.h>
# include <conio.h>

// Main Function
void main ()
{
  int rem,num,temp,reverse=0;

  cout<<" Enter a number \n";
  cin>>num;
  temp=num;

  while (temp !=0 )
        {
                rem = temp % 10;
                reverse = reverse *10 +rem;
                temp = temp /10;
        }

  if (reverse == num)
        {
          cout<<" Palindrome number ";
        }
          else
        {
         cout<<" Not a palindrome number";
        }
```

```
        getch();
}
```

Output Screen

```
Enter a number
31313
palindrome number
```

Example 3.6.9

Write a program to ask the user to input a number and print its table up to the 10th multiple.

Solution of 3.6.9

```
// Header Files
# include <iostream.h>
# include <conio.h>

// Main Function
void main()
{

        int n,i=1,p; // Variable Declrations
    cout<<"Enter a number \n";
    cin>>n;

        while ( i<=10)
        {
                p = i*n;
                cout<<n<<"*"<<i<<"="<<p<<endl;
                i = i +1;
        }

        getch();
}
```

Output Screen

```
Enter a number
5
5 * 1=5
5 * 2=10
5 * 3=15
5 * 4=20
5 * 5=25
5 * 6=30
5 * 7=35
5 * 8=40
5 * 9=45
5 * 10=50
```

Example 3.6.10

Write a program to ask the user to input the marks in 5 subjects. Calculate the student's percentage and print the grade?

Solution of 3.6.10

```
// Header Files
# include <iostream.h>
# include <conio.h>

 void main()
 {

  int m1,m2,m3,m4,m5;
  float tot;

  cout<<" Enter the marks in five subjects \n";
  cin>>m1>>m2>>m3>>m4>>m5;
  tot = m1 + m2 + m3 + m4 + m5;
  cout<<" Your total is \n"<<tot;

  float avg=tot/5.0;
  cout<<"\n Your average is \n"<<avg;

  if (avg>=90)
  {
          cout<<"\n Your grade is A \n";
```

```
}
    else if (avg>=80&&avg<=89)
    {
        cout<<"\nYour grade is  B";
    }
        else if (avg >=70 && avg<=79)
        {
            cout<<"\nYour grade is C";
        }
            else if (avg>=60 && avg<=69)
            {
                cout<<"\nYour grade is D";
            }
                else if ( avg>=50 && avg <=59)
                {
                    cout<<"\nYour grade is E";
                }
                    else
                    {
                        cout<<"\n Your grade is F";
                    }
}
```

Output Screen

```
Enter the marks in five subjects
80
88
56
65
69
Your total is
358
Your aggregate is
71.59998
Your grade is C
```

Example 3.6.11

Write a program to check whether a number entered by the user is an angstrom number or not. The program should carry on executing as long as the user wants?

Solution of 3.6.11

```
// Header Files
# include<iostream.h>
# include<conio.h>

// Main Function
void main()
{
  int sum=0,num,temp,rem;
  char ch='y';

  again:

  cout<<" Enter a number \n";
  cin>>num;
  temp=num;

  while(temp != 0 )
  {
   rem=temp%10;
   sum = rem *rem * rem +sum;
   temp = temp /10;
  }

 if (sum==num)
          cout<<" Angstrom number";
          else
               cout<<" Not an angstrom number";

 cout<<"\n Do you want to continue (y/n)";
 cin>>ch;
 if (ch=='y')
     goto again;
          else
               cout<<" Thank you ";
}
```

Output Screen

```
Enter a number
153
Angstrom number
Do you want to continue (y/n)y
Enter a number
321
Not an angstrom number
Do you want to continue(y/n)n
Thank you
```

Example 3.6.12

Write a program to accept a number from the user and display the following menu:

1. First five multiples
2. Squares of first five multiples
3. Cubes of first five multiples
4. Exit

Depending on the users choice, the appropriate action should be carried out

Solution of 3.6.12

```
// Header Files
# include <iostream.h>
# include <conio.h>

// Main Function
void main()
{
int n1,opt,i=1,p=1;

cout<<" Enter a number \n";
cin>>n1;
cout<<"1. First five multiples\n";
cout<<"2. Squares of first five multiples\n";
cout<<"3. Cubes of first five multiples\n";
cout<<"4. Exit \n";

cout<<"Enter option (1,2,3,4)\n";
cin>>opt;

if (opt==1)
{
        while (i<=5)
        {
```

```
            p = i * n1;
            cout<<n1<<"*"<<i<<"="<<p<<endl;
            i = i + 1;
        }
}
    else if (opt==2)
    {
        while (i<=5)
        {
            p = i * n1;
            p = p * p;
            cout<<p<<endl;
            i = i + 1;
        }
    }
        else if (opt==3)
        {
            while (i<=5)
            {
                p = i * n1;
                p = p * p * p;
                cout<<p<<endl;
                i = i + 1;
            }
        }
            else
                cout<<"Thank you";
  getch();
}
```

Output Screen

```
Enter a number
1
1.First five multiples
2.Squares of first five multiples
3.Cubes of first five multiples
4.Exit
Enter option (1,2,3,4)
3
1
8
27
64
125
```

Example 3.6.15

Write a program to find the sum of the following series:
3 + (3+6) + (3+6+9) … n terms. Assume that the value of n is given by the user during run time.

Solution of 3.6.15

```
// Program to find sum of the series

// Header Files
# include<iostream.h>
# include<conio.h>

// Main Function
void main()
{

  int a,b,c=0,d=3,e,sum=0;
  cout<<"Enter the required number \n";
  cin>>a;

  for (b=1;b<=a;b++)
  {
   c = c + d * b;
   sum = sum + c;
  }

  cout<< " The sum of the series "<<sum;
  getch();
}
```

Output Screen

```
Enter the required number
2
The sum of the series
12
```

Example 3.6.16

Write a program to find the sum of the series

$1-x^3/3! + x^5/5!+x^7/7!$ ... n terms.

The value of n is given by the user.

Solution of 3.6.16

```
// Header Files
# include <iostream.h>
# include <conio.h>

// Main Function
void main()
{

  // Variable Declarations

  int a,b,d=3,g=1,x=1; // Counter Variables

  int sign=1; // Determines the sign of each term in the series

  float sum=0.0,c=1,f=1; // Sum is used to store the sum of the series

  cout<<"Enter the value of x and no of times n \n";
  cin>>x>>a;

  for ( b=1;b<2 * a;b=b+2)
  {
              f=1;
              c=1;

                      for (int t = 1;t<=b;t++)
                      {
                              c = c * t;
                      }
                              for (int y=1;y<=b;y++)
                              {
                                      f = f * x;
                              }

      sum = sum + (float) (f/c * sign); // Type Casting
       sign = sign * -1;
```

```
        g = g+1;
    }

    cout<<" The sum of the series is "<<sum-(x-(x-1));

    getch();
}
```

Output Screen

```
Enter the value of x and no of times n
2
1
The sum of the series is 1
```

3.7 Review Exercise

2/3 Mark questions

Q1) What do you understand by the term 'Exit controlled loop'?

Q2) Differentiate between a while and do-while loop?

Q3) What happens if the break statement in the switch case selection statement is not used?

Q4) What are jump statements?

Q5) Under which header file is the exit() function defined?

Q6) What is the syntax for a while loop explain giving suitable example?

Q7) How is the 'switch case selection statement' different from 'if else conditional statement'?

Q8) Find the errors in the following piece of code:

```
# include <iostream.h>

void main()
{
   clrscr();
    int sum=0, n;
    i=1;
    cout<<" Enter the value of n \n";
    cin>>n;
          while (i<=n+2)

           cout<<i<<endl;
            sum = sum + i

     cout<<" Sum =  "<<sum<<endl;
     getch();
}
```

Q9) What will be the output of the following program:

```
// Header Files
# include <iostream.h>
# include <conio.h>

// Main Function
void main()
{
  int month=4;
  switch(month)
   {
   case 1: cout <<"Jan";
           break;
   case 2: cout <<"Feb";
           break;
   case 3: cout<<"Mar";
           break;
   case 4: cout<<"Apr";

   case 5: cout<<"May";

   case 6: cout<<"June";

   case 7: cout<<"July";
```

```
case 8: cout<<"Aug";
        break;
case 9: cout<<"Sept";
        break;
case 10: cout<<"Sept";
        break;
case 11: cout<<"Nov";
        break;
case 12: cout<<"Dec";
        break;
default: cout<<"Invalid choice";
}
getch();
}
```

Q10) Write the output of the following piece of code:

```
// Header Files
# include <iostream.h>
# include <conio.h>

// Main Function
void main()
{
   int n=7,i=1,p;

        while ( i<=10)
        {
          p = i*n;
          cout<<n<<"*"<<i<<"="<<p<<endl;
          i = i +1;
        }
}
```

4/5 Mark Questions

Q1) Write a program to find the sum of the following series:

$1-y^5/3! + y^7/5!+y^9/7!$..................n terms.

The values of variables 'y' and 'n' are given by the user during program execution.

Q2) Write a program to find the sum of the following series

4+ (4+8) + (4+8+12)…………..n terms.

The value of n is given by the user during program execution.

Q3) Write a program to print the following pattern:

```
0     0
00   00
000 000
0000000
```

Note: The program should use for and while loops to achieve the process

Q4) Write a program to input 5 numbers and print the largest number out of the given 5 numbers on the screen?

Q5) Write a program to accept a number from the user and display the following menu:

First Six Multiples
Lowest Common Factor (L.C.F.)
Highest Common Divisor (H.C.D.)
Exit

Depending upon the user's choice, the appropriate action should be carried out?

Q6) **Encryption and Decryption**

Write a program to encrypt a text message by replacing each letter in the message by another one in the following way:

- If the original letter is uppercase, and its integer value (according to ASCII) is value, replace it by the letter whose integer value is (value + ID)% 26 + 65.
- If the original letter is lowercase, and its integer value (according to ASCII) is value, replace it by the letter whose integer value is (value + ID)% 26 + 97.

Any other characters are left unchanged. Assume ASCII character set is used. ID is student number of your university. (Default ID: 0441673)

3.8 Let us revise!

- ✓ C++ allows the following types of control structures
  - i) If then else control structure
  - ii) The while and do-while loop
  - iii) The for loop
  - iv) Switch multiple-selection statement

- ✓ If then statement:

```
if (condition)
  {
    statement(s)
  }
```

- ✓ Loops have an objective to repeat a statement a certain number of times or till the moment the required condition is fulfilled.

- ✓ The while loop:

```
while (condition)
 {
    statement(s)
 }
```

- ✓ The do-while loop:

```
do
{

 statement(s)

}
while (expression);
```

- ✓ The statements that facilitate the unconditional transfer of program control are called *jump statements.*

- ✓ C++ provides four jump statements: return, goto, break and continue.

- ✓ A goto statement transfers the program control anywhere in the program.

- ✓ The *continue* statement abandons the current iteration of the loop by skipping over the rest of the statements in the loop body. It immediately transfers control to the evaluation of the test-expression of the loop for the next iteration of the loop.

- ✓ The *exit()* function is a library function and it breaks out of the program, abandoning the rest of the execution of the program.

Notes

Part I

CHAPTER 4

FUNCTIONS

AIM

- Introduce the concept of 'functions'.
- To learn declaring and using 'functions'.
- To study method of passing parameters and their relative advantages.
- Defining Global and Local variables.
- Enlist 'Character' and 'Mathematical' functions in C++.

OUTLINE

4.1 Introduction
4.2 Function Definition
4.3 Accessing a function
4.4 Default Arguments
4.5 Constant Arguments
4.6 Arguments as Reference Parameters
4.7 Inline Functions
4.8 Scope of variables
4.9 Character functions in C++
4.10 Mathematical functions in C++
4.11 Recursive Function
4.12 Review Examples
4.13 Review Exercise
4.14 Programming Project
4.15 Let us revise!

4.1 Introduction

Large programs comprising of only a single list of instructions are cumbersome to develop as it is difficult to manage, understand and maintain them. A function in C++ can perform a particular task, and supports the concept of modular programming design techniques. To understand why one needs to use functions let us take up an example.

Suppose that you have created a program which uses the sum of two integers inputted by the user to find the average of the two numbers. How will you approach this piece of problem? To solve the problem we would use the following piece of code:

```
// Header Files
# include<iostream.h>
# include<conio.h>

// Main Function
void main()
{
 clrscr();
 float sum=0;
 int a,b;
 float average=0;
 cout<<" Enter two numbers";
 cin>>a>>b;
 sum = a+b;
 average = sum/2;
 cout<<" \n The average of the two numbers is "<<average;
 getch();
}
```

Now, what happens if we again want to find the sum of two integers to find the percentage of each number in the sum? To solve this problem on basis of our current knowledge, we would generate the following code:

```
// Header Files
# include<iostream.h>
# include<conio.h>

// Main function
void main()
{
 clrscr();
 int ch;
 int a,b;
 float average=0;
 float percentage=0;
```

```
float sum=0;

do
{
 cout<<"\n\n ===== MENU =====\n";
 cout<<" 1. Average of two numbers\n";
 cout<<" 2. Percentage of each number in the sum\n";
 cout<<" 3. Exit\n";
 cout<<" !. Choice\n";
 cin>>ch;
 switch(ch)
 {
  case 1: cout<<" Enter two numbers";
          cin>>a>>b;
          sum= a + b;
          average = sum/2;
          cout<<"\n The average of two numbers is "<<average;
          break;

  case 2: cout<<" Enter two numbers";
          cin>>a>>b;
          sum = a + b;
          percentage= (a/(sum)) * 100;
          cout<<" \n The percentage of "<<a<<" in the sum is: "<<percentage<<"%";
          cout<<" \n The percentage of "<<b<<" in the sum is: "<<(100-percentage)<<"%";
          break;
  }
}
while (ch!=3);
getch();
}
```

What have we done in this program? All we have done in this program is that we have copied the same piece of code (highlighted part in the code) given above to find the sum of two integers and then use it to find the percentage of each in the sum. At this point, we would wish that we could store this repeated piece of code in a block and call it again when required, instead of typing the same piece of code again and again. This is where functions are useful.

A function is named units of a set of program statements which can be invoked from other parts of the program. Much like the copy and paste feature commonly used with Microsoft word. For our example, we can generate a function 'sum' which adds the two integers and returns the sum of the two integers when ever required as shown in program 4.1.

Program 4.1: Function 'sum'

```
// Header Files
# include<iostream.h>
# include<conio.h>

// Function Header: Tells the compiler that the function is declared later in the program.
float sum( int c, int d);

// Main function
void main()
{
 clrscr();
 int ch;
 int a,b;
 float average=0;
 float percentage=0;

 do
 {
  cout<<"\n\n ====== MENU =====\n";
  cout<<" 1. Average of two numbers\n";
  cout<<" 2. Percentage of each number in the sum\n";
  cout<<" 3. Exit\n";
  cout<<" !. Choice\n";
  cin>>ch;
  switch(ch)
  {
   case 1: cout<<" Enter two numbers";
           cin>>a>>b;
           average = sum(a,b)/2;
           cout<<"\n The average of two numbers is "<<average;
           break;

   case 2: cout<<" Enter two numbers";
           cin>>a>>b;
           percentage= (a/(sum(a,b))) * 100;
           cout<<" \n The percentage of "<<a<<" in the sum is: "<<percentage<<"%";
           cout<<" \n The percentage of "<<b<<" in the sum is: "<<(100-percentage)<<"%";
           break;
  }
 }
 while (ch!=3);
 getch();
 }
```

```
/***************************
Name: 'sum'
Parameters: 'c' and 'd'
Return Type: float
Purpose: Returns the sum of two integers
******************************************/
float sum( int c, int d)
{
 int sum_of_integers=0;
 sum_of_integers= c + d;
 return sum_of_integers;
}
```

This piece of code generates a function 'sum' which takes in two integers and returns the sum of the two integers to the main program when ever called by the program. Functions are one of the most fundamental concepts of programming and will be used thoroughly in programs you create later on. We will begin this chapter by teaching you how to declare functions in C++.

4.2 Function Definition

The definition of a function consists of the function header and its body. The syntax of a function definition is as under:

Function header →

type *function_name* (argument1, argument2, ...) statement
{

Body of the function

}

Figure 4.1: Return types in C++

A function definition comprises of the following parts:

- '**type**': It is the type of data returned by the function. The fundamental types of data that can be returned by a function are given in table 4.1.
- '*function_name*': It is the name by function is called.

Table 4.1

Return Type	Type of data returned
'void'	None
'int'	Integer
'float'	Floating points
'char'	Characters and strings

- 'Arguments': Each argument consists of a type of data followed by its identifier as per procedure for declaring variables in chapter 1. Once declared, these variables act within the function like any other variable. They allow us to pass parameters to the functions when a function is called. To enter more than one argument 'commas' are used. A function can have 'none' or multiple arguments depending upon the purpose of the function.
- 'Body of the function': Body of a function could be a single instruction or a block of instructions. If the function contains a block of instructions then the function body should be enclosed in curly brackets `{}`.

We are giving a few solved examples to understand how functions are defined and used in the following section.

4.2.1 Solved Examples

Example 4.2.1.1
Declare a function 'multiply' which takes in two integers as arguments and returns their product as an integer.

Solution of 4.2.1.1

So what do we know about the function we are going to declare?

In this problem, we have already been given the function name 'multiply' and its 'return type'. So let us put the information already given to us about the function in the general form of a function declaration:

```
int multiply ( argument1, argument2, ...)
{
        Body of the function
}
```

Once we have done this then we are only left with the list of arguments and the body of the function. As per the problem statement, the function takes in only two arguments of type 'integer' - we can call these two arguments by any name of our choice but it's a good practice to give names which are context sensitive. We have used 'integer1' and 'integer2' as these arguments in the piece of code given below:

```
int multiply ( int integer1, int integer2)
{
        Body of the function
}
```

These arguments 'integer1' and 'integer2' can now be used for any valid purpose in the function just as we can use any variable after it has been declared in function 'main()'. As per the need of the program, we now have to calculate and return the product of these two arguments. This can be done by declaring and then returning a variable 'product' which stores the product of these two arguments as shown below:

```
int multiply( int integer1, int integer2)
{
 int product;
 product = integer1 * integer2;
 return product;
}
```

One might notice that both 'product' and the return type of the function 'multiply' belong to the same data type. This is not just a mere coincidence but both the return type of the function and the identifier being returned in the 'return' statement always have to be of the same type as they tell the compiler what type of data is being returned by the function. If a function does not return any type of data then we do not need a return statement and we use the keyword 'void' before the function name which means null or empty.

4.2.2 Function prototype

To create and use a function in another function, it becomes necessary that the function being called must be declared before the function in which it is called. Function prototypes allow us to overcome this problem. . The function prototype is a statement, which means it ends with a semicolon. It consists of the function's 'return type', 'name', and the 'parameter list'. In syntax, they are very similar to a function header. The function prototype tells the compiler that the function is defined somewhere later in the program and when this function is called the compiler shifts control to that part of the program. For example, the function header for function 'multiply' in example 4.2.1.1 would look like this.

```
int multiply( int integer1, int integer2);
```

As already mentioned, the function prototype tells us about the 'return type: int', 'name: multiply' and the 'list of parameters and their return types: 'int integer1', 'int integer2''.As a formatting style all function headers are declared after the preprocessor directives, constants and global variables. Many of the built-in functions, we use in C++ have function prototypes which are already defined in files which we include in our programs by using '#include' preprocessor directive. For functions that we create on our own, we must include function prototypes.

4.3 Accessing a function

A function is called (or invoked, or accessed) by providing the function name, followed by its parameters. The parameters are enclosed in parentheses. Program 5.2 declares and uses function 'addition' to calculate the sum of the parameters passed to it as parameters.

Program 4.2: Accessing a function

```
// Header Files
#include <iostream.h>
# include<conio.h>

int addition (int a, int b)
{
 int add;
 add=a+b;
 return (add);
}

void main ()
{
 int sum;
 sum = addition (1,2);
 cout << " The sum of the two numbers is " << sum;
```

```
The sum of the two numbers is 3
```

```
getch();
}
```

Let us study how this program works. The program execution begins from the main function by declaring the variable 'sum' of type integer which is followed by the function call to 'addition' using the following statement.

```
sum = addition (1,2);
```

This statement calls the function addition(), the values '1' and '2' present in this function call are known as 'parameters' and these parameters have a clear correspondence to the variables 'a' and 'b' present in the function declaration.

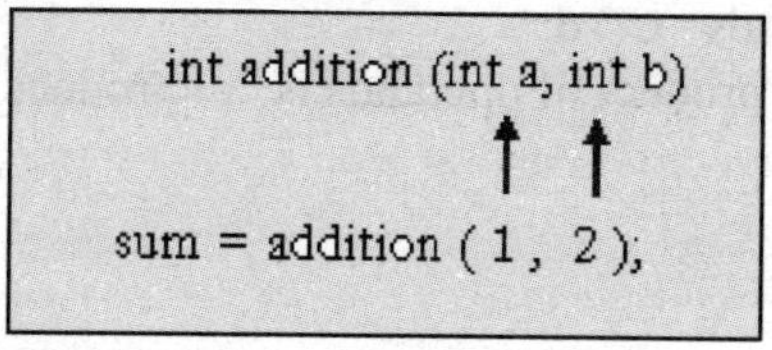

At this point the control of the program is passed from function main to function 'addition'. The values '1' and '2' passed with the function call are assigned to the corresponding variables in the function definition. As a result, the value '1' gets assigned to variable 'a' and the value '2' gets assigned to variable 'b'. Both these variables 'a' and 'b' are termed as local variables as they are defined and can be used only in function 'addition'. In this function, we have declared a variable 'add' which stores the sum of the two parameters passed to it. This variable 'add' is then returned by the function. In this case the function will return the value '3' to the main function which is also known as the return value of the function. The return statement tells the compiler that the role of the function is over as a result of which the control passes back to function 'main' after which the compiler replaces the function call by the value returned by the function.

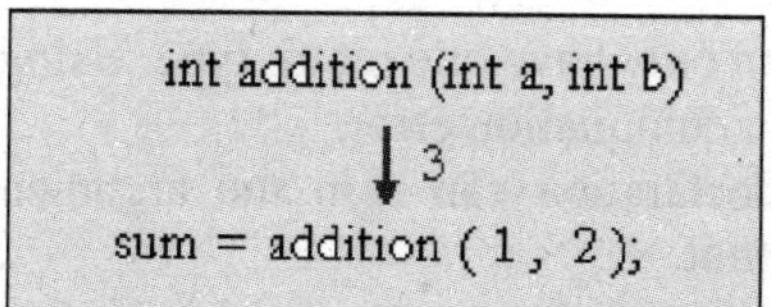

In other words, the statement '**sum = addition (1, 2);**' is simplified to '**sum = 3**' as the function addition returns the integer value '3'. The important thing that one needs to notice is that once the control has been passed back to the function main and the execution begins from the same point from where the control was passed to the function.

A function can be accessed or called as many times as the user wants. As it might be obvious the result of the function depends upon the parameters passed to it. Program 4.3 calls the function 'product' multiple times with different parameters every time.

Program 4.3: Multiple calls to function 'product()'

```
// Header Files
# include<iostream.h>
# include<conio.h>

void product( int c, int d)
{
 int product_operands=0;
 product_operands= c * d;
 cout<<"\n The product of operands is "<<product_operands;
}

// Main Function
void main()
{
 clrscr();
 int a=3,b=4;
 product(a,b);
 product(5,6);
 product(a+3,b+2);
 getch();
}
```

COMMON PROGRAMMING ERRORS

- A function can only have one return type. Using more than one data type will result in a compilation error.
- A function declaration can skip the argument names but a function definition cannot.
- A function prototype always precedes the function definition.
- When the function does not return anything then the return type is void.

4.4 Default Arguments

When declaring variables, C++ also allows us to assign default values for arguments. These parameters are used if this particular parameter is left blank when the function is called. Although if a value is passed with the function call then the parameters default value is overwritten by the value passed in function call. Program 4.4 illustrates how we use default arguments in C++.

Program 4.4: Default arguments in C++

```
# include<iostream.h>
# include<conio.h>

int product (int x, int y=3)
{
 int multiply;
 multiply = x* y;
 return multiply;
}

void main()
{
 clrscr();

 // First call to function 'product'
 cout<<product(10)<<endl;

// Second call to function 'product'
cout<<product(20,12);
}
```

```
30
240
```

In this program, function 'product' has been called twice by function 'main'. In the first call to function 'product', we have only specified one argument '10', so the argument 'x' in this function obtains the value '3' where as argument 'y' takes its default value '3'. As a result of which we obtain the result '30' on the screen. In the second call to the function 'product' two parameters have been passed to the function as a result of which the parameters value '13' overwrites the default value of arguments 'y' resulting in returning a value '240' from the function.

4.5 Constant Arguments

Just like we can declare constant variables, C++ also allows us to declare constant arguments which cannot be modified in the function. For example,

> *float* example (*int day*, *int* month, ***const*** *int* year = 2005);

In this declaration the argument 'year' is declared as a constant variable. The keyword ***const*** preceding this variable is an access specifier and it tells the compiler that the function should not modify the argument.

4.6 Arguments as Reference Parameters

So far, we have studied only to pass parameters to functions by their value. Let us take up an example,

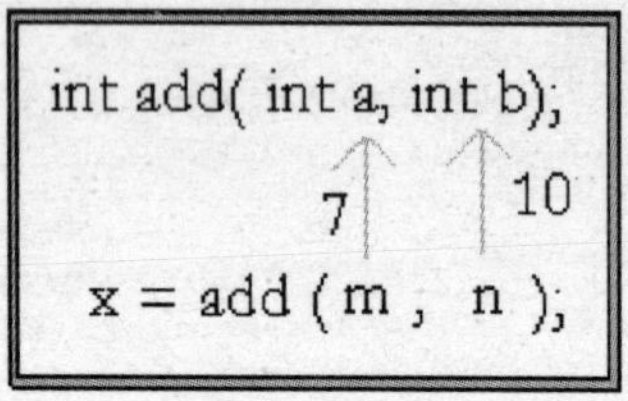

Now in this call to the function 'add' parameters 'm' and 'n' are not passed to arguments 'a' and 'b'. Only values stored in these variables '7' and '10' are passed to arguments 'a' and 'b'. As illustrated in the figure 4.1 given below.

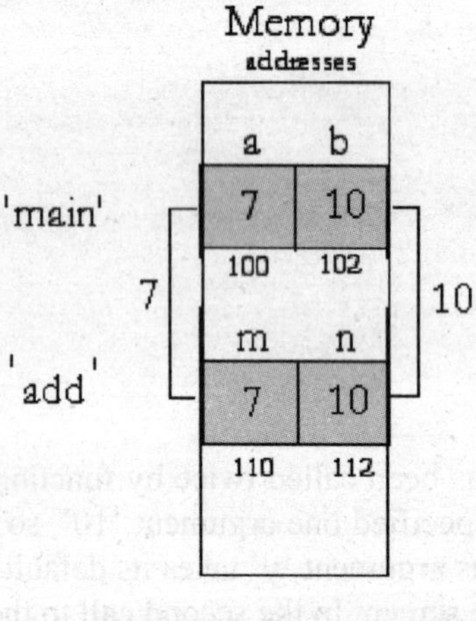

Figure 4.1: Passed by value

Any changes made to these variables 'a' and 'b' in function 'add' are not reflected back to variables 'm' and 'n' declared in the main function. In some cases it might be useful if changes made to arguments could be reflected back to the parameters passed in the function call. C++ allows this by declaring arguments as reference parameters. To understand how this is done look at the following program:

Program 4.5: Declaring arguments as reference parameters

```
// Header Files
# include<iostream.h>
# include<conio.h>
```

```
void reference( int &a, int b)
{
 a=a+10;
 b=b-5;
}

void main()
{
  clrscr();
  int operand1, operand2;
  cout<<" Enter the two operands ";
  cin>>operand1>>operand2;
  reference(operand1, operand2);
  cout<<" Operand1:"<<operand1<<
   "\t Operand2:"<<operand2;
  getch();
}
```

```
Command Prompt - tc
Enter the two operands 5 5
Operand1:15        Operand2:5
```

In this program the function definition for 'reference' might seem a bit peculiar. Here we have declared argument 'a' as a reference parameter this is done by preceding an ampersand '&' sign before the argument identifier. As a result of this, when function 'reference' is called from function 'main' then the parameter 'operand1' will be passed to it by 'reference' where as 'operand2' will be passed to the function by value. The difference between them might become more evident from the figure 4.2 given below.

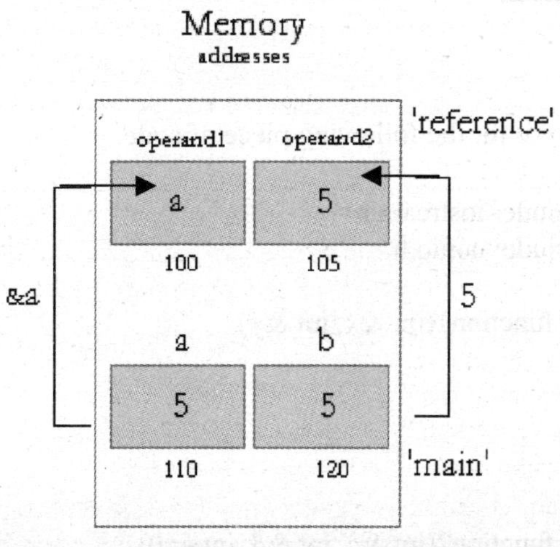

Figure 4.2: Arguments as reference parameters

As parameter 'b' is passed by value to function 'reference', 'operand2' is assigned the value '5' but as 'operand1' has been declared as a reference argument, so variable 'a' is passed to 'operand1' and not just the value stored in variable or parameter 'a'. During this function call variable 'a' is also known as the actual parameter and 'operand1' is also referred to as the formal parameter. As any changes made to the formal parameter 'operand1' are also reflected back to the actual parameter 'a' passed to it in the function call. So when the following operations take place in function 'reference' then variables 'a' and 'operand1' get effected in the following manner (see figure 4.3).

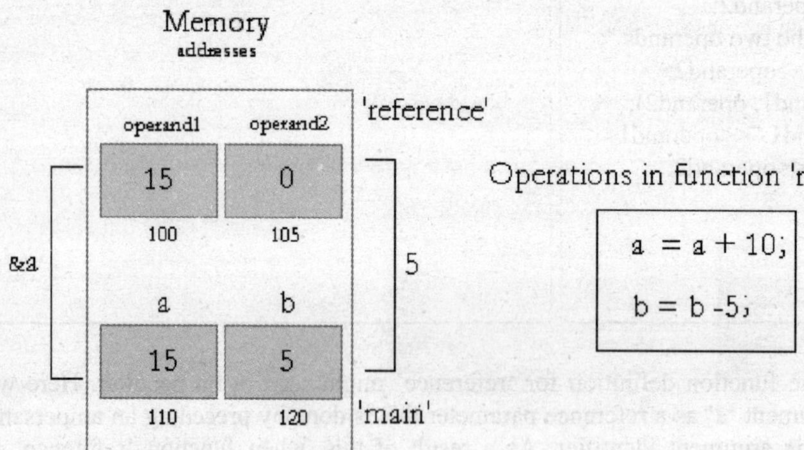

Figure 4.3: Arguments as reference parameters

4.6.1 Solved Examples

Example 4.6.1.1

Determine the output for the following piece of code:

```
# include<iostream.h>
# include<conio.h>

void function1(int &x, int &y)
{
 x++;
 y--;
}

void function2(int &c, int &d, int e=0)
{
 c = c + e;
```

```
d = d - 2;
e = e + c;
}

void main()
{
clrscr();
int var1=2, var2=5, var3=12;
function1(var1, var2);
function2(var1, var3);
cout<<"\n Var1:"<<var1<<"\t Var2:"<<var2<<"\Var3:"<<var3;
getch();
}
```

Solution of 4.6.1.1

Output Screen

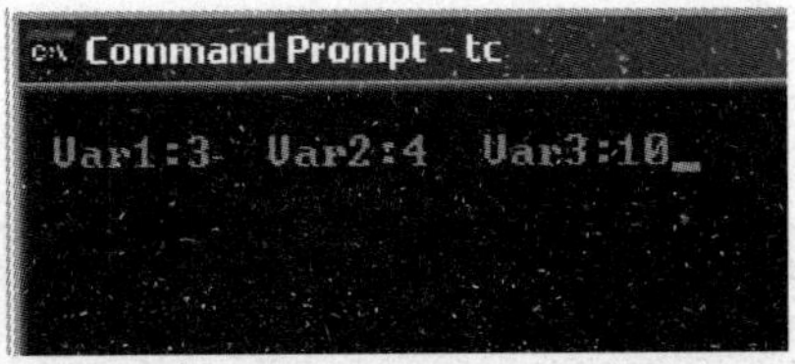

Programming Tips

- When passing the parameter as reference, the parameter is passed to the argument and any changes then made to this argument are reflected back to the passed parameter also known as the actual variable. Where as when passing parameters by value only the value stored in the variable is passed to the argument and changes made to this argument are not reflected back to the actual variable or the actual parameter.

- Parameters are passed to arguments exactly in the order as specified in the call to the function. Changing the order will result in a different output.

- When declaring arguments in the function header, default arguments are always declared at the end of the argument list. The following declaration will result in a compilation error:

```
void xyz( int x = 2, int y, int z)
  {
      .................
  }
```

- Calling a function before its function prototype or definition is declared will result in a compilation error.

4.7 Inline functions

When a function is declared **inline**, the function is expanded at the calling block. The inline specifier forces the compiler to substitute the body of code where function invocation occurs. As a result of which the control of a program is not shifted to the function being called. Inline functions are used to increase program's speed and performance. They are declared using the following syntax:

Syntax:

```
inline return_type  function_name (list of arguments)
    {
      function_body
    }
```

For example,

```
# include<iostream.h>
# include<conio.h>

inline void inline_functions()
{
  cout<<" Inline functions help in increasing programs performance";
}

void main()
{
 inline_functions();
}
```

4.8 Scope of variables

'Scope' of variables refers to the visibility of variables. In other words, it tells us where can we use or access variables. For example, the variables declared within a function or any other closed block of instructions can only be used or accessed in that very function in other words

their scope lies only within the function they are declared in. Let us take up a program to explain this concept.

Program 4.6: Scope of variables

```
# include <iostream.h>
# include <conio.h>

int multiply (int op1, int op2)
 {
  int product=0;
  product = op1 * op2;
  return product;
 }

void main()
 {
  int a, b;
  cout<<" Enter two numbers";
  cin>>a>>b;
  cout<<" The product is "<<multiply(a,b);
  getch();
 }
```

Now if in this program we use variable 'a' or 'b' in function 'multiply' it will give a compilation error. This is so because these variables 'a' and 'b' are local variables and as they have been declared in function main their scope lies only in this function. Similarly, 'op1', 'op2' and 'product' of type integer are also local variables and their scope lies only within function 'multiply'. C++ also allows us to declare 'global variables'. A global variable is a variable that does not belong to any subroutine in particular and can therefore can be accessed from any context in a program. They are declared using the same syntax the only difference being that they have to be declared outside any function or block of instructions. Program 4.7 illustrates how global variables are declared and used in C++.

Program 4.7: Global variables

```
/* To illustrate how to declare and use global variables */
# include <iostream.h>
# include <conio.h>
```

FUNCTIONS

```
// Declration of a global variables 'PI'  and 'radius'
float PI = 3.14;
int radius;

float area()
{
 float evaluate_area=0;
 cout<<"\n Enter the radius of the circle";
 cin>>radius;
 evaluate_area= PI * (radius) * (radius);
 return evaluate_area;
}

float circumference()
{
 float evaluate_circumference=0;
 cout<<"\n Enter the radius of the circle";
 cin>>radius;
 evaluate_circumference= PI * 2 * radius;
 return evaluate_circumference;
}

void main()
{
  clrscr();
  int ch;
  do
  {
   cout<<"\n 1. Calculate the area of the circle";
   cout<<"\n 2. Calculate the circumference of the circle";
   cout<<"\n 3. Exit the program";
   cout<<"\n !  Enter choice";
   cin>>ch;
   switch(ch)
   {
    case 1: cout<<" \n The area of the circle is: "<<area()<<" square units \n";
              break;
    case 2: cout<<" \n The circumference of the circle is: "<<circumference()<<" units \n";
              break;
   }
  }
  while (ch!=3);
  getch();
 }
```

In this program, we have used 'PI' and 'radius' as global variables and used them in functions 'area()' and 'circumference()'. You may observe that declaring these variables as global variables not only saves us the trouble to separately declare these variables in these functions but also saves the computers memory space. Although global variables do allow or increase the chances of accidental changes of data a concept that you will learn in later chapters.

4.8.1 Solved Examples

Example 4.8.1.1
Determine the output of the following piece of code:

```
// Header Files
# include<iostream.h>
# include<conio.h>

void function1(int a, int b)
{
 a++;
 b = b + 5;
 cout<<"\n Function1  a:"<<a<<"\t Function1  b:"<<b;
}

void function2(int a, int c)
{
 a--;
 c=c+5;
 cout<<"\n Function2  a:"<<a<<"\t Function2  c:"<<c;
}

// Main Function
void main()
{
 clrscr();

 int a=7, b=0,c=2;

 function1(a,b);
 function2(a,c);

 cout<<"\n Main a: "<<a<<"\t Main b: "<<b<<"\t Main c:"<<c;
}
```

Solution of 4.8.1.1

We would observe the following output when this piece of code is executed.

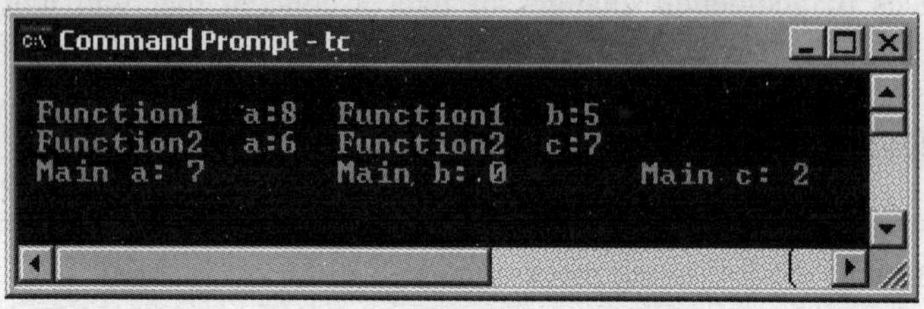

We start by declaring a set of variables 'a = 7', 'b =0' and 'c=2' of type integer in function 'main'. Then, we pass the values stored in variables 'a' and 'b' to 'function1'. The important thing to remember here is that just because 'function1' uses the same named variables 'a' and 'b' it does not mean that they point to the same memory blocks. The scope of variables 'a' and 'b' in function 'main' is limited to that function and hence they are not accessible to 'function1'. When 'function1' is called by the 'main' function, the compiler again declares variables 'a' and 'b' assigning them values '7' and '0' but pointing to different memory blocks as shown in figure 4.4.

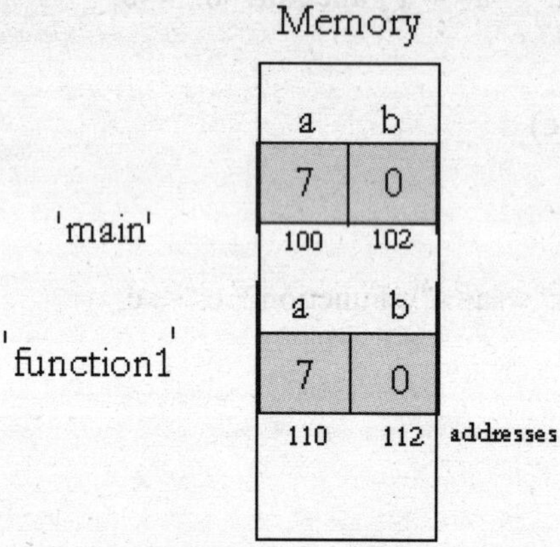

Figure 4.4: Example 4.7.1.1

As a result of this, any changes made to variables 'a' and 'b' of 'function1' do not alter values stored in variables 'a' and 'b' with memory locations '100' and '102' of function 'main' and we obtain the first line in the output screen as `Function1 a:8 Function1 b:5` . This is also illustrated in the figure given below. Using the same logic now try to find the rest of your output on your own.

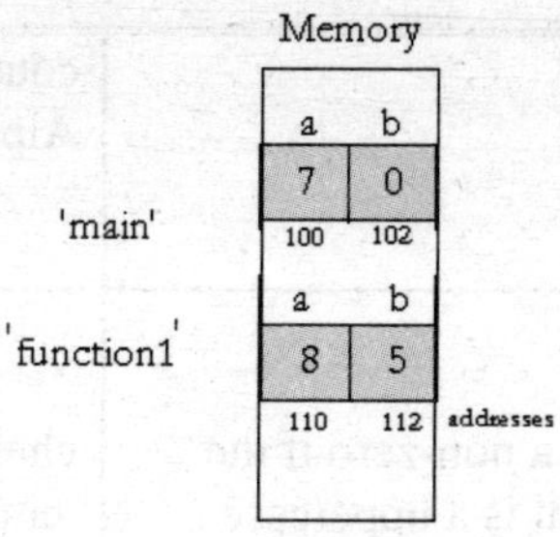

Figure 4.5: Example 4.7.1.1

4.9 Character functions in C++

The table 4.2 summarizes some character functions. To use these, you need to include the header file <ctype.h> in your programs.

Table 4.2: Character functions in C++

Function	Description	Example
isalnum()	Returns a non-zero if the argument is a letter or a digit.	char ch; cin>>ch; if (isalnum(ch)) cout<<"Alphanumeric";
isalpha()	Returns a non-zero if the argument is an alphabet.	char ch; cin>>ch; if (isalpha(ch)) cout<<"Alphabet";
isdigit()	Returns a non-zero if the argument is a digit.	char ch; cin>>ch; if (isdigit(ch)) cout<<"Digit";
islower()	Returns a non-zero if the argument is a lowercase alphabet.	char ch; cin>>ch; if (islower(ch))

		cout<<"Lower case Alphabet";
isupper()	Returns a non-zero if the argument is a uppercase alphabet.	char ch; cin>>ch; if (isupper(ch)) cout<<"Upper case Alphabet";

tolower()	Returns the lowercase equivalent of the argument.	char ch;
		cin>>ch;
		switch(tolower(ch))
		{
		case 'a':
		case 'e':
		case 'i':
		case 'o':
		case 'u': cout<<"Vowel";
		break;
		default;
		cout<<"Consonant";
		}

toupper()	Returns the upper case equivalent of the argument.	char ch; cin>>ch; if(toupper(ch)=='A') cout<<"You entered A"

4.10 Mathematical functions in C++

Table 4.3 summarizes the mathematical functions available in C++. They are defined under the header file <math.h>.

Table 4.3: Mathematical functions in C++

Function	description	Example
fabs(x)	Calculates the absolute value of floating point number x.	float a=-98.987 cout<<fabs(a); returns 98.987

abs(x)	Calculates the absolute value of an integer x.	int a=-76;
		cout<<abs(a);
		returns 76

log(y)	Calculate natural algorithm of y.	cout<<log(2); returns 0.693147
log10(y)	Calculates natural logarithm of y.	cout<<log(2); returns 0.30103
pow(x,y)	Calculates the power x to y	cout<<pow(3,2); returns 9

4.11 Recursive functions

Recursion is a technique where a function calls itself. It is generally used to implement a recursive algorithm. It solves a problem by representing it as an instance of the same problem with a smaller input size in each iteration of the function.

Each recursive function should have the following properties:

- **Base case**: Must have at least one case which can be solved without recursion.
- **Making progress**: At each step there must be some progress toward the base case so that the base case condition is eventually met.
- **Design rule**: during the design of the recursive algorithm, assume that all simpler recursive calls work.

For gaining in depth knowledge on recursive functions please see Appendix F (pp. 589-595).

4.12 Review Examples

Example 4.12.1

Write a program to take two numbers say, 'x' and 'y' from the user and add these numbers using a function and then display the sum of these two numbers on the screen.

FUNCTIONS

Solution of 4.12.1

```
// Header Files
# include<iostream.h>
# include<conio.h>

// Function prototype
int add(int x, int y);

// Main function
void main()
{
 int a,b;
 cout<<" Enter two variables";
 cin>>a>>b;
 cout<<" Sum:"<<add (a,b);
 getch();
}

/******************************
Name:add
Arguments: 'x' and 'y'
Purpose: Calculates the sum of two integers
********************/
int add(int x,int y)
{
 int sum=0;
 sum = x + y;
 return sum;
}
```

Example 4.12.2

Write a program which declares a function 'int accept(int a, int b, int c);' which accepts three parameters 'a', 'b' and 'c' inputted by the user and returns the value obtained by computing value of the expression 'a * b +c' to the main program which displays the returned value.

Solution of 4.12.2

```
// Header Files
# include<iostream.h>
# include<conio.h>

// Function accept
int accept(int a, int b, int c)
```

```
{
   return (a*b+c);
}

// main function
void main()
{
   int x, y, z;
   cout<<" Enter the three integers";
   cin>>x>>y>>z;
   cout<<" Result after evaluation: "<<accept(x,y,z);
   getch();
}
```

Example 4.12.3

Write a program to find the roots of a quadratic equation. Assume that the quadratic equation only has unequal or equal roots. The program should use separate set of functions to determine whether the equation has equal or unequal roots.

Solution of 4.12.3

```
// Header Files
    # include <iostream.h>
    # include <conio.h>
    # include <math.h>

// Function Prototypes
    void exitprogram();
    void equalroots(float, float);
    void unequalroots(float, float, float);

// Main Function
void main()
{
    /********
            Variable Declrations
                    Quadratic Equation: ax^2 + bx + c
                    Discriminant:D
                                                                    ********/
    float a, b, c, D;

    cout<<"Enter the Coefficients of the quadratic equation:";
   cin>>a>>b>>c;
```

FUNCTIONS

```
/*************
  Calculating D= b^2 - 4ac
  case 1: if D = 0 the equation has real and equal roots
        case 2: if D > 0 the equation has real and unequal roots

                  ********/

D = (b*b) - 4*a*c;

if (D<0)
{
        cout<<"\n The quadratic equation has unreal roots.";
        exitprogram();
}
        else if (D>0)
        {
                unequalroots(a,b,D);

                exitprogram();
        }
            else if(D==0)
            {
                    equalroots(a,b);

                    exitprogram();
            }
}

/********
Function: exitprogram

Purpose: To exit the program
******************************/

void exitprogram()
{
  cout<<"\n Thank you... For using the program";
}

/********
Function: equalroots

Purpose: To determine the unique equal root
```

```
*********************************************/

void equalroots(float a, float b)
{
  float root;
  root = (-b/(2*a));
  cout<<"\n The quadratic equation has equal roots:";
  cout<<"\n The only root is "<<root<<" with multiplicity 2";
  return;
}

/********
Function: unequalroots

Purpose: To determine the unequal roots
*********************************************/

void unequalroots(float a, float b, float D)
{
  float root1,root2;
  root1 = (-b + sqrt(D))/(2*a);
  root2 = (-b - sqrt(D))/(2*a);
  cout<<" The quadratic equation has unequal roots: "<<root1<<" and "<<root2;
  return;
}
```


Example 4.12.4

Write a program to display the following type of pattern using functions (The value of n entered by the user)?

```
        *
      * *
    * * *
  * * * *
* * * * *
```

Solution of 4.12.4

```
// Header Files
# include <iostream.h>
# include <conio.h>
```

```
// Function Prototype
void pattern ( int g);

// Main function
void main()
{
   int a;
   cout<<" Enter for how many do the numbers have to be entered ";
   cin>>a;
   pattern (a);
}

/*********************************************************************
// Function Name: Pattern
// Parameters: g (type:int)

// Purpose: To create the required pattern
*********************************************************************/
void pattern (int g)
{
  int t=g;
  for (int b=1;b<=g;b++)
   {
    for (int d = 0 ; d<t;d++)
    cout<<" ";
    for (int c=1;c<=b;c++)
    cout<<"*";
    cout<<"\n";
    t=t-1;
   }
 getch();
}
```

4.13 Review Exercise

2/3 Mark questions

Q1. What is functions single most important role?

Q2. What do you understand by the term 'function argument'?

Q3. Can preprocessor directives be passed as 'parameters' as well?

Q4. What is the difference between arguments passed by value or passed as reference?

Q5. How many values can be returned by a single function?

Q6. What does the function header tell us?

Q7. Overloaded functions are
   i. same named functions
   ii. functions having the same return type.
   iii. functions performing the same process.
   iv. examples of data redundancy.

Q8. A 'function calling statement' must supply arguments that
   i. match the function header in number
   ii. match the function header in number and order
   iii. match the function header in number, order, and data type
   iv. match the function header in number, order, data type, and names
   v. match the function header in number, names, and data type

Q9. How does a function report its answer back to its calling (or boss) function?
   i. by altering or storing the result into one of the variables passed as an argument
   ii. by altering or storing the result directly into the caller's variable
   iii. by cout-ing the result to the screen
   iv. by asking the user via an input function
   v. by executing a **return** statement with the answer.

Q10. Which of the following appear in a function header?
   i. the function name, return type, and argument types
   ii. the function name, return type, argument types and argument names
   iii. the function name, return type, and argument names
   iv. the function name and the supplied arguments

Q11. What is a default argument?

Q12. Write the main function to call the following function:

```
int sum(int a, int b=2)
   {
     return ( a + b);
   }
```

Q13. Assuming that the main program has already been compiled successfully will the following function also compile:

```
float sum ( int b=2, int a)
   {
      return ( a+b);
   }
```

4/5 Mark questions

Q14. Determine the values of y after each of the following statements

a) y = isalnum('a');

b) y = isalpha('b');

c) y= fabs(99.12);

Q15. For each of the following set of integers, write separate functions to find the sum of these series where n (number of terms to be included) is passed as a parameter.

a) 2..4..6..8..10…(2n).

b) 3..5..7..9..11...(2n+1).

c) 6..10..14..18…(2n+4).

Q16. Write a function that displays at the left side of the screen a solid square of dollar signs ($) where the side length (s) is passed as a parameter by the user.

Q17. Write a function which returns the greatest of the three floating point numbers passed to it as parameters.

Q18. Write a function that takes an integer as a parameter and returns 1 if the number with the digits reversed is same as the initial number passed to it as a parameter. (Palindrome Number), For example: 121 is such a number.

Q19. Identify the errors in the following program.

a)
```
int main ( void )
 {
  int sum( void )
   {
    cout<<" The sum is ">>a+b;
   }
 }
```

b) int difference (int x, int y)

```
{
  int diffrential;
  diffrential = x – y;
}
```

c) void remainder(float y)

```
{
  float result;
  result = y % 4;
}
```

Q20. Write the function headers for each of the following:

a) Function 'area' that takes two floating point variables viz. height and side and returns the calculated area as a float parameter.

b) Function 'even' which takes in an integer type and returns the value 1 if the number is even or 0 if the number is odd.

c) Function 'smallest' which takes in 5 parameters and returns the smallest parameter divisible by 3.

4.14 Programming Project

In the 12th century, Leonardo Fibonacci discovered a simple numerical series that is the foundation for an incredible mathematical relationship behind phi. Starting with 0 and 1, each new number in the series is simply the sum of the two before it.

0, 1, 1, 2, 3, 5, 8, 13, 21, 34, 55, 89, 144 . . .

The programming project is to create a program which declares a function after the man who discovered the series to print the terms of the Fibonacci series on the screen, where the number of terms to be displayed is passed as a parameter by the user.

4.15 Let us revise!

- ✓ Function is a named unit of group of program statements.
- ✓ Function call is the statement invoking the function.
- ✓ Function definition is the function declaration plus the body of the function.
- ✓ Actual parameters are the variables passed to a function.
- ✓ Formal parameters are the variables which receive the incoming parameters in the function.
- ✓ Global variable is a variable available to all the functions in the program.
- ✓ Local variable is a variable whose scope lies within the function in which it is declared.
- ✓ Functions help in data organization, increase program efficiency and reduce data redundancy.
- ✓ The general format for a function definition is:

```
return_type function_name ( parameters…)
{
    function definition
}
```

- ✓ Arguments can be passed by value where the functions make a copy of the passed argument and changes made to this copied formal parameters do not affect the actual parameters.
- ✓ A function prototype declares the return type of the function and declares the number, type and the order of parameters.
- ✓ The function which returns no value is a void function.
- ✓ A function can only return a single value.
- ✓ C++ allows function names to be overloaded, i.e. the same identifier name can be used in the same scope of both functions. The compiler decides the function to be used based on the number and types of parameters that are used while invoking the function. Function overloading is an example of 'polymorphism' a concept is explained in Part II, 'Chapter 1' of this book (Object Oriented Programming).

Part I

CHAPTER 5

ARRAYS

AIM

- Introduce the concept of 'Arrays'
- To understand the use of arrays to store, sort, and search lists of data in One/Multi dimensional arrays and strings.
- To be able to pass One/Multi dimension arrays to functions.
- To understand basic sorting techniques and memory allocation of arrays.

OUTLINE

5.1 Introduction
5.2 Declaring Arrays
5.3 Passing arrays as parameters to functions
5.4 Traversing of Arrays
5.5 Searching element in an array
5.6 Merging of arrays
5.7 Sorting with arrays
5.8 Arrays as strings
5.9 Two-dimensional arrays
5.10 Solved Examples
5.11 Review Exercise
5.12 Programming Project
5.13 Let us revise!

5.1 Introduction

Till now, we have studied on writing, printing and inputting single values. Each data type defined so far is stored in a single unique location and referred to as a single variable having its own name like 'sum', 'count', etc. Suppose, we have to make a program to store the names of ten items, we could start creating variables 'item1', 'item2', and 'item3' and so on but what if we have to create a program to store names for say 100 or say a 1000 items then what?

We could use the same approach but then the resulting program will be too long and cumbersome. Now suppose that instead of treating them as 100 similar but separate data items we could set aside a space large enough for storing all 100 values and assign a name to the storage area. Data items stored in this way are termed as 'arrays'.

5.2 Declaring Arrays

Arrays are data structures which hold multiple variables of the same data type. An array is a sequence of objects all of which have the same type. The objects are called elements of the array and are numbered consecutively 0, 1, 2, and so on. These numbers are called the index values or subscripts of the array (see Fig 5.1). The term 'subscript' is used because as a mathematical sequence, an array would be written with subscripts n_0, n_1, n_2, and so on. These numbers locate the elements position within the array, thereby giving direct access into the array.

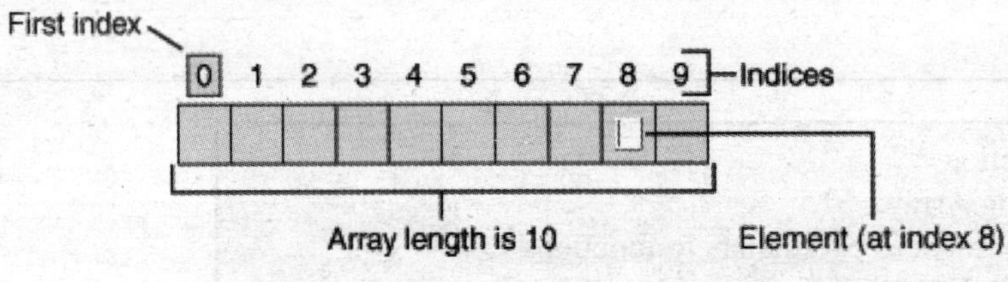

Figure 5.1: Array description

The elements of a one-dimensional array store all the elements in a consecutive order of entry into an array name. The subscripts of array are increased sequentially one-by-one to input the values into the array. A one-dimensional array is a list of variables that are all of the same type and referenced through a common name. An individual variable in the array is called an array element. Arrays form a convenient way to handle groups of related data.

Let's take an example to further understand the concept of arrays. Suppose you want to store 5 different integer values into the memory, and then find the sum of the values. Then you would use the following piece of code:

```
void main()
{
  clrscr();
  int num1, num2, num3, num4, num5;
  int sum=0;
  cout<<" Enter the five values";
  sum=num1+ num2+ num3+ num4+ num5;
  cout<<" The sum of the five values "<<sum;
}
```

The above piece of code declares five different locations in the computer memory for processing five integer values. By using arrays, we can allocate these five memory locations by a single variable name called array with a subscript value '5'. A subscript is a number, within brackets, that differentiates one element of an array from another. Elements are the individual variables in an array. To declare an array the following syntax is used:

Syntax:

data_type **array_name**[*subscripted range*];

Where 'data_type' is any C++ data type, **'array_name'** is the name of the array and '*subscripted range*' is the length of the array.

For example,

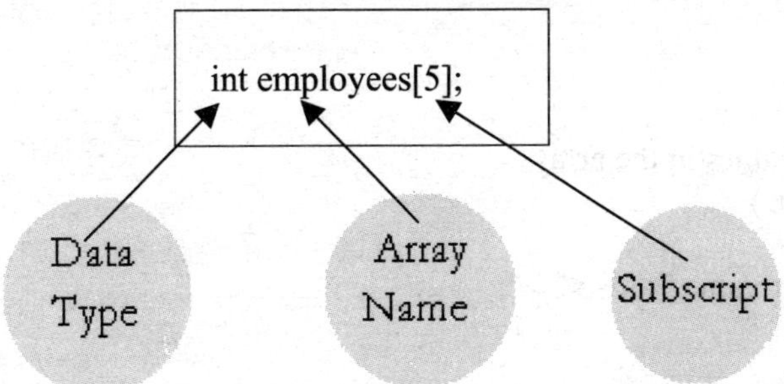

This statement declares an array 'employees' of type integer and it can store '5' integer values. Fig 5.2 shows how this array 'employees' is represented in the computer's memory.

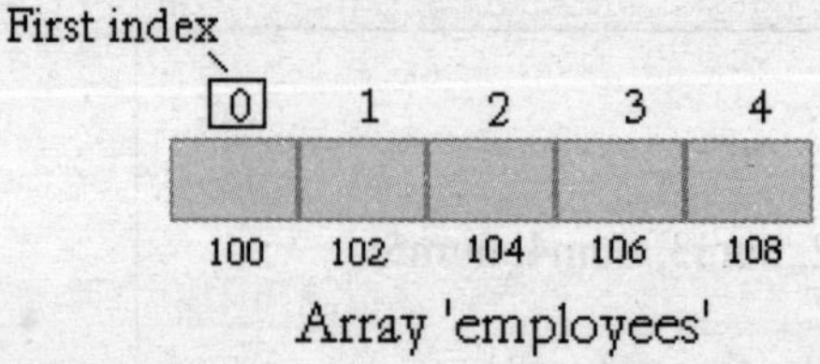

Figure 5.2: Array 'employees' in the computer's memory

The indexing of an array always starts from 'zero till 'size of the array -1'. The array elements are always stored in contagious memory locations ('100','102'...). Data entries in an array are accessed by using square brackets with an index value. For example, to access the first index of array 'employees' we would write 'employees [0];'. Similarly to access the second index of the array we would write 'employees [1];' and so on.

5.2.1 Solved Examples

Example 5.2.1.1

Write a program to enter five integer values from the user and print their sum on the screen.

Solution of 5.2.1.1

```
// Header Files
# include<iostream.h>
# include<conio.h>

// Main Function
void main()
{
  // Declaring an array 'num'
  int num[5];
  int i, sum=0;

  // Inputting the values in the array
  for ( i=0; i<5;i++ )
   {
    cout<<" Enter value "<<i<<"->";
    cin>>num[i];
   }

  // Calculating the sum of the values
  for ( i=0; i<5;i++)
   {
    sum = sum + num[i];
   }
```

```
    cout<<" The sum of all the five elements is"<<sum;
}
```

Output Screen

```
Enter value 0 -> 100
Enter value 1 -> 50
Enter value 2 -> 400
Enter value 3 -> 300
Enter value 4 -> 250
The sum of all the five elements is 1100
```

Let us try to understand how this program actually works. We begin by declaring an array by the statement: 'int num[5];'. This tells the compiler to set aside the memory space for 5 integer variables grouped together under the name 'num'. As one might notice in the figure given below these '5' integer variables which are grouped together are stored in contagious memory locations and can be accessed by changing the subscripts assigned with the array.

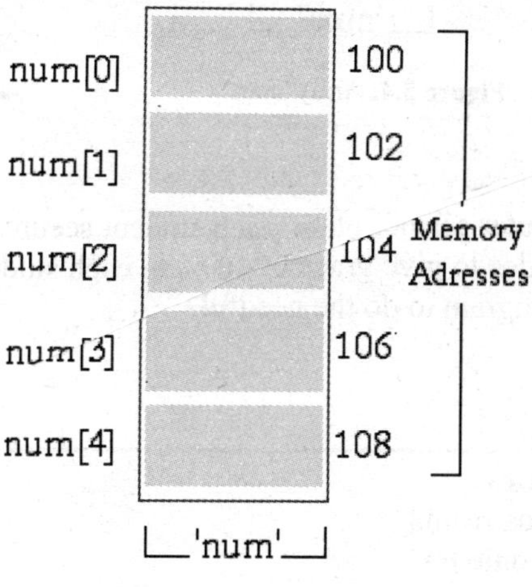

Figure 5.3: Array declaration

Once this is done next comes entering elements in our array 'num'. In example 5.2.1.1 this is done using the following piece of code.

```
// Inputting the values in the array
for ( i=0; i<5;i++ )
{
  cout<<" Enter value "<<i<<"->";
```

```
        cin>>num[i];
    }
```

The index variable 'i' takes values from '0' to '4' within the 'for' loop which are used to enter the array elements of array 'num'. Let us assume that the user enters the values '100', '50', '400', '300' and '250'. These values are then assigned to num[0], num[1], … num[4], i.e., in the order they were entered by the user (see fig. 5.4) which are finally used to calculate the sum of the array elements displayed on the screen.

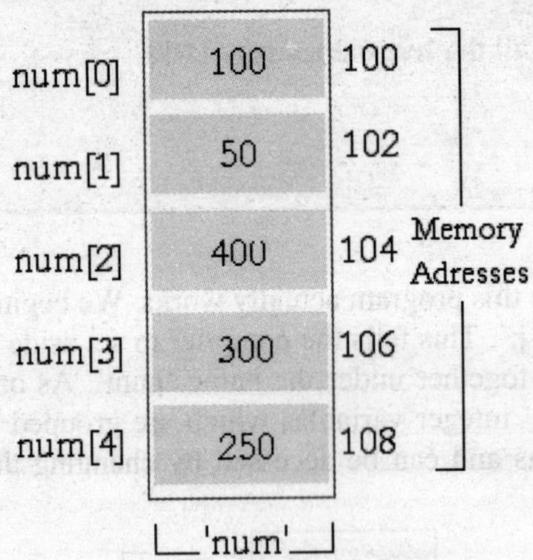

Figure 5.4: Array 'num'

Example 5.2.1.2

Suppose that in your computer science class, each student secures a certain percentage of marks and the teacher decides to give grace of 10 % to each student. If the class contains 20 students, write a C++ program to do the needful?

Solution of 5.2.1.2

```
// Header Files
# include <iostream.h>
# include <conio.h>

// Main Function
void main()
{
        // Variable Declrations
        float per[20];
    int i;
    cout<<" Enter the students percentages for the 20 students";
```

```
    // Entering student information from the student
    for( i=0;i<20;i++)
{
 cin>>per[i];
    }

    // Display the increased percentage of the 20 students
for (i=0;i<20;i++)
    {
      per[i] = per[i] + 10;
      cout<<per[i]<<endl;
    }
getch();
}
```

Common Programming Errors

- The subscripts of all the arrays should always begin with 0. For example in the array int a [5], the subscripts should begin with 0 as explained above.
- When using loops to initialize values into the array one should make sure that the index variable always contains a positive value.
- If the number of values assigned exceeds the size of the array or the program tries to access an index outside the bounds of the array such a statement is an example of a logical error. As the concurrent C++ compilers are very user friendly the compiler may not give an error but it will although produce unexpected results.
  For example,
  int A[3]={9,5,2,3} is an incorrect statement as we are assigning an integer value '3' to unallocated set of memory

5.3 Passing arrays as parameters to functions

Arrays are passed to functions as reference parameters. To pass an array argument to a function the array name is specified without any brackets. The syntax for passing arrays to functions is given below:

Syntax:

```
return_type function_name( data_type array_name)
```

For example, if array 'weeklyupdate' is defined as:

```
int weeklyupdate[10];
```

then the function call for a function 'modifyarray' which takes in an array as a parameter would look like 'modifyarray(weeklyupdate);'. Let us take up a program to further understand the concept of passing arrays to a function.

Program 5.1

```
// Header Files
# include<iostream.h>
# include<conio.h>

void calculate( int arr[5])
{
 for (int i=0 ; i<5 ;i++)
 {
  arr[i] = arr[i] + 10;
 }
}

void main()
{
 clrscr();

 int array_example[5];

 cout<<" Enter the elements of the array";

 for (int a=0; a<5; a++)
 {
  cin>>array_example[a];
 }

 // Modifying array
 calculate(array_example);

 cout<<" The modified array is as follows\n";
```

```
    for (a=0; a<5;a++)
    {
     cout<<array_example[a]<<"\n";
    }
    getch();
}
```

Now in this program, we have passed the array 'array_example' as a parameter to function 'calculate' which increments each array entry by 10 using the concept that

arrays are passed to functions as reference parameters. That is the array 'arr' defined in the function call for functions 'calculate' acts as a formal parameter to 'array_example'.

Hence any changes made to this formal parameter are also reflected back to the actual parameter 'array_example'. The output of this program is given below (Fig. 5.5):

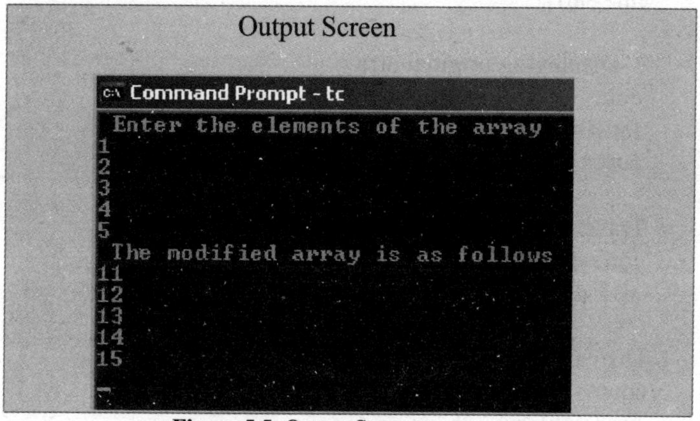

Figure 5.5: Output Screen

5.4 Traversing of Arrays

It is an operation in which each element of an array (i.e. from first element of an array to the last element of the array) is visited. Processing of the visited element can be done according to the requirements of the problem. Program 5.2 shows how traversal of arrays takes place.

Program 5.2: Traversal in an array

```
// Preprocessor Directives
# include <iostream.h>
# include <conio.h>

void main()
```

```
{
  clrscr();
  int  a[15],i,n;
  do
  {
    cout<<" Enter the number of elements in array less than 16";
    cin>>n;
  }
  while(n>15);

  // Traversing
  // Reading the array

  for(i=0;i<n;i++)
{
    cout<<" Enter "<<i+1<<" element : ";
    cin>>a[i];

    // Displaying original array
    cout<<" \n Original Array ";
    for (i=0;i<n;i++)
    cout<<a[i]<<" ";

  // Traversing (a[i]=a[i]*10)
    for(i=0;i<n;i++)
    a[i]=a[i]*10;

  // Displaying the transformed array
    cout<<" \n The transformed array :- \n";
    for (i=0;i<n;i++)
    cout<<a[i]<<" ";
    getch();
  }
```

5.5 Searching element in an array

The process of finding a particular element in an array is called as searching. This process can be carried out in two ways.

5.5.1 Linear Search

In linear search, each element of the array is compared with a search 'key'. The process of carrying out linear search is given below in program 5.3.

Program 5.3: Linear Search

```
// Header Files
# include<iostream.h>
# include<conio.h>

// Function Prototypes
void display (int [], int);
void  input (int [], int &);
int lsearch (int a[],int n, int data);

// Main Function
void main()
{
            // Variable and array declrations
            int a[10], n, data;

            input (a, n);

             cout<<" \n The Array ->"<<endl;
             display (a,n);

            cout<<" \n Enter element to be searched for: ";
            cin>>data;

            int x= lsearch(a,n,data);

            if (x!=-1)
            {
              cout<<data<<" Present at location "<<x<<endl;
            }
              else
              {
                      cout<<" Not present";
               }

            getch();
}


/*****************
 Function:lsearch
 Parameters: a[], n, data
 Purpose: To search for the desired data element
                        entered by the user in the array
```

```
**********************************************/

int lsearch (int a[],int n,int data)
 {
   int c=0,found=0;

           while ((c<n) && !(found))
           {
                  if (a[c]==data)
                  {
                         found++;
                  }
                         else
                              c++;
           }

           if (found)
           {
              return (c+1);
           }
                  else
                  {
                         return (-1);
                  }
         }


/*****************
Function:input
Parameters: a[], n
Purpose: To enter the elements of the array
**********************************************/
void input (int a[],int &n)
{
 int i;
 do
 {
  cout<<" Enter the number of elements <= 10:";
  cin>>n;
 }

 for(i=0;i<n;i++)
 {
   cin>>a[i];
  }
}
```

```
/*****************
Function:display
Parameters: a[], n
Purpose: To display the elements of the array
**********************************************/

void display (int a[], int n)
{
 int i;
 cout<<" The elements of the array are: \n";
 for (i=0;i<n;i++)
          {
          cout<<a[i]<<endl;
          }
}
```

5.5.2 Binary search

To understand the concept of binary search lets take up the following example. Let's say one is looking for the name 'Paul' in a phone book. Open up the phone book approximately half way and look for the name on the opened page. What does it say? Probably one sees a name that begins from 'M'. One would then think does 'Paul' come before or after 'M' in the phone book and realize that it comes in the latter portion of the phone book As a result of this we can ignore the entire first half of the phone book (Part before 'M'). Now open the remaining portion of the book half way. One is probably some where near the data entries starting with the alphabet 'T' in the phone book.

We can then again ask our selves the same question does 'Paul' come before or after data entries starting from alphabet 'T'. As the data entry 'Paul' comes before data entries starting from alphabet 'T', we can ignore the latter half of the phone book and then keep searching in the volume between letters 'M' and 'T'.

Repeating this process, we would eventually find the data entry 'Paul' we are looking for. This is how most of us search for data in huge volumes like a dictionary or a phone book.

This process of searching data through a sorted list is also known as binary search. In brief the process is to search a sorted array by repeatedly dividing the search interval in half. Begin with an interval covering the whole array. If the value of the search key is less than the item in the middle of the interval, narrow the interval to the lower half. Otherwise narrow it to the upper half. Repeatedly check until the value is found or the interval is empty.

The algorithm for binary search is given below:

Algorithm:

- The element to be searched for is taken from the user say the 'Key'.

- The given data array is taken. Any arbitrary lower limit or the lower bound for the data values is taken. Similarly one defines the upper limit or the upper bound. Then we obtain the middle value using.

  Middle = (lower bound + upper bound)/2;

- The search 'key' is compared to the Middle value if 'Key=Middle' then the search is complete. If Key<Middle, the program continues and the search is confined to the first half only. On the other hand if Key>Middle then also the program continues and the search is confined to the latter half. This process is continued till the time 'Key = Middle'.

Using binary search in a phone book containing one million entries, one can locate any specific data entry in at most 20 comparisons. The program to carry out binary search is given below:

Problem 5.4: Binary Search

```
/*************
Name:bsearch
Parameters: 'a', 'n', 'data'
Purpose: To perform binary search to sorted array 'a'
*******************************************/
int bsearch ( int a[], int n, int data)
  {
          int mid,lbound=0,ubound=n-1,found=0;
          while ((lbound<=ubound) && !(found))
           {
            mid = (lbound + ubound)/2;
            if (data > a[mid] )
              lbound = mid +1;
            if (data <a [mid] )
              ubound = mid -1;
            else
              found++;
           }
          if (found)
            return (mid + 1);      // Returning location, if present
          else
            return (-1);    // Returning -1, if not present
```

```
}
```

Common Programming Errors

- Binary search only works when the array to which it is applied is sorted.

5.6 Merging of arrays

This operation merges two sorted arrays into a single sorted array. Suppose 'a' is a sorted array with 'r' elements and 'b' is the sorted array with 's' elements, then the operation that combines the elements of 'a' and 'b' into a single array 'c' is called merging. Program 5.4 provides you with the code to merge two sorted arrays 'a' and 'b'.

Program 5.4: To merge two arrays (sorted in ascending order)?

```
 // Header Files
# include<iostream.h>
# include<conio.h>

// Main Function
void main()
{
  const int r=5;     // size of array A
  const int c=5;     // size of array B
  const int m=10;    // size of the merged array A and array B

  int a[r],b[c],res[m],i,j,k;

  // Enter Details of the first sorted array
  cout<<" Enter the first sorted array ==> "<<endl;
  for(i=0;i<r;i++)
  {
   cout<<" Element "<<i+1<<":";
   cin>>a[i];
  }
  // Enter the details of the second array
  cout<<" Enter the second sorted array ===>"<<endl;
  for(i=0;i<c;i++)
  {
   cout<<" Element "<<i+1<<":";
   cin>>b[i];
  }
```

```
// Initializing all index values to zero
i=0, j=0, k=0;

// Merging Arrays 'A' and 'B'
while ((i<r) && (j<c))
{
 if(a[i]<b[j])
 {
      res[k++]=a[i++];
 }

            else if (a[i]>b[j])
            {
                   res[k++]=b[j++];
            }

                   else
                   {
                          res[k++]=a[i++];
                          j++;
                   }
}

 int t;
 for (t=i;t<r;t++)
      {
            res[k++]=a[t];
      }

      for (t=j;t<c;t++)
      {
            res[k++]=b[t];
      }

      // Displaying Merged Array
      cout<<" Merged array ==>";

      for (i=0;i<k;i++)
      {
            cout<<endl<<res[i];
      }

      getch();
}
```

5.7 Sorting with arrays

Sorting is one of the most important operations performed by computers. The history of sorting goes back to the days when magnetic tapes were used for data storage .Before the emergence of modern databases, sorting was certainly the most common operation performed by computers as most database updating was done by sorting transactions.

Sorting still plays an important part for presentation of data extracted from databases as most people prefer to get reports sorted into some relevant order before wading through series of data. We will discuss two of the simplest method of sorting 'bubble' and 'selection' which will give you an idea of how sorting takes place.

Bubble Sort

Bubble sort is the simplest but unfortunately also the slowest method of sorting arrays. The basic idea when using bubble sort is to compare two neighboring objects and to swap them if they are present in the incorrect order. Given an integer array 'X', of size 'N' the piece of code to employ bubble sort is given below:

```
// Bubble Sort in Ascending Order

for (i=0; i<N; i++)
{
    for (j=0; j<N-1-i;j++)
     {
      if (X[j+1]<X[j]) /* Compare two neighboring elements */
       {
         temp = X[j]; /* Swap X[j] and X[j+1]     */

         X[j] = X[j+1];

         X[j+1]=temp;
       }
     }
}
```

As one might observe the piece of code given above consists of two nested *for* loops. The inner loop having 'j' as the index variable is used to compare adjacent entries in the array ('j' and 'j+1'). While the outer loop causes the inner loop to make repeated passes through the array in the process sorting the array. If the data elements are being sorted in the ascending order then after the first pass the largest element is shifted to the last position in the array. Similarly, after the second pass the second largest data element is placed next to the largest element. Which is the reason that in the inner loop the upper bound for 'j' is stated as 'N-1-I' as one does not need to revisit the end of the array. Let us take an example to understand how bubble sort works better. Suppose the array to be sorted 'X' consists of the following data entries:

21 60 29 52 17

Pass 1:

- Bubble sort begins by comparing the first two data elements in the array. As in this case the data element at 1st index of the array '60' is greater than the data element at the zeroth index '21' no swapping takes place.

- Once this is done the piece of code then compares the data elements at the first and the second index of the array. As '60' is greater than '29' the two data elements are swapped with the help of a temporary variable 'temp'. The result of which is that the largest of the three elements is now at the second index of the array.

21 29 60 52 17

- This process is repeated until all the indexes of the array have been compared with their adjacent indexes as a result of which largest data element bubbles to the end of the array.

21 29 52 60 17
21 29 52 17 60

- This marks the end of the 1st pass. After which the value of 'i' becomes '1' and the upper bound of nested loop with index variable 'j' is decreased by 1 (' N – 1 – i') as now we only have to compare the first 4 data elements in the array.

Similarly in the second pass through the array the second largest element is placed next to the largest. The process again involves the same steps as observed in the 1st pass the only difference being that the effective array size has now been decreased to '4'. This entire process is repeated till the entire array is sorted.

Selection Sort

Selection sort is also one of the simpler methods of sorting. It is almost twice as faster then bubble sort and works best for smaller files. Selection sort begins by first selecting the smallest data element in the unsorted list and then exchanging it with the data element in first position of the array. Once this is done, it then selects the second smallest element and exchanges it with the data element at the second position of the array. This process is carried on till the entire array has been sorted. Given an integer array 'X', of size 'N' the piece of code to employ selection sort is given below:

```
for (i = 0; i < N-1; i++)
{
  min = i;
  for (j = i+1; j < N; j++)
  {

    if (X[j] < X[min])
      min = j;
  }
  temp = X[i];
  X[i] = X[min];
  X[min] = temp;
}
```

Figure 5.6 explains the working of selection sort with the help of an example.

Array X	21 60 29 52 17
Pass 1	17 60 29 52 21
Pass 2	17 21 29 52 60
Pass 3	17 21 29 52 60
Pass 4	17 21 29 52 60

Figure 5.6: Selection Sort

5.8 Arrays as strings

C++ does not have a string data type rather it implements strings as single-dimension character arrays. A string is defined as a character array that is terminated by a null character '/0'. For this reason, the character arrays are declared one character longer than the largest string they can hold. This makes room for the null character at the end of the string. Individual characters of a string can be easily accessed as they make the elements of the character array. The index – refers to the first character, the index 1 to the second, 2 to the third, and so forth. The end of a string is determined by checking for a null character. For example,

A character array can be initialized using a string literal. For example,

```
char myfirststring[] = "Hello";
```

This statement declares a character string 'myfirststring'. The size of the string is automatically determined by the compiler based upon the length of the string. In this example, the compiler would determine the size of the string as '6'. As this string consists of '5' characters and a special null character ('\0') included at the end of each string.

Strings can also be declared using the following syntax:

```
char myfirststring[] = {'H', 'e', 'l', 'l', 'o', '\0'};
```

When assigning the null character '\0' you might think that we are assigning two characters '\' and '0' but this is not true the '\' symbol just tells the compiler that you are dealing with a special character which happens to be the null character '0'. As strings also are array of characters, they can also be accessed as any integer array. For example, myfirststring[0] is the character 'H' and myfirststring[1] is the character 'e'. Figure 5.7 given below shows how strings are stored in the computer's memory.

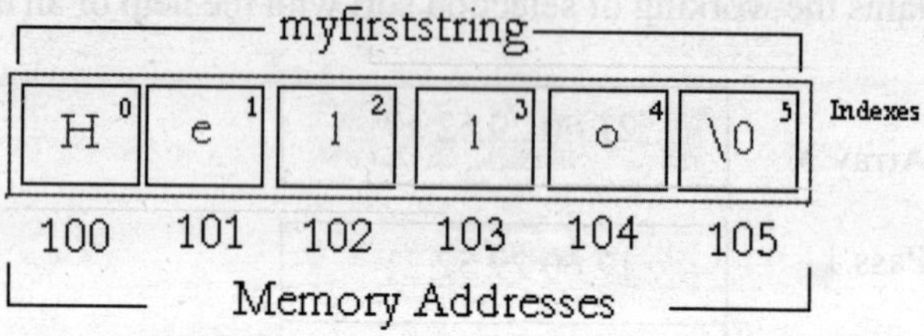

Figure 5.7: 'myfirststring'

The functions to display and print the string on the screen are defined under the <stdio.h> header file and are given in table 5.1.

Table 5.1: The <stdio.h> header file

Function	Usage
gets(string_name);	The function assigns the string inputted by the user to the parameter passed to it. For example, `char string_name[15];`

	gets(string_name); Returns the string inputted by the user to the character array 'string_name'. It works exactly like the 'cin' function defined under the <conio.h> header file which is used to enter integers, floats and characters.
puts(string_name);	The function prints the character array passed to it as a parameter on the screen. It works exactly like the 'cout' function which is used to display integers, floating points and characters on the screen. For example, char string_name[]="This is my first string"; puts(string_name); **Output Screen** 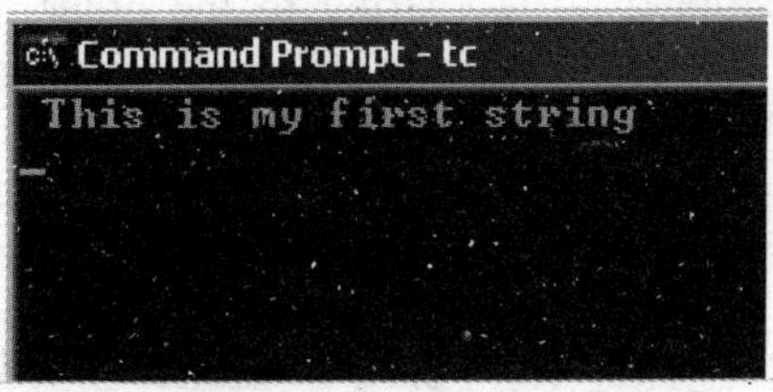

5.8.1 String functions

The <string.h> header file enlists a number of useful functions for dealing with null terminated strings. A brief description of the functions is given in table 5.2.

Table 5.2: The <string.h> header file

Function	Description
▪ strlen(string_name); 'string_name' is a string	The function calculates the length of the string passed to it as a parameter ('string_name') by counting the number of characters from the 0th index of the array to the index containing the null character marking the end of the string.

For example,

```
char string_name[20];
cout<<" Please enter the string: ";
gets(string_name);
cout<<"    The    length    of    the    string
is:"<<strlen(string_name);
```

Output Screen

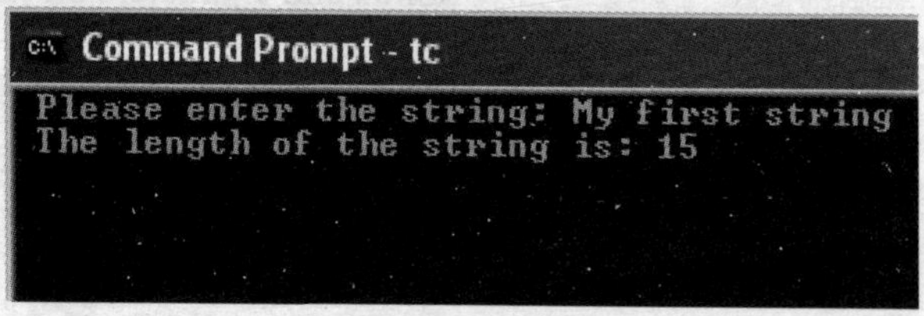

- strcpy(string1,string2)

Where 'string1' is the destination string and 'string2' is the source string.

C++ does not allow the programmer to directly assign one string to the other. For example the statement 'string1 = string2' will result in a syntax error. Hence for copying or assigning strings to a character array the 'strcpy' function is used. The function copies the string stored in 'string2' to the first string 'string1' which are passed to it as parameters. Let us look at a few examples to understand how this function works:

Examples,

-

```
char string1[]="My first string";
char string2[]="My last string";
cout<<strcmp(string1,string2);
```

Output Screen

•

```
char string1[20], string2[20];
cout<<" Enter a string:";
gets(string2);
strcpy(string1,string2);
cout<<" The entered string is:";
puts(string1);
```

Output Screen

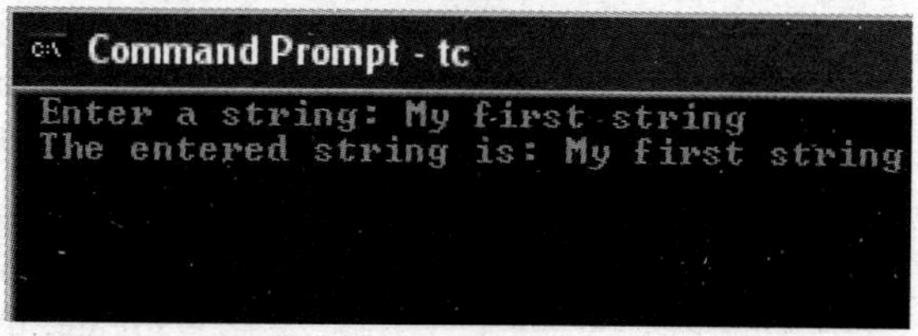

• Strcmp(string1,string2

The function is used to compare two strings passed to it as parameters by the programmer. The function starts comparing from the first character in each string and continues with subsequent characters until the corresponding characters differ or until the end of the strings is reached. Based upon this comparison the function returns the following values.

Return Value	Comparison

'0'	It returns a value '0' if both the strings passed to it as parameters ('string1', 'string2) are equivalent.
	Example,
	`char string1[]="My first string";`
	`char string2[]="My last string";`
	`cout<<strcmp(string1,string2);`

'>0'	It returns a value '>0' if 'string1' is greater than 'strings2'. The magnitude of the value returned is the difference between the ASCII values of the first dissimilar characters observed during the

String comparison

For example,

```
char string1[]="My first string";
char string2[]="My last string";
cout<<strcmp(string1,string2);
```

The function will return the value '6' as a result of the comparison between the strings passed to it. This is so because the first difference between the two strings occurs at the 4th index. As '1' and 'f' are not equivalent the difference in their ASCII values comes out to be '+6'.

The functions returns a value (<0) if 'string2' is greater than 'string1'.

For example,

```
char string1[]="My first string";
char string2[]="My last string";
cout<<strcmp(string1,string2);
```

When this piece of code is executed then a value of '-6 is observed on the screen instead of '+6' as in the previous example when 'string1' was greater than 'string2'.

- Strcat(string1,strings2);

  Where 'string1' and 'string2' are both strings.

The functions strcat appends a copy of 'string2' at the end of 'string1'. As a result of which the length of 'string1' becomes (strlen(string1) + strlen (string2)).

For example,

```
Char string1 []="My first";
char string1[20];
strcpy(string1,"My first string");
puts(string1);
```

	Output Screen
	My first string

5.8.2 Solved Examples

Example 5.8.2.1

Write a program to check whether the string entered by the user is a palindrome or not?

Solution 5.8.2.1

```
// Preprocessor Directives
  #include<iostream.h>
  #include<conio.h>
  #include<stdio.h>
  #include<string.h>

// Main Function
  void main()
  {
   clrscr();
   char string[40],i;
   int j=0,flag=0;
   cout<<" Enter string";
   gets(string);
   j=strlen(string)-1;
   for (i=0;i<strlen(string)-1;i++)
   {
      if (string[i] != string[j])
      {
        flag++;
      }
     j--;
   }

   if (flag==0)
```

```
    {
    cout<<" \n |Entered string is palindrome|";
    }
    else
        cout<<" Entered string is not a palindrome";
        getch();
}
```

OUTPUT SCREEN

```
Enter the string MaM

|Entered string is a palindrome|
```

Example 5.8.2.2

Write a program to enter a string from the user and then display the inputted string with all the spaces converted into '#'s?

Solution of 5.8.2.2

```
// Preprocessor Directives
# include<iostream.h>
# include<conio.h>
# include<string.h>
# include<stdio.h>

// Main Function
void main()
{
 clrscr();
 char string[15];
 cout<<" Enter the string";
 gets(string);
 for (int i=0;i<strlen(string);i++)
 {
   if (string[i]==' ')
   {
    string[i]='#';
   }
 }
 cout<<" \n Displaying the converted string \n";
 puts(string);
```

```
   getch();
  }
```

Output Screen

```
Enter the string My sisters name is Deepti

Displaying the converted string
My#sisters#name#is#Deepti
```

Example 5.8.2.3
Write a program to count the no. of vowels in the given string?

Solution of 5.8.2.3

```
// Header Files
# include<iostream.h>
# include<conio.h>
# include<string.h>
# include<stdio.h>

  void main()
  {
     clrscr();
     char string[15];
     int vowels=0;
     cout<<" Enter the string";
     gets(string);
     for (int i=0;i<strlen(string);i++)
     {
       if (string[i]=='a' || string[i]=='e' || string[i]=='o' ||string[i]=='i' ||  string[i]=='u')
      {
        vowels++;
       }
     }
     cout<<" \n The no. of vowels are"<<vowels;
     getch();
  }
```

OUTPUT SCREEN

```
Enter the string Ankit

The no. of vowels are 2
```

5.9 Two-dimensional arrays

A two-dimensional array is an array in which each element is itself an array. For instance, an array A[M][N] is an M by N table with M rows and N columns containing M * N elements figure 5.8.

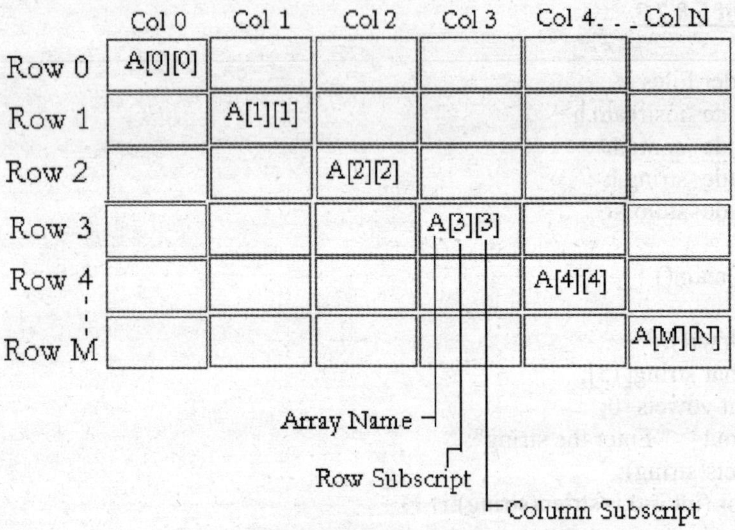

Figure 5.8: Two Dimensional Arrays

The number of elements in a 2-D array can be determined by multiplying number of rows with number of columns. For example, the number of elements in an array A[5][3] is calculated as 15.

This two-dimensional array may also be visualized as a one-dimensional array of arrays. An alternative view of this array is given in the figure 5.9.

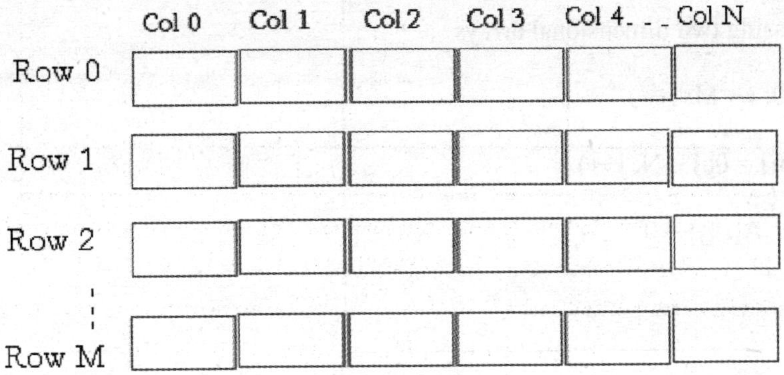

Figure 5.9: Two dimensional Arrays

The simplest form of a multi-dimensional array, the two-dimensional array, is an array having single-dimension arrays as its elements. The general form of a two-dimensional array declaration in C++ as follows:

Type array-name*[rows][columns]*

Where type is the base data type of the array having name *array-name; rows,* the first index, refers to the number of rows in the array and *columns,* the second index, refers to the number of columns in the array. The following declaration declares a character array 'name' having '5' rows and '25' columns.

```
char name[5][25];
```

Just like one dimensional arrays two dimensional arrays can also be initialized at the time of declaration. The following declaration assigns values for three grades for each of the first two students in the array.

```
int grades[Student_Number][Grades_achieved] = { {55, 60, 65},{95, 90, 85}};
```

Note: Data entries for each row are enclosed in individual curly braces.

5.9.1 Accessing Two Dimensional Arrays

Two dimensional arrays are accessed/ initialized with the help of two square brackets. The following piece of code given below is used to access an array 'A' of size 'M*N' ('M rows, N columns) and initialize all its members to zero.

```
...
{
 ...
 // Accessing two dimensional arrays
 int i, j;
 for(i = 0; i < M; i++)
   {
     for(j = 0; j < N; j++)
       {
         A[i][j] = 0;
       }
   }
}
```

When accessing two dimensional arrays it is important to put each subscript in its own, correct pair of brackets. Trying to initialize or access elements of a two dimensional array would produce syntax errors. For example,

```
/* Incorrect Statements */
        int A[M, N];
        A[i, j] = 0;
        A[j][i] = 0;
```

5.9.2 Passing Two Dimensional Arrays as a Parameter to Functions

As one dimensional array, two dimension arrays are also passed to functions by reference automatically. Program 5.5 declares a two dimensional array 'actual_2darray' which is initialized by the user and then passed to the function 'display' where it is displayed in matrix form.

Program 5.5: Two dimensional arrays as function arguments

```
// Header Files
# include<iostream.h>
# include<conio.h>

// Function prototype
 void display(int formal_2darray[3][3]);

// Main Function
void main()
{
 clrscr();
 int actual_2darray[3][3];

 // Enter 2d Array
```

```
cout<<" Enter the elements of the 2 dimensional array:";

for (int i=0; i<3; i++)
  {
    for (int j=0; j<3; j++)
      {
        cin>>actual_2darray[i][j];
      }
  }

//Passing 2d array to function
 display(actual_2darray);
}

/******************************
Name: display
Purpose: To display the 2d array in Matrix form
*************************************/

void display(int formal_2darray[3][3])
{
 cout<<endl<<" Displaying the 2d array in Matrix Form... \n"<<endl;
 for (int i=0; i<3; i++)
   {
   for (int j=0; j<3; j++)
       {
       cout<<"\t"<<formal_2darray[i][j]<<" ";
       }
       cout<<endl;
   }
}
```


The following output is observed when the program 5.5 is executed:

OUTPUT SCREEN

```
Command Prompt - tc
Enter the elements of the 2 dimensional array: 1 2 3 4 5 6 7 8 9

Displaying the 2d array in Matrix Form...

        1       2       3
        4       5       6
        7       8       9
```

5.9.3 Mapping of Two Dimensional Arrays

Although, we visualize two dimensional arrays by rectangular tables this is not the way two/multi dimension arrays are stored in the computers memory. The computer's memory only supports a linear placement of data items akin to a one-dimensional array as a result of which the memory simulates the two/multi dimensional array as a one dimensional array. This process is called as Mapping of an array. For example, for a two dimensional array 'Two_dimension_array[M][N];' having 'M*N' as the maximum number of elements that can be stored into it. The computer maps the two dimensional array into one dimension using the following formula:

Two_dimension_array[i * N + j]

Where 'i' represents the corresponding row, 'j' represents the corresponding column and 'N' represents the maximum number of columns allowed in the two dimensional array 'Two_dimension_array'.

Assuming 'N' to be '10' the data entry stored at 'Two_dimension_array[2][3]' is mapped into a one dimensional array say, Single_dimension_array[2*10 +3]. Hence, we can also use this for 'Single_dimension_array[i * N+j]' in place of 'Two_dimension_array[i][j]' as both point or reflect to the same memory block. The entire process of mapping is explained in the part III of the book.

5.9.4 Solved Examples

Example 5.9.4.1

Write a program to accept a sequence of strings, storing them in a two dimensional array, and then print them on the screen?

Solution of 5.9.4.1

```
// Header Files
# include<iostream.h>
# include<string.h>
# include<stdio.h>

// Main Function
void main()
{
  clrscr();
  char name[5][25];
```

```
cout<<"Enter the names with a maximum of 24 characters";
 for(int i=0;i<5;i++)
gets(name[i]);

cout<<" \n The names stored are";
for (i=0;i<5;i++)
puts(name[i]);

getch();
}
```

OUTPUT SCREEN

```
Enter the names with the maximum of 24 characters
Ankit Asthana
Kartik Gupta
Deepti Asthana
Karan Chopra
Neha Maheshwari

The names stored are
Ankit Asthana
Kartik Gupta
Deepti Asthana
Karan Chopra
Neha Maheshwari
```

5.10 Solved Examples

ARRAYS

Example 5.10.1

Write a program to create a matrix of order 4*4 containing integer elements using a function swap which swaps the value of two integers print the transpose of this matrix (without using a 2nd matrix)?

Solution of 5.10.1

```
// Header Files
# include <iostream.h>
# include <conio.h>
# include <iomanip.h>

// Function Prototype
void swap(int e, int f);
```

```
// Main Function
void main()
{
int a,b,c,d,e,f;
int trans[5][5];
cout<<"Enter the size of the 2-dimensional array A(Rows(<5) and Columns(<5))";
cin>>a>>b;
swap(a,b);
cout<<"Thank you for using the program ";
getch();
}

/*******************************
Name: swap
Parameters: int e, int f
Purpose: Transpose the matrix
*******************************/
void swap( int e, int f)
{
 int arr1[5][5];
 int arr2[5][5];
 int a,b,c,d;

 // Transposing the array
 cout<<" Enter array A";
 for (int p=0;p<e;p++)
 for (int q=0;q<f;q++)
 cin>>arr1[p][q];

 for (int i=0;i<e;i++)
 for (int j=0;j<f;j++)
 arr2[j][i]=arr1[i][j];

 cout<<" Displaying";
 for (int t=0;t<10;t++)
 {
  cout<<".";
 }
 cout<<" Elements of A"<<endl;

 for (i=0;i<e;i++)
 {
  for (int j=0;j<f;j++)
  cout<<setw(8)<<arr1[i][j];
  cout<<endl;
 }
```

```
cout<<" Transposed array A as follows  \n\n";

for (int j=0;j<f;j++)
{
 for (i=0;i<e;i++)
 cout<<setw(8)<<arr2[j][i];
 cout<<endl;
}
}
```

OUTPUT SCREEN

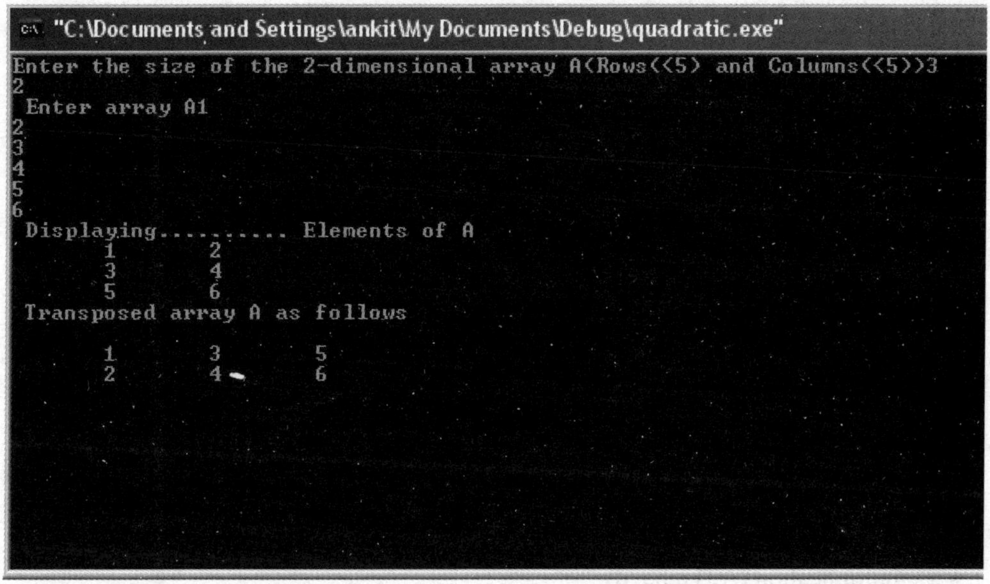

Example 5.10.2
Write a program to create two matrices A and B and to store the product of these two matrices into another matrix C. The program should use a separate function to calculate the product of the two matrices.

Solution of 5.10.2

```
// Header Files
# include <iostream.h>
# include <conio.h>
# include <dos.h>

// Function Prototype
```

```
void multiplication (float arr1[5][5], float arr2[5][5], int s, int t, int u, int v);

// Main Function
void main()
{
  float A[5][5],B[5][5];
  int a,b,c,d;
  cout<<"\n Enter the size of array 1 ";
  cin>>a>>b;
  cout<<" Enter the elements of array 1";

  for (int e=0;e<a;e++)
  {
      for (int f=0;f<b;f++)
      {
              cin>>A[e][f];
      }
  }

  cout<<"\n Enter the size of the array 2";
  cin>>c>>d;

  cout<<" Enter the elements of the array 2";
  for (e=0;e<c;e++)
  {
      for (int f=0 ; f<d;f++)
      {
              cin>>B[e][f];
      }
  }

  multiplication (A,B,a,b,c,d);

}

/*********************
Name: multiplication

Purpose: To calculate the product of two matrices passed to it as parameters
**************************************************************/
void multiplication (float arr1[5][5], float arr2[5][5], int s, int t, int u, int v)
{

 int C[5][5];
```

```
if (t==u)
{
 for (int i=0;i<s;i++)
 {
     for (int j=0;j<v;j++)
             { C[i][j]=0;
                 for (int k=0;k<t;k++)
                             C[i][j]= C[i][j] + arr1[i][k] * arr2[k][j];
             }
}

// Displaying array 1
cout<<" \nArray 1 in matrix form is as follows \n\n";
for (i=0;i<s;i++)
{
     for (int j=0;j<t;j++)
     {
             cout<<"\t"<<arr1[i][j]<<" ";
     }

 cout<<endl;
}

//Displaying array 2
cout<< "\nArray 2 in matrix form is as follows \n\n";
for (i=0;i<u;i++)
   {
             for (int j=0;j<v;j++)
             {
                     cout<<"\t"<<arr2[i][j]<<" ";
             }
    cout<<endl;
   }

// Displaying array 3
cout<<"\nArray C = A * B in  matrix form is as follows \n"<<endl;
for (i=0;i<s;i++)
   {
             for (int j=0;j<v;j++)
             {
             cout<<"\t"<<C[i][j]<<" ";
             }
    cout<<endl;
   }
}
else
```

```
{
cout<<"\n Matrices not Compatiable";
}
}
```

Example 5.10.3

Write a program to create a matrix of the order of '5 * 5' containing integer elements. Write user defined functions to do the following:

(1) Find the sum of the elements lying on the left diagonal
(2) Find the sum of the elements lying on the right diagonal
(3) Find the sum of the elements lying on both the diagonals

Solution of 5.10.3

```
// Header Files
# include <iostream.h>
# include <conio.h>

// Function Prototypes
void suml ( int arr1[ ][5], int c, int d) ;
void sumr ( int arr1[ ][5], int c, int d) ;
void sumb ( int arr1[ ][5], int c, int d) ;
void display (int arr1[ ][5],int c ,int d);

// Main Function
void main()
{
  int a,b,e,f;
  int arr[5][5];

  do
  {
    cout<<"\nEnter the dimensions of the square matrix(rows and columns):";
    cin>>a>>b;
    if (a!=b)
    {
          cout<<"\nInvalid Dimensions.\n";
    }
  }while (a!=b);

  cout<<"\nEnter the elements of the array:";
  for (e=0;e<a;e++)
  for (f=0;f<b;f++)
  cin>>arr[e][f];

  display(arr,a,b);
```

```
  suml(arr,a,b);

  sumr(arr,a,b);

  sumb(arr,a,b);

  getch();
}

/*********
Name:suml
Parameters: arr1[][], c, d
Purpose: To calculate the sum of the left diagonal
***************************************************/
void suml( int arr1[5][5], int c,int d )
 {
   int lsum=0;
   int i;
   int j;

   // sum of left diagonal
   for (i=0; i<c; i++)
   {
      for (j=0; j<d; j++)
            if (i==j)
              {
                     lsum+= arr1[i][j];
              }
   }
   cout<<"\nSum of the elements on the left diagonal "<<lsum<<endl;
 }

/*********
Name:sumr
Parameters: arr1[][], c, d
Purpose: To calculate the sum of the right diagonal
***************************************************/

void sumr(int arr1[5][5],int c,int d)
{
  int rsum=0;
  int j=d-1;

  // Sum of the right diagonal
  for (int i=0;i<c;i++)
```

```
    {
            rsum+=arr1[i][j];
            j--;
    }
  cout<<endl<<"The sum of the elements on the right diagonal
"<<rsum<<endl;
}

/*********
Name:sumb
Parameters: arr1[][], c, d
Purpose: To calculate the sum of both diagonal
*************************************************/

void sumb(int arr1[5][5], int c,int d)

{
  int lsum=0;

  // Sum of left diagonal
  for (int i=0;i<c;i++)
    {
            for (int j=0;j<d;j++)
                    if (i==j)
                    {
                            lsum+=arr1[i][j];

                    }
  }

  int lrsum=0;
  int rsum=0;
  int j=d-1;

  // Sum of the right diagonal
  for (i=0;i<c;i++)
  {
    rsum+=arr1[i][j];
    j--;
  }

  // Sum of both the diagonals
  if (c%2==0)
  {
      lrsum= lsum+rsum ;
  }
```

```
        else
            {
                  int b=c/2;

                  lrsum= lsum + rsum - arr1[b][b];
            }

  cout<<endl<<"The sum of both the diagonals "<<lrsum<<endl;
}

/*********
Name:display
Parameters: arr1[][], m, n
Purpose: To display the matrix
**************************************************/
void display (int arr1[5][5], int m,int n )
{
   // To clear the screen
   cout<<"\nMatrix -> \n"<<endl;
   for (int i=0;i<m;i++)
   {
         for (int j=0;j<n;j++)
               {
                     cout<<arr1[i][j]<<" \t ";
               }

         cout<<endl<<endl;
   }
}
```

5.11 Review Exercise

1/2 mark questions

Q1) Is the following declaration valid?
'unsigned int arr(7);'

Q2) State whether the following statements are true or false:
(i) An array element is accessed using a dot operator.
(ii) An array can store many different types of values.
(iii) This is an syntactically correct statement int arr[2.3];
(iv) An individual array element is passed to a function and not the entire array.

Q3) Arrays are passed to functions as:
(i) reference parameters.
(ii) formal parameters.

ARRAYS

(iii) actual parameters
(iv) (i) and (iii) are correct
(v) None of the above

Q4) The number of bytes occupied by the two dimensional array A[10][10] are:
a) 100 bytes
b) 10 bytes
c) 20 bytes
d) 40 bytes
e) None of the above

Q5) State whether the following are true or false:
a) Arrays can have more than two dimensions
b) There is no difference between a character array and a string.
c) Arrays are a collection of elements belonging to the same data type.
d) An array element is accessed using the dot operator.

Q6) Write C++ statements for the following questions:
a) *Array* birds having 50 elements of type *int.*
b) A *float* array sum of index value 23.
c) A statement that checks for the occurrence of string "Dog" in the *string* s1.

Q7) Are the following statements syntactically correct:
a) int x[2][2] = { {0,1},{1,2}};
x[1,1]=5;
b) int name1[15];
char name2[15];
strcat(name1,name2);
c) int x[4][0] = { (0,0)};

Q8) Write statements to accomplish the following:
i) Display the value of the fifth element of array 'A'.
ii) Print a value into element 5 of single-subscripted *long int* array A.
iii) Initialize each of the eight members of single subscripted *array* A to 0.
iv) Print the grand total of integer array 'num' containing 100 elements.
v) Copy all the elements of integer array 'A' into floating-point array 'B'.
vi) Determine the smallest and the largest integer values from a character array 'A' containing 15 elements. Hint: Use type casting (ASCII Values)

Q9) Consider a 5 by 5 integer array 'A'.
a) Write C++ statement to define this array?
b) How much space (in bytes) does this declaration involve using the declaration?
c) How many columns does it have?
d) How many rows does it have?
e) How many elements does it have?
f) Write the names of all the elements in the second row in array A.

g) Using loops initialize each member of array A to a value of 0.
h) Using loops input values for each member of Array A.
i) Determine the sum of elements on the main diagonal of this array A inputted in the above statements.
j) Print this array A in matrix (tabular) form.

Q10) Using binary search how many comparisons will the array of following size take
i) 1023 elements
ii) 1048576 elements
(**Hint:** Binary search eliminates one half of the elements in a sorted array after each comparison)

4/5 mark Questions

Q11) Write a program to initialize an integer array **numbers** containing 100 elements. Initialize these elements values from 1 to 100 in ascending order. Create another array **even** which stores those elements of array numbers that are even. Also display all the elements of array even?

Q12) Write a program to create two matrices a of the order m*n and matrix b of the order p *q. Write a user defined functions to do the following:
a. Create another matrix 'c' where each element of 'c' is the sum of the corresponding elements of the array 'a' and 'b'.
b. Create another matrix'd' where each element'd' is the difference of the corresponding elements of the arrays 'a' and 'b'.
c. Write a function display to display the following matrices 'a', 'b', 'c' and 'd'.
d. Find the transpose of matrix a and display it

Q13) Write user defined functions to do the following
a. Create 2 matrices 'x' & 'y' of the order 'a*b', 'c*d' respectively containing integer values
b. Create a 3rd matrices which has the sum of the array X and array Y

5.12 Programming Project

In section 5.8.4, we studied how the computer memory stores two dimension arrays by simulating them in a single dimension. The programming project for this chapter is to state how C++ maps a three dimensional array (i.e. array_name[row][col][depth]) to one dimensional memory. Write a fully commented and structured ANSI C++ program that uses a single looping structure (of your choice) and your 3-D to 1-D mapping to print out the following array: int map_3d[2][2][2] = {5,10,15,20,25,30,35,40}.

5.13 Let us revise!

- ✓ An array is a collection of variables of the same type that are referenced by a common name.
- ✓ Arrays can be one dimensional, two dimensional or multi dimensional.
- ✓ An array is declared by specifying its base type, name and size.
- ✓ An array of type *char* can be used to store a character string.
- ✓ In C++, arrays are passed to functions as reference that is any changes made to the formal array will be reflected back to the actual array.
- ✓ To receive an array argument the formal array should be of the same type as the actual array.
- ✓ The data type of array elements is known as the base type of the array.
- ✓ In C++, array indices start from 0, and are up to size 1.
- ✓ C++ considers strings as single dimension arrays.
- ✓ The total number of bytes stored in a two dimensional array is given by the formulae: number of rows (1st index) * number of columns (2nd index) * sizeof(base type).
- ✓ Linear search compares each element of the array with a specific element (Search key). Works very well for smaller arrays or unsorted arrays.
- ✓ Binary search also a method for searching elements in an array. The algorithm for the binary search eliminates one half of the array after each comparison. If and when element is found the elements position is stored. Binary search works great for larger arrays but the only limitation is that the array should be sorted.
- ✓ The data type of array elements is known as the base type of the array.
- ✓ In C++, array indices start from 0, and are up to size 1. The total number of bytes stored in a two dimensional array is given by the formulae: number of rows(1st index) * number of columns(2nd index) * sizeof(base type).
- ✓ Sorting is to arrange the various elements of an array in either ascending or descending order. It is of three types bubble, insertion, selection
- ✓ C++ considers strings as single dimension arrays. The total number of bytes stored in a two dimensional array is given by the formulae: number of rows(1st index) * number of columns(2nd index) * sizeof(base type).
- ✓ Sorting is to arrange the various elements of an array in either ascending or descending order. It is of three types bubble, insertion, selection

Part I

CHAPTER 6

STRUCTURES

AIM

- Introduce the concept of 'Structures'
- How to declare and use Structures, Arrays of Structures and Nested Structures.
- Close comparison between Structures and arrays
- How to create Pointer to a Structure
- Pass and return structures to functions
- Appreciate the concept of Structures

OUTLINE

6.1 Introduction
6.2 Structure Definitions
6.3 Structure Variables
6.4 Accessing Members of a Structure
6.5 Structure Arrays
6.6 Structures with Functions
6.7 Nested Structures
6.8 Solved Examples
6.9 Review Exercise
6.10 Programming Project
6.11 Let us revise

6.1 Introduction

Suppose one has lots of different but related data, one would prefer to store this data together in a single unit. Let me take a very common example, which we have often observed while using computers. Think about random folders and icons lying on your desktop like 'Recycle Bin' which stores all the deleted files together, 'My Documents' which stores all documents and spread sheets and 'My Network Places' which stores all files related to 'Networking'. All in all, these icons consist of similar files which are put together making up these single units to help organize data and files.

This process in C++ is achieved by the help of structures. A structure is a heterogeneous collection of data. It is a collection of data of different data types. A structure empowers us to create our own data types by using the collection of fundamental and derived data types available in C++ which serves as an efficient way of grouping several pieces of related information together. Just the same way as random lying papers are grouped in a file and words are put together to form sentences.

6.2 Structure Definition

Till now, we have learnt about simple data types like *int*, *char*, and *float*. Structure allows us to declare user defined data types thus increasing the number of data types. A structure is declared using the following C++ statements:

Syntax:

```
struct < tag name>
{
  data_type1 var1;
  data_type2 var2;
  data_type3 var3;
};
```

The structure definition tells us about how the structure is organized. It informs the compiler about the various data members present inside the structure.

Figure 6.1 helps in understanding structure declaration.

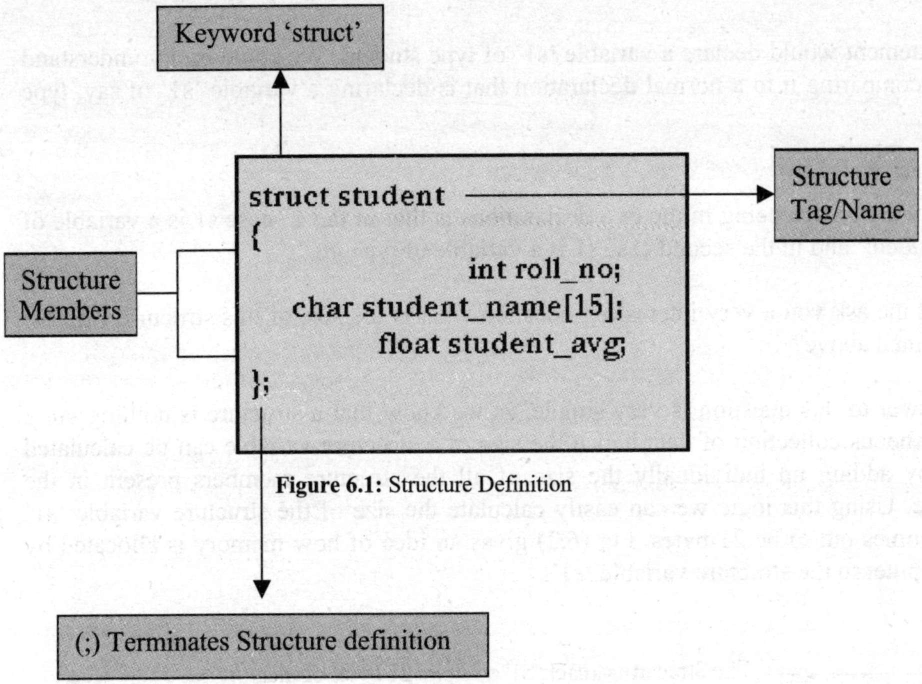

Figure 6.1: Structure Definition

To declare a structure one has to start with the keyword 'struct'. The keyword 'struct' informs the compiler that a structure is being declared. The identifier 'student' is the structure name. The variables within the structure 'student', 'roll_no' of type integer, a character array 'student_name' and a floating variable 'student_avg are known as structure's members which are enclosed between a pair of curly braces ({ }). The semicolon (;) is used to terminate the structure definition.

The important thing to understand at this point is that this structure definition alone does not actually create any variables in other words no memory has been assigned to these variables. With this declaration one has declared a type of structure which we will use further to create structure variables. They are used to declare new data types.

6.3 Structure Variables

As we already know that the structure definition does not declare any variables. To do this we need to declare a structure variable for the defined structure. This is done by again starting with the structure name already defined with the structure variable name.

For example, if one wishes to create structure variables for the structure 'student' defined above one would just write the following c++ statement.

student s1;

This statement would declare a variable 's1' of type student. We could easily understand this by comparing it to a normal declaration that is declaring a variable 's1' of say, type integer.

int s1;

The only difference being in the two declarations is that in the 1st case s1 is a variable of type 'student' and in the second case s1 is a variable of type *int*.

Now let me ask you a very interesting question what is the size of this structure variable 's1' defined above?

The answer to this question is very simple, as we know that a structure is nothing but a heterogeneous collection of data hence the size of a structure variable can be calculated easily by adding up individually the size of all the structure members present in the structure. Using this logic we can easily calculate the size of the structure variable 's1' which comes out to be 21 bytes. Fig (6.2) gives an idea of how memory is allocated by the computer to the structure variable 's1'.

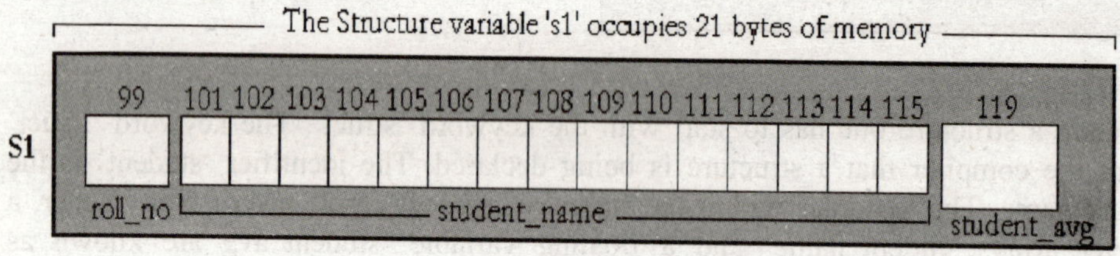

Figure 6.2: Memory allocation for structure variables

(s1 occupies memory locations say, from 99 to 122, i.e., 21 bytes)

In addition to this one can also define multiple data structures, also all the information stored in one structure can also be copied into another structure of the same type which we will study in more detail in the next section.

6.3.1 Solved Examples

Example 6.3.1.1

(a) Declare a structure 'date' having the following members:

day -- A string of size[3]
Represents the day part of the date

month -- A string of size[20]
Represents month name of a date

year -- A string of size [4]
Represents the year part of the date

(b) What is size of a variable of type date hence created?

Solution of 6.3.1.1

a)

```
struct date
{
  char day[3];

  char month[20];

  char year[4];

};
```

b) The size of a structure variable of type 'date' will occupy 27 bytes of computers memory.

Note: The size of structure might differ from one machine to another also the size of the structure is also determined by a concept known as 'word alignment' although this concept is out of the scope of the book.

Example 6.3.1.2
(a) Declare a structure 'Employee' having the following members:

Emp_Name	--	A string of size[15] Represents the name of the employee
Emp_IdNo.	--	A Long int variable Represents the employees Id number
Emp_Designation	--	A string of size[20] Represents the designation of the employee
Emp_salary	--	A float variable Represents the salary of the employee

(b) Declare C++ statement to declare two structure variables 'Emp1', 'Emp2' of type 'Employee'

Solution of 6.3.1.2
(a)

```
struct Employee
{
```

```
char Emp_Name[15];
 long int Emp_IdNo;
 char Emp_Designation[20];
 float Emp_salary;
};
```

(b) Employee Emp1,Emp2;

We can also define the structure variables after the structure, in such a case the tag name becomes optional but then one cannot declare any more structure variables in the main function.

For example, consider the structure 'Employee', for this structure we can also declare the structure variables 'Emp1', 'Emp2'without giving a name to the structure as shown below.

```
struct <optional tag/name>
 {
   char Emp_Name[15];
   long int Emp_IdNo;
   char Emp_Designation;
   float Emp_salary;
 }Emp1,Emp2;
```

The only disadvantage using this feature is that now we cannot create any more structure variables of this type.

6.4 Accessing members of a structure

We can access members of a structure with the help of two operators in C++. The operator **(.)** and the structure pointer operator **(->)** also known as the arrow operator. The structure member is accessed with the help of the structure name. Lets take an example, to access the structure member 'Emp_salary' of structure variable Emp1 of type Employee defined in the example above one would write the following C++ statement.

```
Emp1.Emp_salary = 2000.20 ;
```

The important thing to note here is that the part of the statement before the **(.)** operator is the structure variable name 'Emp1' and the part after the dot operator 'Emp_salary' is the name of the structure member to be accessed. The result of this statement is that the structure member 'Emp_salary' is given a value of '2000.20'.

Structures members can be treated just like any other ordinary variables available in C++.

That is all the various operations which can be done on any ordinary variables are also valid with structure members. Consider the following figure 6.3 given below.

This figure(6.3(a)) contains the structure definition for the structure 'Hospital'. The members of this structure can be accessed using the (.) operator figure (6.3(b)).

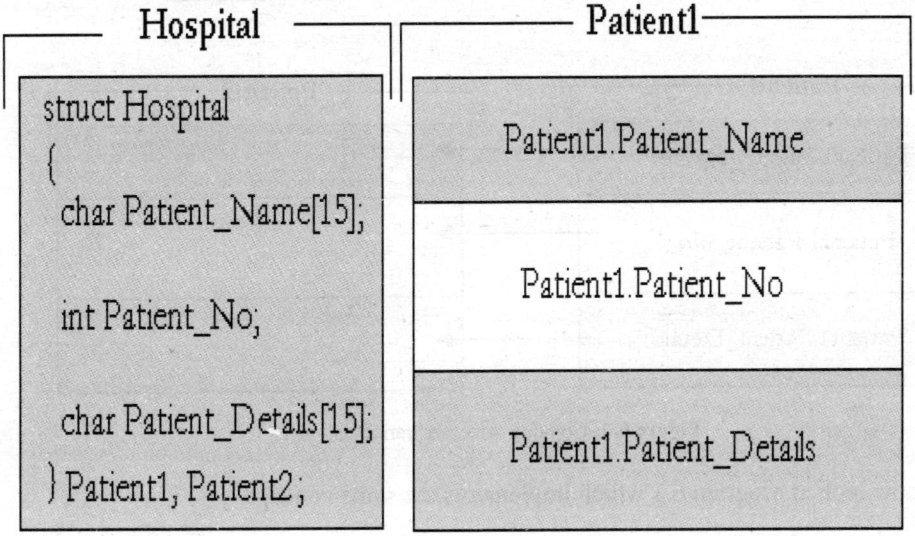

(a) (b)

Figure 6.3(a): Structure Definition for 'Hospital'

(b): Structure Variable 'Patient1'

As we already know that one can create several structure variables using the same structure. Suppose we create two structure variables for structure 'Hospital' 'Patient1' and 'Patient2' and we assign some particular 'Patient_Name', 'Patient_No' and 'Patient_Details' to 'Patient1' then if we say:

```
Patient2 = Patient1;
```

Then this statement will assign the structure variable 'Patient1' to the other structure variable 'Patient2' figure(6.4) and all the following conditions will hold.

```
Patient2.Patient_Name   = Patient1.Patient_Name

Patient2.Patient_No = Patient1.Patient_No

Patient2.Patient_Details = Patient1.Patient_Details
```

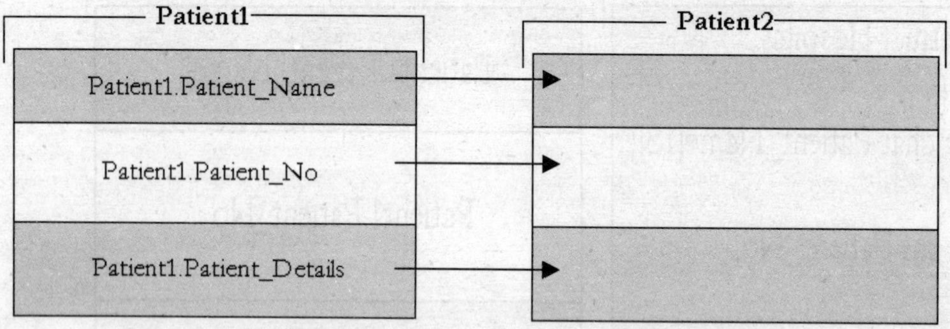

Figure 6.4: Copying structure variables

We can now look at program 6.1 which implements the same concept.

Program 6.1

```
// Header Files
// Program 6.1: Structure Variables

# include<iostream.h>

# include<conio.h>

# include<stdio.h>

/********************************************
Structure definition

Name: Student
```

```
Structure Members and Type:   roll_no: int

                              student_name[15]: char

                              avg: float
*******************************************/
```

```
struct student
{

 //Data_type1 Variable1

              int roll_no;

 //Data_type2 Variable2

              char student_name[15];

 //Data_type3 Variable3

              float avg;
};

//Main Program

void main()

{

 // Declaring structure variable s1 of type student

 student s1;

 cout<<" ENTER DETAILS";

 // Entering Data for student

 cout<<endl<<" Enter Roll No:";

 cin>>s1.roll_no; // Accessing the Structure member 'roll_no'
```

```
cout<<endl<<" Enter Student Name:";
 gets(s1.student_name); // Accessing the structure member 'student_name'
 cout<<endl<<" Enter Student Average";
 cin>>s1.avg;  // Accessing the structure member 'avg'
 cout<<endl<< " PRINTING DERAILS";
 cout<<endl<< " Roll No:"<<s1.roll_no;
 cout<<"\t"<< " Student Name:"<<s1.student_name;
 cout<< " Student Avg"<<s1.avg;
}
```

When this program is executed at first the compiler creates a structure 'student' with the above mentioned structure members. Then the compiler declares a structure variable 's1' of type student. In this program, the user enters the details of a student which include students roll number, name and average and then the program displays these details on the screen. The program could be easily understood by reading the comment entries provided with the program.

PROGRAMING TIPS

- Tag Names for structures should always be initialized to increase the scope of creating structure variables at time of structure declaration.
- All structure members should have different names to prevent logical errors.

6.4.1 Solved Examples

Example 6.4.1.1

Using the structure definition for structure 'Library' having the following members write a c++ program which declares a structure variable L1:

Book_Name	--	A string of size[15] Represents the name of the book
Book_IdNo	--	A int variable Represents the books Id number
Book_Shelf	--	A string of size[5] Represents the Book shelf number where the book is stored.

The user should then be asked to enter the details for the structure variable. The program should also check whether the book name is "Cleopatra" if so, the program should print a suitable message on the screen.

Solution of 6.4.1.1

```
// Header Files
# include <iostream.h>
# include <conio.h>
# include <string.h>
# include <stdio.h>

// Structure Library
struct Library
{
 char Book_Name[15];

 int Book_IdNo;

 char Book_Shelf[5];
};

// Main Function
void main()
{
 Library L1;
 char str[]="Cleopatra";

 cout<<"Enter Respective Details:";
 cout<<endl<<"Book Name";
```

```
gets(L1.Book_Name);
cout<<endl<<"Book_IdNo";
cin>>L1.Book_IdNo;

cout<<endl<<"Book Shelf";
gets(L1.Book_Shelf);

if (strcmp(str,L1.Book_Name)==0)
{
 cout<<endl<<"Condition Satisfied";
}
      else
      {
             cout<<endl<<"Condition not Satisfied";
      }
}
```

COMMON PROGRAMMING ERRORS

- Not ending the structure definition with a (;) semicolon is a compilation error.
- Not using the dot operator (.) to reference to structure members is a compilation error.

6.5 Structure Arrays

Before we learn about arrays of structures lets compare arrays and structures. Both arrays and structures are collection of data types. The major difference in them being that an array is a collection of data of the same type, where as a structure helps to group together data that may vary in type. Let us look at the following comparison between array and structures.

Structures	Arrays

struct Employee
{
char Emp_Name[15];
int Emp_IdNo.;
char Emp_Designation[15];
};
	char Emp_Name [15];
	char Emp_Designation[15];

Now as we can see the structure 'employee' groups data of three different data types: *char*, *int* and *float* where as the *array* 'name[15]' is a collection only of character type of data. Structures allow us to build data bases, especially if one considers the possibility of building arrays of them but is it possible to have arrays of structures?

The answer to this question is 'Yes'. Arrays of structure are declared by declaring the structure variables as arrays. Let us look at program 6.2 given below:

Program 6.2:

```
// Header Files
# include <iostream.h>
# include <conio.h>
# include <stdio.h>

// Structure Employee
struct Employee
{
 char Emp_Name[15];

 int Emp_IdNo;

 char Emp_Designation[15];
};

// Main Program
void main()
{
 Employee E1[10]; // Array of structures

 for (int i = 0; i<10;i++)
 {
        cout<<" Enter Respective Details for Employee"<<i+1;
        cout<<endl<<"1. Name";
        gets(E1[i].Emp_Name);

        cout<<endl<<"2. Employee Id No.";
        cin>>E1[i].Emp_IdNo;

        cout<<endl<<"3. Employee Designation";
        cin>>E1[i].Emp_Designation;
 }

 cout<<endl<< " Printing Employee database";
```

```
for (i=0;i<10;i++)
{
cout<<endl<<"1. Name"<<E1[i].Emp_Name;

cout<<endl<<"2. Employee Id No."<<E1[i].Emp_IdNo;

cout<<endl<<"3. Employee Designation"<<E1[i].Emp_Designation;
}
}
```

Arrays of structure have the properties same as a normal array the only difference being is that this time they are collection of a 'struct' data type. All operations valid on ordinary Arrays are also valid with arrays of structure. For example, in the program above we have declared an array 'E1' with index value 10 of type 'Employee'. This array of structure helps us to create a database for a set of 10 employees with the name, designation and Id No. for each employee. Each index value in this array of structure is accessed in a similar manner with the help of the (.) operator. Let us look at the following C++ statements from program 6.2 above.

```
for (int i = 0; i<10;i++)
{

        cout<<" Enter Respective Details for Employee"<<i+1;

        cout<<endl<<"1. Name";

        cin>>E1[i].Emp_Name;
        . . .
}
```

One uses ***for*** loop to enter the details for employee name into each index of array 'E1'. Each index entry of this array is accessed using '**E1[i]**.Emp_Name'. The variable 'i' refers to each index of the array **'E1'** and the part after the (.) operator refers to the 'Emp_Name' of the structure variable 'E1'**.** Similarly, the other ***for*** loop is used to print the details of this database on the screen.

An array of structure is very similar to a two-dimensional array, it can be thought as if it consists of columns, each of which may consist of distinct data types. Fig 6.3 given below represents the array 'E1' in such a manner.

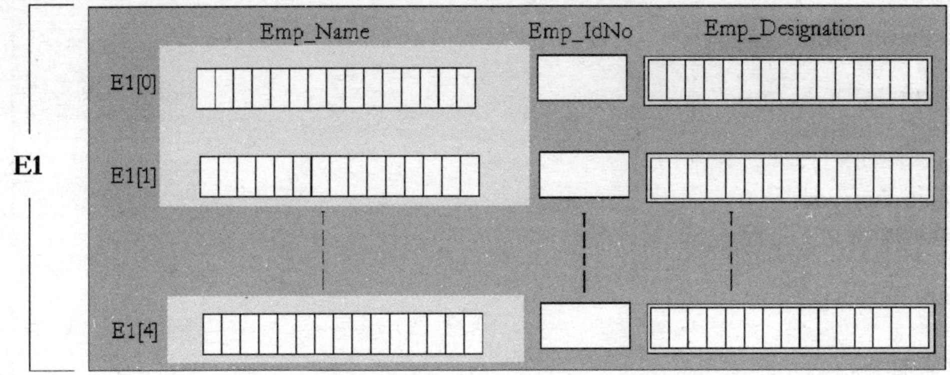

Figure 6.3: Memory Allocation for Structure variable E1

6.5.1 Solved Examples

Example 6.5.1.1

(a) Declare a structure 'Team' having the following members:

Player_Name	--	A string of size[15] Represents the name of the employee
Player_No.	--	An integer variable Represents the employees Id number
Player_Type	--	A string of size[20] Represents the designation of the employee

(b) Write C++ statements to declare an array of structure variables 'Players' for a team of 11 players and create a menu driven program which takes in details from the user for creating a team, displays the created team and also searches for a specific player in the created team using the Player_No. as the search key?

Solution of 6.5.1.1

```
// Header Files
# include <iostream.h>
# include <conio.h>
# include <stdio.h>

// Structure Definition
struct team
{
 char Player_Name[15];
```

```
 int  Player_No;

 char Player_Type[20];
};

// Main Function
void main()
{
 team Players[11];

 int flag=0;
 int search=0;
 int ch;

 do
 {
 cout<<endl<<"1. Create Team";
 cout<<endl<<"2. View Team";
 cout<<endl<<"3. Search for a player";
 cout<<endl<<"4. Exit";
 cin>>ch;

 switch(ch)
        {
        case 1:
                        {
                                for (int i=0; i<11;i++)
                                {
                                        cout<<" Enter Details for player "<<i+1;

                                        cout<<endl<<" Enter Name:";
                                        gets(Players[i].Player_Name);

                                        cout<<endl<<" Enter Player No.";
                                        cin>>Players[i].Player_No;

                                        cout<<endl<<" Enter Player Type";
                                        gets(Players[i].Player_Type);

                                        flag++;
                                }

                                break;
```

```
            }
    case 2:
            if (flag!=0)
            {
            cout<<"===  TEAM  ===";
              for (int i=0;i<11;i++)
                {
                 cout<<endl<<" Player No:"<<Players[i].Player_No;
                 cout<<endl<<" Player Name:"<<Players[i].Player_Name;
                 cout<<endl<<" Player Type:"<<Players[i].Player_Type;
                }
            }
           break;

    case 3:
         cout<<" Enter the Player No. to be searched";
         cin>>search;

         for (int i=0;i<11;i++)
         {
                  if (search == Players[i].Player_No)
                  {
                           cout<<" Player Found";
                           cout<<endl<<" Name"<<Players[i].Player_Name;
                           cout<<endl<<" Type"<<Players[i].Player_Type;
                           cout<<endl<<" Player No."<<Players[i].Player_No;
                     break;
                  }
         }
   }
 } while (ch!=4);
}
```

6.6 Structures with functions

As variables of any other data type, structure variables can also be passed to functions. Structure variables can be passed to functions in the following ways:

- Passing the entire structure variable as a parameter
- Passing individual structure members to the function
- Passing a pointer to a specific structure*

* Topic of pointers is introduced and explained in Chapter 7.

STRUCTURES

In addition to all this, we can also have functions which return structures. The important thing to note is that whenever structure variables or individual structure members are passed to the functions they are passed by value. So any changes made to the formal

parameters are not reflected back to the actual parameters. Structures can be passed by reference by preceding the structure variable with an '&' sign when the function is being called. Arrays of structures are automatically called by reference.

6.6.1 Passing structure variables as parameters

Program 6.3 shows structure variables being passed as parameters. In this example, the structure variable 'point_actual' is passed by value. The result of the program is that it plots '**'on the screen at a specified location by the user.

Program 6.3:

```
// Header Files
# include<iostream.h>
# include<conio.h>

// structure graph
struct graph
{
 int x;
 int y;
};

// Function Header for function plot
void plot (graph point_formal);

// Main Function
void main()
{

 // Declaring structure variable point_actual
 graph point_actual;


 // Passing structure variable 'point_actual' to function 'plot', by value.
 plot(point_actual);

 getch();
```

```
}

/***************************************
Name: plot
Purpose: Prints '**' at the specified location
*************************************************/
void plot (graph point_formal)
{
 cin>>point_formal.x;
 cin>>point_formal.y;

 /*
     The 'gotoxy' function
     General Syntax: gotoxy(xcoordinate,ycoordinate):
     Purpose: Sets the cursor to the specified x and y coordinate specified in its call. It
              is defined under the <conio.h> header file. It works exactly like the
              locate command in some other programming languages.
 */
 gotoxy(point_formal.x,point_formal.y);
 cout<<"**";
}
```

COMMON PROGRAMMING ERRORS

- Equating structures variables belonging to different structures is an compilation error
- Assuming that structure variables are passed by reference when being passed to functions is a logical error.

6.6.2 Passing structure members as parameters

Members of structure variables declared can also be passed as parameters to a function. Again, these parameters can be passed by value or passed by reference as per need of the program. Let us take an example,

Program 6.4:

```
// Header Files
# include<iostream.h>
# include<conio.h>
```

```
// Example of a structure variable being passed to a function
struct graph
{
  int x;

  int y;
};

void plot (int x, int y);

void main()
{
 clrscr();
 // Declaring structure variable point_actual
 graph point_actual;
 cout<<" Enter required points to plot the graph";
 cin>>point_actual.x;
 cin>>point_actual.y;

 // Passing structure variable 'point_actual' to function 'plot'
 plot(point_actual.x,point_actual.y);
 getch();
}

/***************************************
Function Name: plot
Purpose: Plot the point at the specified location
***************************************/
void plot (int x,int y)
{
  /*
    gotoxy: function defined under the <conio.h> header
     file. It allows the user to display text at any specified
     location on the screen
  */
  gotoxy(x,y);
  cout<<"**";
}
```

You might have already noticed that Program 6.4 is very similar to Program 6.3. Both these programs perform the same function. The only difference being that in Program 6.3 the entire structure 'point_actual' is not passed as a parameter where as in this program we have instead passed only the members of this structure 'x' and 'y' to the function.

6.6.3 Passing a pointer to the structure as a parameter

Pointers pointing to structures can also be passed as parameters to the function. An example of such a case is shown in Program 6.5.

Program 6.5

```
// Header Files
# include<iostream.h>
# include<conio.h>

// Structure 'graph'
struct graph
{
  int x;
  int y;
};

void plot (graph *ptr1);

void main()
{
 clrscr();

 // Declaring structure variable point_actual
 graph point_actual;

 graph *ptr;
 ptr = &point_actual;

 cout<<" Enter required points to plot the graph";
 cin>>ptr->x;
 cin>>ptr->y;

 // Passing structure variable 'point_actual' to function 'plot'
 // Passing the structure by reference
 plot(ptr);
 getch();
}

void plot (graph *ptr1)
{
 gotoxy(ptr1->x,ptr1->y);
 cout<<"**";
```

```
}
```

6.7 Nested Structures

A nested structure is a structure which contains other structures variables as its members. Once we have created a structure we can use the *struct* keyword to create nested structures. Consider the two structure definitions given below.

```
struct Date
{
 int day;
 int month;
 int year;
};
```

```
struct Telephone
{
int Telephone_Number;
int Telephone_Bill;
 struct Date Date_Bill;
 } Mobile;
```

We can observe that in the structure declaration for structure 'Telephone' we have declared a structure variable 'Date_Bill' for another structure 'Date' also shown in figure 6.5.

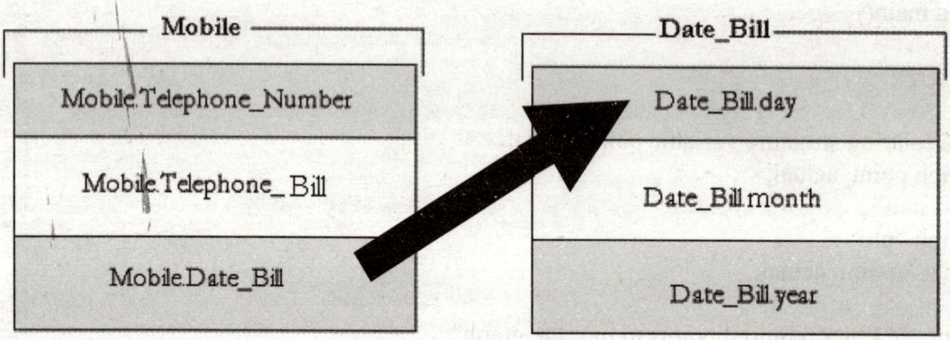

Figure 6.5: Nested Structures

We can initialize the members of the structure variable 'Mobile' with the extended use of again the dot operator(.). This operator is also used to access members of structures that are themselves members of a larger structures in other words in our example, we use this operator to access the structure members (day, month, year) of the structure 'Date'. To be more clear say; we want to access the member 'day' of structure 'date' from a structure variable of structure 'telephone' and intialize it to a value of '4' then one would write the following C++ statements.

```
Telephone Bill1;

Bill1.Date_Bill.day=4;
```

Now let me ask you a very interesting question can a structure contain an instance of its own type?

The answer to this question is 'no' we cannot. We can only declare structures as structure members to a structure provided the structure whose variable is a member to the nested structure is already defined.

6.7.1 Solved Examples

Example 6.7.1.1
Write a structure definition for structure 'Race' having the following attributes. A character array 'Player_Name' which represents the name of the player playing in the race, an integer variable 'Player_No' representing the player number and a structure variable 'Player_Time' of structure 'Time' which represents the time taken by each player in the race. The definition for structure 'Time' is given below:

```
struct Time
{
  int hrs;
  int mins;
  int secs;
 };
```

Solution of 6.7.1.1

```
struct Time
{
 int hrs;
 int mins;
 int secs;
};
struct Race
{
 char Player_name[20];
 int Player_No;
 struct Time Player_Time;
 };
```

6.8 Solved Examples

Example 6.8.1

Write a program to create an array of the given structure 'Emp'

```
struct Emp
{
 int Emp_No;
 char Emp_Name[15];
 float Emp_Basic;
};
```

Create user defined functions to

(a) Sort the array of structures declared in ascending order of Emp_Basic

(b) Calculate the net salary of each employee using :

Net Salary = Basic + H.R.A.+ D.A. – P.F.

H.R.A. = 25 % of Basic
D.A = 10 % of Basic
P.F. = 10% of Basic

Solution of 6.8.1

```
/* Header Files */
# include <iostream.h>
# include <conio.h>
# include <stdio.h>

// Structure 'Employee'
// Structure Members: Employee_No: Represents Employee Number
//                   : Employee_Name: Represents Employee Name
//                   : Employee_Basic:  Represents Employee Basic

struct Employee
{
 int Employee_No;
 char Employee_Name[15];
 float Employee_Basic;
};

// Function Headers
void accept (Employee E1[], int index);
void display (Employee E1[], int index);
void sort (Employee E1[], int index);
```

```
void Netsalary (Employee E1[], int index);

// Main Function
void main()
{
 clrscr();
 Employee E[50];
 int ch;
 int flag=0;
 int Array_index;
 do
 {
  clrscr();
  cout<<"\n =========== DATABASE: EMPLOYEE =============="<<endl;
  cout<<" 1. Create Employee database"<<endl;
  cout<<" 2. Print Enteries form database"<<endl;
  cout<<" 3. Sort the Employees in Order of Basic Salaries"<<endl;
  cout<<" 4. Calculate the Net salary of each Employee"<<endl;
  cout<<" 5. Exit Database"<<endl;
  cout<<" !. Press Choice";
  cin>>ch;

  switch (ch)
  {
  case 1:
        if (flag==0)
        {
        clrscr();
        cout<<" For how many employees should the database be created";
        cin>>Array_index;
        accept(E,Array_index);
        flag++;
        }
        else
        {
        cout<<" Option Not Available";
        getch();
     }
        break;
  case 2:
        clrscr();
        display(E,Array_index);
        break;
  case 3:
```

```
        sort(E,Array_index);
           break;
   case 4:
           Netsalary(E,Array_index);
           break;
  }
 }
 while (ch!=5);
 getch();
}

/*******************************************
Name: accept
Formal Parameters: E1[], index
Purpose: Enter values into structure array
*******************************************/

void accept( Employee E1[], int index)
{
 cout<<" Enter the following Details";
 for (int i=0; i<index;i++)
 {
  cout<<endl<<" Employee No:";
  cin>>E1[i].Employee_No;
  cout<<" Employee Name:";
  gets(E1[i].Employee_Name);
  cout<<" Employee Basic:";
  cin>>E1[i].Employee_Basic;
  cout<<"----------------";
  }
}
/*******************************************
Name: display
Formal Parameters: E1[], index
Purpose: Display the structure array
*******************************************/

void display( Employee E1[], int index)
{
 for (int i=0; i<index;i++)
 {
  cout<<endl<<" Employee No:"<<E1[i].Employee_No;
  cout<<endl<<" Employee Name:";
  puts(E1[i].Employee_Name);
```

```
  cout<<" Employee Basic:"<<E1[i].Employee_Basic;
  cout<<endl<<"--------------------";
  }
  getch();
}

/*******************************************************************
Name: sort
Formal Parameters: E1[], index
Purpose: Sort the  structure array in ascending order of basic salary
*******************************************************************/

void sort (Employee E1[], int index)
{
 clrscr();

 struct Employee temp;

 for (int i=0; i<index;i++)
 for (int j=0; j<index-i-1;j++)
 if (E1[j].Employee_Basic>E1[j+1].Employee_Basic)
 {
    temp = E1[j];
    E1[j]=E1[j+1];
    E1[j+1]=temp;
 }
 cout<<"Sorting Complete";
 getch();
}

/******************************************
Name: Netsalary
Formal Parameters: E1[], index
Purpose: Calculate the Net salary of the employees
         using Net Salary = Basic + 25 % Basic(H.R.A) + 10%Basic(D.A.) -10%
Basic(P.F.)
******************************************/

void Netsalary (Employee E1[], int index)
{
 clrscr();
 cout<<"=====================================<<endl;
 cout<<"Net Salaries for all employees"<<endl;
 float Salary[50];
```

```
for ( int i=0; i<index;i++)
 {
 Salary[i]= (1.25) * E1[i].Employee_Basic;
 cout<<"Employee No: "<<E1[i].Employee_No<<"  Net Salary: "<<Salary[i]<<endl;
 }
getch();
}
```

Example 6.8.2

Write a program to define a structure called 'Award' with the following data members

(i) Name of the winner: String of length 30 characters

(ii) Prize Money of Award: Long integer variable

Declare an array of the structure with **n** elements. Write user defined functions for:

(a) Input data values into structure members;

(b) Display the contents in tabular form;

(c) Display the details of students who have achieved awards having prize money > $50000; and

(d) Display details of the student achieving the highest prize money.

Solution of 6.8.2

```
// Header Files
# include <iostream.h>
# include <conio.h>
# include <stdio.h>

// Structure definition for'Award'
struct Award
{
 char Name[30];
 char type[15];
 long prize;
};

// Function Headers
void input (Award A[], int n);
void display (Award A[],int n);
void details (Award A[],int n);
void largest (Award A[],int n);

// Main Function
void main()
```

```
{
 Award A[50];
 int n;
 int flag=0;
 int ch;
 do
 {
 clrscr();
 cout<<" ================== Award Database ======================";
 cout<<endl<<" 1. Input Award Information ";
 cout<<endl<<" 2. Display Award Information";
 cout<<endl<<" 3. Details: Awards awarded for prize money > 50000$";
 cout<<endl<<" 4. largest Prize money award";
 cout<<endl<<" 5. Exit";
 cout<<endl<<" Enter Choice :?: ";
 cin>>ch;

 switch(ch)
 {
  case 1:
        if (flag==0)
        {
        clrscr();
        cout<<" For How Many Awards";
        cin>>n;
        input (A,n);
        flag++;
        }
        else
        cout<<" Option not available";
      getch();
        break;
 case 2:
        display (A,n);
        getch();
        break;
 case 3:
        details (A,n);
        break;
 case 4:
        largest (A,n);
        break;
 }
}
```

```
while (ch!=5);

getch();

}

/****************************************************
Name: input
Parameters: A[], n
Purpose: Input data in structure array 'A[]'
****************************************************/
void input ( Award A[], int n)
{
 clrscr();
 for (int i=0; i<n;i++)
  {
  cout<<" Enter Name of person";
  gets(A[i].Name);
  cout<<" Enter type";
  cin>>A[i].type;
  cout<<" Enter Prize Money $";
  cin>> A[i].prize;
  cout<<"======================="<<endl;
  }
}


/****************************************************
Name: Details
Parameters: A[], n
Purpose: Print all members of array structure 'A[]'
****************************************************/
void display (Award A[], int n)
{
 clrscr();
 for (int i=0; i<n;i++)
  {
  cout<<"Name :";
  puts(A[i].Name);
  cout<<"Type :"<<A[i].type<<endl;
  cout<<"Prize Money :"<<A[i].prize;
  cout<<endl<<"===================="<<endl;
  }
}
```

```
/*************************************************
Name: Details
Parameters: A[], n
Purpose: Print details  of structure members of Array 'A[]'
        where prize money>50000$
*************************************************/

void details (Award A[], int n)
{
  clrscr();
  for (int i=0;i<n;i++)
  {
  if (A[i].prize>50000)
   {
   cout<<endl<<"Name:"<< A[i].Name;
   cout<<endl<<"Type:"<< A[i].type;
   cout<<endl<<"Prize Money:"<<A[i].prize;
   }
  }
  getch();
}

/*************************************************
Name: largest
Parameters: A[], n
Purpose: Print details  of structure array 'A[]' with
        the largest prize money
*************************************************/

void largest (Award A[], int n)
{
  clrscr();
  int  max=A[0].prize;
  int index=0;
  for (int i=0;i<n;i++)
  {
    if (max<A[i].prize)
    {
        max = A[i].prize;
        index = i;
    }
  }
```

```
    cout<<" Name:"<< A[index].Name;
    cout<<endl<<" Type: "<<A[index].type;
    cout<<endl<<" Prize: "<<A[index].prize;
    getch();
}
```

Example 6.8.3

Using the following structure definition for nested structure 'Ticket' given below, Write a program to enter the details of 5 tickets and calculate the ticket fares for each of the following depending on distance traveled (Table Given Below).

```
struct person
{
   char Name[15];
   int age;
};
```

Distance Traveled	Fare
< =200 Miles	$5/Mile
>200&<300 Miles	$4/Mile
>=300 Miles	$3/Mile

Ticket

Members	Type
PNR	string
DOT	date
Passenger	person
From	string
To	string
Traversed	int

```
struct date
{
  int day;
  int month;
  int year ;
};
```

Solution of 6.8.3

```
  // Header Files
# include<iostream.h>
# include<conio.h>

// Comments: Use Header File <stdio.h> and use functions gets(), puts() to
//              manipulate with strings for better results
```

```
// Structure Definition for structure 'person'
struct person
{
 char Name[15];
 int age;
};

// Structure Definition for structure 'date'
struct date
{
 int day;
 int month;
 int year;
};

// Structure Definition for structure 'ticket'
struct ticket
{
 char PNR[15];
 date DOT;
 person Passenger;
 char From[15];
 char To[15];
 int Traversed;
};

// Function Headers
void accept( ticket T[], int n);
void fare (ticket T[], int n);
void display(ticket T[], int n);

// Main Function
void main()
{
 clrscr();
 int choice;
 ticket T[50];
 int index;
 do
```

```
{
clrscr();
cout<<"######## Ticket Booking ########"<<endl;
cout<<"!1! Enter Passenger information"<<endl;
cout<<"!2! Ticket fare for passengers"<<endl;
cout<<"!3! Print Tickets"<<endl;
cout<<"!4! Quit Program"<<endl;
cout<<"!?! Enter Choice"<<endl;
cin>>choice;

switch(choice)
{
 case 1:
        clrscr();
        cout<<" For how many Passenger(s) the ticket(s) to be booked for <50";
        cin>>index;
        accept(T,index);
        break;
 case 2:
        clrscr();
        fare(T,index);
        break;
 case 3:
        clrscr();
        display(T,index);
        break;

 default: if (choice!=4)
         cout<<"\n Please Press Valid Choice";

 }
}
while (choice != 4);
getch();
```

```
cout<<"Enter the following details:"<<endl;
 for (int i=0; i<n;i++)
   {
   cout<<"Enter the PNR Number";
   cin>>T[i].PNR;
   cout<<endl<<"Enter Date:";
   cout<<endl<<"      Day:";
   cin>>T[i].DOT.day;
   cout<<endl<<"      Month:";
   {
    cout<<"\n PNR:"<<T[i].PNR;
   cout<<"\n Fare:"<<4*T[i].Traversed;
   }


  if (T[i].Traversed>=300)
   {
cin>>T[i].DOT.month;
   cout<<endl<<"      Year:";
   cin>>T[i].DOT.year;
   cout<<endl<<"Enter Passenger Details:";
   cout<<endl<<"              Name   :";
   cin>>T[i].Passenger.Name;
   cout<<endl<<"              Age    :";
   cin>>T[i].Passenger.age;
   cout<<endl<<"Source Station:";
   cin>>T[i].From;
   cout<<endl<<"Destination Station:";
   cin>>T[i].To;
   cout<<endl<<"Distance Traversed:";
   cin>>T[i].Traversed;
   cout<<endl<<"^^^^^^^^^^^^^^^^^^^^^"<<endl;
   }
}
/*****************************************
Name: Fare
Parameters: T[], n
Purpose: To calculate Ticket Fare
*****************************************/
void fare (ticket T[], int n)
{
  clrscr();
  for (int i=0;i<n;i++)
```

```
  {
   if (T[i].Traversed <=200)
   {
    cout<<"\n PNR:"<<T[i].PNR;
    cout<<"\n Fare:"<<5*T[i].Traversed;
   }
   if (T[i].Traversed >200 && T[i].Traversed<300)
    cout<<"\n Fare:"<<3*T[i].Traversed;
    cout<<"\n PNR:"<<T[i].PNR;
   }
   cout<<"--------------";
  }
  getch();
}

/*************************************
Name: display
Parameters: T[], n
Purpose: To display ticket details
*************************************/
void display(ticket T[],int n)
{
   int i;
   for ( i=0; i<n;i++)
   {
   // Entering Ticket Details
   cout<<endl<<" Entry :"<<i+1;
   cout<<endl<<" PNR Number: "<<T[i].PNR;
cout<<endl<<" Date:";
   cout<<endl<<"      Day:"<<T[i].DOT.day;
   cout<<endl<<"      Month:"<<T[i].DOT.month;
   cout<<endl<<"      Year:"<<T[i].DOT.year;
   cout<<endl<<" Passenger Details:";
   cout<<endl<<"            Name  :"<<T[i].Passenger.Name;
   cout<<endl<<"            Age   :"<<T[i].Passenger.age;
   cout<<endl<<"Source Station:"<<T[i].From;
   cout<<endl<<"Destination Station:"<<T[i].To;
   cout<<endl<<"Distance Traversed:"<<T[i].Traversed;
   cout<<endl<<"^^^^^^^^^^^^^^^^^^^^"<<endl;
   }
   getch();
   }
```

6.9 Review Exercise

1 Mark/ 2 Mark

Q1) When referencing structure members, the identifier before the (.) operator is the
  a) Structure Variable
  b) Structure Tag
  c) Key word 'struct'
  d) None of the above
  e) All of the above
  f) None of the above

Q2) A structure is a collection of
  a) Variables of different data types
  b) Variables of similar data types
  c) Variables of same data types
  d) Smaller nesting structures
  e) All of the above

  f) None of the above

Q3) Write a C++ statement which sets the 'secs' member of time structure to '10'.

Q4) Write C++ statements to accomplish the following:
  a) Write structure definition for structure 'Computer' having integer variable 'ComputerNo', character array 'ComputerName' with names as long as 20 characters.
  b) Declare a structure variable 'Num1' for structure 'Computer'.
  c) Initialize the structure member 'ComputerName' to "I B M".

Q5) Give the output for the following piece of code:

```
struct graph1
{
 int x;
 int y;
 int z;
};

graph1 increment (graph1 g1)
{
 g1.x*= g1.y-- + ++g1.z;
 g1.y++;
```

```
  g1.z++;
  return g1;
}

void main()
{
  clrscr();
  graph1 g1;
  graph1 g2;
  g1.x=1;
  g2.x=2;
  g1.z=2;
  g1.y=0;
  g2=increment(g1);
  cout<<g2.x<<g2.y<<g2.z;
  getch();
}
```

Q6) Find the error(s) in the following piece of code:

```
# include<'iostream.h'>
# include<'conio.h'>
structure car
{
 char car_name[15];
 int car_number
 char car_type;
}; diesel, petrol;

main()
{
 \\ Program to enter details for structure variables
 cout<<" Enter Car Name";
 gets(diesel.car_name);
 cout<<" Enter Car type";
 gets(car_type);
 cout<<" Car number";
 cin>>petrol.car_type;
}
```

Q7) State whether the following statements are true or false.
a) Nested structures are collection of structures having same data types.
b) Structures are similar to two-dimensional arrays.
c) The name of the structure is also known as structure tag.
d) (.) operator is used to create structure variables.
e) One can create recursive structures.

Q8) How are structures more advantageous than arrays explain giving suitable examples?

Q9) Create a structure of type 'time' that contains three integer members: 'hour', 'minute' and 'second'. Then write a program that should take in time from the user in the following format 'hrs.min.sec' and display this time entered by the user on the screen.

Q10) Using the following structure definition for structure 'coordinate' given below, Write a function which takes a structure of type 'coordinate' as a parameter it swaps the x and the y coordinate of the structure variable without using any other external variables and returns a structure of type coordinate.

```
struct coordinate
{
  int x;
  int y;
};
```

<u>Hint</u>: Take 2 variables A and B, we can swap there values without using any other variable using the following method:

```
A = A+B
B = A-B
A = A-B
```

Use similar trick to solve this problem.

<u>4 Mark/ 5 Mark</u>

Q11) Write a program (WAP) to create a structure of type 'Team' given below. Write user defined functions to:

a) Input values of all the members of the structure for 'n' elements of the array.
b) Display function to show data of all the cells entered separately in tabular form

```
struct team
{
    char name[20];
    int num;
    int age;
    float avg;
    char category;
};
```

Q12) Write a program to create an array of given structure 'Train':

```
struct Train
{
    int Train_No;
    char Train_Name[10];
    int Train_fare;
};
```

Write user defined functions to:

a) Sort the array in ascending order of Train_fare, Train_No

b) Print the sorted array in tabular form

Q13) Write a program to define a structure called 'Scholarship' with the following data members.

i) Name of the scholarship: string
ii) Type of scholarship : char type
iii) Number of scholarships : short Int type

Declare an array of the structure with 'N' elements write user defined functions for the following:

a) Input: To read in structure members from the user
b) Display: To display the contents in the array in a tabular form
c) Display_Selective: To display the details of all the Scholarships whose number is greater than 10.
d) Display: To display the name of the scholarship having the highest occurrences.

Q14) Declare a structure Air_Canada having the following members:

Flight_Name : A character array
Flight_Fare : A long int
Flight_No: 'int' Type:

Write a menu driven program to create an array of the above structure and read in values for these members from the user. Write a function and pass the structure using a pointer to the structure and search for an entry with flight name "AC084'.

6.10 Programming Project

Complex numbers are an extension of real numbers, in which all non-constant polynomials have roots. Every complex number consists of a real part and an imaginary part. They have the form a + bi where a and b are real numbers and i satisfies the equation $i^2 = -1$. Multiplication is denoted by (a+bi)(c+di) = (ac-bd) + (ad+bc) i , and addition is denoted by (a+bi) + (c + di) = (a+c) + (b+d) i.

Given the structure Complex:

```
struct Complex
{
    float real;
    float img;
};
```

Write a program which consists of user defined functions to perform the following functions with the help of a menu driven program.

(i) Accept: To accept values into an array of type 'Complex' for a set of 10 complex numbers.

(ii) Add: To add any two complex numbers passed to a function the function should return a structure variable

(iii) Multiply: To multiply any two complex numbers passed to the function and return the resultant complex number

(iv) Sort: To sort the list of complex numbers present in the structure array and print the sorted list on the screen (Sorting Key: Real Part).

(v) Largest: To print the largest complex number on the screen

(vi) Insert: To insert a complex number (Using Pointers)

6.11 Let us revise!

- ✓ Structures are collection of heterogeneous type of data
- ✓ Structures are very similar to arrays the only difference being that arrays are only collection of same type of data
- ✓ Structures are defined using the following format

```
struct <tag/name>
{
   data type var1; ...
   data type var4;
};
```

- ✓ Key word 'struct' introduces the structure definition which is followed by the structure name. The body or the list of variables making up the structure are enclosed in {} brackets. The structure definition is terminated using the (;) operator.
- ✓ The tag name of the structure is optional. If the structure is defined without a tag name, the structure variables should be defined in the structure definition.
- ✓ It is also possible to create array of structures which are very similar to two dimensional arrays. The major use of arrays of structures is to create databases. Arrays of structures can be created by creating structure variables as arrays.
- ✓ Structure variables and their members can also be passed to functions. They can be passed by value or passed by reference. In addition to this, we can also have functions having structures as there return types.
- ✓ Structure variables are passed by reference by passing their address in the call to the function.
- ✓ Arrays of structures are automatically passed by reference.
- ✓ It is also possible to embed a structure within another structure.
- ✓ To reference variables of the nested structure the (.) operator is used.
- ✓ Structures are a powerful and an efficient way of grouping data from different fields into a single entity.

PART I

CHAPTER 7

POINTERS

AIM

- To introduce the concept of 'Memory Management'
- To understand the concept of 'Pointers'
- Learn to use 'Pointer' and 'Pointer Operators'
- Comparison between 'Arrays' and 'Pointers'
- To introduce and use concept of 'Dynamic Memory Allocation' using the 'new' and 'delete' operators.

OUTLINE

7.1 Introduction

Pointers are among C++'s most difficult concepts to understand and master. In the earlier chapters, we have already seen how variables are stored in the computer memory in a series of memory cells that can be accessed by the use of identifiers. What is though more important to know is the fact that the computer memory is nothing but also a series of successive 1 byte cells, and each of these cells is assigned a unique address?

We can compare the structure of the computer memory to a street in a city. In a street every house has a unique address for example, say 110 Winston Street which can be compared to an identifier in programming terminology. Now if want to find this house we can easily find this house without any trouble since there is only one house by the address of 110 Winston street and it must lie between 109 and 111.

Similarly, in a computer each memory location has a unique address. The addresses are in ascending order (in succession of 1 Byte), so if we wish to locate memory location say 110, the operating system knows that there is only one location with that specific address and that it lies between 109 and 111.

Pointers are nothing but variables that hold memory addresses in C and C++. They provide much power and utility for a programmer to access and manipulate data in ways not seen in some other languages. Pointers enable us to create data structures, such as, linked lists, stacks, queues which grow and shrink in size during execution of programs.

7.2 Addresses and Pointers

Till now we have worked with variable types which store characters, integers and floating point numbers. Addresses are also stored in a similar manner with the use of pointers or pointer variables.

A pointer that holds an address of a variable is called a pointer variable. Look at the following statement:

```
int *ptr;
```

In this statement, we are declaring a pointer variable where 'ptr' is the name of the variable. The '*' informs the compiler that we want a pointer variable, i.e., to set aside however many bytes is required to store an address in the memory. The *int* says that we intend to use our pointer variable to store the address of an integer and such a pointer variable is called as a pointer to an integer. We have already learnt that as soon as a variable is declared it is stored in a distinct location in adjacent cells (the memory).

In some cases, it might be interesting to know the exact location of where this variable is stored. C++ makes this possible with the use of the 'address of' operator. It is a unary operator and it is used by preceding a variable identifier by an *ampersand sign* ( ). Let's look at the following statement:

```
int *address;
address = &unknown;
value = unknown;
```

This statement would assign to the pointer variable **'address'** the address of the variable **'unknown'**. It is important to know that whenever one sees an ampersand (&) sign preceding the name of a variable, it implies that we are not referring to the content stored in the variable but to the address of the variable at which it is stored in the memory. This is further explained in Figure 7.1 given below:

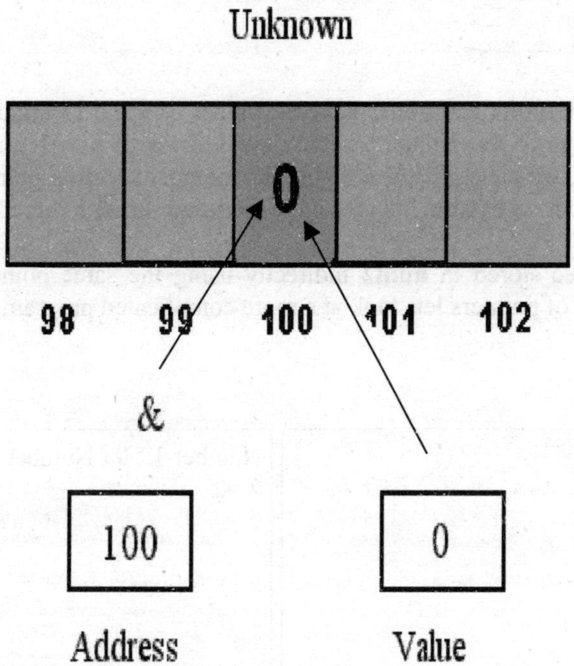

Figure 7.1: Address of operator

Now that we know what pointer variables are let's look at the following program and try to understand its working:

Program 7.1:

```
// Pointer Examples
#include <iostream.h>
#include <conio.h>
void main ()
{
 int num1 = 5, num2 = 15;
 int * ptr;
 ptr= &num1;
 *ptr = 0;
 ptr = &num2;
 *ptr = 2;
 cout << " Number 1:>" << num1 << "/ Number 2:>"
<< num2;
 }
```

```
Number 1:>0 / Number 2:>2
```

When this program is executed, **num1** and **num2** have the values of 5 and 15 initially. As the program goes on, we assign to the pointer variable the address of **num1** using the address of (&) operator. Then, we have put value **'0'** in the memory location pointed by **ptr**, which is pointing to the address of **num1**, so we have modified **num1** indirectly.

Similarly, we change the value stored in **num2** indirectly using the same pointer. To further understand the concept of pointers lets look at a more complicated program.

Program 7.2:

```
// Pointers Examples
# include <iostream.h>
# include <conio.h>

void main ()
{
 int num1 = -5, num2 = 0;
 int *ptr1, *ptr2;

 ptr1 = &num1;    // ptr1 = address of num1
 ptr2 = &num2;    // ptr2 = address of num2
 *ptr1 = 0;       // value pointed by ptr1 = 0
 *ptr2 = *ptr1;      // value pointed by ptr2 = value
pointed by ptr1
```

```
Number 1:>0 / Number
2:>2
```

```
 ptr1 = ptr2;        // ptr1 = ptr2 (value of pointer
copied)
 *ptr1 = 2;        // value pointed by ptr1 = 2

 cout << " Number 1:>" << num1 << "/  Number 2:>"
<< num2;
}
```

It is easy to understand the working of the program by reading the comments assigned to the program statements. The important thing to note is that Program 7.1 & 1.2 generate the same output.

PROGRAMING TIPS FOR POINTERS

While learning pointers, the most important advice that can be offered to any beginner is that draw a lot of Figures. The relationship between the address of a cell and the value it contains is easier to understand if one can see that relationship depicted on a page. The following simple rules will help:

- Draw boxes for every variable in the part of the program that one is trying to understand. The positioning of these boxes is immaterial but the only thing to keep in mind is that these array elements are laid out contiguously in memory. Thus, if working with an array variable, one should draw that array as a connected series of boxes.

- All pointer variables occupy 4 bytes of computers memory.

- Assign arbitrary address numbers to the boxes drawn. It doesn't matter whether one knows what the real addresses are, just invent some for the purpose of understanding what is going on in the program.

- As you assign addresses, remember that variables require different amounts of memory depending on their type. That is an integer variable type will occupy two bytes of memory where as a float type will occupy 4 bytes of memory.

As an example, let us look at the following piece of code.

```
int  x, y, *z, *w;
z=&x;
w=&y;
```

One should be able to create the following diagram using the steps given:

- Draw boxes for integer variables 'x' and 'y' and give them any arbitrary addresses (1000, 1002) in our case.
- Draw similar boxes for pointer variables 'z' and 'w' having addresses of x and y respectively stored in them.
- Introduce arrows between the pointer variables and those variables whose addresses are stored by these pointer variables.
- Now look at the following Figure:

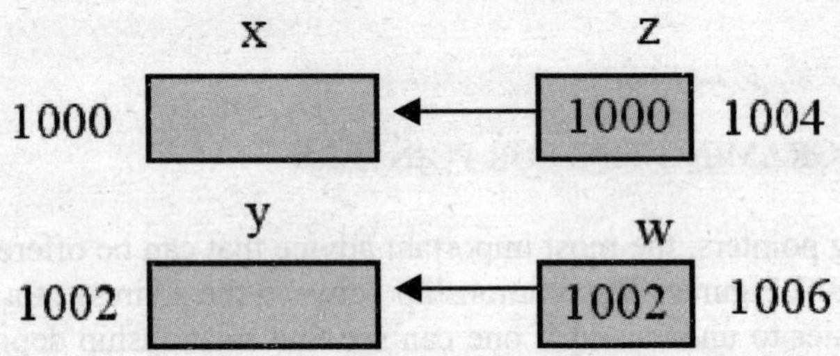

Figure 7.2: Pointer Diagrams

This Figure also known as 'Pointer Diagram' depicts that 'x' and 'y' are integer variables having addresses '1000' and '1002' respectively. It also shows that 'z' and 'w' are pointer variables having the addresses of 'x' and 'y' stored in them. The arrows marked denote the relationship between 'x', 'z' and 'y', 'w'.

Let us now come to a slightly different problem. What happens if we want to access the content stored in the memory block to which a pointer points to?

To solve this problem one can take help of the indirection operator (*). For example,

```
int temp;
int value;
int *ptr;
ptr = &value;

temp = *ptr;
```

Now when we use the indirection operator with the pointer name except when we are declaring the pointer then we are referring to the memory block whose address this pointer stores or in other words to the memory block to which this pointer points to. So by initializing ‘temp=*ptr’, what we are actually doing is pointing to the address stored in the pointer ‘ptr’ which is the integer variable ‘value’. The net result of this statement is that what ever value is stored at this location to which the pointer ‘ptr’ points to is stored in the temporary variable ‘temp’.

Let us take-up the following example to under stand this concept better.

7.2.1 Solved Examples

Example 7.2.1.1

What will be the output for the following piece of code?

```
int amt = 900;
int *p;
p=&amt;
amt+=100;
(*p)-=50;
cout<<”amt=”<<amt<<” *ptr=”<<ptr<<endl;
cout<<”&amt=”<<&amt<<” p=”<<p<<endl;
```

Solution of 7.2.1.1

The above program will display the following output as ‘**p**’ holds the address of ‘**amt**’ and hence any change in ‘**amt**’ will be same as change in ***p**.

OUTPUT SCREEN

```
amt=950 *ptr=950
&amt=0*8ffebab4 p=0*8ffebab4
```

Now let’s review the ‘Pointer diagrams’ and learn how to use them with the indirection operator with the help of the following example.

PROGRAMING TIP EXAMPLE

Draw pointer diagrams and hence determine the output for the following piece of code.

```
# include<iostream.h>
# include<conio.h>
```

```
void main()
{
clrscr();
int a=10, b=20;
int *ptr1, *ptr2;

ptr1=&a;
 (*ptr1)++;

ptr2=&b;
(*ptr2)++;

*ptr1= *ptr2;
cout<<*ptr1<<" "<<*ptr2<<" "<<a<<" "<<b;
getch();
}
```

We start with the basic steps, i.e., first make boxes for the integer variables 'a' and 'b' containing values 10 and 20 having any arbitrary addresses.

Step 1:

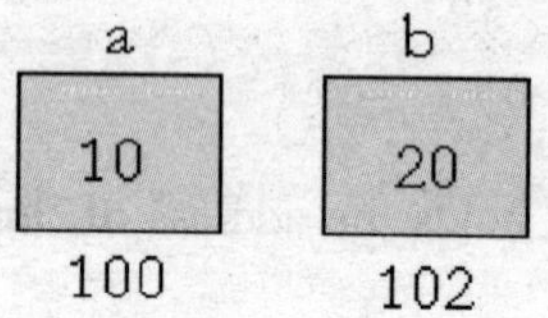

Now make similar boxes for the pointer variables 'ptr1' and 'ptr2'

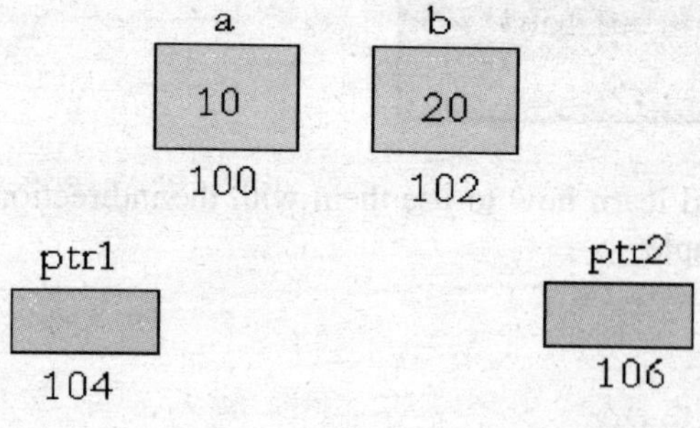

Step 2:

Now take a look back at the piece of code provided to us and observe the following statements

```
ptr1=&a;
(*ptr1)++;
```

In the first statement, we assign the address of the integer variable '**a**' to the pointer variable '**ptr1**'. In other words, the pointer is now pointing to the integer variable '**a**'. In the second statement, we have used the indirection operator, which signifies that we are now referring to the variable to which the pointer variable '**ptr1**' is pointing to and incrementing it by a value of '1'. To make things look even simpler one can also replace '***ptr1**' by '**a**' as both the operations will produce same result. So we will observe the same result even if we replace the statement **(*ptr1)++**; by **a++**; as the pointer '**ptr1**' is currently pointing to the integer variable '**a**'.

Let us now make a pointer diagram for these statements:

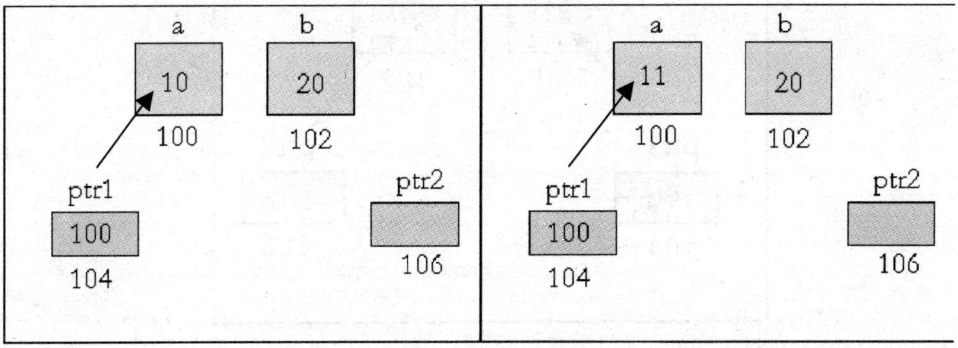

We can now follow the same steps for these statements and arrive to the following pointer diagrams.

```
ptr2=&b;
(*ptr2)++;
```

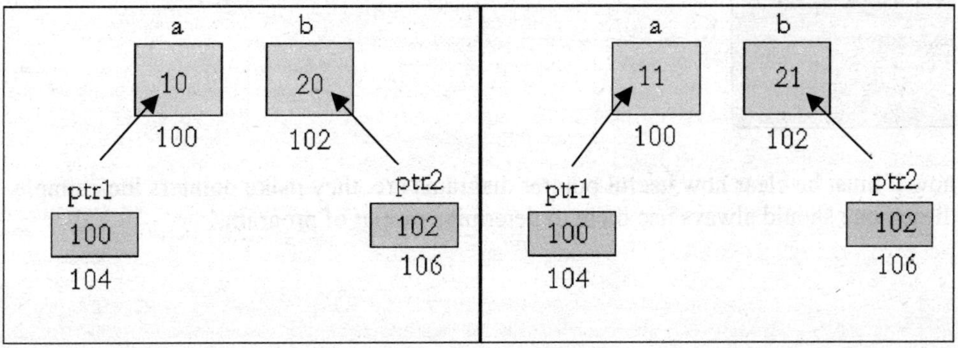

Step 3:

Now in the next statement:

```
*ptr1= *ptr2;
```

We have assigned the value stored in the integer variable to which the pointer **'ptr2'** is pointing to the value stored in the variable to which the pointer **'ptr1'** points to. In simple terms, we can also say that we have assigned the integer variable **'a'** the value of integer variable **'b'** indirectly and the statement can also be written as **a= b;** as long as **'ptr1'** points to 'a' and **'ptr2'** points to **'b'** as also clear in our pointer diagram.

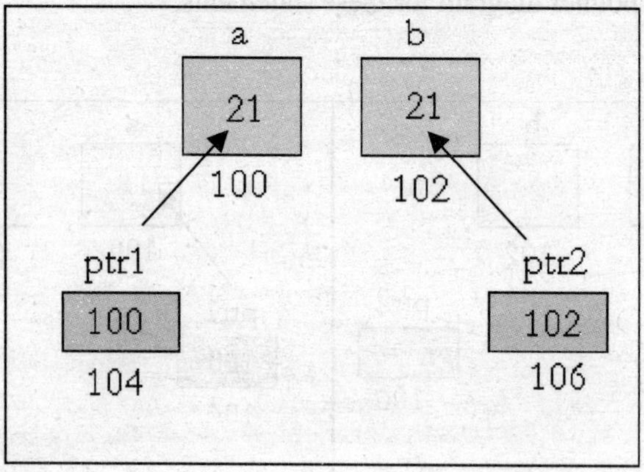

Step 4:

In the last step, we just print the values stored at the specified locations provided in the program on the screen using our pointer diagram, to observe the following output.

Output Screen

```
21 21 21 21
```

By now it must be clear how useful pointer diagrams are, they make pointers look simple and hence one should always use them to determine output of programs.

7.2.2 The 'size of' operator

The 'sizeof' operator is used to calculate the size of an object/variable belonging to any data type, structure or class. The 'sizeof' operator yields the size of its operand with respect to the size of type char. It has the following syntax:

Syntax: sizeof (object/variable_name);

The result of the sizeof operator is of type size_t, an integral type defined in the include file <STDDEF.H>.

For example,

```
...
int var;
cout<<sizeof(var);
```

When these statements are executed the program will display '4' on the screen. The sizeof operator can also be applied to arrays. In such a case the size of operator will return the size of the entire memory block occupied by the array passed to it as a parameter.

For example,

```
...
float var[10];
cout<<sizeof(var);
```

As expected when the following statements are executed the integer '40' is displayed on the screen (4 * '10' bytes).

7.2.2.1 Importance of the 'sizeof' operator

To understand the importance of the 'sizeof' operator look at the following program:

```
// Header Files
# include <iostream.h>
# include<conio.h>

/
// Main Function
void main()
{
        Test test1;

        cout<<sizeof(test1);
```

```
}
/ Structure Definition
struct Test{
        int var1;
        char var2;
      };
```

Now when this program is executed one should expect ‘5’ to be displayed on the screen as the structure definition for structure ‘Test’ has an integer variable (‘4’ bytes) and a character variable (‘1’ byte) but to our surprise we notice that a number ‘8’ is displayed on the screen. Now this is not the compilers fault, but this is because of a concept known as ‘data wrapping’. A concept introduced briefly in the previous chapter.

What happens is that the compiler always tries to align all the variables to the word boundary ‘4 or multiples 4 bytes’ for better performance of your programs. So if the amount of space occupied by a variable is say ‘5’ the compiler then aligns it to the nearest multiple of ‘4’ which happens to be ‘8’ in this case. The overall understanding of this concept is however out of the scope of the book but with this example, it should be clear now as why we need the ‘sizeof’ operator.

7.3 Pointer to an Array

A pointer can also be used to point to an array. A pointer, which stores the address of an array, is called as a pointer to an array. In fact, there is a close relationship between pointers and arrays.

An array name can be thought of as a constant pointer. Actually, the identifier of an array is equivalent to the address of its first element, like a pointer is equivalent to the address of the first element that it points to. Look at the following piece of code:

```
int  num[10];
int *ptr;
```

Now the array name ‘**num**’ is a constant pointer. As we already know that arrays are self reference parameter so while using a pointer to point to an array we do not use ‘*The address of (&) operator*’ as we have done in the case of variables earlier in this chapter.

The following statement sets the pointer ‘**ptr**’ to point to the array ‘**num**’:

```
ptr = num;
```

This statement is equivalent to taking the address of the first element of the array ‘**num**’ as follows:

```
int *ptr=num;
      or
int *ptr;
ptr=&num[0];
```

Let us now review the comparison between arrays and pointers. At this point the pointer '**ptr**' and the array '**num**' are exactly equivalent and they have the same properties, the only difference is that we could assign another value to the pointer `'ptr'` as it is a pointer variable whereas `'num'` will always point to the zeroth index of the array '**num**'.

COMMON PROGRAMMING ERRORS

- Ignoring the '*' variable while declaring a pointer variable will result in a logical error.
- Not dereferencing a pointer to obtain a value to which the pointer points to will result in a syntax error

7.3.1 Pointer expression and pointer arithmetic

Pointer arithmetic is quite different than conventional arithmetic. To begin with, only addition and subtraction operations are allowed to be conducted, the others make no sense in the world of pointers. But both addition and subtraction have a different behavior with pointers according to the <u>size</u> of the data type to which they point. The important ones which are commonly used are the increment (++) and the decrement (--) operators.

Let's take up an example to understand the use of these operators with pointer variables. Assume an array say, **int x[5]** and say that it is stored at a position 100 in the memory. Now as the data type is 'int' so each variable of this type would occupy 2 bytes of memory (see Figure 7.3). We can now initialize the pointer '**ptr**' to point to the array '**x**' with either of the equivalent statements.

```
int *ptr=x;
ptr = x;
ptr = &x[0];
```

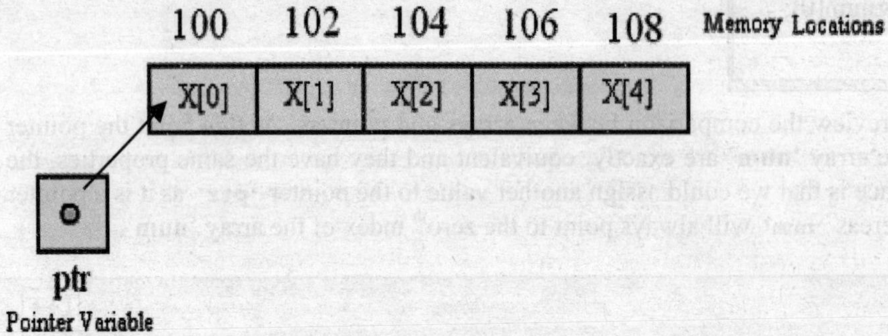

Figure 7.3(a): Pointer to an array

In simple arithmetic 100 + 2 would give 102 but this is not the case when one is operating using pointer arithmetic. When using pointer variables as operands then in such a case they are not just incremented or decremented by the value of an integer but size of object the pointer refers to times the value of the integer. So in the following statement

```
ptr+=2;
```

it would produce final address as 104 (100 + 2*2) and not 102 and hence after this statement the pointer will now point to X[2].

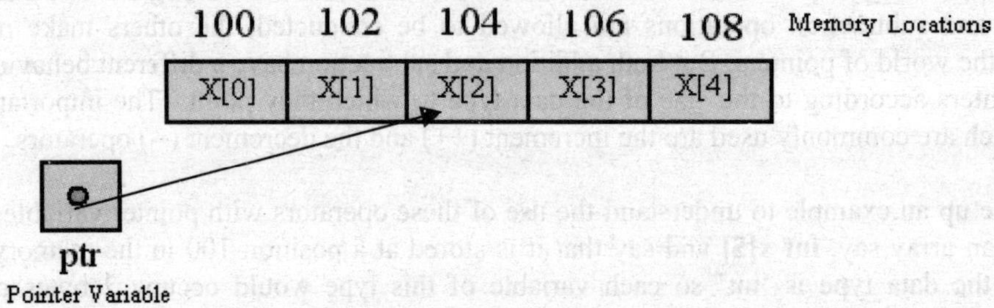

Figure 7.3 (b): Pointer to an array

An array pointer can also be alternatively referenced with the following pointer expression.

```
* ( ptr + 2)
```

Note: One should remember to use parenthesis as the precedence of operators that is * is of higher precedence than +. Let us better understand pointer arithmetic with the help of the following example:

Program 7.3

```
// Program 7.3: Pointer to an array
// Header Files
# include <iostream.h>
# include <conio.h>

// Main Function
void main ()
{
 int x[5];
 // Pointer Variable 'ptr'
 int * ptr;
 ptr = x;

 *ptr = 10;
 ptr++;

 *ptr = 20;
 ptr = &x[2];

 *ptr = 30;
 ptr = x + 3;

 *ptr = 40;
 ptr = x;

 *(ptr+4) = 50;

 for (int y=0; y<5; y++)
  {
   cout << x[y] << ", ";
  }
}
```

```
10, 20, 30, 40, 50,
```

The working of this program is explained with the help of Figure 7.4.

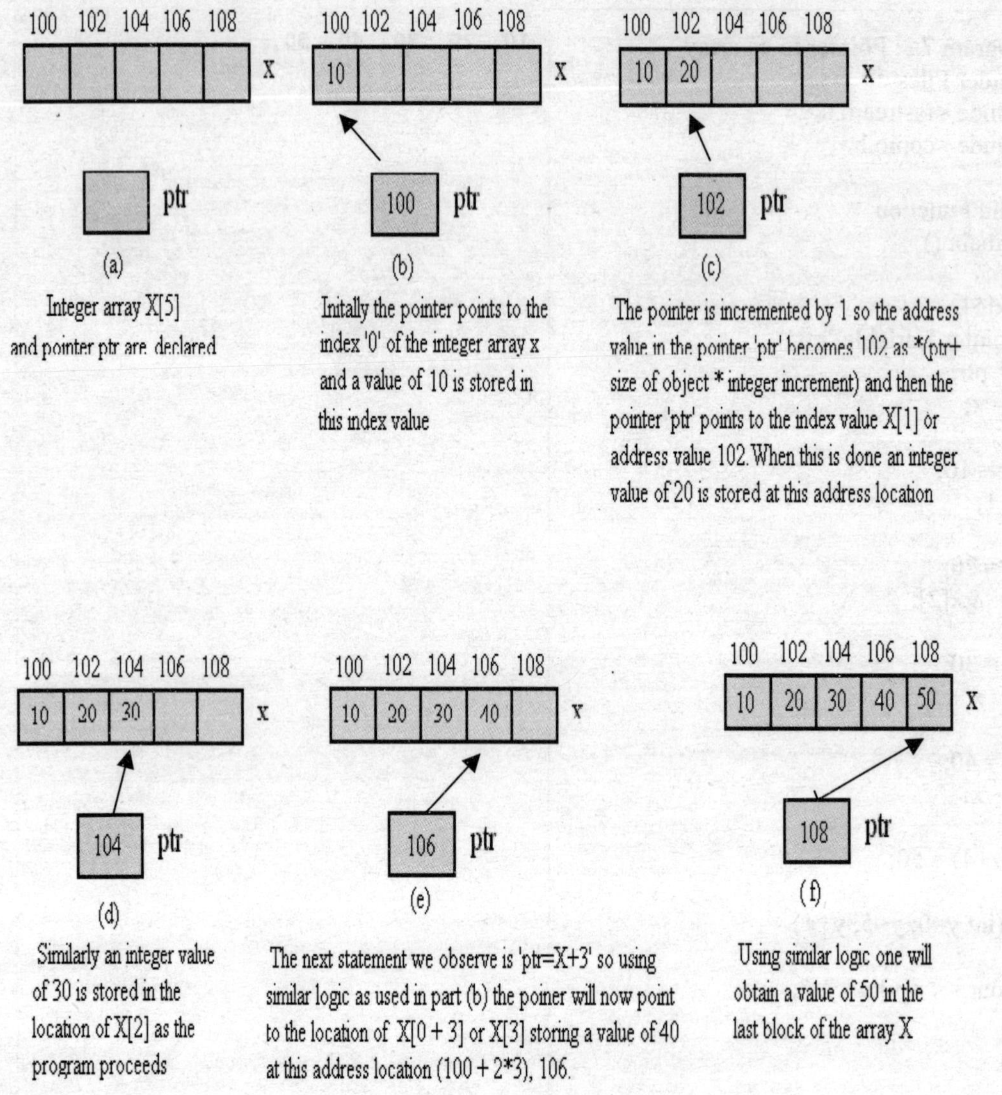

(a) Integer array X[5] and pointer ptr are declared

(b) Initally the pointer points to the index '0' of the integer array x and a value of 10 is stored in this index value

(c) The pointer is incremented by 1 so the address value in the pointer 'ptr' becomes 102 as *(ptr+ size of object * integer increment) and then the pointer 'ptr' points to the index value X[1] or address value 102. When this is done an integer value of 20 is stored at this address location

(d) Similarly an integer value of 30 is stored in the location of X[2] as the program proceeds

(e) The next statement we observe is 'ptr=X+3' so using similar logic as used in part (b) the poiner will now point to the location of X[0 + 3] or X[3] storing a value of 40 at this address location (100 + 2*3), 106.

(f) Using similar logic one will obtain a value of 50 in the last block of the array X

Figure 7.4: Pointer Arithmetic

COMMON PROGRAMMING ERRORS

- Using Pointer arithmetic with a pointer to refer to an address which does not exist
- Using 'Multiplication' or 'Division' with pointer variables is not valid.

- Forgetting to use parenthesis when undergoing pointer arithmetic will result in an logical error.
  For Example: *ptr + 3; instead of *(ptr +3);

7.4 Pointers to Pointers

'Pointers to Pointers', the topic name might seem very complicated but in reality it is very simple. In order to create pointers to a pointers all we need to do is add another asterix (*) for each level of reference. This concept is explained through C++ statements in Program 7.4.

Program 7.4

```
char a;

char *pa; // Pointer to 'a'

char **ppa; // Pointer to pointer 'pa'

a = 'I';

pa = &a; // Pointer 'pa' stores address of character variable 'a'

ppa = &pa; // Pointer 'ppa' stores address of character variable 'pa'
```

We can also explain this concept with the use of memory addresses (see Figure. 7.5). Suppose that **a, pa, ppa** have the following memory locations 100, 200, 300.

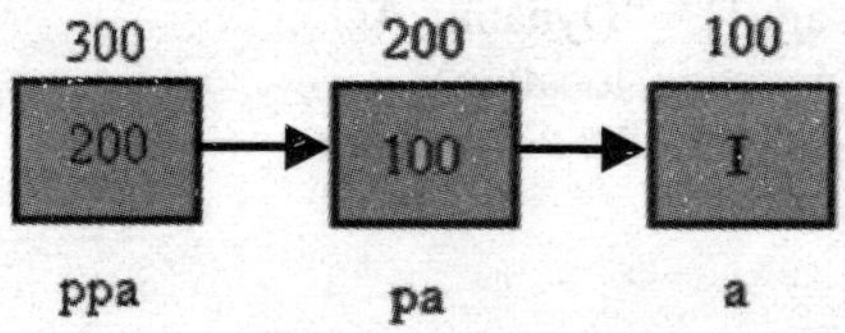

Figure 7.5: Pointers to pointers

Then,

ppa is a variable of type (char **) having value '200'

***ppa** refers to the integer value stored in variable 'pa' i.e. 100

****ppa** refers to the character value stored in variable 'a' i.e. 'I'

7.4.1 Solved Examples

Example 7.4.1.1

Find the output for the following piece of code:

```
# include <iostream.h>
# include <conio.h>
# include <ctype.h>
# include <string.h>

void newtext (char string [], int &position)
{
    char *pointer = string;

    int length = strlen (string);

    for ( ; position <length -2; position +=2 , pointer ++)
    {
     *(pointer + position ) = toupper (*(pointer + position));
    }
}

void main ()
{
   clrscr();
   int location = 0;
   char message [] = "Dynamic Act";
   newtext (message, location);
   cout<<message<<" # "<<location;

}
```

Solution of 7.4.1.1

OUTPUT SCREEN

```
DynAmiC ACt# 10
```

Example 7.4.1.2

Give the output of the following program segment

```
# include<iostream.h>
# include<conio.h>
# include<ctype.h>

void main()
{
 clrscr();

 char *s = "MeTropoliTan";

 for ( int x =0; s[x] != '\0';x++)
 {
  if (x%2!=0 && islower(s[x]))
    s[x] = toupper(s[x]);
  else
    if (isupper(s[x]))
    s[x] = tolower (s[x]);
  else
    s[x]= s[x]--;
 }
  cout<<s<<endl;
}
```

Solution of 7.4.1.2

In this piece of code'**s**' is declared as a pointer variable pointing to the first character of the string 'MeTropoliTan'. The program converts some of the characters to upper case and some to lower case depending upon the condition provided in the if else loop construct. The working of this program should be easily understood as we already observed similar problems above.

OUTPUT SCREEN

```
mEtRoPoLitaN
```

7.5 Pointer with functions

As we have already studied in the earlier chapters that there are two ways to pass arguments to a function 'Call by Value' and 'Call by reference'. In C++ 'Call by reference' is practiced by using either the address of operator or by the use of the pointers. In part I chapter 3 if we recall we were using the address of operator (&) when we were calling functions by reference. What we were actually doing though was passing the address of the variable to the function and hence reflecting any changes made in the formal parameters to the actual parameters. Call by reference can also be replicated by the use of pointers in C/C++.

The programs 7.5 (a), (b) present similar functions being called by reference by using the address of operator (&) in the 1st case and using the indirection operator (*) in the other. The important thing to note is that both these programs are equivalent and give the same result.

Program 7.5

(a) Using Function with Pointers	(b) Using Functions as Reference

// Header Files
# include<iostream.h> 	
# include<conio.h> 	
# include<string.h> 	
# include <stdio.h> 	
 	
/****************************
Name: pointer_example
Arguments: char *ptr, int length
****************************/
 	
void pointer_example(char *ptr, int length);
 	
// Main Function
 	
void main()
 	
{
	// Header Files
	# include<iostream.h>
	# include<conio.h>
	# include<string.h>
	# include <stdio.h>
	
	/**********************
	Name: reference_example
	Arguments: char string[]
	**********************/
	
	void reference_example(char string[]);
	
	// Main Function
	
	void main()
	
	{
	    clrscr();
	    char string_actual[15];

```
        clrscr();
        char string[15];
        int length_string;
        cout<<" Enter String (<15
)"<<endl;
        gets(string);
        length_string=strlen(string);
        // Call to the function
pointer_example
        pointer_example(string,
length_string);
        getch();
}

// Function Definition and Body
void pointer_example( char *ptr, int
length )
{
   for (int i=0; i<length; i++)
   {
        cout<<*ptr;
        ptr++;
   }
}
```

```
        cout<<" Please enter the string (<15
characters>)"<<endl;
        gets(string_actual);
        // Call to the function
reference_example
        reference_example(string_actual);
        getch();
}
// Function Definition and Body

void reference_example(char
string_formal[])
{
  puts(string_formal);
}
```

When these programs are executed, one would notice that they result in the same outcome. In fact, both these programs are equivalent piece of code.

Let us try to understand why is it so? In program 7.4 (a) if we notice we have used a character pointer in the function definition for function 'pointer_example'. When the character array 'string' is passed to it as a parameter. The pointer points to the 1st character of this character array 'string'. When we enter the function body we fall into a for loop which executes till the length of the string passed to it and the pointer 'ptr' is incremented every time in each iteration and hence the whole string is printed on the screen as a result of this loop (Figure III1.2) loop. In program 7.4 (b) the same thing happens the only difference being that in this case we have passed the character array as a reference parameter using the address of operator (&).

PROGRAMING TIPS

- Always use parenthesis to avoid compilation and logical errors when using pointer arithmetic.
- Pointer arithmetic is different from conventional arithmetic. In pointer arithmetic only 'addition' and 'subtraction' using operators is allowed.
- Pointers and arrays are very similar concepts
- Using the address of (&) operator is same as using pointers.

7.6 New and Delete Operators

To understand the use of the new and delete operator let us look at the following array program 7.6.

Program 7.6

```
// Program Prints the Name of a person
// Header Files
# include <iostream.h>
# include <conio.h>
# include <stdio.h>

// Main Function
void main()
{
    clrscr();
    char string [15];
    cout<<" Enter the Name of the person ";
    gets (string);
    puts(string);
}
```

All this program does is input a name from the user and then print that name in the next line. What is though more important to observe is that when we declare the character array string with an index value 15. The computer reserves space for 15 characters.

Now when we input the string say 'Computer'. It has 8 characters and should occupy 8 characters but instead it would too use up all the space assigned for 15 characters as at time of declaration for this string we declared it for a set of 15 characters. Hence we are wasting the rest space for 7 characters and hence the computers memory. C++ does not allow us to specify the array size at the time of program execution. The compiler requires the array size to be a constant. Hence, while declaring an array you need to know how big the array is likely to be which may always not be possible as we just saw in the previous program. C++ overcomes this problem by providing the 'new' and the 'delete' operators which allow us to use the computer memory efficiently.

7.6.1 The New Operator

'New operator' in C++ returns the addresses of a block of unallocated bytes (depending on data type a pointer is pointing to). In simple words it helps in obtaining blocks of memory returning a non zero pointer pointing to its starting point.The following program shows how the new operator can be used in C++.

Program 7.7:

```
// Header Files
# include <iostream.h>
# include <conio.h>
# include <stdio.h>


// Main Function
void main()
{
        clrscr();// Clear Screen
        char *ptr; // Pointer to char
        int size;
        cout<<" Enter the number of characters in the persons name";
        cin>> size;

        ptr = new char [size+1]; // Set aside memory: size

        cout<<endl<<" Enter the Name of the person ";
        cin>>ptr;
        cout<<endl<<ptr;

        delete [] ptr; // Frees the allocated block of memory

        getch();
}
```

Let us take a look at this expression:

ptr = new char [size+1];

returns a pointer to a section of memory equal to size bytes just large enough to hold the name of the person to be inputted. By adding +1 to the size we also make sure that it has enough space to even include the null operator '\0' at the end of the string.

7.6.2 The Delete Operator

As we know that the computers memory is limited therefore while working with these operators one has to be careful of the amount of memory a program occupies. As if a program uses large chunks of memory then all the available memory will be reserved for the program and the program will eventually crash. So for safe and efficient use of memory, the 'new' operator has a counter part known as the 'delete' operator which returns all the memory blocks allocated to the program using the 'new' operator back to the operating system.

Syntax:

```
delete pointer_name;
```

Let us look at following statement in program 7.7:

delete [] ptr;

This statement returns to the operating system whatever memory pointed to by our pointer 'ptr'. The square brackets tell the compiler that we are deleting the entire array block.

7.7 Array of pointers

An array, who's each element is a pointer type, is known as an array of pointers. Arrays of pointers are used to create arrays of strings. Each entry in the array is a string and this pointer points to the 1st character of a string. Consider the following definition of a character array 'flowers'.

char * flowers[3] = { " ROSE", "LILY", "LOTUS" };

The highlighted part (char *) indicates that each element of the array flowers is a pointer to char. All entries in the array 'flowers' store addresses of these strings Each index entry of this array points to the 1st character of their corresponding string (see Figure 7.6).

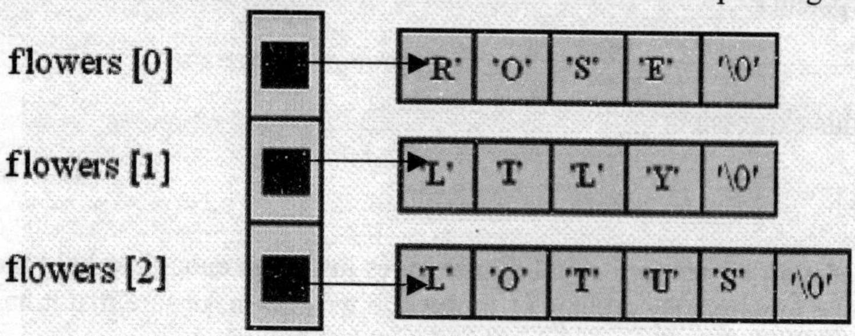

Figure 7.6: Array of pointers

We can now also look at Program 7.8 which also shows the use of array of pointers in C++.

Program 7.8

```
# include <iostream.h>
# include <conio.h>

void main()
{
 clrscr();

 int *a[3]; // Declaring an array of pointers

 for (int i=0;i<3;i++)
 {

   a[i] = new int; // Allocating block of memory for the character array
  *a[i]= i * 25;

 }

 for (i=2;i>=0;i--)
 cout<<"*A["<<i<<"]="<<*a[i]<<endl;

 for (i=0;i<3;i++)
 delete a[i];  // De allocating block of memory for the character array
 getch();
}
```

In this program, a[i] is an array of pointers and each element of this array a[0], a[1], a[2] points to a memory block of type int. Again each element of this just stores the pointers which point to their respective memory blocks.

'Array of pointers' displays the data structuring capabilities of C++. We will further learn about them in later chapters.

7.8 Pointer to a structure

A pointer which stores the address of struct type data is known as pointer to structure. An example of a pointer to a structure is shown in the following program 7.9.

Program 7.9

```
# include <iostream.h>
# include <conio.h>
```

```
struct graph
{
 int x, y;
};

void main()
{
 clrscr();

 grpah *g;

 g = new graph;

 // *g.x = 24; Not allowed

 // g.*x = 24; Not allowed

 // g.x = 24;  Not allowed

 g->x=24;

 g->y=g->x*2-2;

 cout<<" G->X="<<g->x<<" G->Y="<<g->y<<endl;

 delete g;

 getch ();
 }
```

OUTPUT SCREEN

```
G->X=24 G->Y=46
```

When using pointer to a structure the only difference is that we do not use the deference operator instead we use a '–' and a greater than '>' to refer to the values pointed by the pointer 'g'. Hence if say we are referring to the data member 'x' in the structure 'graph' the following c++ statements are invalid.

```
*g.x = 24; // Not Valid
g.*x = 24; // Not Valid
g.x = 24; // Not Valid
```

One has to use the '->' to refer to data member 'x' of the structure as also shown in the program above.

7.9 Solved Examples

Example 7.9.1

Find the output for the following piece of code:

```
# include <iostream.h>
# include <conio.h>

void main()
{
 clrscr();

 int a = 100, *b=&a;
 cout<<*b<<a<<endl;

 (*b)+=10;
 a-=100;
 cout<<*b<<a<<endl;

 int *c;
 c = new int;
 *c=100;
 *c=a;
 a+=100;
 cout<<*c<<a<<endl;
 c=b;
 (*b)+=90;
 a+=10;
 cout<<*c<<*b<<a<<endl;
 getch();
}
```

Solution of 7.9.1

OUTPUT SCREEN

```
100100
1010
10110
210210210
```

Example 7.9.2

Consider the given declarations and give the outputs. All parts of code are independent of each other.

```
# include <iostream.h>
# include <conio.h>

void main()
{
 clrscr();
 int s=10, t=90, *u, *v;

 //(i)
  u=&s;
  v=&t;

  cout<<*u<<*v<<t<<s<<endl;

 //(ii)
  u = &t;
  v=u;
  (*v)++;
  s=s+t;
  t=t+s;

  cout<<s<<t<<*u<<*v<<endl;

 //(iii)
  s++;
  --t;
  v=&t;
  cout<<s<<*v;
  u=v;
  v=&s;
  s=t-s;

  cout<<*u<<*v<<endl;

 getch();
}
```

Solution of 7.9.2

OUTPUT SCREEN

```
i) 10909010
ii) 101192192192
iii)11898978
```

Example 7.9.3

What will the user see when the following piece of code is executed.

(i)

```
# include <iostream.h>
# include <conio.h>

struct point
{
 int x,y;

 }polygon[]={{1,2},{1,4},{2,4},{2,2}};

void main()
{
 point *a;
 a= polygon;
 a++;
 a->x++;
 cout<<polygon[0].x<<polygon[0].y<<endl;
 cout<<a->x<<a->y<<endl;
 getch();
}
```

(ii)

```
# include <iostream.h>
# include <conio.h>
void main()
{
 clrscr();
 int x=20, y=30, *b=&x;
 (*b)+=15;
 cout<<x<<*b<<endl;
```

```
 x++;
 cout<<*b<<x<<endl;
 b=&y;
 y+=x;
 int *c=b;
 b=&x;
 y+=12;
 x*=4;
 cout<<*b<<*c;
 getch();
}
```

(iii)

```
# include <iostream.h>
# include <conio.h>
void main()
{
 clrscr();
 int a[]={2,4,6,8,10};
 int *k,*p1;
 p1=a;
 k = new int;
 (*p1)+=10;
 *k=55;
 (*p1)++;
 *p1=*k;
 (*k)*=2;
 cout<<*p1<<*k<<endl;
 getch();
}
```

(iv)

```
# include <iostream.h>
# include <conio.h>
void main()
{
 clrscr();
 char *p = "Difficult";
 char c;
 c=++*p++;
 cout<<c<<*p<<endl;
 getch();
}
```

(v)

```
# include <iostream.h>
# include <conio.h>
```

```
void main()
{
  clrscr();
  int a=32, *ptr=&a;
  char ch='A';
  char &f= ch;
  f+=a;
  *ptr+=ch;
  cout<<a<<" "<<ch<<endl;
  getch();
}
```

Solution of 7.9.3

(i)

Output Screen

```
12
24
```

(ii)

Output Screen

```
3535
3636
14478
```

(iii)

Output Screen

```
55110
```

(iv)

Output Screen

```
Ei
```

(v) **Output Screen**

```
129 a
```

Example 7.9.4

Write a program which reads in a group of 10 numbers and places them in an array of type int. It then calculates the sum of all the odd numbers in the set of these 10 numbers and prints the odd numbers and their sum on the screen. Use pointer notation where ever possible.

Solution of 7.9.4

```
# include <iostream.h>
# include <conio.h>

void main()
{

  clrscr();
  int *ptr[10];
  int sumodd=0;
  int flag=0;
  cout<<" Enter the 10 numbers in the array";
  for (int i=0; i<10;i++)
  {
   ptr[i] = new int;
   cin>>*ptr[i];
  }
  for (i=0; i<10;i++)
  {
   if (*ptr[i]%2!=0)
    {
     if (flag==0)
     cout<<" The odd numbers are";
     sumodd = sumodd + *ptr[i];
     cout<<*ptr[i]<<endl;
     flag++;
    }
  }
  cout<<" The sum of odd numbers in the array is"<<sumodd;
  getch();
}
```

Example 7.9.5

Declare an array of pointers to strings representing the 5 week days. Also, declare a function to sort these strings in alphabetical order using bubble sort. Sort the pointers to the string as and not the actual strings?

Solution of 7.9.5

```
// Header files
# include <iostream.h>
# include <conio.h>
# include <stdio.h>
# include <string.h>

// Function: b_sort
// Purpose: To sort the array passed to it as a paramter
void b_sort(char *str_pointers[])
{
 char *temp;
 for (int j=0;j<5;j++)
 for (int i=0;i<4-j;i++)
 {
        if (strcmp (str_pointers[i],str_pointers[i+1])>0)
        {
                temp = str_pointers[i+1];
                str_pointers[i+1]=str_pointers[i];
                str_pointers[i]=temp;
        }
 }
}

// Main Function
void main()
{
 char *weekdays[5]={"Monday","Tuesday","Wednesday","Thursday","Friday"};

 puts("\nWeekdays: Before Sorting");

 for (int i=0; i<5; i++)
        {
                puts(weekdays[i]);
        }

 b_sort(weekdays);
 puts("\nWeekdays: After Sorting");

 for (i=0; i<5; i++)
```

POINTERS

```
 {
  puts(weekdays[i]);
 }
 getch();
}
```

Example 7.9.6

Find the output for the following piece of code:

```
# include <iostream.h>
# include <conio.h>

void main()
{
 clrscr ();
 int *ptr;
 int number = 5;
 ptr = &number;
 cout<<ptr<<endl;
 cout<<&number<<endl;
 cout<<*&ptr<<endl;
 cout<<*(*&ptr)<<endl;
 cout<<*&*&*(*&ptr)<<endl;
 getch();
}
```

Solution of 7.9.6

OUTPUT SCREEN

```
0x1fa70ffa
0x1fa70ffa
0x1fa70ffa
5
5
```

7.10 Review Exercise

1 Mark/ 2 Mark Questions

Q1) A pointer stores
   a. an address of a variable
   b. the values of the variable it points to
   c. is a set of unallocated bytes of memory
   d. a data type of an address variable

Q2) The expression *post;
   a. is a pointer to the variable post
   b. holds the address of variable post
   c. refers to the contents of the post.
   d. refers to the contents stored to the variable to which post points to.

Q3) Will the following piece of code compile without errors:

```
int ptr;
int *ptr1;
int **ptr2
ptr1=&ptr;

ptr2=*ptr1;
ptr = ptr2;
```

Q4) Are the following c++ statements equivalent:

i) int ptr[2] and *(int ptr +2)

ii) int *ptr; and int *ptr;
    ptr = &add; ptr = *& add;

Q5) Is pointer arithmetic the same as conventional arithmetic. If not how is it different from conventional arithmetic? Give suitable examples?

Q6) Write c++ statements
   i. to input a set of two integers say, 'a' and 'b' from the user and
   ii. swap their values using pointers.

Q7) Assuming the code given below, find the error in each of the program segments a), b) and c).

Code:

```
int *ptr, number;
int num[5] = { 5,10 ,15 , 20, 25, 30};
ptr = num;
```

Statements:

a) // Use pointer to get the address of first value of array.
```
number  = ptr;
```

b) // Change the value '10' at the index position to 2 of array num to '5'
```
*(ptr+1)=5;
```

Q8) Find the output for the following piece of code.

```
# include <iostream.h>
# include <conio.h>

struct coordinate
{
 int x
 int y;
 };

void display ( coordinate n)
            {
               cout<<" Row ="<<n.x<<"\t Column = "<<n.y<<endl;
            }

            void main()
{
 clrscr();
 coordinate A = {20,50}, B;
 coordinate *c;
 c=&b;
 c->x += 20;
 display (b);
 c = &a;
 c->y +=20;
 display (a);
 getch();
}
```

Q9) Write a program which reads in a group of 10 numbers and places them in an array of type int. It then calculates the sum of all the even numbers in the set of these 10 numbers and prints the even numbers and their sum on the screen. Use pointer notation where ever possible.

Q10) Write a program to input an array of strings. The program should also contain a function to convert all the characters of the string to upper case and also count the number of lower case characters. Use pointer notation where ever possible.

3 Mark/ 4 Mark Questions

Q1) Find the output for the following piece of code:

```
int arr[] = {2,3,4,5};

int *arrptr=array;
int val =  *arrptr;

cout<< val<<endl;
val = * arrptr++;

cout<<val<<endl;
val=*arrptr;

cout<<val<<endl;
val= *++arrptr;

cout<<val<<endl;
```

Q2) Find errors in the following piece of code:

```
/***************************
 The program swaps the values of two integers with the help of pointers
 ***************************/
// Header Files
# include <iostream.h>
 # include <conio.h>
 // Main Function
void main ()
 {
  clrscr ();
  int *ptr;
  int num1;
  int num2;
  num1=&ptr;
  num2= *ptr;
```

Q3) Create a database for 20 employees in a company, the database should include employee name, employee number, employee designation, employee salary, employee department. Create separate functions to sort the database in ascending order with employee name, employee id and employee salary. Also create function Emp_search to search any employee with employee number as the search key. Use structures and pointer notation where ever possible?

Q4) Write C++ statements for the following:

i) Initialize a pointer to an integer.

ii) Initialize a pointer to a string.

iii) Initialize a pointer to an array of 10 characters.

iv) Initialize a pointer to a pointer to a character, a floating point.

v) Initialize a pointer to the following structure:

```
struct graph
{
int x;
int y;
};
```

Also then initialize x = 5, y =10 using the pointer variable.

Q5) Read a sequence of words from the user. Keep reading the sequence till the point the user enters the word 'STOP'. Print these words in the order of sequence do not print any word starting from the character 's'. Also write a function Seq_sort which returns a sorted list of words to be printed on the screen. Use pointer notation where ever possible.

Q6) State the difference between an array of characters and a string. How is size of an array of characters different from a string? What is the size of the array 'str'?

```
char str[] = "This is Question 6";
```

Declare an array of strings in which the strings contain the names of all the days. Ask the user to input a set of 10 random strings. Print those days in order of occurrence. Use pointer notation where ever possible.

7.11 Programming Project

A very popular puzzle which most of us have played when we were young is the '10-puzzle'. This puzzle's frame can hold 10 tiles. It consists of blocks number from digits 1 to 9 and an empty space. The purpose of the game is to slide the blocks. The goal is to slide the blocks using the empty space block such that each block is arranged in the ascending order when observed row wise. For example if 'X' represents the empty space given a valid initial configuration one should achieve the final configuration as shown in Figure 7.6.

Our project is to write c++ a program for which the user inputs the set of 9 integers in the order of sequence. The program should print all the moves to reach the desired configuration of blocks. Use pointers and structures where ever possible.

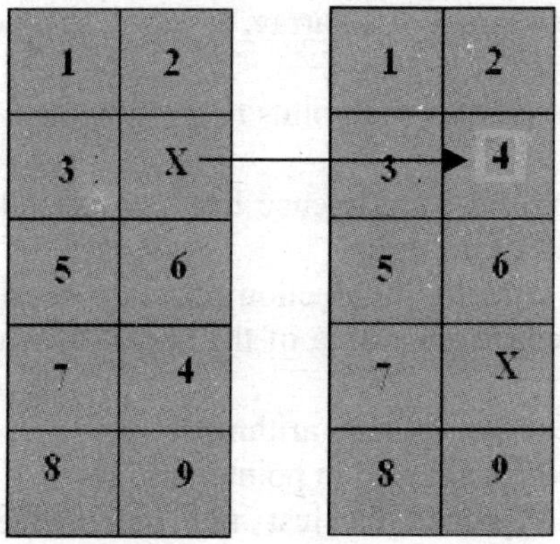

Figure 7.6: The '10's Puzzle

7.12 Let us revise!

- The address (&) of operator returns the address of its operand.
- A pointer that holds an address of a variable is called a pointer variable.
- The pointer definition is:

  int *ptr;

- A pointer, which stores the address of an array, is called as a pointer to an array
- An array name is a constant pointer and points to the first element of the array.
- Arrays are automatically passed by reference because the value of the array name is the address of the array.
- The '*' operator, referred to as the indirection operator when used with the pointer variable returns the value of the object to which it points.
- Pointer arithmetic is different than general arithmetic.
- Only addition and subtraction is allowed in pointer arithmetic.
- In pointer arithmetic, the pointer is just not incremented or decremented by the value of the integer instead it is incremented or decremented by the value of the integer times the size of the data type the pointer points to.
- The 'new' operator in c++ returns the address of a block of unallocated bytes.
- The 'delete' operator in c++ reverses the process of the new operator, by releasing the memory location from a pointer.
- We can also have pointers to pointers. These variables are defined using double or triple asterix (*) depending upon the degree of branching, for example, int ** ptr (for degree of branching 2).
- An array of pointers is an array who's each element is a pointer type.
- A pointer which stores the address of a *struct* data type is known as a pointer to a structure.

PART II

OBJECT ORIENTED PROGRAMMING

Part II

CHAPTER 1

OBJECT ORIENTED PROGRAMMING

AIM

- To introduce the concept of Object Oriented Programming (OOP)
- To understand the difference between procedural and object oriented programming.
- To understand the various features and advantages of OOP
- To appreciate the concept of OOP

OUTLINE

1.1 Introduction
1.2 Basic features of Object Oriented Programming
1.3 Classes and Objects
1.4 Constructors and Destructors
1.5 Review Examples
1.6 Review Exercise
1.7 Let us revise

1.1 Introduction

As programming languages evolved there occurred many problems with the procedural programming language. In procedural programming language emphasis was on doing things that were functions, it consisted of global variables, and there existed always a possibility of accidental change in data. Hence, a new system of programming was developed which was named as Object Oriented Programming. In short it was termed as 'OOP'. OOP enables the programmers to group together data and the code that uses data into discrete units. In OOP the stress is given on the object in spite of the procedure.

An object is defined by two terms: attributes and behaviors. If you look at a person and visualize him as an object, you will find that a person has attributes, such as, eye color, age, height, and so on. A person also has behaviors, such as walking, talking, breathing, and so on. In its basic definition, an *object* is an entity that contains *both* data and behavior. The word *both* is the key difference between the more traditional programming methodology, procedural programming, and OOP.

In procedural programming, code is placed into totally distinct functions or procedures. Ideally, as shown in Figure 1.1, these procedures then become "black boxes," where inputs go in and outputs come out. Data is placed into separate structures, and is manipulated by these functions or procedures.

Figure 1.1 Black boxes.

1.1.1 Difference between OO and Procedural Programming

In Object Oriented design, the attributes and behavior are contained within a single object, whereas in procedural or structured design, the attributes and behavior are normally separated.

As illustrated in Figure 1.2, in procedural programming the data is separated from the procedures, and sometimes the data is global so it is easy to modify data that is outside your scope. This means that access to data is uncontrolled and unpredictable (i.e. several functions may have access to the global data). Further, because you have no control over who has access to the data; testing and debugging are much more difficult. Objects address these problems by combining data and behavior into a nice, complete package.

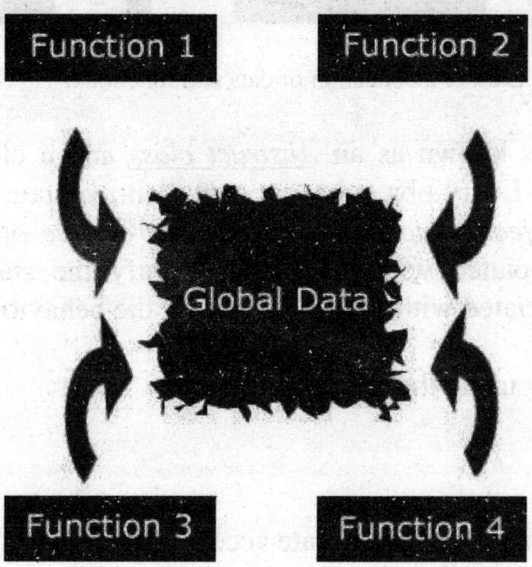

Figure 1.2 Using global data.

1.2 Basic Features of Object Oriented Programming

- Emphasis is on data
- It follows a bottom-up approach in program design
- It has concepts like data hiding which prevents the accidental change of data
- It has properties like
    - Polymorphism
    - Inheritance
    - Encapsulation

  These properties are explained later in this chapter.

1.3 Classes & Objects

An object has a similar relationship to a class that a variable has to a data type. In short an object is an instance of a class. A class is a user defined data type used to implement an abstract object. It contains members of three types: 'private', 'public' or 'protected' by default the data members of the class are private. Contents of a class are known as members of the class, data declared inside the class is known are known as data members and functions included inside the class are known as member functions.

An object is said to be instance of a class, in the same way 'keyboard' and 'mouse' belong to the class 'hardware', or 'me' and 'you' are instances of a class 'HUMAN'.

Figure 1.3: Classes a collection of data and functions

A class with no object is known as an *Abstract class* and a class having object(s) is known as *Concrete class*. Every object has its own identity, state and behavior. **Identity** *is the property of the object, which distinguishes it from the other objects*. Static and Dynamic properties associated with the object signify the state of the object. The operations/functions associated with the object exhibit the behavior of the object.

A class can be declared by using the following syntax:

```
class  Class-name
{
    private:     // its optional to write private access specifier
        data-member;
        data-member;
        member-function

    protected:
        data-member;
        data-member;
        member-function

    public:
        data-member;
        data-member;
        member-function
};
:
class_name List-of-objects;
```

For example:

```
class HUMAN
{
    int HIEGHT,EYECOLOR,AGE;

    char TYPE;  // M: Man
                // W: Women
```

```
public:
    void input();
                              MEMBER FUNCTIONS
    void output();
};
:
HUMAN  Steve, Jordan ;
```

In the above example Steve and Jordan are object declarations. Members can be kept in any of the three accessibility modes private, public and protected. Members in the public visibility mode of the class are accessible to the objects of the class whereas members in the private accessibility mode are not accessible to the objects of the class. They are only accessible inside the class to the member functions of the class.

NOTE: Protected members will be explained later in Chapter 2 entitled 'Inheritance'.

Program 1.1 illustrates the use of classes and objects:

Program 1.1

```
/***********************************************************************
Program 1(1).cpp
Explaining the concept of classes and objects
***********************************************************************/

// Header files
# include <iostream.h>
# include <stdio.h>

// Declration of class hospital
class hospital
{
  private:
  int patientno,wardno;          //private data members
  char patient_name[20];

  public:
  void register_patient();          //public member function prototype

  void showstatus()        //public member function declaration
     {
       cout<<patientno<<":"<<patient_name<<":"<<wardno<<endl;
     }
};                              //semicolon is a must
```

```
/**********************************************************************
Name: register_patient
Class: hospital
Purpose: Input patient information
**********************************************************************/

void hospital::register_patient()
     {
        cout<<"patient no ?";
        cin>>patientno;
        cout<<"name ?";
        gets(patient_name);
        cout<<"Ward no ?";
        cin>>wardno;
     }

// Main function
void main()
  {
     hospital  p1,p2;
     p1.register_patient();
     p2.register_patient();
     p1.showstatus();
     p2.showstatus();
  }
```

```
// cin>>p1.wardno;    ** not accessible as wardno is a private member
// cin>>p1.patientno; **not accessible as patientno is a private member
```

In the above example, one can see that a class Hospital is defined with

i. Three private data members patientno, wardno and patient_name; and
ii. Two public member functions register() and showstatus().

Member functions can be defined inside the class as well as outside the class as shown in the example, member function showstatus() is defined inside the class whereas the member function register() is defined outside the class by using the scope resolution operator (::) with the name of the class it belongs to. Figure 1.4 pictures the use the of the scope resolution operator. The objects of the class can call both these functions in the same way. Generally single lined functions are defined inside the class and multiple line functions or functions containing control structures (if then else or while loops) are defined outside the class to have clarity in understanding the behavior of the class.

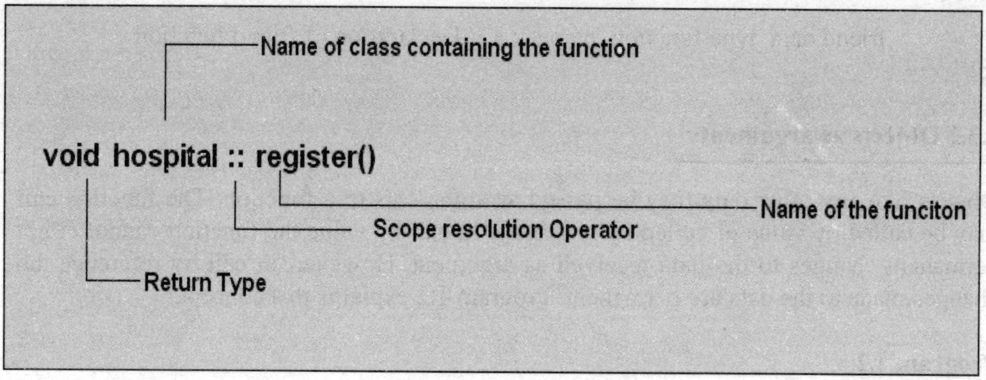

Figure 1.4: A function declared outside the class

Note: The size of the object (in bytes) depends upon the data members present in the class it belongs to. In the above example the object p1 occupies 24 bytes.

COMMON PROGRAMMING ERRORS

- Declaration of member functions outside the class definitions without the scope resolution operator (::) will lead to an error.
- The class definitions must end with a semicolon. Ignoring this will lead to an error

1.3.1 Friend Function

Only a member function of a class can access data declared in the private access specifier in a class declaration as a result of which there is no chance of accidental change of data. However there are cases where the user wants to access data of an object by a function which is not a member function of the class to which the objects belong. This is possible by declaring a function as a friend function of the class. The syntax for such a function is given below

```
class class_name
{
    private:
        ............................ //private members
        ............................
    public:
        .......................... // public members
```

```
        .........................

        friend data_type function_name();    // Declaration of friend function
};
```

1.3.2 Objects as arguments

Objects like any other data may be passed as arguments to a function. The function call may be called by value or called by reference. In call by value the function cannot effect permanent changes to the data received as argument. However, in call by reference the changes made to the data are permanent. Program 1.2 explains this concept.

Program 1.2

```
/**************************************************************************
Program 2(2).cpp
 The program displays objects being passed as arguments for class time and objects
undergoing basic arithmetic operations.
**************************************************************************/

// Header Files
# include <iostream.h>
# include <conio.h>

class time
{
 int hrs,mins;

 public:

 // Function to get time from the user
 void gettime()
   {
        cout<<"Enter the hours !";
        cin>>hrs;
        cout<<" \nEnter the minutes !! ";
        cin>>mins;
   }

 void settime (int h ,int m)
   {
    hrs=h; mins=m;
   }

 // Function to show time on the screen
```

```
void showtime()
  {
 cout<<hrs<<":"<<mins<<endl;
  }

// Function to sum two objects of class time
void sum (time t1,time t2)
   {
     int minutes=t1.mins +t2.mins;
     hrs = t1.hrs+t2.hrs +minutes/60;
     mins=minutes%60;
   }
};

// Main function
void main()
{
  clrscr();
  time t1,t2,t3;
  t1.gettime();          // Call to function gettime
  t2.settime(3,45);      // Call to function settime
  t3.sum(t1,t2);         // Objects being passed as arguments
  cout<<"\nt1=";
  t1.showtime();         // Call to function showtime
  cout<<"t2=";
  t2.showtime();
  cout<<"t3=";
  t3.showtime();
  getch();
}
```

OUTPUT SCREEN

```
Enter the hours !10

Enter the minutes !! 10

t1=10:10
t2=3:45
t3=13:55
```

In this program class time has hrs, mins as its private members and hence cannot be accessed from the function main. Class time also has public member functions through which these private members can be accessed.

When this program is executed t1, t2, t3 objects of class time are created. The function 'gettime' is invoked for object t1 and the user is asked to enter the hours and the minutes for this object. The values entered by the user '10' and '10' are stored as this objects values for hours and minutes. Similarly for object t2 function settime is invoked and values '3' and '45' are stored as objects value for hours – 'hrs' and minutes-'mins' respectively. For object t3 however the function sum is invoked in which objects t1 and t2 are being passed as arguments. The values for t3s private members 'hrs' and 'minutes' is the sum of the values for private members of t1 '10' ,'10' and that of t2 '3','45' respectively.

PROGRAMING TIPS

- Declare all member function as **const** if object remains unchanged. This can help to remove many errors.
- Languages like C++ are still evolving languages. Avoid using loaded words like 'Object'. Even though "Object" is not a keyword in future might become one.

1.3.3 Encapsulation

To understand the concept of encapsulation better take an example of a simple quadratic equation,

$$Ax^2 + Bx + C = 0$$

All quadratic equations constitute an example of a class. As all quadratic equations have unique identity (degree '2'), state (coefficients: A, B and C) and similar behavior (2 roots). In OOPS we create objects by combining data members and data functions for input, output and data manipulation.

As it might be obvious each and every object of the class 'Quadratic Equation' will have three coefficients (A, B and C) and two roots and in order for data manipulation each object will also have some member functions to read these coefficients, calculating the roots and displaying them on the screen. This method or practice of wrapping up of data and functions in a single unit is known as *'Encapsulation'*. Figure 1.5 given below further enlightens this concept.

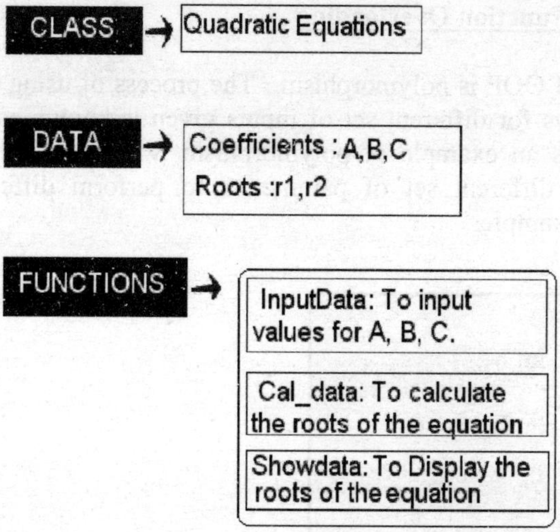

Figure 1.5: Data and member functions required by a class quadratic equations

1.3.4 Data Abstraction and Data Hiding

Data abstraction is defined as bringing the data down to its essentials. For example, consider that an automobile company has come up with a new design for an automobile to make it fuel efficient. Now before they launch their product in the market they want to make the customers aware of the fuel efficiency that this new automobile will provide them. For instance they want to make the customers aware of the fact that this newly designed automobile will be 40% more fuel-efficient than any other automobile available in the market. However, they do not want to give away the intricate details of the design owing to the fear of the design being replicated by the competitors in the market.

Therefore, the management decides that the company should only give away those basic details, which are essential and only includes features like how would this new design enhance the fuel efficiency of the automobile keeping the intricate details regarding the engine design hidden. Now this process in which only the essential features of the new automobile design are highlighted and thus, represented to the outside world without including the intricate features is termed as abstraction.

In C++, the *private* class members initialized remain hidden from the outside world and hence all the intricate details can be stored in these members whereas the *public* members form the interface by providing the essential and relevant information to the outside world. This process is also termed as **data hiding**.

1.3.5 Polymorphism & Function Overloading

One of the key feature of OOP is polymorphism. The process of using an operator or a function in different ways for different set of inputs given is known as polymorphism. **Function overloading** is an example of polymorphism, where the functions with the same name work with different set of parameters to perform different operations. Consider the following example,

```
\\ Function 1
int maximum (int a, int b);
\\ Function 2
int maximum (int a, int b, int c)
\\ Call to function 1
maximum (10, 12);
\\ Call to function 2
maximum (10, 12, 13);
```

Now when this piece of code is executed and the compiler reaches the 1st call to the function, function 1 is called as this function call matches the function header of function 1 as it has the same number of parameters. Similarly when the compiler reaches the call for the 2nd function, function 2 is called as the function call matches the function header for the 2nd function. This is an example of function overloading, where same named functions behave differently for different kind of inputs given to them by the user.

When defining functions having same names it is becomes absolutely necessary that they should differ in **number, type and order.**

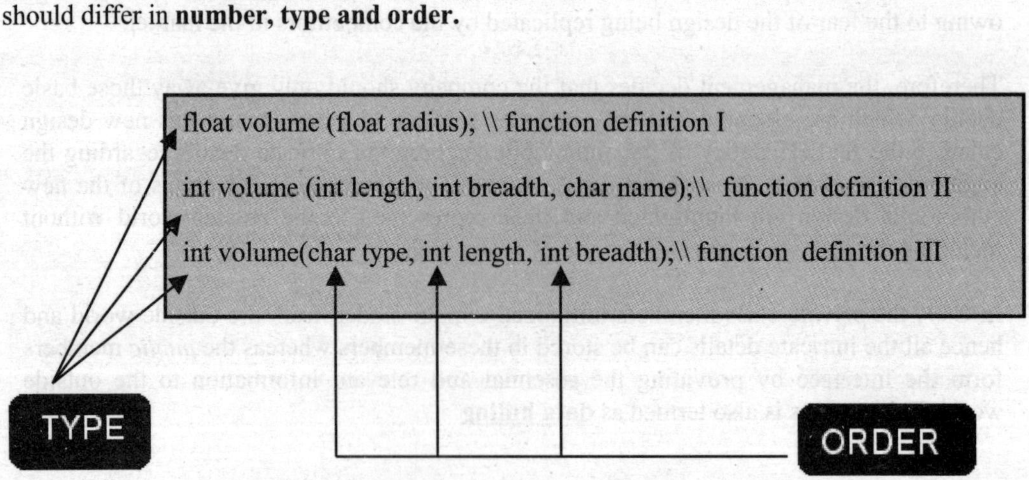

Figure 1.6: Function overloading

For example consider figure 1.6. This figure shows three function definitions. These function definitions differ in type, number and order as shown in the following table 1.1.

Table 1.1: Function Definitions

Function Defintion	Number of parameters	Type of parameters	Order of parameters
I	1 radius	float datatype	float
II	3 length, breadth, name	int datatype, int datatype, char datatype	int, int, char
III	3 type, length, breadth	char datatype, int datatype, int datatype	char, int, int

The various functions of these function definitions will behave differently for different types of input given to them. However, sometimes the following also happens. For example,

```
\\ function 1
int maximum(a, int b);
\\ function 2
int maximum(int a , int b , int c=5);
maximum(10,12);
```

During execution of this program, when the compiler reaches the call to the function maximum the compiler is not sure which function out of above two to invoke, function 1 or function 2 as both the functions 1 and 2 satisfy the function call **maximum(10,12);**

When this type of a situation occurs in which the compiler is not sure about which of the 2 functions to invoke it is referred to as **Function Ambiguity**. If such a case occurs during a program execution the program will hang during its execution. Another case of function ambiguity may take place when one is using 'float' and 'double' or 'int' and 'long' as data types for the local variables in the function header.

1.3.6 Solved Examples

Example 1.3.6.1

Define a class in C++ with the following description

Private members

- A data member Flight Number of type integer
- A data member Destination of type string
- A data member Distance of type float
- A data member Fuel of type float
- A member function CALFUEL() to calculate the value of fuel as per the following criteria

Distance	**Fuel**
<=1000	500
more than 1000 and <=2000	1100
more than 2000	2200

Public members

- A function FEEDINFO() to allow the user to enter values for flight number, destination, distance & call function CALFUEL() to calculate the quantity of fuel
- A function SHOWINFO() to allow user to view the content of all the data members

Solution of 1.3.6.1

```
class FLIGHT
    {
      int Fno;                    // Represents Flight Number
      char Destination[20];       // Represents Destination
      float Distance;             // Represents Distance
      float Fuel;                 //Represents Fuel
      void CALFUEL();

      public:
     void FEEDINFO();
     void SHOWINFO();
    };

void FLIGHT::CALFUEL()
    {
      if(Distance<=1000 )
     Fuel=500;
```

```
    if(Distance>1000 && Distance<=2000)
    Fuel=1100;
        else
            Fuel=2200;
    }


void FLIGHT::FEEDINFO()
    {
        cout<<" Flight No:";
        cin>>Fno;
        cout<<" Destination:";
        gets(Destination);
        cout<<" Distance:";
        cin>>Distance;
        CALFUEL();
    }


void FLIGHT::SHOWINFO()
    {
        cout<<" Flight no:"<<Fno <<endl;
        cout<<" Destination:"<<Destination<<endl;
        cout<<" Distance:"<<Distance<<endl;
        cout<<" Fuel:"<<Fuel<<endl;
    }
```

Example 1.3.6.2

Define a class TEST in C++ with the following description:
Private members

- Test code of type Integer
- Description of type string
- Nocandidate of type integer
- Centerreqd (no of centers reqd) of type integer
- A member function CALCNTR() to calculate the no of centers as number of candidates/100+1

Public members

- A function SCHEDULE() to allow user to enter the values of testcode.
- Description , nocandidate & call function CALCNTR to calculate the number of center
- A function DISPTEST() to allow user to view the content of all the data members

Solution of 1.3.6.2

```
class TEST
    {
        int TestCode;
        char Description[20];
        int Nocandidate;
        int Centerreqd;
        void CALCNTR();

        public:
        void SCHEDULE();
        void DISPTEST();
    };


void TEST::CALCNTR()
    {
        Centerreqd=Nocandidate/100+1;
    }

void TEST::SCHEDULE()
    {
        cout<<" Test code:";
        cin>>TestCode;
        cout<<" Description:";
        gets(Description);
        cout<<"Number:";
        cin>>Nocandidate;
        CALCNTR();
    }
```

Example 1.3.6.3

WAP (Write a program) to create an array of objects of class stud

```
class stud
            {
            int rno;
            char nam[10];
            float avg;

             public:
             void in();
```

```
void out();
};
```

Write a user defined function to sort the array of class stud in ascending order of roll no?

Solution of 1.3.6.3

In this class we will have to create a function retroll() which will return the Rollno ('rno') of the particular objecT

```
class stud
{
      int rno;
      char nm[10];
      float avg;

   public:

      void in();
      void out();
      int  retroll ()
       {
       return rno;
       }
};

void stud :: in()
   {
      cout<<" Roll no    :";
      cin>>rno;
      cout<<" Enter the name";
      gets(nm);
      cout<<" Enter the avg";
      cin>>avg;
   }

void stud ::out()
   {
      cout<<" Roll no:"<<rno;
      cout<<" Name:";
      puts(nm);
      cout<<"Avg:"<<avg;
   }
```

```
void accept ( stud s[],int n);
void display( stud s[],int n);
void sortroll( stud s[],int n);

void main()
{
      stud a[50];
      int n;
      cout<<"enter the no of students";
      cin>>n;
      accept(a,n);
      cout<<" The contents of the array";
     display(a,n);
     sortroll(a,n);
     cout<<" The array in sorted form of roll nos is ";
    display(a,n);
}
```

Example 1.3.6.4

Give the output for the following questions

(a)
```
class parts
{
      char pnm[20];
      float prc;
public:
      void assign(char p[],float pr)
                  { strcpy(pnm,p);prc=pr;}

      void show()
                  {cout<<pnm<<"@"<<prc<<endl;}

      void price( int l=0)
                  { prc=(l==0)?prc+90:prc-90;}
};


void main()
{
         parts p,q;
         p.assign("bolts",900);
         q.assign("clamps",345);
```

```
        p.price();
        q.price(1);p.show();q.show();
        p.price(1);p.show();
    }
```

b)

```
class account
{
    int balance,accno;

public:
    account(){balance=0;}
    account(account &s)
                {
                  balance = ++s.balance;
                  accno=0;
                }
    void assign( int u)
                {
                  balance = 110; accno = u;
                }
    void disp()
                {
                  cout<<"Balance"<<balance<<endl;
                  cout<<" Acc no."<<accno<<endl;
                }
};

void main()
{
        account a1;
        a1.assign(9);
        a1.disp();
        account a2(a1);
        a2.disp();
        account a3(a2);
        int y=10;
        a3.assign(-y);
        a3.disp();
}
```

Solution of 1.3.6.4

a) OUTPUT SCREEN

```
bolts@990
clamps@255
 bolts@900
```

b) OUTPUT SCREEN

```
Balance110
 Acc no. 9
Balance111
 Acc no. 0
Balance110
 Acc no. -10
```

1.4 CONSTRUCTORS AND DESTRUCTORS

Constructors and destructors determine how the objects of a class are created, initialized, copied, and destroyed. They are member functions whose names are distinguished from all other member functions because they have the same name as the class they belong to. Constructors and destructors have many of the characteristics of normal member functions.

You declare and define them within the class, or declare them within the class and define them outside--but they have some unique features.

1.4.1 CONSTRUCTORS

Constructors are special member functions, which can be included in the class for automatic initialization at the time of object creation, these special member function(s) is/are known as Constructors or Constructer function(s). Constructor functions have the unique following features:

- Name of the constructor function is same as that of the class they are part of.
- No return type is required for the constructor function.
- Constructor functions are automatically called at the time of object creation/declaration.
- Constructor functions are always defined in the public type access specifier.
- Constructor functions can be overloaded.

With the use of a constructor variables can be given initial values which otherwise would be having junk values.

Program 1.3

```
/*************************************************************************
 Program 1(3).cpp
 Shows the declaration of a constructor
**************************************************************************/
// Header Files
# include <iostream.h>
# include <conio.h>

// Declaration of class trial
class Trial
{
  int a, b;

  public:

      Trial()  ───────────►  Constructor for class trial
  {
  a=0;b=0;
  }

 void disp()
  {
      cout<<a<<b<<endl;
  }

 void raise()
        {
          a+=10;
          b+=10;
        }

 void down()
```

```
        {
            a-=5;
            b-=5;
        }
};

// Main Function
void main()
{
    Trial T;          ——▶  Automatic call to the Constructor
    T.disp();
    T.raise();
    T.disp();
    T.down();
    T.disp();
}
```

OUTPUT SCREEN

```
00
1010
55
```

In program 1.3 we have a initialized a class **trial** which has two private data members **a** and **b.** This class also has a public member function **Trial()** but if we notice carefully this is a special member function as this is a constructor. Member function **Trial()** has the same name as that of the class of which it is a part of. Now when an object of class is declared the constructor of the class is automatically called. In this case when T an object of class Trial is declared the constructor **trial()** is automatically called for and private data members of the class **trial a** and **b** are given initial values of zero respectively.

1.4.1.1 DEFAULT CONSTRUCTOR

If a constructor is not provided in a class, the compiler automatically creates a constructor, for the class and the constructor created is known as the default constructor.

Program 1.4: Showing the declaration of a Default constructor by the compiler

```
class try
```

```
{
  int a, b;
  public:
  try(){}
  void getit();
  void  show();
};
```

try() is the default constructor of the class try.

PROGRAMING TIPS

- Constructors should be initialized in a class even though it is not necessary it is important to do so as it removes away the risk of variables having junk values and restricting many errors.
- Destructors should also be initialized to free the memory space occupied by constructors.

1.4.1.2 PARAMETERIZED CONSTRUCTOR

A parameterized constructor can take values as arguments into the constructor function at the time of object declaration. A parameterized constructor is defined in the same way as any other constructor, the only difference between an ordinary constructor and a parameterized constructor is that the function headers of these constructors will have parameters and hence different initial values can be given to objects of the same class with the use of this constructor.

Program 1.5:

```
/************************************************************************
 Program 1(5).cpp
 Object Declaration of a parameterized constructor
************************************************************************/

# include<iostream.h>
# include<conio.h>

 class employee
 {
     private:
     int employeeNo;
     public:
     employee(int n ) //  parameterized constructor
```

```
    {
    employeeNo = n;
    }
};

void main()
{
  clrscr();
  employee E1(10);
  getch();
}
```

1.4.1.3 COPY CONSTRUCTOR

A constructor, like any other function can take arguments. A copy constructor can take as argument an object of the same class to which it belongs. To understand the copy constructor lets look at the following program

Program 1.6:

```
/**********************************************************************
 Program 1(6).cpp
 Shows the declaration of a Copy Constructor
**********************************************************************/
// Header Files
# include<iostream.h>
# include<conio.h>

// Declaration of class play
class play
{
  int count, number;
  public:

  play()      // constructor
  {
    count=0;
    number=0;
  }
  play ( play &p) // copy constructor
  {
   count=p.count +10;
   number= p.number+20;
  }
```

```
    void disp()
    {
     cout<<count;
     cout<<number<<endl;
    }

    void change ( int c, int n)
    {
     count = c;
     number=n;
    }
};

void main()
{
 play  p; // call for the constructor
  p.disp();
  p.change(90,80);
  play q(p); // copy constructor call
  q.disp();
}
```

A copy constructor is *an overloaded constructor function in which an object of the same class is/are passed as reference parameter(s)*. It is used when an objects data value is related to or is initialized using another objects data value, of the same class. In the above example the values of data members of object q are dependent on the values of data members of object p.

1.4.1.4 CONSTRUCTOR OVERLOADING

Constructors are just like other functions, they can also be overloaded, that is same named constructers can be used to give different set of outputs depending upon the kind of input given to them. The concept of constructer overloading can be easily understood by the program given below.

Program 1.7:

```
/*********************************************************************
 Program 1(7).cpp
 Depicts the concept of constructor overloading.
*********************************************************************/
// Header Files
# include<iostream.h>
# include<conio.h>
```

```
class work
{
  int X,Y;
  public:
  work() //1
      {
      X=10;Y=30;
      }

   work(int c)  //2
      {
       X=c;
       Y=2*c;
      }

   work (int x,int y) //3
      {
       X=x;
       Y=y;
      }
};

void main()
{
  work w;           // 10: Call for constructor 1
  work r( 30,60);   //  20: Call for constructor 3
  work rr(30);      //  30: Call for constructor 2
}
```

The class work initialized in this example has 3 different overloaded constructors, which behave, differently on the types of inputs given to them. When this program is executed and the compiler reaches line 10 in the program then the 1st constructor is called as it matches the function header of this constructor. Similarly as the compiler reaches the lines 20 and 30 constructor 3 and constructor 2 are called respectively.

COMMON PROGRAMMING ERRORS

- Declaring a constructor with a return type (even void) will lead to a compilation error.
- Constructors should always be declared in public access specifier.

- In case of copy constructor the parameter passed has to passed as reference parameter.

1.4.1.5 Solved Examples

Example 1.4.1.5.1

Find error, if any in the following program

```
class num
{
        int n;
        int num()
            {
              n=4;
            }

        public;
            void display ()
            {
              cout<<n;
            }
};
```

Solution of 1.4.1.5.1

i) Constructer can only be present in Public access specifier
ii) Constructor does not have a return type
iii) After public there should be a colon (:) instead of a semicolon (;)

Example 1.4.1.5.2

Write a program to generate a Fibonacci series using constructor to initialize the data members.

Hint: Fibonacci series is a series in which the data members present in the series can be obtained by adding the previous 2 data members.

Solution of 1.4.1.5.2

```
/**********************************************************************
 Solved Example 1.7
 Fibonacci Series
**********************************************************************/
// Header Files
```

```
# include<iostream.h>
# include<conio.h>

 class series
 {
     int a,b,c,i,n;
     public:
             series()
             {  a = 1;
                b = 1;
                i = 2;
             }
             void read();
             void calc();
};

void series::read()
{
     cout<<" Enter the value of n";
     cin>>n;
}

void series::calc()
{
             cout<<endl<<a;
             cout<<endl<<b;
             while(i<n)
             {
                c=a+b;
                a=b;
                b=c;
                cout<<"\n"<<c;
                i++;
             }

};

void main()
{
    series f;
    f.read();
    f.calc();
    getch();
}
```

Example 1.4.1.5.3

Write the output of the following program:

```
a) class sum
   {
     int x,y,total;

     public:

            sum( int a,int b)
            {
              x=a;
              y=b*2;
             }

             void display()
             {
                    total = x + y;
                    cout<<total;
              }
   };

   void main()
   {
     sum s(9,5);
    s.display();
   }
```

a) OUTPUT SCREEN

```
19
```

b)

```
// Header Files
# include<iostream.h>
# include<conio.h>

class variable
{
  int x;
```

```
int y;

public:
variable()
{
  x = 10;
  y = 20;
}

variable (int a, int b)
{
  x = 2 * a;
  y  = b;
}

void increase ()
{
  x+=10;
  y++;
}

void decrease()
{   x--;
    y--;
}

void output()
{
  cout<<" Value of x "<<x<<"\t";
  cout<<" Value of y "<<y<<endl;
}

};

void main()
{
  clrscr();
  variable v1 ;
  variable v2(10,20);
  v1.increase();
  v2.decrease();
  v1.output();
  v2.output();
  getch();
}
```

b)

OUTPUT SCREEN

```
Value of x 20   Value of y 21
Value of x 19   Value of y 19
```

1.4.2 DESTRUCTORS

The destructor is the counterpart of a constructor. It is a member function that is called automatically when a class object goes out of scope. It has same name as that of the class , proceeded by a tilde (~). A destructor destroys an object. Destructors are declared in the header files of their class, or are inherited from the base class of that class.

Typical syntax of a destructor is as given below:

```
classname::~classname();
```

A destructor has the same features as that of the constructor that are

- Name of the destructor function is same as that of the class they belong to
- No return type is required for the destructor function
- Destructor functions are automatically called when the object goes out of scope
- Destructor functions are always defined in the public type access specifier

When an object is created, sufficient amount of memory is allocated to it. When the scope of an object comes to an end, resource allocated to it must be freed so that it can be used elsewhere. This process can be achieved by the use of a destructor. This function is automatically invoked when the scope of an object comes to an end.

Note: In case the programmer does not provide for a destructor manually, the compiler provides a default destructor just as the default constructor.

Program 1.8:

```
/*********************************************************************
Solved Example 1.8
Elucidates the concept of Destructors.
*********************************************************************/
```

```
// Header Files

# include<iostream.h>
# include<conio.h>

class trial
{

 private:
  int t1;
  int t2;

 public:
    trial (int a,int b)  // constructor function
    {
    t1=a;
    t2=b;
    cout<<" This is a trial program";
    }

    void output()
     {
      cout<<endl<<" The sum of the variables entered is "<<t1+t2;
     }


 ~trial()    // destructor function
   {
  cout<<" \n The trial program is over";
   }
};
void main()

{
 clrscr();
 trial t(1000,2000);
 t.output();
 getch();
}
```

OUTPUT SCREEN

```
This is a trial program
The sum of the variables entered is 3000
The trial program is over.
```

1.5 Review Examples & Questions

Example 1.5.1
Find the errors in the following programs.

```
a) # include<iostream.h>

   class xyz
   {
     int a;
     int b;
    public:
     xyz(int x,int y)
     {
      a=x;
      b=y;
     }
    void output()
    {
    cout<<" Variable 1 "<<a;
    cout<<" Variable 2 ">>b;
    }
   }
   void main()
   {
    xyz x1;
    xyz x2(15,15);
    x2.output();
    getch();
   }
```

a) Errors

- <conio.h> header file is missing.
- Illegal class declaration, semicolon (;) is missing.

- Arguments have to be passed with object x1.
- Extraction operators are to be used with cout.

The correct program is given below

```
# include<iostream.h>
# include<conio.h>

class xyz
{
 int a;
 int b;
 public:
 xyz(int x,int y)
 {
  a=x;
  b=y;
 }

 void output()
 {
  cout<<" Variable 1 "<<a;
  cout<<" Variable 2 "<<b;
 }

};


void main()
{
 xyz x1(10,10);
 xyz x2(15,15);
 x2.output();
 getch();
}
```

b)

```
# include<iostream.h>
# include<conio.h>

class Integer
   {
   private:
```

```
        int n;
public:
        Integer (Integer x)
        {
                n=x.n;
        }
        void show()
        {
         cout<<n;
        }
};

void main()
{
Integer k(8);
k.show();
}
```

b) Error

- The argument passed in copy constructer has to be passed as a reference parameter: That is, Integer (Integer &x).
- Also when declaring 'k' the parameter passed to the constructor has to be an object of class 'Integer'.

```
c) class circle
   {
   private
         float radius;

   public:
       void getdata();
       {
        cout<<" Enter the radius ";
        cout<<radius;
       }
       float area();
   }

circle:: float area()
       {
        return (3.14 *radius*radius);
       }
```

c) Errors

- Line 3 Colon(:) missing after key word private
- Line 7 Extra semicolon following function name header
- Line 13 Missing semicolon at the end of the class definition
- Line 15 The function should be declared with return type preceding the class name the correct code is: float circle::area().

Example 1.5.2

Declare a class max, which has 3 integer data type members, a function read to input the values of the data members and a function display to display, the greatest number between them?

Solution of 1.5.2

```
// Header Files
# include<iostream.h>
# include<conio.h>

class maximum
{
 int x,y,z;
 public:
 void read();
 void display();
};

void maximum::read()
{
  cout<<" Enter the three numbers";
  cin>>x>>y>>z;
}


void maximum::display()
{
 if ( (x>y) && (x>z))
 cout<<" Maximum number is "<<x;
 else

if ((y>x)&&(y>z))
cout<<" Maximum number is"<<y;
else
cout<<" Maximum number is"<<z;
}
```

Example 1.5.3

What will be the output of the following questions?

```
a)
// Header Files
# include<iostream.h>
# include<conio.h>

int area(int s)
{
 return (s*s);
}

float area(int b,int h)
{
 return (0.5*b*h);
}

void main()
{
  clrscr();
  cout<<area(5)<<endl;
  cout<<area(4,3)<<endl;
  cout<<area(6,(area(3)))<<endl;
  getch();
}
```

a)

OUTPUT SCREEN

```
25
6
27
```

b)

```
# include<iostream.h>
# include<conio.h>
struct salary
{
 float gross;
 float GPF;
```

```
float tax;
float net;
};

void main()
{
 clrscr();
 salary x= {5800,10,500,0};
 float deductions;
 deductions=x.GPF+x.tax;
 x.net=x.gross-deductions;
 cout<<" Net amount payable ="<<x.net;
 getch();
}
```

b) OUTPUT SCREEN

```
Net amount payable =5290
```

c)

```
# include<iostream.h>
struct SCORE
{
 int point,bonus;
};

 void calculate(SCORE &S,int N=10)
 {
    S.point++;
    S.bonus+=N;
 }

 void main()
 {
  SCORE SC={20,5};
  calculate(SC);
  cout<<SC.point<<";"<<SC.bonus<<endl;
```

```
  calculate(SC);
  cout<<SC.point<<";"<<SC.bonus<<endl;
  calculate(SC,15);
  cout<<SC.point<<";"<<SC.bonus<<endl;
  }
```

c) OUTPUT SCREEN

```
21;15
22;25
23;40
```

d)

```
// Header Files
# include<iostream.h>
# include<conio.h>
# include<string.h>
# include<stdio.h>

// Declaration of class student
class student
{
 char name[15];
 int rollno;
 public:
 student()
   {
   strcpy(name,"Ankit");
   rollno=1;
   }
 student(int a)
   {
   strcpy(name,"Neha");
   rollno=a;
   }
 void output();
 void increase();
};

void student::output()
```

```
{
 cout<<" The roll no of the student "<<rollno;
 cout<<" The name of the student ";
 puts(name);
 }

void student::increase()
 {
 rollno++;
 }

// main function
void main()
{
 student s;
 student s1(5);
 s.increase;
 s1.increase;
 cout<<"##### ---- Student program ---- #####";
 s.output;
 s1.output;
 getch();
}
```

d)

OUTPUT SCREEN

```
##### ---- Student program ---- #####
```

e)

```
# include<conio.h>
# include<iostream.h>

class class1
{
 public:
 int i,j;
```

```
 class1(int a, int b)
 {i=a; j=b;}

 void show()
 {
   i = 2;
   i--;
        if (i==1)
        {
              cout<<"class1:i:"<<i<<"j:"<<j<<endl;
              return;
        }
        show();
 }
};

int main()
{
 class1 x(20,20);
 x.show();
 getch();
}
```

e)

OUTPUT SCREEN

```
class1:i:1j:20
```

f)

```
# include<iostream.h>
# include<conio.h>

class example
{
 static int x;
 int y,z;
 public:
 example(int i,int j)
```

```
{
 y=i;
 z=j;
 x++;
}
void display()
{
 cout<<"y="<<y<<endl;
 cout<<"z="<<z<<endl;
}
static void dis()
{
 cout<<"x="<<x<<endl;
}

};
int example::x;

void main()
{
 clrscr();
 example o1(7,5),o2(8,6),o3(2,0);
 o1.display();
 example::dis();
 o2.display();
 o3.display();
 getch();
}
```

f)

OUTPUT SCREEN

```
y=7
z=5
x=3
y=8
z=6
y=2
z=0
```

g)

```
# include<iostream.h>
# include<conio.h>
int c =0; // Global Variable
// Declaration of class block
class block
{
 public:
 block()
 {
        cout<<"Total object created"<<endl;
  }
 ~block()
 {
   cout<<"Total object destroyed"<<endl;
 }
};
void main()
{
 clrscr();
 block M1,M2,M3,M4;
 cout<<"Block1"<<endl;
 block m5;
 cout<<"Block 2"<<endl;
 block m6;
 cout<<"Block 3"<<endl;
 getch();
}
```

g)

OUTPUT SCREEN

```
Total object created
Total object created
Total object created
Total object created
Block1
Total object created
Block 2
Total object created
Block 3
Total object destroyed
Total object destroyed
Total object destroyed
Total object destroyed
Total object destroyed
Total object destroyed
```

Question 1.5.4
Define a structure? Declare a structure in c++ with name, roll number and age as its components.

Answer of 1.5.4

A structure is a collection of variable having different data types. The declaration as

```
struct student
{

  char name[15];
  int roll;
  int marks;

};
```

Exercise: Now think how classes and structures are different and similar to each other.

Example 1.5.5
Declare a structure client containing the following members:

- The character quantity of the client
- The integer quantity called clientid
- The integer quantity called no_of_items
- The long integer quantity called Client_total

Solution of 1.5.5

```
struct client
{
  char name[15];
  int clientid;
  int no_of_items;
  long client_total;
};
```

Example 1.5.6
Write a program to add and subtract complex numbers using the structure given below:

```
struct complex
      {
        int real;
        int imag;
      };
```

Solution of 1.5.6

```
// Header Files
# include<iostream.h>
# include<conio.h>

// Structure definition
struct complex
{
 int real;
 int imag;
};

// Function definition
void add(complex c1,complex c2)
{
  complex c3;
  c3.real=c1.real+c2.real;
  c3.imag=c1.imag+c2.imag;
  cout<<" The Sum of the 2 complex numbers is "<<c3.real<<" + "<<c3.imag<<"i";
}
// Function Definition
void sub(complex c1,complex c2)
{
  complex c3;
  c3.real=c1.real-c2.real;
  c3.imag=c1.imag-c2.imag;
  cout<<" The Sum of the 2 complex numbers is "<<c3.real<<" + "<<c3.imag<<"i";
}

// Main Program
void main()
{
 int choice;
 char r;
 complex num1,num2;
 cout<<"Enter the real part";
 cin>>num1.real;
 cout<<"\n Enter the imaginary part";
 cin>>num1.imag;
 cout<<"\n Enter the real part";
 cin>>num2.real;
 cout<<"\n Enter the imaginary part";
```

```
cin>>num2.imag;
do
{
        cout<<" #### MENU ####"<<endl;
        cout<<" 1) Add"<<endl;
        cout<<" 2) Subtract"<<endl;
        cin>>choice;
        switch(choice)
        {
         case 1 : add(num1,num2);
  break;
  case 2 : sub(num1,num2);
  break;
        }
  cout<<" Do you want to continue";
  cin>>r;
}while(r!='n');
getch();
}
```

Question 1.5.7
What is a class and are the private members of class accessible to the object?

Answer of 1.5.7
A class is a user defined data type used to implement an abstract object, giving you the capability to use object oriented programming with c++. No the private members of a class are not accessible to the object.

Question 1.5.8
What are the differences between the following?
a) Object oriented programming and procedural programming
b) Public and private members of a class

Answer of 1.5.8
a) In object oriented programming the stress is given on the object, whereas in procedural programming the stress is given on the subject.

b) The public members are accessible to objects of a class whereas private member are not accessible outside the class or to objects of the class.

Example 1.5.9
Write a program to solve a quadratic equation? Use guidelines in section 1.3.3 to solve this particular problem?

Solution of 1.5.9

```
// Header Files
#include<iostream.h>
#include<conio.h>
#include<math.h>

// Definition of class q
class q
{
 int a,b,c;
 float r1,r2,d;
 public:
 void read();
 void calculate();
};

void q::read()
{
  cout<<" Enter the values of a,b,c";
  cin>>a>>b>>c;
}

void q::calculate()
{
 d= (b*b)-(4*a*c);
 if (d>=0)
 {
  r1= (-b + sqrt(d))/(2*a);
  r2= (-b - sqrt(d))/(2*a);
  cout<<"\n Root 1 is"<<r1;
  cout<<"\n Root 2 is"<<r2;
 }
 else
 {
   cout<<"\n  Roots are imaginary ";
 }
}
// main function
void main()
{
 q q1; // object of class q
 q1.read();
 q1.calculate();
}
```

Question 1.5.10

Define the following terms:

a) OOP
b) Procedural Programming
c) Object
d) Class
e) Class declaration
f) Private section
g) Data Hiding
h) Scope Resolution Operator (::)
i) Abstraction
j) Friend Function
k) Constructor
l) Default Constructor
m) Copy Constructor

Answer of 1.5.10

a) OOP

Object oriented programming enables the programmers to group together data and code that uses data into discrete units. In OOP the stress is given on the object in spite of procedure.

b) Procedural programming

In procedural programming, we think about functions and the execution flow these functions.

c) Object

An object is a self-contained abstraction of an item. An instance of a class.

d) Class

A class is a user defined data type used to implement an abstract object. It contains members of three types: private, public and protected. By default the data members of the class are private. Classes enable the programmer to model objects with attributes and behaviors. Class types can be defined in c++ using the key word 'class' and 'struct', but key word class is normally used for this purpose.

e) Class declaration

The class is declared with a keyword class

```
class <class_name>
 {
  private:
      data_members;
            member_functions;
  public:
      data members;
            member_functions;
 };
```

f) **Private section**

Private members are available to only members of class and not accessible to the objects or functions outside the class. The default access mode for classes is private so all members after the class header and before the first member access specifier are considered to be private.

g) **Data hiding**

The variables and functions declared in a class as private are not accessible to any outside function. This feature of a class is called as data hiding.

h) **Scope resolution operator (::)**

This operator is used in situations where a global variable exists with the same name as a local variable. Also, this is used in c++ class when the number functions are declared outside the class definition, the function name is preceded by the class name and the binary scope resolution operator (::)

i) **Abstraction**

The class members, which are private, remain hidden from the outside world, the public members form the interface by providing the essential and relevant information to outside world. Thus only the essential features are represented to outside world without including the background details, which is called abstraction.

j) **Friend Function**

A function outside of a class can be defined to be a friend function by the class. By doing so the class gives the friend function, free access to the private members of the class.

k) **Constructor**

A constructor is a special initialization function that is called automatically whenever instance of the class is declared. The name of the constructor is same as that of class and it returns no value.

l) **Default constructor**

A default constructor is one, which accepts no parameters:

```
class student
{
 private:
 int rollno;
 public:
 student() //Default constructor
      {
      rollno=1;
      }
};
```

m) **Copy constructor**

A copy constructor is that constructor which is used to initialize one object with the values from another object of same class during declaration.

Question 1.5.11

Is data hiding same as encapsulation?

Answer of 1.5.11

No. Data hiding is the property of a program where vital data remains safely hidden from functions which do not use or manipulate them. On the other hand, encapsulation is the mechanism through which data hiding is achieved.

Example 1.5.12

An automobile dealer has given identity number(idno) to all spare parts. The following class was defined to store information about identity number and listed price of a spare part:

```
class product
{
 private:
 int idno;
 public:
 float price;
 public:
 void getdata(int n, float p)
   {
    idno = n;
    price=p;
   }
};
```

Write a program to edit the existing class definition for 'class product' to include tax in the listed price and then calculate and display the net price including tax for the following spare parts:

(a) id no=1013 price=345.0
(b) id no=2314 price=125.0

Note: tax is 10% of the listed price

Solution of 1.5.12

```
class product
{
  private:
  int idno;
  public:
  float price;
  float tax ;
  public:
  void getdata(int n, float p)
   {
     tax = .10 * p;
     idno = n;
     price=p+tax;
   }
};

void main()
{
   product p1,p2;
   p1.getdata(1013,345.00);
   p2.getdata(2314,125.00);
   cout<<" Net amount payable for spare part1:"<<p1.price<<"$"<<endl;
   cout<<" Net amount payable for spare part2:"<<p2.price<<"$";
}
```

Example 1.5.13

Which function is called during each function call in the program given below:

```
...
long total(int x);                    //………. I
char choose( char a, char b);         //……….II
char choose (char a);                 //……….III
float total (int x, float y);         //……….IV

void main()
{
  ...
  total(n);          // ……….1
  choose('c');       // ……… 2
  choose('c','d');   // ……….3
  total(n,n1);       // ……….4
}
```

Solution of 1.5.13

Call 1 invokes function (I)
Call 2 invokes function (III)
Call 3 invokes function (II)
Call 4 invokes function (IV)

Example 1.5.14
Observe the following program

```
...

long total(int x);                    // .......... I
int total (int x, int y=10);          // .........II
void main()
{
 ...
 total(n);          //..........1

}
```

Which function will the compiler invoke when the following program is executed?

Solution of 1.5.14

When the following program is executed function ambiguity takes place as the compiler is not sure which function to invoke and as a result of this the compiler hangs.

Note: The result of this program is compiler dependent.

Example 1.5.15

Define a class student with the following specification:

admno	integer
sname	20 character
eng,math,science	float
total	float
ctotal()	A function to calculate 'total = eng + math + science'

Public member function of a class student

takedata()	To accept values for admno, sname, eng, math, science and invoke ctotal() to calculate total
showdata()	To display all the data members on the screen

Solution of 1.5.15

```
class student
{
        int admno;
        char sname[20];
        float eng,math,science;
        float total;
        void ctotal();
        public:
                void takedata();
                void showdata();
};

void student::takedata()
{
        cout<<" \n Enter the admission number of student ";
        cin>>admno;
        cout<<"\n Enter the name of the student";
        gets(sname);
        cout<<"\n Enter the marks in English";
        cin>>eng;
        cout<<"\n Enter the marks in  Maths";
        cin>>math;
        cout<<"\n Enter the marks in Science";
        cin>>science;
        ctotal();
}

void student ::ctotal()
{

        total = eng + math + science;
}


void student::showdata()
{
        cout<<"\n Name "<<sname;
        cout<<"\n Admission no"<<admno;
        cout<<"\n Total marks"<<total;
}
```

Example 1.5.16

Define a class batsman with the following specifications:-

Private members

bcode	(4 digit code number)
bname	(20 characters)
innings, notout, runs	integer type
batavg	it is calculated according to the formula: batavg = runs/(innings – notout)
calcavg()	function to compute batavg

public members

readdata()	function to accept values for bcode, name, innings, notout and invoke the function calcavg()
displaydata()	function to display the data members on the screen

Solution of 1.5.16

```
class batsman
{
  int bcode;
  char bname[25];
  int innings, notout, runs;
  float batavg;
  float calcavg()
  {
    return (runs/(innings-notout));
  }
 public:
   void readdata();
   void displaydata();
};
void batsman::readdata()
{
  clrscr();
  cout<<"Enter the batsman code";
  cin>>bcode;
  cout<<"Enter the batsman name";
  gets(bname);
  cout<<"Enter total innings";
  cin>>innings;
  cout<<"Enter total notout";
  cin>>notout;
  cout<<"Enter total runs";
  cin>>runs;
  batavg=calcavg();
}
void batsman :: displaydata()
{
```

```
clrscr();
cout<<" Batsman Code"<<bcode;
cout<<endl<<" Batsman Name"<<bname;
cout<<endl<<" Total innings "<<innings;
cout<<endl<<" Total notout "<<notout;
cout<<endl<<" Total runs"<<runs;
cout<<endl<<" The batting average"<<batavg;
}
```

1. 6 Review Exercise

1 Mark questions

Q1) Which data members of a class is accessible to the outside world?

Q2) What is data abstraction?

Q3) What is the significance of the scope resolution operator (::)?

Q4) What is wrong with the following declaration:

```
Class{
        int a,b,c,sum;
        private
        void read();
        void display();
    }
```

Q5) How is the memory allocated to a class and to its objects?

Q6) Is encapsulation a security technique?

Q7) How does the compiler decide which function to invoke in case of function overloading?

Q8) Is it possible to have an overloaded function with different return types but same number and type of arguments?

Q9) Define an object?

Q10) What is the relation between an object and a class?

2 Mark questions

Q1) How is object oriented programming different from procedural programming? Give proper examples for differentiating?

Q2) Differentiate between a constructor and a destructor function?

Q3) What is the purpose of the constructor function in a class? Give a suitable example of a constructor function in a class?

Q4) Why is a destructor function required in a class illustrate with the help of a suitable example?

Q5) Discuss the different ways by which we can access public members of an object?

Q6) What do you understand by the term copy constructor give suitable examples to illustrate how it is useful?

Q7) Differentiate between the following:

a) a structure and a class
b) an object and a structure variable

Q8) Is polymorphism an example of function overloading, explain giving suitable examples?

Q9) Can we use the same function name for a member function of a class and an outside function in the same program file? If yes, how are they distinguished? If no, give reasons.

Q10) Find the syntax error(s), if any, in the following program:

```
# include <"conio.h ">
# include<iostream.h>
void Main()
{
        int ch;
  cin<<ch;
  if ch>=9
  cout<<ch;
  for (int i=0;i<2;i++)
  cout<<end;
}
```

4 Mark questions

Q1) Declare a class employee having the following members:

Data Members:

Employee name
Employee address
Employee number

Member Functions

To read data members
To display the data members

Q2) Define a class teacher with the following specification:

private members of class teacher

name	20 characters
subject	10 characters
basic, hra, da	float
netpay	float // Obtained by the sum of float variables 'basic' 'hra' and 'da'
calculate	A function computes and returns the net salary ('netpay') a

public member function of class teacher

readdata() Function to accept data values and invoke the calculate function

displaydata() Function to prints the teacher information on the screen

Q3) Declare a structure date having members as

day	-	a string of size[2] represents day part of a date
month	-	a string of size [20] represents month name of a date

year -	a string of size[4]; represents year part of a date

Declare a class medicine with the following specifications

private members of a class

medicine_name	-	a string of size[25]
priceperunit	-	float
mfgdate	-	of type date
expdate	-	of type date

public members of the class

medentry() - A function to accept values of the data members from user

ShowWarning() - A function that displays the name of the medicine along with warning message as "Use within 2 Months", if the expiry date is 2 months after manufacturing date

ShowAll() - A function that displays above details of a medicine properly formatted in a single line

Q4) Define a class to represent a bank account. Include the following members:

Data members:

Name of the depositor
Type of the account
Account number
Balance amount in the account

Member functions:

To deposit an amount
To withdraw an amount.
To display the name, type of account and the balance of the account holder

Write the main() block to test the program. Use constructors to initialize the data members?

Q5) What is function overloading? Use the concept of function overloading to compute the area of rectangle (given length of two sides) ,area of triangle (given length of the three sides using Heros formula) and area of a circle (given length of a radius)

1.7 Programming Project: Mechanical Engineering

An automobile company, "FORD" is trying to launch a new car. The company is although not sure about which engine design to implement in their new car. The company currently has option of two engines (fig 1.7) A and B.

Engine efficiency is determined by the following formula:

E = ((x+y)*y)/z + ((x+z)/w)*i;

The parameters for both engine designs are given below in table 1.2. Using the criteria's given create a C++ object oriented program to determine the efficiency of the two engines. Which engine should the company use for the launch of its new Ford V9.12?

(A) (B)

Figure 1.7: Car Engines

Engine Features	Engine A	Engine B
Volume (x)	4.20	5.30
Horse Power (y)	190	260
Valves (z)	Quad 4	Quad 4
Height (w)	0.98	0.89
HEAD C.C. (i)	45.5	46.6

Table 1.2: Engine Specifications

1.8 Let us revise!

- ✓ A **class** is a user defined data type used to implement an abstract object.
- ✓ An **object** is as instance of a class.
- ✓ A class having no objects is known as an **Abstract Class**.
- ✓ A class definition has members which could be data members or member functions.
- ✓ A **member function** is a function which is a part of a class. A member function has access to private members of a class which other external functions do not have.
- ✓ A class has 3 kinds of access specifiers, private, public, protected.
- ✓ **Private Members** are those members which can only be accessed by the member functions.
- ✓ **Public Members** are those members which can be accessed by any function in the entire program.
- ✓ The practice of wrapping up of data and functions together in a single unit is known as Encapsulation.
- ✓ **Data Abstraction** is defined as bringing the data down to its essentials.
- ✓ The process of using an operator or a function in different ways for different set of inputs given is known as **polymorphism.**
- ✓ **Constructors** are special member functions which can be included in the class for automatic initialization at the time of object creation.
- ✓ **Constructors** have the same name as that of the class they are initialized in. They also have no return type and are automatically called at the time of object creation.
- ✓ A **copy constructor** is *an overloaded constructor function in which an object of the same class is/are passed as reference parameter(s).*

- ✓ The **destructor** is the counterpart of the constructor. It is a member function that called automatically when a class object goes out of scope.
- ✓ OOPS has various advantages over procedural programming. OOPS has close relation between the real world objects and user created classes.
- ✓ Compilers for Object Oriented programs are able to detect conceptual errors hence increasing program reliability.
- ✓ Its various features like *encapsulation, Inheritance, data abstraction, polymorphism* make it much more advantageous than procedural programming hence object oriented languages like C++, Java are experiencing a rapid increase in popularity among other programming languages.

Notes

Part II

CHAPTER 2

INHERITANCE

AIM

- Introduce Inheritance, the most powerful concept of Object Oriented Programming
- To learn about base classes and derived classes
- To understand and use concept of inheritance and study its advantages

OUTLINE

2.1 Introduction
2.2 Base and Derived Classes
2.3 Inheritance in C++
2.4 Types of Inheritance
2.5 Solved Examples
2.6 Review Exercise
2.7 Programming Project
2.8 Let us revise

2.1 Introduction

We already know that modern Object Oriented languages provide three main capabilities, viz., 'Data Abstraction', 'Polymorphism' and 'Inheritance'. We have already covered 'Abstraction' and 'Polymorphism' in previous chapters. In this chapter, we will deal with the most powerful concept in object oriented programming called 'Inheritance'

Inheritance is the concept of creating a new class referred to as derived class from an already existing class (called Base Class). The derived class inherits the properties of the base class. In addition to this, the derived class can also have properties of its own.

Let us understand this concept through an example involving development of software for 'School Administration'. To do this, we would consider 'Teachers' and 'Students' classes - both these classes would be implemented differently as they have separate identity. However, there are some members which are common to both these classes, such as, 'Name', 'Home Address' and 'Age' including common functions for initiating these members.

We can observe that both classes have common members and functions. We, therefore, need a concept which when implemented copies the code for these common members from one class to the other and then change the class name. This concept is implemented through 'Inheritance'. Inheritance allows reusability of code of a class which is already debugged and tested. Inheritance also allows us to save on programming effort and enhances maintainability of the program.

2.2 Base and Derived Classes

Inheritance is used to create hierarchical structures. Look at the category Animals in figure 2.1, there are three divisions of animals who eat only leaf and vegetables (Herbivores), animals who eat other animals as well as leaf and vegetables (Omnivores) and animals who eat only other animals for food (Carnivores). Each of these categories has further subcategories and under them even more subcategories exist. The important thing to note in this example is that once a category is defined all the elements in these categories and other subcategories satisfy the characteristic under which they were defined. The advantage of doing this is that once a member of a category is determined we do not need to learn again that whether the animal is an herbivore or an omnivore or a carnivore.

In this example, 'Animals' is referred to as the base class and 'Herbivores', 'Omnivores' and 'Carnivores' are termed as derived classes. One may find that in other books, authors have also referred to 'Base Classes' as 'Super Class' and 'Derived Classes' as 'Sub Class'. Derived classes also have the potential of becoming Base class, e.g., 'Herbivores' which is a derived class of class 'Animals' is also a base class for classes 'Elephant' and 'Giraffe'. Generally derived classes are larger than their base classes as they contain data members and member functions of their own as well as they may use all the functionality of the base class as well.

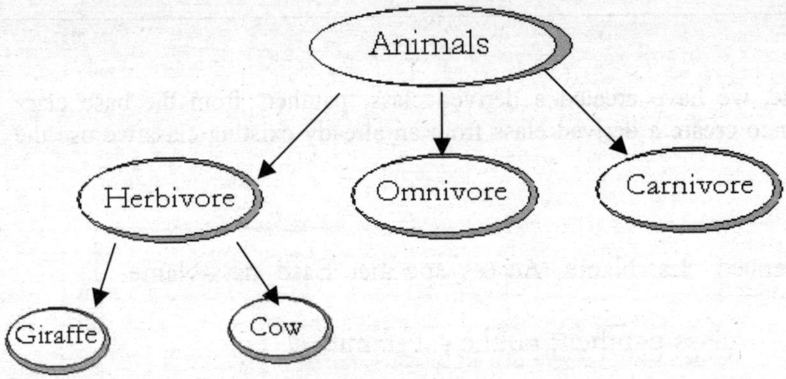

Figure 2.1: Inheritance Hierarchy

2.3 Inheritance in C++

Let us look at the Program 2.1 to understand how inheritance is used in C++.

Program 2.1:

```
class cat_family
{
  public:    // The data and methods can be accessed directly
  char category[10];
  char legs;
  int age;
  cat_family();
  ~cat_family();
  void food_habits();
  void place_of_stay();
};

class panther : public cat_family
{
  public:
  void sex_of_specie()
  {
    if (strcmp(category,"White Panther")==0)
    {
      cout<<" White Panther is an endangered specie";
```

```
    }
  }
void color();
};
```

In this piece of code, we have created a derived class 'panther' from the base class 'cat_family'. In order to create a derived class from an already existing class we use the following format:

```
class Derived_class-Name : Access_specifier Base_class-Name

class panther : public cat_family
```

As you know, C++ class contains up to three sections: *private*, *protected* and *public*. Let us see how access specifiers work.

- The data and member functions declared in the *private* section of a class are not accessible outside the class. Only the member functions declared within the class have access to the private data and functions of the class.
- The data and member functions declared in the *protected* section of a class are not accessible outside the class except within sub-classes (or derived classes) given from the given parent (or base) class.
- The data and member functions declared in the *public* section are of a class are available outside the class, i.e., when using the *public* type access specifier, all the *public* members of the base class are inherited by the derived class. These public members are also accessible by the objects of base and derived classes hence created.

A hierarchy of abstractions can be established using derived classes. Objects of a derived class can be defined so as to inherit all the methods of the parent class or only a few selected methods of the base class. Further, new methods - not present in the base class - can also be specified that are peculiar to the derived class. Every object of a derived class contains field of data from the base class as well as its own *private* data.

One can also observe in Program 2.1 that the derived class 'panther' accesses the *public* data members of its base class 'cat_family'. Similarly, the *protected* members and functions under the 'protected' key word of the base class are also passed on as 'protected' members to the derived class. Though, these members cannot be accessed from instances or objects of this class.

The relationship between the access specifiers and the inheritance allowed by them is also summarized in the table (2.1) given below.

Inheritance Type	Access Specifier	Members in Derived Class
Private	Private	Not Accessible
	Protected	Not Accessible
	Public	Not Accessible
Protected	Private	Private
	Protected	Protected
	Public	Protected
Public	Private	Private
	Protected	Private
	Public	Public

PROGRAMING TIPS

- Create hierarchical models to understand the concept of inheritance for each of the sample problems provided. Hierarchical models allow us to understand better the flow of data members inherited by there derived classes.

- C++ also offers ways to save space and computer memory by using virtual base classes which allows us to save space and avoid data ambiguities in class hierarchies involving multiple inheritance. It eliminates the procedure in which each non virtual object contains a copy of all the data members defined in the base class.

Now that we understand the concept of inheritance let us look at the following examples.

2.3.1 Solved Examples

Example 2.3.1.1

Answer the questions (i) to (iv) on the basis of the following code:

(i) Write the names of data members which are accessible from objects belonging to class 'branch'.

(ii) Write the names of all the member functions which are accessible from objects belonging to the class employee.

(iii) Write the names of all the members which are accessible from member functions of class 'employee'.

(iv) How many bytes will be required by an object belonging to the class 'employee'?

```
class company
{
char website[12];
char name[20];

protected:
int noemployees;

public:
company();
void register();
void status();
};

class branch:public company
{
long nocomputer;

protected:
float expense;

public:
branch();
void enter();
void show();
};

class employee:private branch
{
```

```
 int eno;
  char ename[20];
  float salary;

  public:
  employee();
  void joining();
  void showdetail();
 };
```

Solution of 2.3.1.1

(i) None of the data members are accessible from objects belonging to class branch.

(ii) The names of member functions which are accessible from objects belonging to class 'employee' are joining(), showdetail().

(iii) The members accessible from objects belonging to class 'employee' are
<u>Data Members:</u> eno, ename, salary, expense, noemployees
<u>Member Functions:</u> register(), status(), enter(), show(), joining(), showdetails().

(iv) The amount of bytes required by an object belonging to class 'employee' is summation of all the bytes required by the objects of all the base classes and the class 'employee' which comes out to be '68' bytes.

Note: 'register' also happens to be a keyword in C. Hence some C/C++ compilers might give an error in executing the program. Here the author assumes that this is understood and lays stress only on the concept of inheritance.

COMMON PROGRAMMING ERRORS

- Assuming that private members of a base class can be inherited directly by the derived classes and then using them as a part of the derived class is a logical and a compilation error.
- Declaring the constructors and destructors in the private access type specifier is an compilation error.

Example 2.3.1.2
Given the following class definitions answer the questions that follow:

```
class publisher
{
char pub[12];
double turnover;

protected:
void register();

public:
publisher();
void enter();
void display();
};

class branch: protected publisher
{
char city[20];
protected:
float employee;
public:
branh();
void haveit();
void giveit();
};

class author: private branch
{
 int acode;
 char aname[20];
 float amount;

 public:
 author();
 void start();
 void show();
};
```

(i) Write the names of data members which are accessible from objects belonging to class author.

(ii) Write the names of all the member functions which are accessible from objects belonging to the class branch.

(iii) Write the names of all the members which are accessible from member functions of class author.

(iv) How many bytes will be required by an object belonging to class author?

Solution of 2.3.1.2

(i) None of the data members are accessible from objects belonging to class author.
(ii) The names of the member functions which are accessible from objects belonging to class author are haveit(), giveit().

(iii) The members accessible from the member functions of class 'author' are:
Data Members: employee, acode, aname, amount
Member Function: register(), haveit(), giveit(), start(), show()

(iv) The number of bytes occupied by an object belonging to class author are 70.

At this point let me ask you a very interesting question. What happens to the constructors and destructors of the base class can they also be inherited by their derived classes?

Well the constructors or destructors are not inherited by their derived classes but when even an object of a derived class is declared or initialized the default constructor for the base class is automatically called.

Program 2.2 further enlightens the same concept.

Program 2.2:

```
// Header Files
# include <iostream.h>
# include <conio.h>

// Class Definition for Class A
class A
{
private:
int a;
int b;
int c;
public:
A()
{
cout<<" This is the constructor for class A \n";
}
~A()
{
cout<<" This is the destructor for class A \n";
}
```

Output Screen

```
This is the constructor for class A
This is the constructor for class B
This is the destructor for class B
This is the destructor for class A
```

```
};

/*
  Class definition for Class B
  Base Class: A
  Access Specifier: public
*/

class B: public A
{
 public:
 B()
  {
  cout<<" This is the constructor for class B \n";
  }
  ~B()
  {
  cout<<" This is the destructor for class B \n";
  }
};

void main()
{
 clrscr();
 B object1;
 getch();
}
```

In this program as soon as the 'object1' an object of class B is created, the default constructors for A and then B are called for. Similarly, as the scope of the class ends the message "This is the destructor for class B" is displayed followed by a similar message for class A.

COMMON PROGRAMMING ERRORS

- Private members and Protected members of the base or derived classes are never accessible to the objects of these classes.
- The difference between the private and protected members lies only in the type of inheritance allowed by them. The members under the protected access specifier can be inherited by derived classes whereas the private members of a class can never be inherited properly.

2.4 Types of Inheritance

Inheritance exists in two forms depending upon the number of parent or base classes a derived class has.

a) Single Inheritance (Figure 2.2):

When a class inherits only from a single parent or in other words each derived class has a single parent. A good example of single inheritance is the tree structure [see Figure II (2.2(b))].

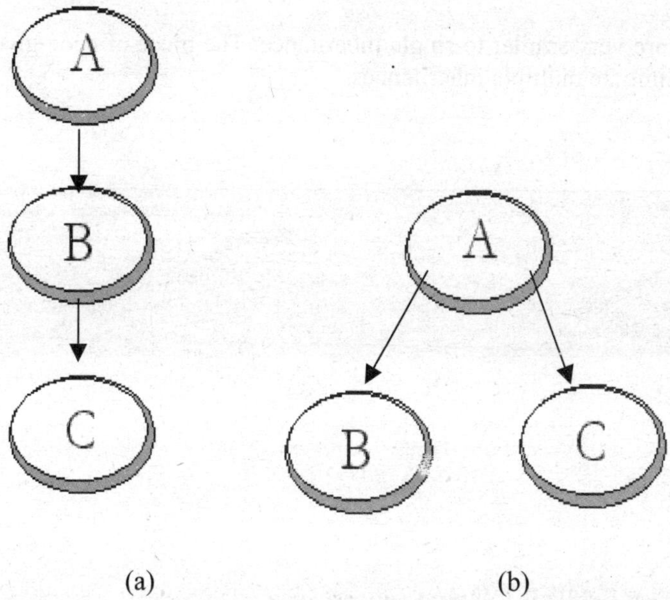

(a) (b)

Figure 2.2: Single Inheritance (SI)

b) Multiple Inheritance

Multiple Inheritances are observed when the derived class inherit properties from more than one parent or base class. This is a very common practice used in object oriented programming as it allows each class to inherit and combine all useful features from a range of classes. Figure 2.3 shows few examples where multiple inheritances are observed.

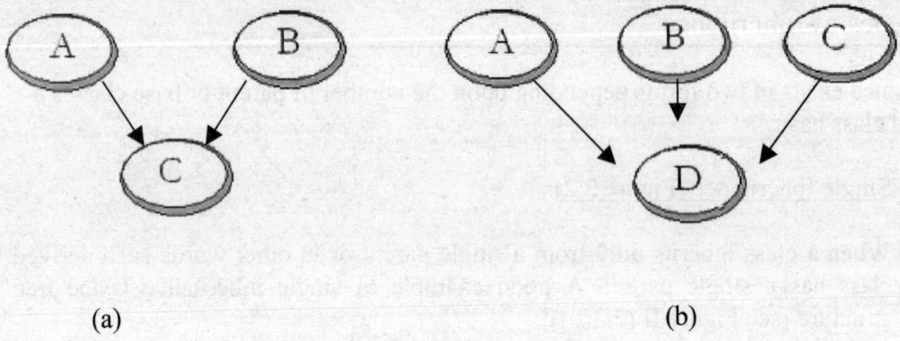

Figure 2.3: Multiple Inheritances

Multiple inheritances are very similar to single inheritance. The piece of code given below displays the syntax to initiate multiple inheritances.

Syntax:

```
class A
  {
   ...
  };

class B
  {
   ...
  };

class C : public A, public B // Multiple Inheritance
  {
   ...
  };
```

2.5 Solved Examples

Example 2.5.1

```
class mydata
{
 int data1;
 protected:
 float val;
 void guess();
 public:
 void get_mydata();
 void manipulate();
};

class yourdata:protected mydata
{
 int data2;
 protected:
 void access();
 public:
 long value();
 int catch();
 void miss();
};

class ourdata:public yourdata
{
 float data3;
 public:
 void have();
 void give();
};
```

(i) Name the data members accessible from functions of class 'ourdata'?
(ii) How many bytes will be occupied by an object belonging to 'classyourdata'?
(iii) Define the function catch() which displays all the data members accessible to it.
(iv) Name the member functions which are accessible from objects of class 'ourdata'.

Solution of 2.5.1

(i) The data members accessible from functions of class 'ourdata' are 'data3' of class 'ourdata' and value of class 'yourdata'.

(ii) An object belonging to class 'yourdata' will occupy 12 bytes.

(iii) The function definition for 'catch()' which displays all the data members accessible to it is as follows.

```
void yourdata::catch()
{
  cout<<value<<data2<<val<<endl;
}
```

(iv) The member functions accessible class ourdata are catch(), miss() of 'yourdata' and have(), give() of class 'ourdata'.

Example 2.5.2

Given the following class definitions answer the questions that follow:

```
class myclass
{
 char data1[20];
 int data2[5];

 public:
 void read();
 void show();
};

class myfirstclass : private myclass
{
 int deriveddata1;
 float deriveddata2;
 protected:
 int standard;
 public:
 void read_firstderived();
 void show_firstderived();
};

class mysecondclass : public myfirstclass
{
 float deriveddata3;
 public:
 void read_secondderived();
 void show_secondderived();
};
```

(i) Name the members which can be accessed inside class myfirstclass.
(ii) Name the members which can be accessed by an object of mysecondclass.
(iii) Name the members which can be accessed by an object of class myfirstclass.
(iv) What will be the size of an object mysecondclass in bytes ?

Solution of 2.5.2

(i) The members which can be accessed inside class myfirstclass:

```
void read();
void show();
int deriveddata1;
float deriveddata2;
int standard;
void read_firstderived();
void show_firstderived();
```

(ii) The members which can be accessed by an object of class mysecondclass.

```
void read_firstderived();
void show_firstderived();
void read_secondderived();
void show_secondderived();
```

(iii) The members which can be accessed by an object of class myfirstclass are:

```
void read_firstderived();
void show_firstderived();
```

(iv) The size of an object of class 'mysecondclass' is 42 bytes.

Example 2.5.3

(a) Both private as well as protected members of a class are not accessible to the object of the class. So what is the significance of using members inside the protected specifier?

(b) Will the following piece of code compile:

```
# include <iostream.h>
# include <conio.h>

class X
```

```
{
 protected:
 int var1;

 public:
 int var3;

 private:
 int var 2;
};

void main()
{
 X x1;
 getch();
}
```

Solution of 2.5.3

(a) Although both, the private as well as protected members of a class are not accessible to the objects of the class, the significance of protected members lies in inheritance. The members declared in the protected specifier of the base class are accessible to the derived class, where as the derived class cannot access the members under the private specifier of the base class.

(b) Yes, the piece of code given will compile as the order of placement of type specifiers does not matter and hence we can follow any format for type specifiers when defining a class.

Example 2.5.4

Determine the output for the following piece of code:

```
# include <iostream.h>
# include <conio.h>
# include <stdio.h>
# include <string.h>

class electronics
{
 private:
 int equipment_no;
```

```
public:
char equipment_name[15];
int equipment_price;
electronics()
{
 cout<<endl<<" An object of type Electronics has been declared";
}
~electronics()
{
 cout<<endl<<" The scope of the created object is now over";
}
 void enter();
 void display();
};

class computer: public electronics
{
 public:
 computer()
 {
  cout<<endl<<" Computer is a derived class of electronics";
 }
 char motherboard;
 int modelno;
};

void electronics::enter()
{
 cout<<" Enter Equipment Name";
 gets(equipment_name);
 cout<<endl<<" Enter Equipment Price";
 cin>>equipment_price;
}

void electronics:: display()
{
 cout<<endl<<" Equipment Name ->"<<equipment_name;
 cout<<endl<<" Equipment Price ->"<<equipment_price;
}

void main()
{
 clrscr();
 computer c1;
 electronics e1;
```

```
strcpy(c1.equipment_name,"Computer");
strcpy(e1.equipment_name,c1.equipment_name);
c1.equipment_price = 2000;
c1.display();
e1.equipment_price=c1.equipment_price;
e1.equipment_price--;
e1.display();
getch();
}
```

Solution of 2.5.4

Output Screen

```
An object of type Electronics has been declared
Computer is a derived class of electronics
An object of type Electronics has been declared
Equipment Name ->Computer
Equipment Price ->2000
Equipment Name ->Computer
Equipment Price ->1999
The scope of the created object is now over
The scope of the created object is now over
```

2.6 Review Exercises

1/2 Mark Questions

Q1) What are the advantages of inheritance which make it the most powerful tool available in object oriented programming?

Q2) What are the different types of inheritance, explain briefly by giving examples?

Q3) How are members declared under private and protected access specifiers of a class different from outside the class declaration?

Q4) Write the class declaration for a class 'mouse' derived from class 'hardware' using the public type access specifier, having a character array 'type' and an integer variable 'cost' as its data members.

Q5) Write the class declaration for 'Mirror' from class 'Glass' and 'Silica'. The class 'Mirror' should also include two character arrays 'type', 'shape' along with an integer variable 'thickness' as its data members.

Q6) Find the error(s) for the constructors in the following code fragments:

```
i) class sample1
{
  float a,b,c;
  public:
  float sample1();
};
```

```
ii) class sample2
{
  float a,b,c;
  sample2();
};
```

Q7) Is it possible for a derived class to access the private members of the base class indirectly. If yes then create a base class and a derived class then use these classes to illustrate your point?

4/5 Mark Questions

Q8) Given the following class definitions:

```
class world
{
char continents[10];
protected:
char oceans[10];
public:
void input (char[]);
void output();
};

class country : private world
{
char cname[20];
protected:
char capital[20];
public:
void indata();
void outdata();
};
  class state: public country
{
char sname[20];
```

```
public:
void display();
};
```

(i) Name the base class and the derived class of the class 'country'.
(ii) What will be the size of an object of class 'world'.
(iii) What will be the size of an object of class 'country'.
(iv) What will be the size of an object of class 'state'.
(v) Name the data members that can be accessed from member functions of class 'world'.
(vi) Name the data members that can be accessed from member functions of class 'country'.
(vii) Name the data members that can be accessed from member functions of class 'state'.
(viii) Name the members that can be accessed by an object of class 'world'.
(ix) Name the members that can be accessed by an object of class 'country'.
(x) Name the members that can be accessed by an object of class 'state'.

2.7 Programming Project

The food chain shows how each living thing gets its food. Some animals eat plants and some eat other animals to survive. Your project is to create first inheritance hierarchy models of all the food chains that you can think of starting with 'forest' as the base class. Then create a menu driven program which displays the food chains of the various animals as per the 'food chain' hierarchy. An example of food chain of a 'Wolf' is given below. Use inheritance concept where ever possible.

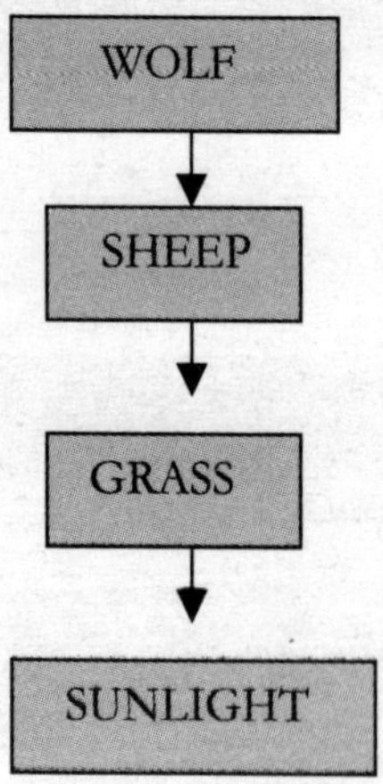

Food Chain of a 'Lion'

2.8 Let us revise!

- ✓ Inheritance is the concept of creating a new class, (derived class) from an already existing class (Base Class)
- ✓ The derived class can contain all the features of its base class and additional features of its own.
- ✓ A derived class is declared using the following format in C++:
  Syntax: class derived_className: Access_specifier Base_className.
- ✓ There are three type of access specifiers 'Public', 'Protected' and 'Private'.
- ✓ The 'Public' type access specifier allows minimum amount of data hiding to take place.
- ✓ The 'Protected' type access specifier provides levels of data protection between that of 'public' or 'private' type access specifiers.
- ✓ The members under the 'Protected' type access specifier can be passed on to the derived classes but cannot be accessed by objects of classes.
- ✓ The 'Private' type access specifier provides highest level of data protection. Members under the 'Private' type access specifiers cannot be inherited by derived classes neither can they be accessed by objects of these classes.
- ✓ Constructors and Destructors of base classes cannot be inherited by derived classes.
- ✓ When ever an object of a derived class is declared or initialized the default constructor for the base class is automatically called for.
- ✓ A class can be derived from one or more base classes. When the derived class inherits its properties from a single base class it is defined as 'Single Inheritance' where as when a derived class derives its properties from more than one base class 'Multiple Inheritance' is said to be observed. The code for initiating multiple inheritances is given below:

```
class A
{
   ...
};

class B
{
   ...
};
class C : public A, public B // Multiple Inheritance
{
   ...
};
```

Notes

PART III

DATA STRUCTURES & FILES

Part III

CHAPTER 1
DATA STRUCTURES

AIM

- Introduce the concept of Data Structures
- Learn to declare and use Structures, Arrays of Structures and Nested Structures.
- Comparison structures and arrays.
- Learn about Pointer to a structure
- Pass and return structures to functions.
- Appreciate the concept of 'Structures'

OUTLINE

1.1 Introduction
1.2 Data Structures
1.3 Arrays
1.4 Operations on static data structures
1.5 Solved Examples
1.6 Review Exercise
1.7 Programming Project
1.8 Let us revise!

1.1 Introduction

A computer programmer creates programs which are series of instructions to manipulate and organize data in a desired manner. Organizing data and establishing a relationship among its members is called structuring data or in simpler words any mathematical and logical model of data is known as data structure. In programming, the term *data structure* refers to a scheme for organizing related pieces of information. The basic types of data structures include files, lists, arrays, records, trees and tables. Each of these basic structures allows operations to be performed on the data.

Arrays are the simplest data structures. Some operations are common to all the data structures. These include accessing each member for some operation (traversal), search for locating a given record, insertion or deletion of records, sorting of records and merging of data structures. In the following sections, we shall discuss about the basic concepts of data structures, dynamic data structures and some more data structures known as linked lists, stacks and queues.

1.2 Data Structures

Given below are some basic definitions related to data structures:

- Primitive data structure

  The data structures, whose definitions are available in the compiler, are known as the primitive data structures.

- Non Primitive data structure

  The data structures, whose definitions are not available in the compiler, are known as non primitive data structures.

- Linear data structure

  Linear data structures are those data structures where each element has access to a maximum of one predecessor and one successor element. For example: Stacks and Queues.

- Non-linear data structure

  They are the data structure in which each element can access any number of predecessor elements and any number of successor elements. For example: Tree, Graphs, etc.

- <u>Static Data structure</u>

  The data structure in which the numbers of elements are fixed is known as static data structure. Example: Arrays

- <u>Dynamic data structures</u>

  The data structures in which the numbers of elements are not fixed are known as dynamic data structure. Example: Linked List, Dynamic stack and Dynamic Queue.

1.3 Arrays

Arrays are examples of static homogeneous data structures as the number of elements in array remain fixed. They are also commonly known as subscripted variables. We have already studied in previous chapters about how arrays are stored in consecutive memory locations. In this section, we will learn how we can determine the address of the memory locations occupied by an array. Let us begin with One Dimensional arrays.

1.3.1 One Dimensional Array

Suppose we declare a one dimensional array 'int A[i],' where 'i' can take up any integer value. Now the number of elements in this array can also be found by subtracting the last index of the array also known as the 'Upper Bound' with the first index of the array also known as the 'Lower Bound'. In this example, we have 'i' as the upper bound and '0' as the lower bound. We can use the following general formula to determine the memory location of any index of a array.

Memory location of A[i]:

Location (A[i]) = Base_address (A) + W*(i-LB)

Where,

Number of elements = Upper Bound – Lower Bound
= i - 0
= i

Where 'W' is the size of the object created.

1.3.2 Two Dimensional Arrays

As discussed in Part I that the computer memory only supports a linear placement of data items akin to a one-dimensional array as a result of which the memory simulates the two/multi dimensional array as a one dimensional array only. Two dimensional arrays are also stored at contagious memory locations similar to that of the one dimensional array. The only difference between them being that two dimensional arrays can be stored in the following two ways:

- Row major
- Column Major

Let us consider a two dimensional array A[i][j].

Number of elements = i * j = (UB(i) – LB(i) + 1) * (UB(j) – LB(j) +1)

Where UB is the upper bound and LB is the lower bound.

- **<u>Row Major</u>**

Let us take a two dimensional array A[i][j] of size M*N that is having M rows and N columns (Figure 1.1).

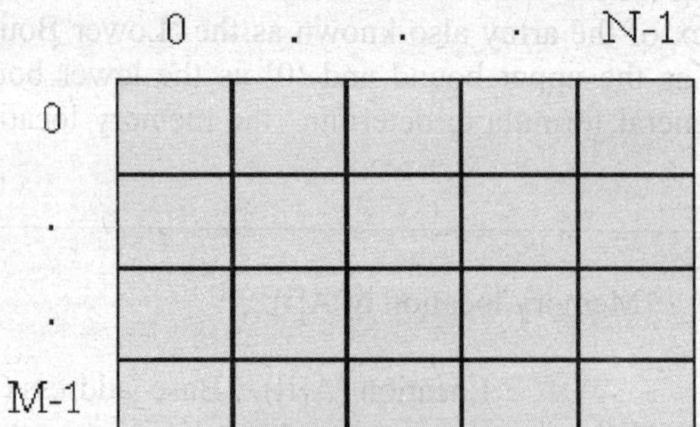

Figure 1.1: An array having M rows and N columns

The computer always keeps track of the base address only. So, by knowing the base address (Base (A)) and size of each element (W) one can calculate the address of any [I,J] element. The algorithm for a row major two dimensional array is given below:

Algorithm: For Row Major

For Two dimensional array A[i][j] of size M rows and N columns.

Base Address : Base (A), Address of the 1st element of the array

No. of Column s: N = UB (j) – LB(j)
UB(j) is the upper bound of column
LB(j) is the lower bound of the column

No. of Rows: M = UB(i) – LB(j)
UB(i) is the upper bound of the row
LB(j) is the lower bound of the column

Size of object: W is the size of the object

Memory Location: Loc(A[I][J]) = Base(A) + W*(M*I+J)

- **Column Major**

'Column Major' is also similar to the 'Row Major' order the only difference being that in the column major the elements are stored along the column. That is first the elements of the first column are filled and then the other ones are filled sequentially. To explain the functionality of column major order let us suppose an array A[i][j] with M rows and N columns.

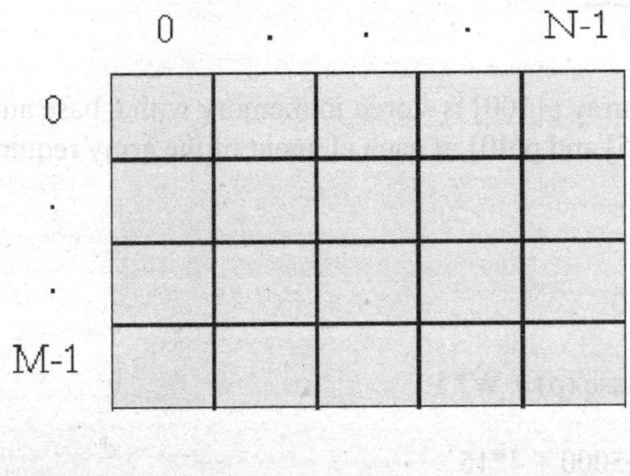

The algorithm given below explains the functionality of column major order.

Algorithm: For Row Major

For Two dimensional array A[i][j] of size M rows and N columns.

Base Address : Base (A), Address of the 1st element of the array

No. of Columns: N = UB (j) – LB(j) + 1
UB(j) is the upper bound of column
LB(j) is the lower bound of the column

No. of Rows: M = UB(i) – LB(j) + 1
UB(i) is the upper bound of the row
LB(j) is the lower bound of the column

Size of object: W is the size of the object

Memory Location:

Loc(A[I][J]) = Base(A) + W*(N*(J-LBJ) + (I-LBI))

If we assume LB(i), LB(j) as '0' then we obtain a much simplified formula:

Loc (A[I][J]) = Base(A) + W*(N*J+I)

1.3.3 Solved Examples

Example 1.3.3.1

A one-dimensional array p[100] is stored in memory with a base address as 5000. Find out addresses of p[15] and p[40], if each element of the array requires 4 bytes.

Solution of 1.3.3.1

Given

Base(p) = 5000
W = 4
Loc (p[I]) = Base (p) + W* I

Loc (p[15]) = 5000 + 4*15

= 5000 + 60
= 5060
Loc (p[40]) = 5000 + 4*40

= 5000 + 160
= 5160

Solved Example 1.3.3.2

A one dimensional array A[-5,…,25] is stored in the memory with each element requiring 2 bytes. If the base address is 8000, find out the following:

a) Address of A[5] and A[-3]
b) Total no. of elements present in the array

Solution of 1.3.3.2

Given,

Base(A) = 8000
W = 2
LB = -5
Loc(A[I]) = Base(A) + W*(I-LB)
Loc(A[5]) = 8000 + 2*(5-(-5))
= 8000 + 20
= 8020
Loc(A[-3]) = 8000 + 2*(-3-(-5))
= 8000 + 4
= 8004

Total
No of elements = UB – LB + 1 = 25 – (-5) +1 = 31

Solved Example 1.3.3.3

A two dimensional array Q[5][15] is stored in memory along the row with each element requiring 2 bytes. If the base address is 6500, find out the following:

a) Addresses of q[5][10] and q[3][5]
b) Total no. of elements present in the array

Solution of 1.3.3.3

Given,
Base (q) = 6500
W = 2
M = 5

Row major, Loc (Q [I][J]) = Base (Q) + W*(M*I+J)

Loc (Q[5][10]) = 6500 + 2 * (15 *5 +10)
= 6500 +170
= 6670

Loc (Q[3][5]) = 6500 + 2 * (15*3 +5)
= 6500 +100
= 6600

Total number of elements = N * M = 5 * 15 = 75

Solved Example 1.3.3.4

R[-4, …, 4, 7, …,17] is a two dimensional array, stored in the memory along the column with each element requiring 4 bytes. If the base address is 5000, find out the following

a) Addresses of R[2][10] and R[3][15]
b) Total no of elements in the array

Solution of 1.3.3.4

Given,

Base(R) = 5000
W = 4
N = UBI – LBI + 1 = 4 – (-4) +1 = 9
M = UBJ – LBJ + 1 = 17 – 7 + 1 = 11

Column Major,
Loc (R[I][J]) = Base (R) + W * (N * (J – LBJ) + (I – LBI))
Loc (R[2][10]) = 5000 + 4*(9 * (10 -7) + (2 – (-4))
= 5000 + 132
= 5132
Loc (R [3] [15]) = 5000 + 4*(9*(15-7) + (3 – (-4))
= 5316
Total
No of elements = N * M = 9 *11

1.4 Operations on static data structures

1.4.1 Insertion

The insertion operation is performed by inserting an element at a desired location in an array. However, to add an element in between the array, all elements from the location of insertion need to be moved one location forward to accommodate the new element. This operation is shown in figure 1.2.

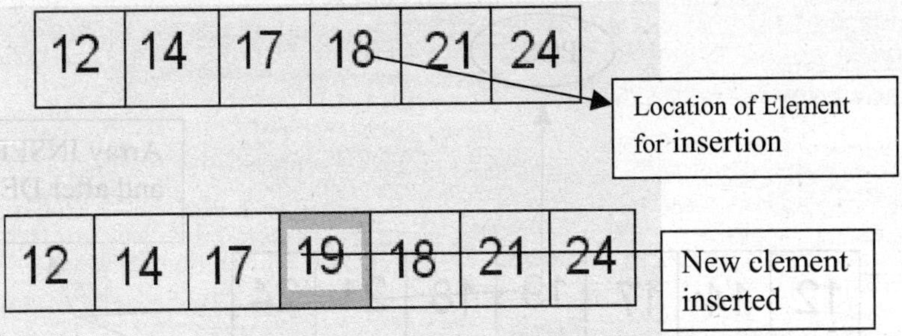

Figure 1.2: Insertion of new element '19' in array INSERTION

The program 1.1 gives the function to insert an element at a desired location into an array.

Program 1.1: Function to insert Data at 'Pos' in the array 'arr'.

```
void insert (int arr[], int &l, int data)
{
  if (l<max)
  {
   for (int c=l;c>pos;c--)
     arr[c]=arr[c-1];
     arr[pos]=data;
     l++ ;// After insertion of an element increases L
  }
  else
  cout<<" Array is Full"<<endl;
}
```

Note: 'Pos' is presumably defined as global variable and 'pos' is the position from which insertion will take place.

1.4.2 Deletion

As the name suggests the 'deletion' operation is used to delete an element from a specified position ('pos' in figure 1.3) in the static data structure. When the selected element is deleted from the data structure, then the elements stored at subsequent positions in the structure shift either one step forward or shift one step backward towards the position from where the element was deleted as also shown in the figure 1.3.

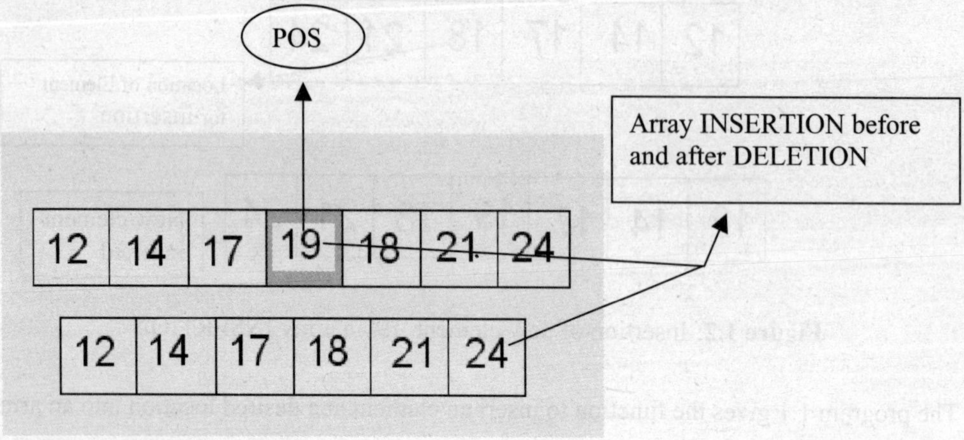

Figure 1.3 Element 19 deleted from array INSERTION

The program 1.2 given below enlists the piece of code used to delete an element from an array.

Program 1.2: Function to delete data from POS in the array 'arr'

```
void delete (int arr[], int &l, int pos)
{

    for (int c=pos;c<l-1;c++)
    arr[c]=arr[c+1];
    l--;
}
```

1.5 Solved Examples

Example 1.5.1

The base address of a two dimensional array A with 5 rows and 4 columns is 2000. If each element requires 4 bytes for its storage, find the address of element a[3][3] if arrangement is row major?

Solution of 1.5.1

Now we have been given the Base address (A) = 2000

Size of each element (w) = 4
Number of columns (N)= 4
Now, the elements have been stored as row major
Address of element A[i][j]= A + w(N*I + j)
= 2000 + 4 * (4*3+3)
= 2060

So, the required address is 2060.

Example 1.5.2

For an array of real numbers Realarr[20][20] find the address of Realarr[10][12] if Realarr[1][1] is stored in location 1000. Assume each real number requires 4 bytes. Show the various steps of calculation?

Solution of 1.5.2

We use following formula to compute the address:

A[i][j] = B + w(n(I-LI) + (J-L2))
Now, Base address (B) = 1000
Size of each element = 4

L1=L2=1

A[10][12]= 1000 + 4(20(20-1) + (20-1))
= 1000 + 4(20(19) + 19)
= 1000 + 4(380 +19)
= 1000 + 4(399)
= 1000 + 1596
= 2596

Example 1.5.3

Write an algorithm which finds the location and values of largest and second largest elements in two dimensional array DATA with N rows and M columns.

Solution of 1.5.3

Let us assume an array A[][] having M rows and N columns.
Step : 1. Max = A[0][0]
2. Min = A[0][0]

```
        3. i=0
        4. while (i<m) repeat 5 to 10.
        5. j=0
    6. while (j<N) repeat step 7 to 9

    7. if (Max<A[i][j])
            Max= A[i][j]
    8. if (Max>A[i][j])
            Max=A[i][j]
    9. j= j+1
   10. i= i+1
   11. cout<<" Maximum value is"<<Max
   12. cout<<" Maximum value is"<<Min
   13. End.
```

Example 1.5.4

Each element in an array DATA[20][50] requires 4 bytes of storage. Base address of data is 2000, determine the location of DATA [10][10] when the array is stored as

(a) Row major
(b) Column major

Solution of 1.5.4

Base Address = 2000
Size of the element = 4

(i) Row major Order

N=50

DATA[10][10]= 2000 + 4(50(10-1) +(10-1))
= 2000 + 4(50 (9) + 9)
= 2000 + 4(454)
= 2000 + 1816
= 3816

(ii) Column major Order

M = 20

DATA[10][10]= 2000 + 4(20(10-1) + (10-1))
= 2000 + 4(20(9) + 9)
= 2000 + 4(180 +9)
= 2000 + 4(189)
= 2000 + 756
= 2756

Example 1.5.5

Given an array A[6][16] whose base address is 100. Calculate the location A[2][5] if each element occupies 4 bytes and array is stored row wise?

Solution of 1.5.5

Base address = 100
W=4
L1 = 1 L2 = 1
N = 16
A[2][5] = B + W(n(I- L1) + (J – L2))
= 100 + 4(16(2-1) + 5-1)
= 100 + 4(16 + 4)
= 100 + 80
= 180

Example 1.5.6

Explain how bubble sort will sort the following array:

11 6 26 9 8 24 18

Solution of 1.5.6

Bubble sort compares adjacent elements and swaps them if necessary and then compares the next pair of adjacent elements.

The method when applied to the given array gives the following result:-

Pass 1: Swap numbers 11 and 6 to give 6 11 26 9 8 24 18
Swap numbers 26 and 9 to give 6 11 9 26 8 24 18
Swap numbers 26 and 8 to give 6 11 9 8 26 24 18
Swap numbers 26 and 24 to give 6 11 9 8 24 26 18
Swap numbers 26 and 18 to give 6 11 9 8 24 18 26

Pass 2: Swap numbers 9 and 11 to give 6 9 11 8 24 18 26
Swap numbers 11 and 8 to give 6 9 8 11 24 18 26
Swap numbers 24 and 18 to give 6 9 8 11 18 24 26

Pass 3: Swap numbers 9 and 8 to give 6 8 9 11 18 24 26

Example 1.5.7

It is required to sort the following array by method of insertion sort. Show the status of the array after each insertion:

40 23 15 67 55 84 32

Show the status of the array after each insertion?

Solution of 1.5.7

Iteration							Array
0	23	40	15	67	55	84	32
1	15	23	40	67	55	84	32
2	15	23	40	67	55	84	32
3	15	23	40	55	67	84	32
4	15	23	40	55	67	84	32
5	15	23	32	40	55	67	84

Example 1.5.8

The following numbers (89, 20, 31, 56, 20, 64, 48) are required to be sorted using selection sort showing how the list would appear at the end of each pass.

Solution of 1.5.8

The example has the following solution:

89	20	31	56	20	64	48
20	89	31	56	20	64	48
20	20	31	56	89	64	48
20	20	31	56	89	64	48
20	20	31	56	89	64	56
20	20	31	48	56	64	89

1.6 Review Exercise

1/2 Mark Questions

Q1) Define data structure and give its physical significance?

Q2) Describe the following operations on an array with suitable examples:

- Traversal
- Linear search
- Bubble sort
- Merging

Q3) Which of the two ('bubble' and 'selection') sort is the most efficient and why?

Q4) The base address of a two dimensional array X with 15 rows and 4 columns is 2000. If each element requires 4 bytes for its storage, find the address of element X[10][4] if arrangement is row major?

Q5) The following numbers are required to be sorted using bubble and selection sort showing how the list would appear at the end of each pass.

a) 20 40 30 10 50
b) 10 2 3 4 -2 1 5

Q6) If 2 dimensional array C[5…10,-5…9] is stored using column major representation, then calculate the address if C[8,-2], if the base address is 10 and each array element requires 2 bytes of memory.

2/3 Mark Questions

Q7) Each element of an array DATA[20][50] requires 2 bytes of storage. Base address of DATA is 2000. Determine the location of DATA[10][22] when the array is stored as
(a) Row Major
(b) Column Major

Q8) Given two dimensional array A[10][20], base address of A is 100 and width of each element is 4 bytes. Find the location of A[12]

Q9) If two dimensional array C[5, …, 9,-4,…, 10] is stored using column major representation, then calculate the address if C[8,-2], if the base address is 10 and each array element requires 2 bytes of memory.

4/5 Mark questions

Q10) Write a menu driven program in C++ to sort an array using selection and bubble sort.

Q11) Write a menu driven program to search the array using linear and binary search?

Q12) Explain the following terms primitive and non primitive data structures and differentiate between them giving suitable examples.

1.7 Programming Project

The programming project for this chapter involves the creation of a telephone directory for a set of 50 subscribers. The directory should include subscriber names listed in alphabetical order, together with their street address and telephone numbers. The program created should also have an option to search for any specific data entry and enlist the details involved with that data entry.

Hint: Use 'Selection' sort and 'Binary' search for better results

1.8 Let us revise!

- The data structure, which is available in the compiler, is known as a primitive data structure.
- The data structure, which is not available in the compiler, is known as non primitive data structure.
- The data structure in which each element has access to maximum of one predecessor element and maximum of one successor element is known as linear data structure. Example: stack, queue, etc.
- The data structure in which each element can access any number of predecessor elements and any number of successor elements known as non linear data structure. Example: Tree, Graphs, etc.
- The data structure in which the numbers of elements are fixed is known as static data structure. Example: Arrays
- The data structures in which the numbers of elements are not fixed are known as dynamic data structure. Example: Linked List
- <u>One dimensional array</u>
  Number of elements N= UB – LB + 1
  Where LB- lower bound, UB – upper bound
  Memory location of A[i]: Loc (A[i]) = Base (A) + W*(i-LB)
  Loc (A[i])=Base(A) + W*I
  Where N is given as in c++, LB is assumed as 0
- <u>Two dimensional array</u>
  A two dimensional arrays can be stored in the following two ways.
    - Row major
    - Column Major

  Number of elements = N * M = (UBI – LBI + 1) * (UBJ – LBJ +1)

- <u>Binary search</u>
  The prerequisite condition to search as element from an array using binary search technique is that the array should be sorted in ascending or descending order.

- The deletion operation is used to delete an element from any position (pos).

- The insertion operation is used when a new element is inserted into an existing array, but to insert a data entry in between the array all elements from the inserted place will move one place forward to accommodate the new data element.

Part III

CHAPTER 2
LINKED LISTS

AIM

- Introduce the concept of 'Linked Lists'.
- Able to create and perform various operations on 'Linked Lists'
- To create 'Linked' data structures using pointers, self referential structures.
- Use applications of 'Link Lists' such as 'stacks' and 'queues'.

OUTLINE

2.1 Introduction
2.2 Linked lists
2.3 Linked lists as stacks
2.4 Linked lists as queues
2.5 Solved examples
2.6 Review exercise
2.7 Programming project
2.8 Let us revise!

2.1 Introduction

Till now, we have only studied about linear data structures like arrays and structures. This chapter introduces dynamic data structures which have distinct advantages over traditional linear data structures. The most obvious being that the size of elements in an array was limited to the number provided at the time of declaration. The next being that in order to avoid the danger of running out of allocated memory we would declare huge array sizes but hardly ever, would use the entire space allocated to these arrays. Hence, we were deprived of using a lot of potential memory which could have been allocated to and utilized by other applications. Further, operations like 'insertion' and 'deletion' of data were also very time consuming and inefficient, as order of all the elements had to be changed depending upon the operation applied. 'Linked Lists' introduce practical solutions to all these problems. This chapter introduces the concept of 'Link Lists' and describes algorithms and their implementation through programs.

2.2 Linked Lists

Linked Lists are dynamic data structures which can shrink and expand during program execution. In theory, they are very similar to arrays. The difference lies in the construction of their structures. An array can be described as a huge unit of data where all its elements are grouped together as a single block of memory. Where as, linked lists allocate different blocks of memory to each element called 'node' where each node contains two fields the 'data' field to store data parameters and 'next' field which is a pointer which points to the next node in the list. The figure 2.1 given below shows the cases of sequential (array type) and linked memory allocations.

Sequential		Linked		
A1	Data 1	A1	Data 1	A2
A1 + C	Data 2	A2	Data 2	A3
A1 + 2C	Data 3	A3	Data 3	A4
A1 + 3C	Data 4	A4	Data 4	NULL

Where C is the size of the object

Figure 2.1: Sequential and Linked memory allocation

Linked lists have various advantages over traditional arrays. Firstly, when declaring linked lists, we are not confined to a fixed space as in arrays. For example, if one observes carefully in the figure given above the pointer part in node 'A4' of the linked lists contains a NULL value. If we want to add another node to the list one can replace this null value with the address of the next node. Hence, we need to allocate memory only when required. In addition to this, one can also group more data in the data part of the node to save additional memory. Linked lists are also very useful as the process of 'insertion' or 'deletion' of data is fairly simple and can be achieved without shifting the entire data structure depending upon the operation applied. Figure 2.2 depicts how the deletion operation works. In this figure, we have deleted the node 'A2' by just changing the address stored in the pointer part of the node 'A1' from 'A2' to 'A3'.

Linked List

A1	Data 1	A3
A2	Data 2	A3
A3	Data 3	A4
A4	Data 4	NULL

Figure 2.2: Deletion of node

As described earlier, linked lists consist of 'data' part for storing data and pointer variables which store the address of the next node in the list, so they can also be expressed with the help of pointer diagrams. For example, figure 2.3 shows pointer diagrams for the linked list declared in figure 2.1.

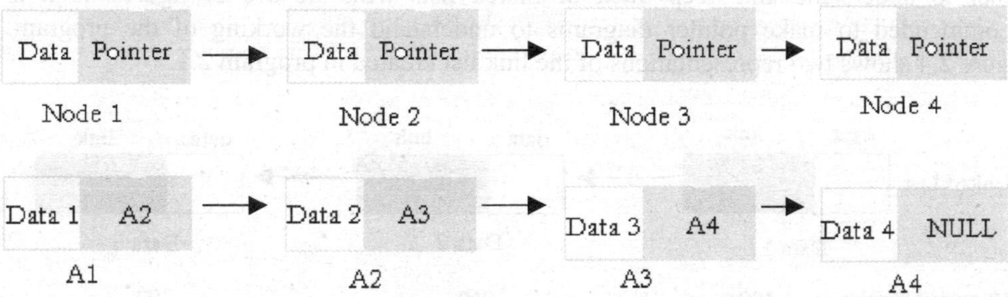

Figure 2.3 Pointer Diagram

In this figure, each box represents a 'node' and each arrow represents a 'pointer'. Let us now learn how to create and use linked lists.

2.2.1 Creation of Linked Lists

We already know that linked lists are a linear collection of self referential structures. So in order to generate a linked list, we first have to declare a self referential structure. Program 2.1 illustrates the creation of a linked list.

Program 2.1:

```
/********************************
Structure Name: list
Structure Variables: data, link (pointer to structure)
*******************************************************/

struct list
{
 int data;

 list *link;
}data1,data2,data3;

data1.link=&data2;     // link to data 2

data2.link=&data3;     // link to data 3

data3.link=NULL;       // Marks the end of the list
```

In this program, we have declared a self referential structure 'list' having 'data1', 'data2' and 'data3' as its variables which have been used to generate a linked list. It is always easier to understand and keep track of linked lists with the use of figures so it is recommended to make pointer diagrams to understand the working of the program. Figure 2.4 shows two representations of the link list created in program 2.1.

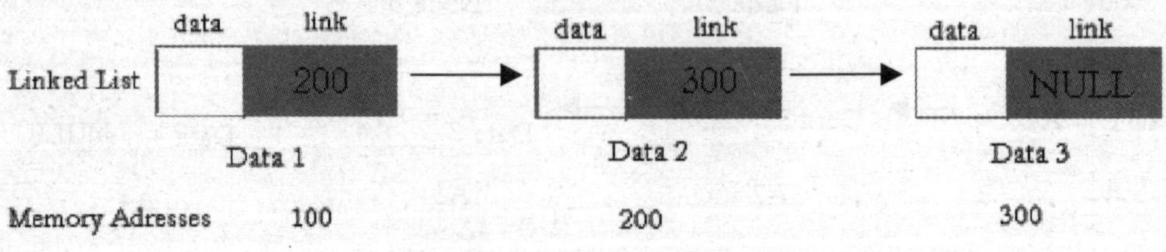

Figure 2.4 (a): Pointer Diagram

Node	Points To
Data 1	Data 2
Data 2	Data 3
Data 3	NULL

Figure 2.4 (b): Linked List Table

PROGRAMMING TIPS

- Using dynamic data structures is far more efficient than using traditional data structures as dynamic data structures can grow or shrink in size as per the need of the program.
- Insertion and deletion of elements in an array is time consuming as the entire array has to be shifted accordingly. Hence, using link list is a more efficient method for data storage.

2.2.2 Traversing a linked list

To access the data contained in the nodes of the list, we take the pointer to the first node of the list and then use the pointer in the link field of the first node to locate the second node. This procedure is repeated until we encounter the last node which has the entry NIL in its link field. The process of going through Node1, Node 2 and so on of the list is called as traversing a linked list.

Now that we understand what one means by traversing a linked list let us develop an algorithm to perform this operation.

Algorithm

Prerequisite: This algorithm works for a linked list in which each node stores the address of its preceding node.

Steps

1. Declare a pointer, pointing to the last node.

2. Assign the pointer variable declared in step 1, the address stored in the pointer part of the self referential structure.

3. Repeat the process described in step 2 until the pointer is assigned a NULL value which marks the end of the link list.

It might be easier to understand this algorithm with the help of an example. Program 2.2 creates a linked list which fulfils the prerequisite for our algorithm and then traverses the link list using the algorithm given above.

Program 2.2: Traversing a linked list

```
/************
Program 2.2: Traversing a linked list
*****************************************/

// Header Files
# include<iostream.h>
# include<conio.h>

/****************
Self Referential structure
Name: List
Data Members: integer variable 'data', pointer variable 'ptr'
**********************************************************/
struct list
{
 int data;
 list *ptr;
};

// Main Function
void main()
{
 clrscr();
 int i=1;

 // Pointer variable pointing to memory block of type List
 list *l1 = new list;

 // Pointer variable l2 of type list
```

```
list *l2;

l1->ptr=NULL;

int counter=1;

char ch = 'y';

while (ch != 'n')
{
 cout<<" \n Enter data for node"<<counter;
 cin>>l1->data;

 l2 = l1;
 l1=new list;

 l1->ptr=l2;
 cout<<"\n Do you want to add another node (y/n)";

 cin>>ch;
}

// While loop traversing the Linked List
while ( i != 0)
{
        if (l2->ptr == NULL)
        {
                i=0;
        }
   l2=l2->ptr;
 }
getch();
}
```

In this program we have created a linked list as a collection of self referential structures of type 'list' using two pointer variables 'l1' and 'l2'. At first when these pointers are declared 'l1' points to a dynamically allocated block of memory or to the first node of type 'list' (figure 2.5(a)). The pointer part 'ptr' of this node is initialized to NULL and data value say '10' is inserted in the data part 'data' of the node by the user. A copy of this nodes address is then assigned to the other pointer variable 'l2' which then also starts pointing to the this node (figure 2.5(b)).

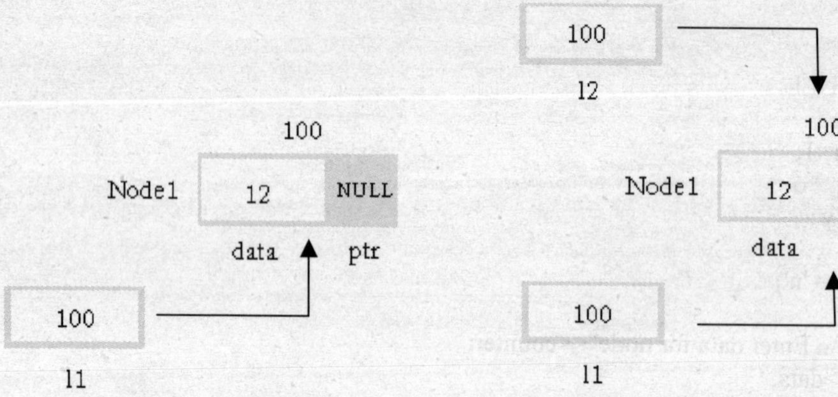

(a) (b)

Figure 2.5: Creating link lists using pointer variables

When this is done, the pointer 'l1' is then intialized to point to another memory block of type 'list' or create the second node of the 'list' (figure 2.6(a)) and the address stored in the pointer variable 'l2' is assigned to pointer part 'ptr' of the second node (figure 2.6(b)).

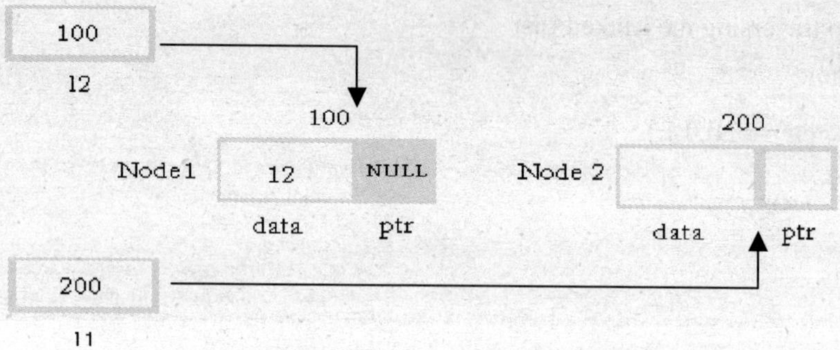

Figure 2.6(a): Creating Linked Lists

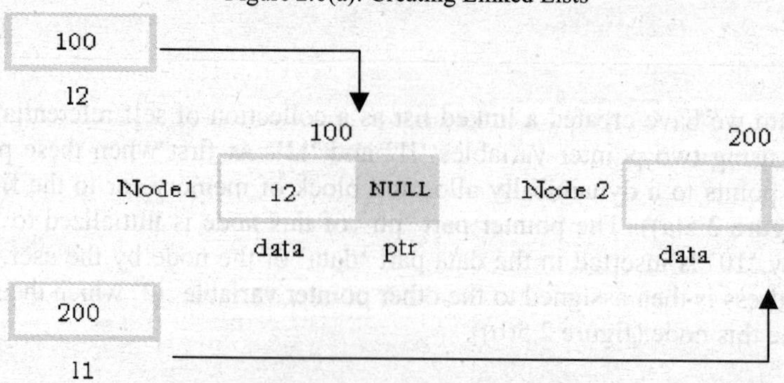

Figure 2.6 (b): Creating linked lists

This entire process can continue till the user wants and allows us to create link lists of any size but what do we achieve by applying this complicated process?

Well, with the help of this piece of code we have created a linked list in which each node stores the address of its preceding node as per the prerequisite required in the algorithm we studied in section 2.2.2. Let us now try to understand how the program given above traverses the link list that was created.

```
while ( i != 0)
{
        if (l2->ptr == NULL)
        {
                i=0;
        }
   l2=l2->ptr;
}
```

Program 2.2 uses the above piece of code to traverse the link list. In this piece of code the pointer 'l2' is used to traverse the linked list and during each loop it is assigned the address of the node to which it points to, which happens to be the address of the preceding node. This process is carried on till the point the first node containing 'NULL' value stored in the pointer part is encountered where it comes out of the while loop achieving its purpose.

COMMON PROGRAMMING ERRORS

- Not initializing the pointer in the last node of the link list can lead to a runtime error.
- Loosing the memory address of a node in a 'Linked List' can lead to a logical error.

2.2.2.1 Solved Examples

Example 2.2.2.1.1

Create a linked list for the structure 'Employee' given below. The program should input the 'Name' and the 'Age' of the Employee and then display the linked list on the screen. The program should keep inserting nodes till the user wants.

```
strcut Employee
{
    char Name[15];
    int Age;
    Employee *ptr;
};
```

Solution of 2.2.2.1.1

```
/************
Solved Example: 2.2.2.1.1
******************************************/

// Header Files
# include<iostream.h>
# include<conio.h>
# include<stdio.h>

/****************
Self Referencial structure
Name: Employee
Data Members: character array Name[]
              integer variable 'Age'
              pointer variable 'ptr'
*******************************************************/

struct Employee
{
 char Name[15];
 int Age;
 Employee *ptr;
};

// Main Function
void main()
{

 clrscr();
 int i=1;

 // Pointer variable pointing to memory block of type Employee
 Employee *E1 = new Employee ;

 // Pointer variable l2 of type Employee
```

```
Employee *E2;

E1->ptr=NULL;

int counter=1;

char ch = 'y';

while (ch != 'n')
{
 cout<<" \n Enter data for Employee "<<counter;
 cout<<" \n Enter Name of Employee";
 gets(E1->Name);

 cout<<" Enter the age of the Employee";
 cin>>E1->Age;

 E2 = E1;

 E1=new Employee;

 E1->ptr=E2;

 cout<<"\n Do you want to add another Employee (y/n)";

 cin>>ch;
 counter++;
}

// While loop printing the Employee List
cout<<" \n \n ######## EMPLOYEE LIST ########";
while ( i != 0)
{
 if (E2->ptr == NULL)
 {
 i=0;
 }
 cout<<"\n Employee Name :"<<E2->Name;

 cout<<" \t \t Age :"<<E2->Age;

 E2=E2->ptr;
 }
getch();
}
```

In this program, we have created a link list using the structure 'Employee'. The important thing to notice in this example is that it uses two pointers 'E1' and 'E2' where 'E1' is used to point to the new dynamic memory blocks or the new nodes and the pointer 'E2' is used to store the address of the previous node and assign it to the pointer part 'ptr' of the node just as we did in program 2.2.

2.2.3 Inserting nodes in linked lists

In this section, we will study about insertion of a node in the middle of a linked list given in figure 2.7.

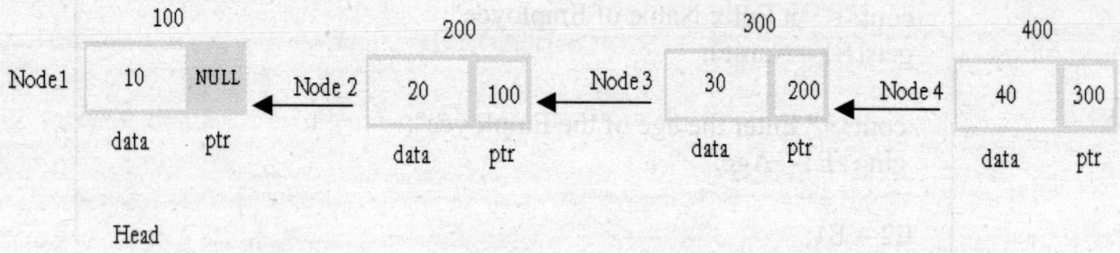

Figure 2.7: Link List

Let us insert a node between 'Node 3' and 'Node 4'. To do so, we have to keep two things in mind. Firstly, we need the address of the preceding node 'Node 3' and the node which is being inserted say 'Node X'. Further, we need to use two pointers: one which will hold the address of 'Node3' and the other which will hold the address of the newly inserted node 'Node X' so that we can maintain the chain of links in the link list. Figure 2.8 shows how the link list would look like when 'Node X' is inserted in the link list.

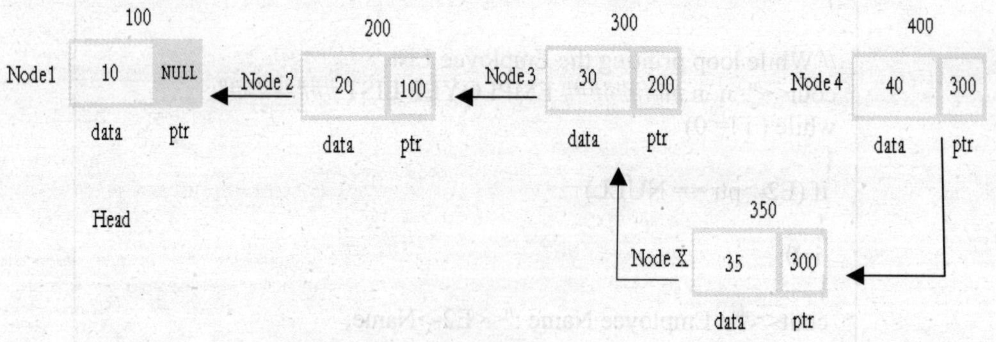

Figure 2.8: Insertion of Node 'X' in the already created link list

2.2.4 Deleting nodes from linked lists

The process of deletion of a node from the linked list is quite simple. Let us again take the same link list which we took to understand the insertion operation (Figure 2.7). Say, we want to delete 'Node 3' of the link list then all one has to do is change the address stored in 'Node 4' from 300 to 200 and 'Node 3' will be deleted. Figure 2.9, shows how the link list would look after 'Node 3' has been deleted from it.

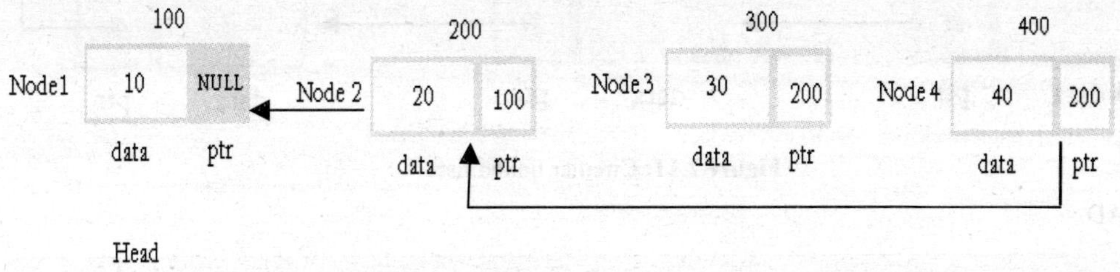

Figure 2.9: Deletion of nodes from a link list

2.2.5 Circular or ring linked lists

Circular or ring linked lists are special linked lists. They have the special property that the last node links to the first node (see figure 2.10). Therefore, this link list does not have a node having a NULL pointer. The advantage of this structure is that the list can be accessed at any given node. There is no first or last node. The node structure is similar to linked list and can also be easily updated. Insertion of a new node at a desired place can be done by rearranging the links to include the new node in the ring. Deletion of a node is performed by adjusting the links as in the case of ordinary linked lists.

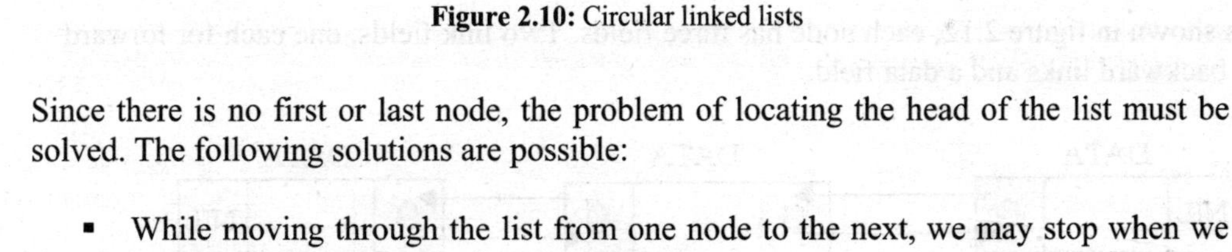

Figure 2.10: Circular linked lists

Since there is no first or last node, the problem of locating the head of the list must be solved. The following solutions are possible:

- While moving through the list from one node to the next, we may stop when we return to the node from where we started.

- We can also include a special recognizable node into each circular list as a convenient stopping place. This special node is often called the list head, as shown in figure 2.11.

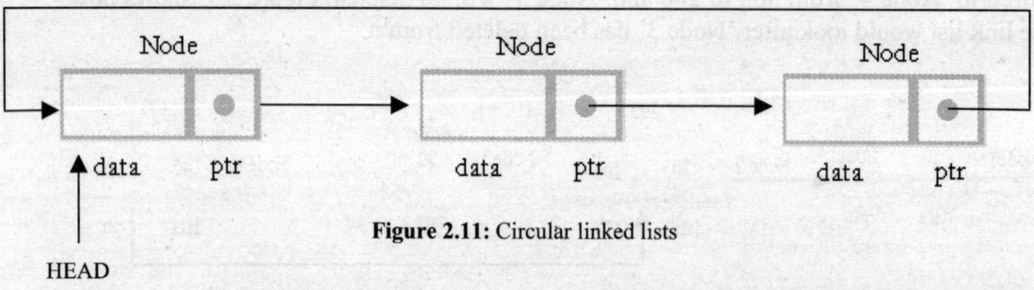

Figure 2.11: Circular linked lists

COMMON PROGRAMMING ERRORS

- Declaring a NULL pointer in the last node of a ringed link list can lead to an logical error
- Loosing tracks of pointers while inserting or deleting link list well result in a logical or a runtime error.

2.2.6 Multi-Lists

Singly linked lists pose problems as they are one-directional. One can only traverse these linked lists in the direction of the links but what happens if we want to traverse linked lists in both directions?

For this purpose, we need to define a more general list structure - one in which data elements belong to several lists. This type of structure is called a multi-list. The nodes of such lists have more than one link. For example, we can include two links in each node, pointing to the items on both sides of the node. This structure is referred to as a doubly-linked (two-way) list.

As shown in figure 2.12, each node has three fields. Two link fields, one each for forward & backward links and a data field.

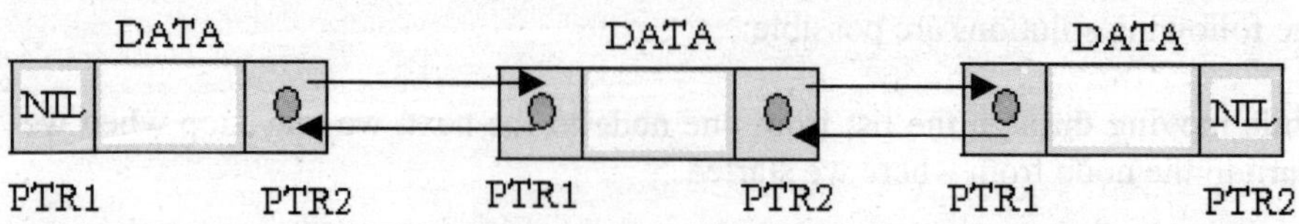

Figure 2.12: Doubly linked list

As one might observe in the figure above, both the left and the right nodes of the list have NIL links. We can also have a ringed doubly linked ring structure as shown in the figure

2.13. The only change we will observe in such a structure is that no node will contain NIL values stored in the link part of their structure.

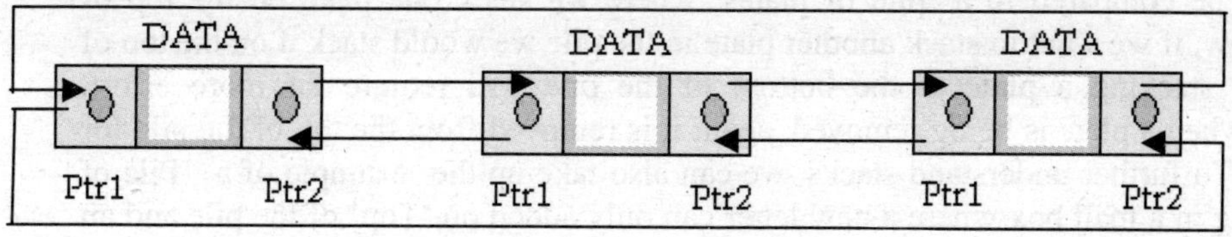

Figure 2.13: A doubly linked ring structure

The cost of creating such structures is the need for extra memory to keep the second link. The process of deletion and insertion in doubly linked lists is very similar to the one we have already followed for singly linked lists. Figure 2.14 shows the modification in the linked list when a new node X is inserted into the link list and Figure 2.15 shows the effect on the link list when this element X is deleted from the linked list.

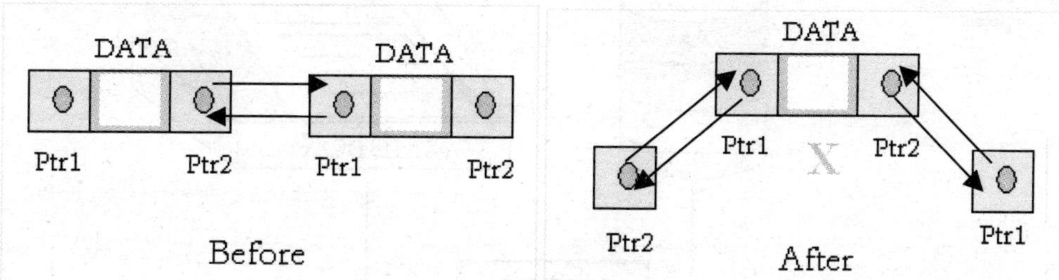

Figure 2.14: Insertion operation in Double Linked Lists

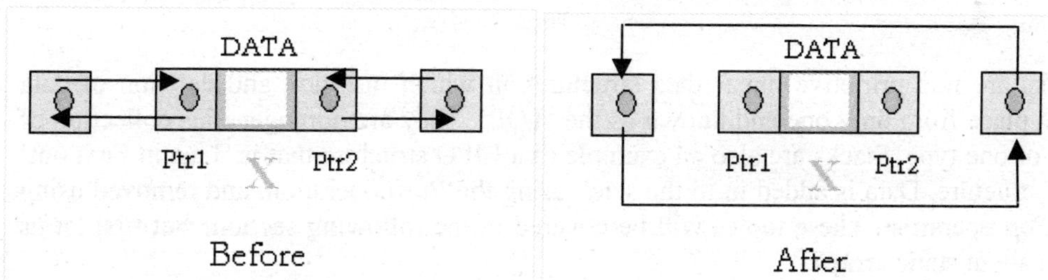

Figure 2.15: Deletion operation in doubly linked lists

These sections describe linked lists and the various operations possible on them. Later in this chapter, we will learn about the practical applications of linked lists like creating stacks and queues which involve singly linked and doubly linked lists.

LINKED LISTS

2.3 Linked Lists as Stacks

Stacks can be compared to a 'pile of plates' where we stack one plate on the top of another. Now, if we want to stack another plate in the pile we would stack it on the top of the pile as stacking a plate at the bottom of the pile will require far more effort. Similarly, when a plate is being removed, again it is removed from the top of the pile for simplicity. To further understand stacks, we can also take up the example of a 'Pile of letters' lying in a mail box where a new letter can only added on 'Top' of the pile and an old letter can be removed from the same point 'Top' as also shown in figure 2.16.

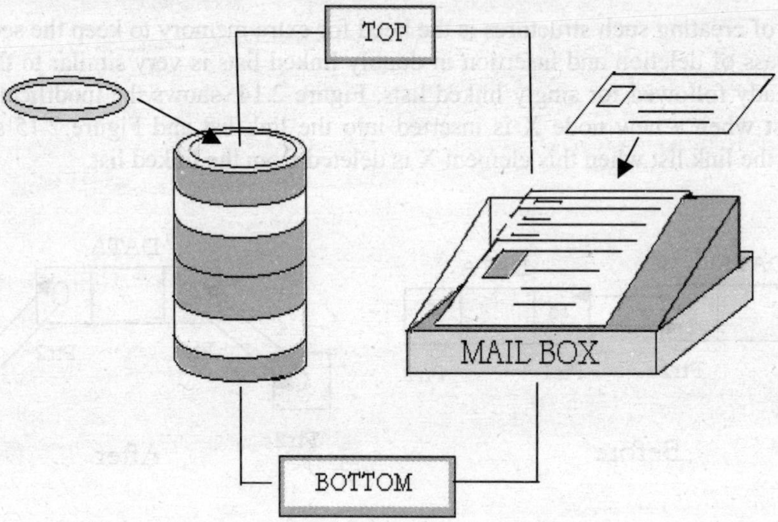

Figure 2.16: An example of a stack

Stacks are non primitive linear data structures in which insertion and deletion of data takes place from only one end known as the 'TOP'. They are homogeneous collection of data of one type. Stacks are also an example of a LIFO structure that is 'Last in First out' data structure. Data is added in to the stack using the *Push* operation, and removed using the *Pop* operation. These topics will be covered in the following sections but first let us learn about static arrays.

2.3.1 Static Stacks

Stacks can also be implemented as one dimensional arrays known as 'Static' stacks. 'Static' stacks have a fixed amount of data which can be entered into them and generally used when we know how much space the data would occupy. 'Static' stacks are created by declaring a linear one dimensional array in which insertion or 'Pushing' and deletion or 'Popping' of data is allowed only from one single location known as the 'TOP'. Let us take an example of a static stack by declaring an array 'Static_Stack' which can store 8 integer data values. What happens if we want to insert or 'push' data into our static stack? Say we push the data value '5' into our stack then our linear array would look like figure 2.17.

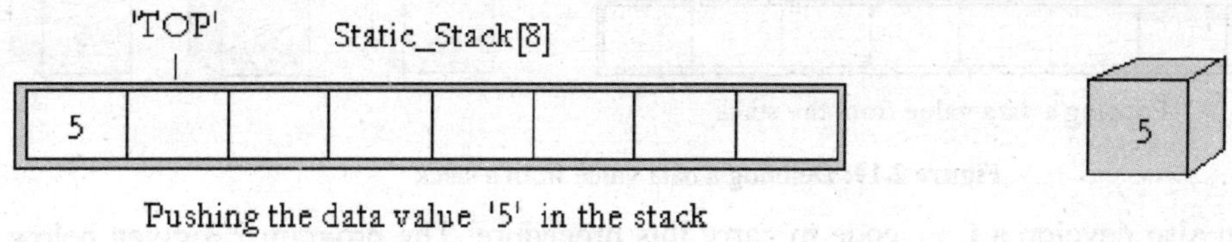

Figure 2.17: Pushing data into the stack

Now after the insertion of the data value the position from where insertion and deletion takes place 'TOP' shifts to the proceeding memory location, just like in our 'Pile of Plates' example where once a plate is inserted or pushed in the pile the next plate can only be inserted on top of the previous plate. Now let us see what happens if insert another data value say '10' into the array what will be the effect of this insertion in our stack.

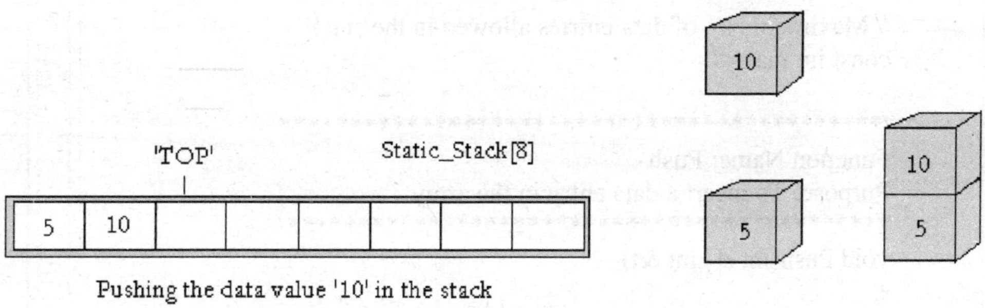

Figure 2.18: Insertion of data entry into the stack

Our stack would then appear as figure 2.18 given above. Again if we notice carefully 'TOP' is shifted to the next memory location. Similarly, we can add more data values in our stack but what happens if we want to pop or delete a data entry?

When using stacks, we can only delete the preceding entry that is the data entry at the location 'TOP – 1'. So if we want to delete the data entry '5', we will first have to delete the data entry '10' as insertion and deletion in a stack is only allowed from a single location. It might be more apparent now that why stacks are also known as LIFO structures. Figure 2.19 shows the effect on the stack when the data entry '10' is deleted or in other words 'popped' from the stack. After the data entry has been deleted the position 'TOP' is decremented and then signifies the preceding index of the linear array.

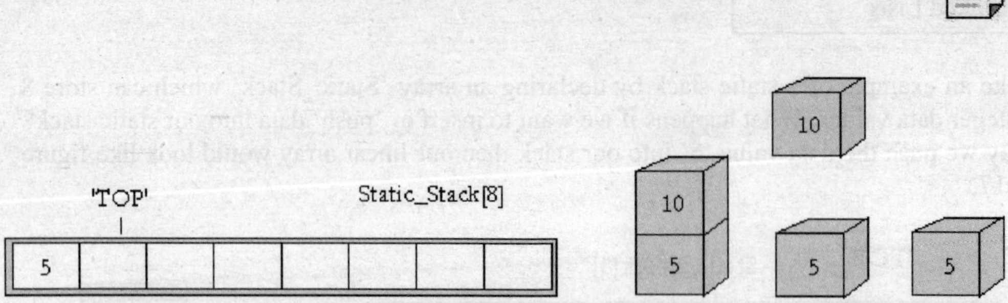

Popping a data value from the stack

Figure 2.19: Deleting a data value from a stack

We can also develop a C++ code to carry this procedure. The program 2.3 given below represents stack as an array.

Program 2.3

```
// Header Files
# include<iostream.h>
# include<conio.h>

// Maximum No. of data entries allowed in the stack
const int max=8

/*******************************************
Function Name: Push
Purpose: To insert a data entry in the array
*******************************************/
void Push(int s[],int &t)
{
  if (t<max)
  {
    cout<<" Data to be entered";
    cin>>s[++t];
    cout<<endl<<"Data has been entered";
    cout<<endl<<"________________";
  }
  else
  cout<<"\n The stack is full"<<endl;
}

/*******************************************
Function Name: Pop
Purpose: To delete a data entry from the array
```

```
******************************************/
void Pop(int s[],int &t)
{  if (t!=-1)
  {
   cout<<endl<<" The data entry "<<s[t]<<" has been
deleted";
   t--;
  }
}


/******************************************
Function Name: display
Purpose: To display data entries in the stack
******************************************/
void display(int s[],int &t)
{
 cout<<endl<<"Displaying data entries in the stack";
 for (int i=t;i>=0;i--)
 cout<<endl<<s[i];
}


//Main Function
void main()
{
 clrscr();
 int static_stack[max], top=-1;
 int ch;
 do
 { cout<<endl<<"\n 1) Push";
  cout<<"\n 2) Pop";
  cout<<"\n 3) Display";
  cout<<"\n 4) Quit";
  cin>>ch;
  switch(ch)
  {
   case 1:Push(static_stack,top);
   break;
   case  2:Pop(static_stack,top);
   break;
   case  3:display(static_stack,top);
   break;
  }
```

```
    } while (ch!=4);

    getch();
}
```

Let us closely examine this program. In this program, we have declared a one dimensional array 'static_stack' which can hold 8 integer data values represented by the constant variable 'max'. The variable 'Top' is initialized to value '-1' and is used to keep track of the position from where data values are inserted and deleted. The function 'Push' is given below:

Function 'Push'

```
void Push(int s[],int &t)
{
  if (t<max)
  {
   cout<<" Data to be entered";
   cin>>s[++t];
   cout<<endl<<"Data has been entered";
   cout<<endl<<"___________________________";
  }
  else
  cout<<"\n The stack is full"<<endl;
}
```

This function is used to insert data entries into the stack. The linear array and the variable 'Top' are passed to it as reference parameters. Which means that any changes made to the formal parameters 's' and 't' are also reflected back to the actual parameters. The function inserts the data entry at the index 't+1' of the linear array. This is also the reason why the variable 'top' is initialized to -1 when it is being declared.

This process carries on as long as the number of data entries inserted is less than the maximum number of data entries allowed in the stack.

Function 'Pop'

```
void Pop(int s[],int &t)
{
  if (t!=-1)
  {
   cout<<endl<<" The data entry "<<s[t]<<" has been deleted";
   t--;
```

```
}
}
```

This function is used to delete or pop data entries from the static stack. It also receives the static array and the variable 'top' as reference parameters which are used to pop a data entry from the stack. This process can carry on as long as the stack has data entries in it or in other words as long as the value of 't' is not -1. The important thing to note in this function deletes only one data entry at a time and it always deletes the last data entry.

Function 'Display'

```
void display(int s[],int &t)
{
 cout<<endl<<"Displaying data entries in the stack";
 for (int i=t;i>=0;i--)
 cout<<endl<<s[i];
}
```

All this function does is that it prints all the data entries present in the stack on the screen.

2.3.2 Dynamic Stacks

Stacks which are implemented as arrays are very useful if we know the number of data entries from before, in other words they are useful when a fixed amount of data is to be accessed. To get an idea of this imagine a recursive loop. A menu driven stack program might be a good example. Now in this loop, we do not know how many times this loop might recur or how many data entries the user is willing to enter. The decision entirely rests on the user and might vary every time the program is executed. Using a stack represented as an array might be a poor solution as one will have to declare a very large block of memory so that there is no danger of the program running out of memory. This can waste a significant amount of computer's memory if the loop only repeats itself a few times during the execution of the program. How do we solve this problem?

In such a case, we have to use the concept of dynamic memory allocation. As stacks are represented as arrays, they can also be represented as pointers by creating a linked list with the use of which one can create 'Dynamic stacks', whose size can increase or decrease during the execution of the program.

Program 2.4 demonstrates a 'Dynamic Stack' with its various operations.

Program 2.4: Dynamic Stack

```
// Header Files
# include <iostream.h>
# include <conio.h>

/****************************
Self Referential Structure
Name: Node
Members: integer variable 'data'
      : pointer 'ptr' to type node
************************************/
struct node
{
  int data;
  node *ptr;
};

/*********************************************
Class: Stack
Private Members: top: pointer to type node
Public Members: void push()
                void pop()
                void display()
Constructor: stack()
Destructor: ~stack()
*******************************************/
class stack
{
  node *top;
  public:
  stack(){ top = NULL;}
  void push();
  void pop();
  void display();
  ~stack(){};
};

/***************************
Name: push
Parameters: None
Purpose: Insert data entry in to dynamic stack
**********************************************/
```

```
void stack::push()
{
 node *temp= new node;
 cout<<endl<<"Enter Value";
 cin>>temp->data;
 temp->ptr=top;
 top=temp;
}

/***************************
Name: pop
Parameters: None
Purpose: Delete data entry from dynamic stack
**********************************************/
void stack::pop()
{
 node *temp=top;
 if (temp != NULL)
  {
   cout<<endl<<top->data<<" Deleted";
   top=top->ptr;
   delete temp;
  }
 else
  {
  cout<<"\n The stack is empty";
  }
}

/***************************
Name: display
Parameters: None
Purpose: Display data entries of the dynamic stack
**********************************************,

void stack::display()
{
 node * temp= top;
 while (temp != NULL)
  {
  cout<<temp->data<<endl;
  temp=temp->ptr;
  }
}
```

```
/******************
Main Function
******************/
void main()
{
 clrscr();
 stack dynamic_stack;
 int choice;
 do
 {
  cout<<endl<<" 1. Push";
  cout<<endl<<" 2. Pop";
  cout<<endl<<" 3. Display";
  cout<<endl<<" 4. Exit"<<endl;
   cout<<"\n Enter Choice";
   cin>>choice;
  switch(choice)
   {
   case 1: dynamic_stack.push();
           break;
   case 2: dynamic_stack.pop();
           break;
   case 3: dynamic_stack.display();
           break;
   }
  } while (choice != 4);
  getch();
 }
```

Let us start from the very beginning of this program. At first, we have declared a self referential structure 'node' which contains an integer variable 'data' and a pointer variable 'ptr' of type 'node'. What we have done with this declaration is that we have created a pointer which can hold an address of structure variable of type 'node' as also shown in figure 2.20.

```
struct node
{
 int data;
node *ptr;
};
```

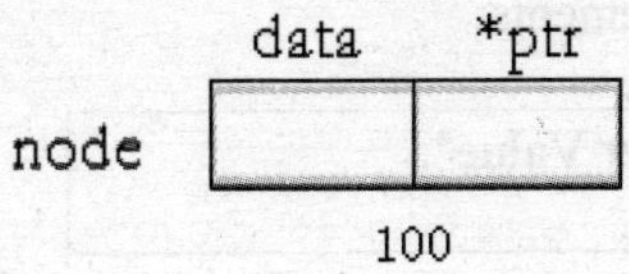

Figure 2.20: Self referential structure

Following the structure declaration, we have declared a class stack consisting of a pointer variable of type 'node' as its private member and contains 'push', 'pop' and 'display' as its public member functions. We will take up these functions in the next section of this chapter. The important thing to remember here is that whether one represents stacks as arrays or stacks as pointers it does not change the concept of 'stacks'.

2.3.2.1 Functions of a dynamic stack

- **The 'push' function**

```
   void stack::push()
{
 node *temp= new node;
 cout<<endl<<"Enter Value";
 cin>>temp->data;
 temp->ptr=top;
 top=temp;
}
```

When this function is called then a pointer variable 'temp' is declared pointing to type 'node'.

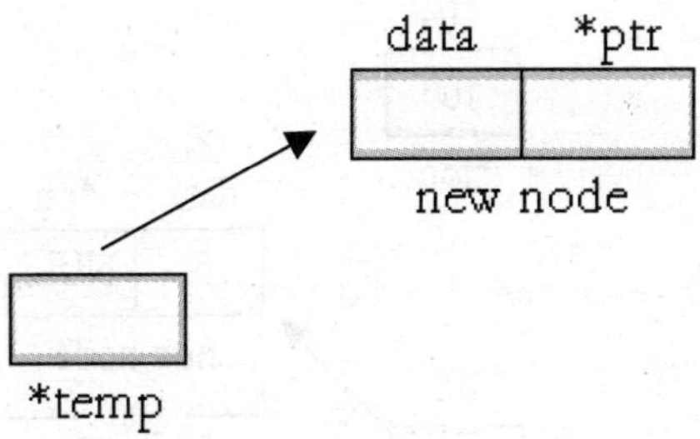

Figure 2.21: Pointer 'temp' of type 'node'

For understanding the concept, let us say we enter the data value '5' then how does this data entry get pushed on to the array?

To comprehend how insertion of a data entry takes place in a dynamic stack let us look at the following statements:

```
cout<<endl<<"Enter Value";
cin>>temp->data;
```

To begin with, we have stated 'cin>>temp->data', this statement is used to enter data entries into the 'data' part of the new node.

We can also visualize this by looking at the figure 2.22 assuming that the user enters '5' into the dynamic stack.

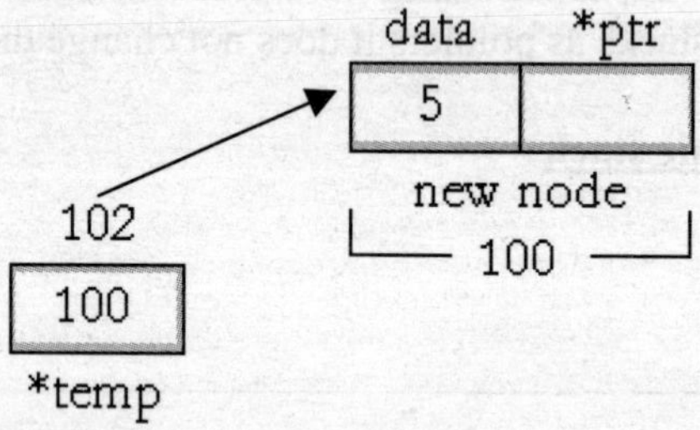

Figure 2.22: Insertion of a data entry in a node

In the next few statements, we have assigned the address 'NULL' stored in pointer variable 'top' initially to the pointer variable 'ptr' of the new node and then we have assigned the address stored in the pointer variable 'temp' to the pointer variable 'top'

```
temp->ptr=top;
 top=temp;
```

as shown in figure 2.23.

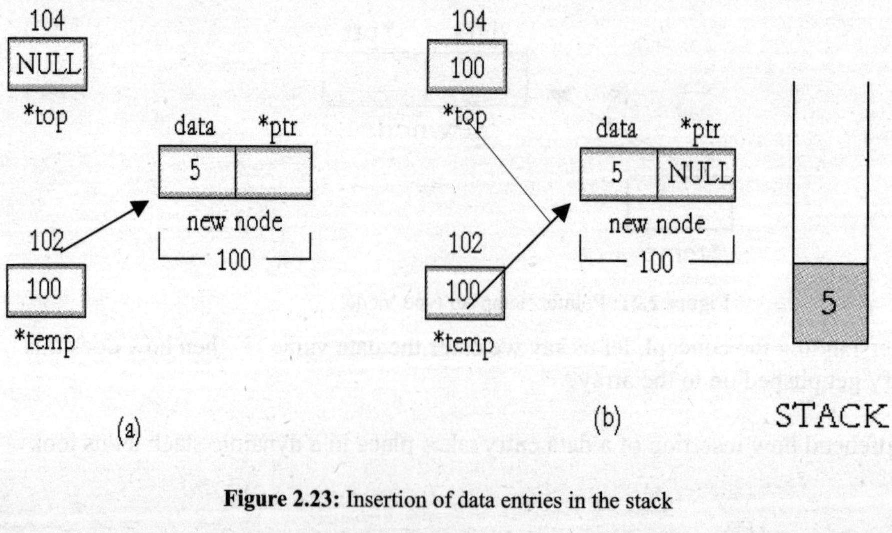

Figure 2.23: Insertion of data entries in the stack

Now what happens if we insert another data entry '10' into the stack?

To know how this works, we will again follow the same steps as we did when we pushed our first data entry into the stack.

The pointer 'temp' is again initialized pointing to a new memory block of type node in which the new data entry '10' (see figure 2.24) is entered into the stack.

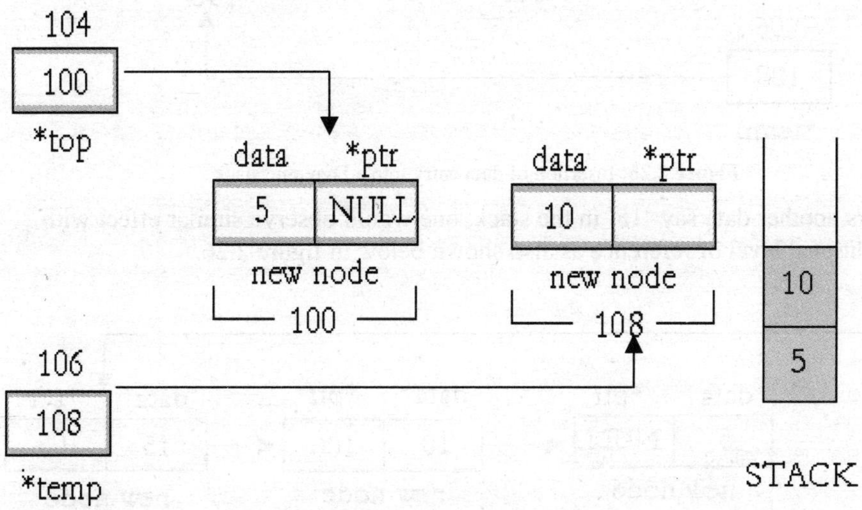

Figure 2.24: Insertion of data entry into the stack

Again, we execute the same set of statements given below which assign the address stored in the pointer 'top' to the pointer part of the new node and the address stored in pointer 'temp' to the pointer variable 'top'.

```
temp->ptr=top;
top=temp;
```

The only change one will observe with this data entry is that now the new node with the memory address '108' will start pointing to the preceding node with the memory address '100' (see figure 2.25).

LINKED LISTS

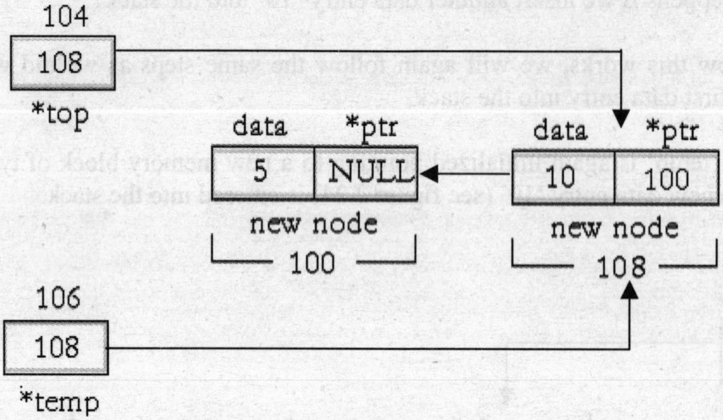

Figure 2.25: Insertion of data entry into a Dynamic stack

If one enters another data say '15' in the stack, one would observe similar effect with only an additional level of reference as also shown below in figure 2.26.

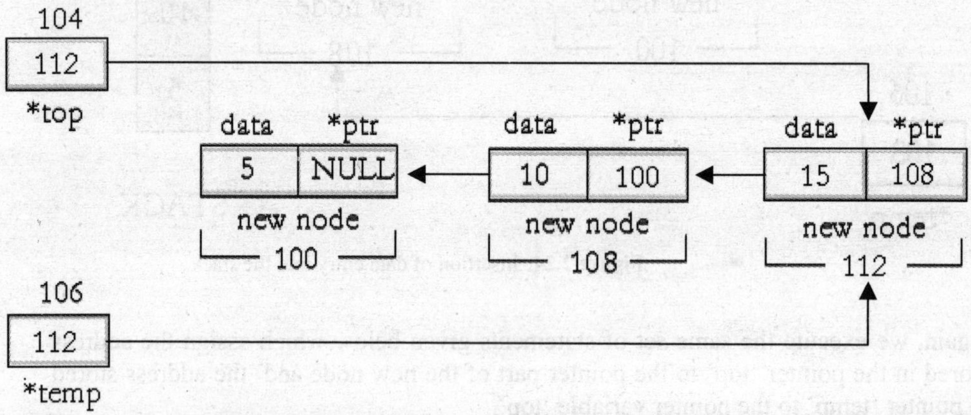

Figure 2.26: Insertion of data entry into a Dynamic stack

- **The 'pop' function**

```
void stack::pop()
{
 node *temp=top;
 if (temp != NULL)
 {
  cout<<endl<<top->data<<" Deleted";
  top=top->ptr;
  delete temp;
 }
 else
 {
```

```
   cout<<"\n The stack is empty";
  }
}
```

To understand the working of this function, we will carry on with the same link list which we created using our push function. So how does this function work?

When this function is called at first, this program creates a pointer variable 'temp' of type 'node' and assigns it the address of the latest data entry in the stack stored in the pointer variable 'top' to the last node or the last data entry. Let us now come back to the stack we created in the previous section with integers '5', '10', '15' as data entries. Say, now we want to pop a data entry then how does this work and how does the stack look like at each step?

The entire process of how a data entry is popped and how does the stack look like in each step is explained in the figure 2.27 given below:

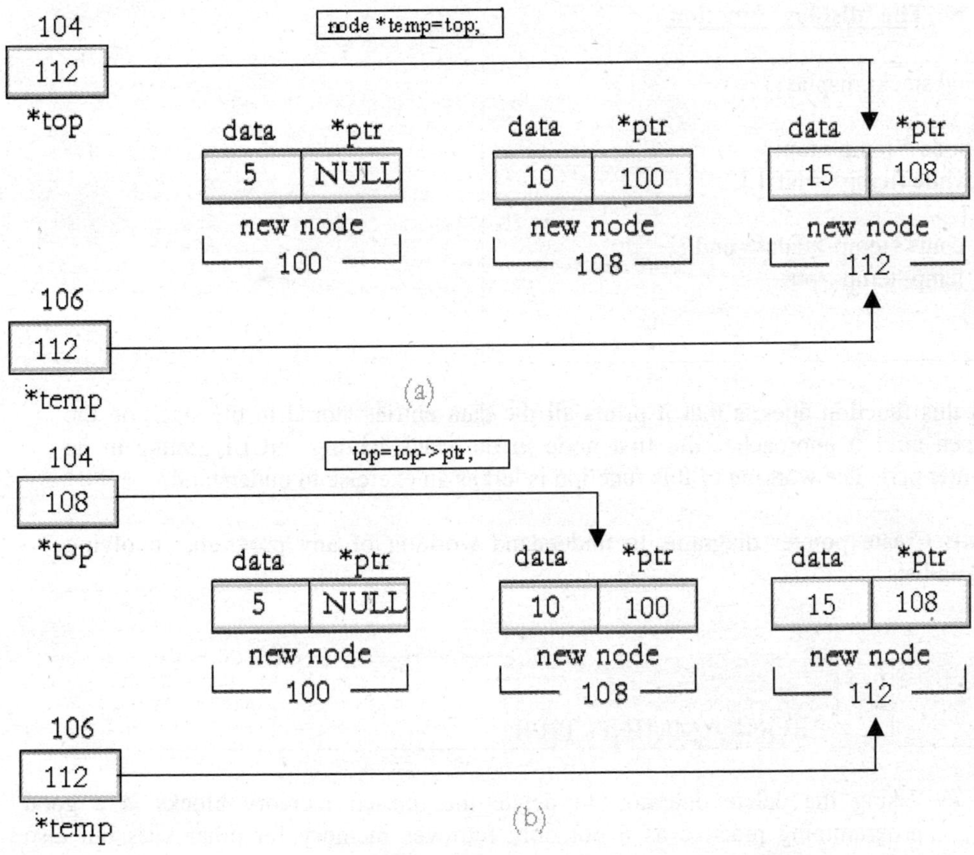

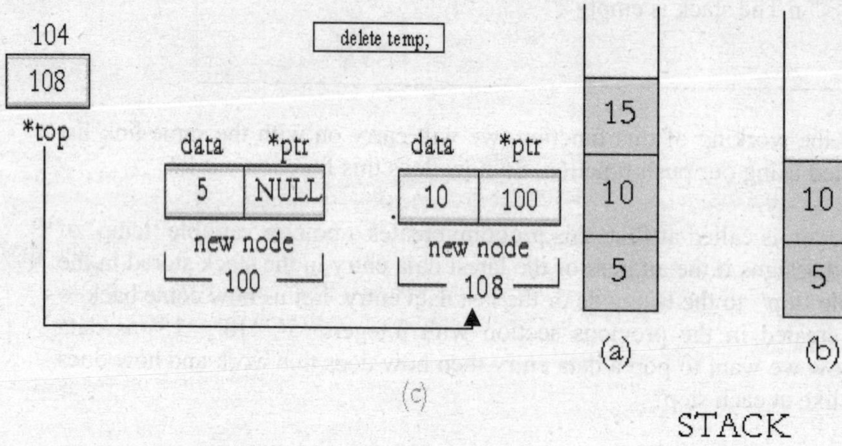

Figure 2.27: Popping of data entry from dynamic stack

- <u>**The 'display' function**</u>

```
void stack::display()
{
 node * temp= top;
 while (temp != NULL)
 {
  cout<<temp->data<<endl;
  temp=temp->ptr;
 }
}
```

All this function does is that it prints all the data entries stored in the stack on the screen until it approaches the first node in the stack having 'NULL' value in its pointer part. The working of this function is left as an exercise to understand?

Hint: Create pointer diagrams to understand working of any programs involving linked lists

PROGRAMMING TIPS

- Using the delete operator, to delete the unused memory blocks is a good programming practice as it not only retrieves memory for other uses but also reduces potential errors.
- Constructors should always be accompanied with destructors to save memory.

2.3.3 Uses of stacks

One might wonder where stacks are used in programming languages. One common use of stacks is for converting an infix expression to postfix and finding the value of an postfix expression but what does one mean by an infix or postfix expression?

An infix expression is an expression which we all have commonly observed in conventional algebra, for example '4+3', which is an expression representing the sum of two integers '4' and '3'. Infix expressions place their (binary) operators between the two values to which they apply. In the above example, the addition operator was placed between the '4' and the '3'. On the other hand, a post fix expression places each operator after the two operands to which it applies as its name might suggest as 'post' means after. So if we want to convert our infix statement '4+3' as a postfix statement it would become '4 3 +'. Figure 2.28 given below enlists few examples of 'Infix' and 'Postfix' operations.

Infix:	**Postfix:**
8 / 2	8 2 /
(8+7) * 2	8 7 + 2 *
(2+4)/(3+4)	2 4 +3 4 + /
8 * (5 + 4)	8 5 4 + *

Figure 2.28: Infix and Postfix expressions

The important thing to note in the table given above is that postfix expressions do not require () parenthesis for operations. Infix statements on the other hand require parenthesis to force certain order of evaluation.

At this point, it might be interesting to develop an algorithm for evaluating a postfix expression. Let's start with an empty stack. Whenever one observes a data entry, one uses the push function to push the data entries into the stack. On the other hand whenever an operator is observed, we pop the last two numbers say A and B. Then, we push the value obtained using the formula 'B operator A' on to the stack. This process should carry on as long as only one number is left which is popped out of the stack. That would be the result of the post fix operation provided one used a valid postfix expression.

Let's take up an example to understand the given algorithm better. Say, one wants to evaluate the post fix statement **'1 7 + 2 *'**.

All one needs to do is to follow the algorithm we developed, i.e., we push the first two data entries '1' and '7' into the stack. Now, once this is done we move to the next point in our postfix expression. This time we observe a '+' operator so we pop the last two data entries '7' and '1' where '7' would correspond to A and '1' would correspond to 'B' and we apply the formula 'B operator A', '1+7' to obtain the result as '8' which being a number is again pushed back into the stack as also shown in the figure 2.29.

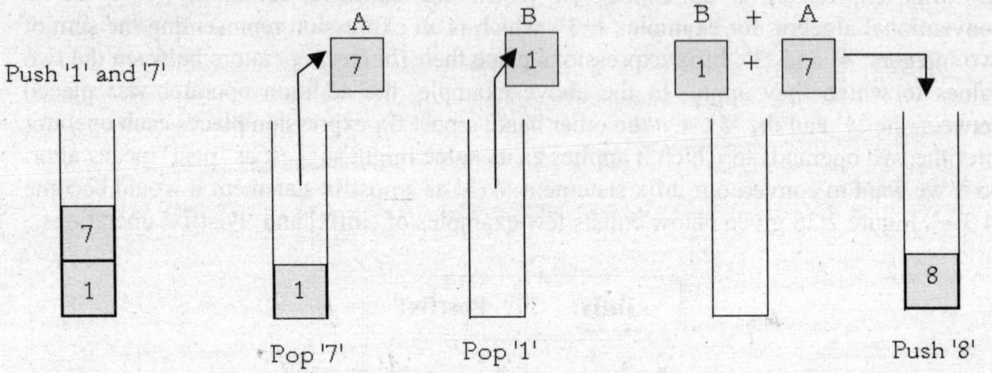

Figure 2.29: Postfix expression

Now we again move to the next point and observe the number '2' in the stack which is again pushed into the stack. Next, we observe the operator '*'. So we again pop the last two numbers '2' and '8' and obtain the result '16' using the formula 'B operator A'. Which is also the result of the postfix expression **'1 7 + 2 *'** (Figure 2.30).

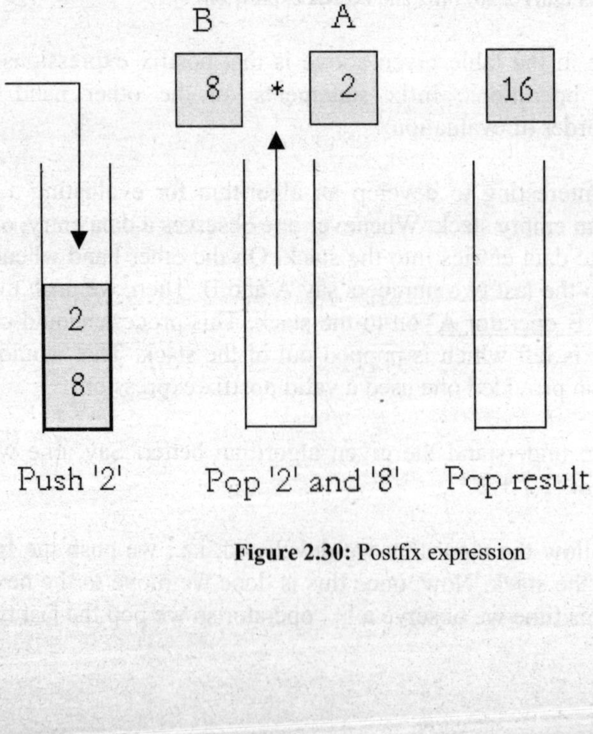

Figure 2.30: Postfix expression

COMMON PROGRAMMING ERRORS

- Not initializing a constructor to assign NULL values to starting pointers when declaring class stack for dynamic stacks might result in runtime errors
- Not using the correct order of parenthesis while solving infix to postfix problems will result in an error.

2.3.4 Solved Examples

Example 2.3.4.1

Write a function in C++ to perform the Push operation on a dynamically allocated stack containing real numbers.

Solution of 2.3.4.1

```
struct node
{
 float data
 node *link;
}

class stack()
{
 node *top;
 public:
 stack();
 void push();
 void pop();
};

void stack::push()
{
   node *temp;
   temp=new node;
   cin>>temp→data;
   temp→link=top;
   top=temp;
}
```

Example 2.3.4.2

Convert the expression given in infix form to postfix form:

A+B*C^D-(E/F – G)

Show the status of the stack after each step.

Solution of 2.3.4.2

STEP	INPUT	STACK STATUS	OUTPUT
-			
1.	A	EMPTY	A
2.	+	+	A
3.	B	+	AB
4.	*	+*	AB
5.	C	+*	ABC
6.	^	+*^	ABC
7.	D	+*^	ABCD
8.	-	+*	ABCD^
		+	ABCD^*
		EMPTY	ABCD^*+
		-	
9.	(	-(	ABCD^*+
10.	E	-(	ABCD^*+E
11.	/	-(/	ABCD^*+E
12.	F	-(/	ABCD^*+EF
13.	-	-(-	ABCD^*+EF/
14.	G	-(-	ABCD^*+EF/G
15.	)	-(-	ABCD^*+EF/G-
16.		EMPTY	ABCD^*+EF/G-

Example 2.3.4.3

Evaluate the following postfix expression using stack and show the contents of the stack after execution of each step.

50, 40, +, 18, 14, -, 4, *,+

Solution of 2.3.4.3

STEP	INPUT	STACK STATUS
1.	50	50
2.	40	40
3.	+	40 is popped 50 is popped Empty 90
4.	18	90 18
5.	14	90 18 14
6.	-	14 is popped 18 is popped 90 90 4
7.	4	90 4 4
8.	*	90 4 90 90 16
9.	+	90 Empty 106
10. End of Input		EMPTY
Result		106

2.4 Link Lists as Queues

A queue is an example of an abstract data type structure similar to a stack. The difference being that the first data element to be inserted is the first to be removed which can be abbreviated as FIFO (first in, first out) or LILO (last in, last out). Thus, items are removed from the queue in the very same order in which they were put into the queue in the first place. A queue is a homogeneous collection of elements in which placing of data elements is called as 'insertion or enqueue' which is done at the end of the list called the 'rear' and 'deletion or dequeue' is done at the other opposite end known as the 'front'. The figure 2.31 given below shows various features present in a queue.

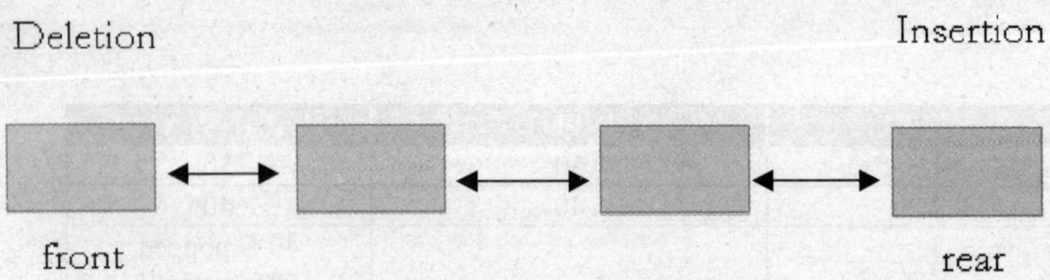

Figure 2.31: An empty Queue

One of the major applications of queue is to create job queues for 'job scheduling' by an equal-priority operating system. A job queue has the following features:

- Jobs present in a job queue are processed in order they enter the system;
- To delete later jobs, one has to delete previous jobs first; and
- As jobs enter and leave the system, the queue gradually shifts to the right.

An example of 'job scheduling' can be observed when we command computer say, to print 4 articles stored in the computers memory then the computer prints them by first creating a job queue having the jobs assigned to it and then it uses the above defined features of 'job scheduling' to complete each job individually.

2.4.1 Static Circular Queues

Queues can also be implemented as one dimensional arrays known as 'Static circular' Queues. 'Static' queues have a fixed amount of data which can be entered into them and generally used when we know how much space the data would occupy. 'Static' queues are created by declaring a linear one dimensional array in which insertion or 'enqueue' of data is allowed from a single location known as the 'Rear' and deletion or 'dequeue' of data elements is allowed only from one single location known as the 'Front'. Let us take an example of a static queue by declaring an array 'static_queue' (shown in figure 2.32) which can store 5 integer data values.

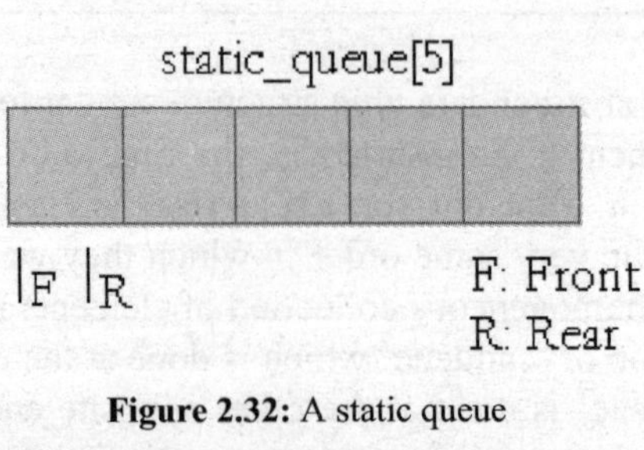

Figure 2.32: A static queue

One of the important things to note from the figure above is that in an empty queue both the 'Front' and the 'Rear' ends of the queue share the same memory address or point to the same index of the array. Let us now observe, what happens if we insert a data entry say '5' into the queue?

As we have learnt before that in a queue all the data insertions takes place from the 'Rear' end so the data entry '5' is assigned to the 1st index of the array 'static_queue[]' (see Figure 2.33), which is the index the 'Rear' end points to. At this point, one might wonder, why is the data entry added to the 1st index of the array and not to the zero th index of the array? This question will be answered later in this section. For now just try to understand how stacks work.

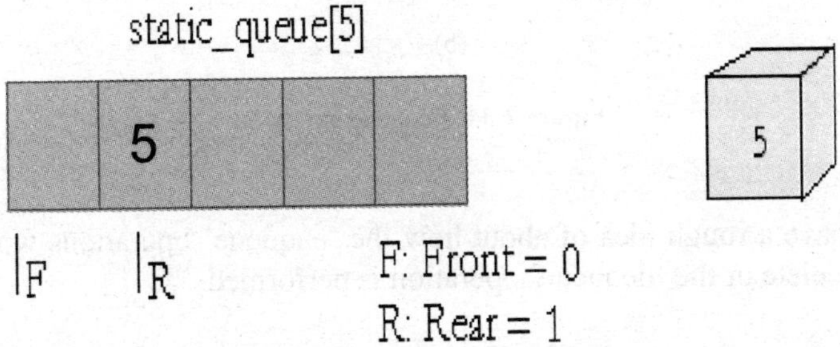

Figure 2.33: Insertion of a data element in a queue

We can further use this operation to enter more data entries like '10' and '15' in the queue. Figure 2.34 shows the effect of this operation on the queue.

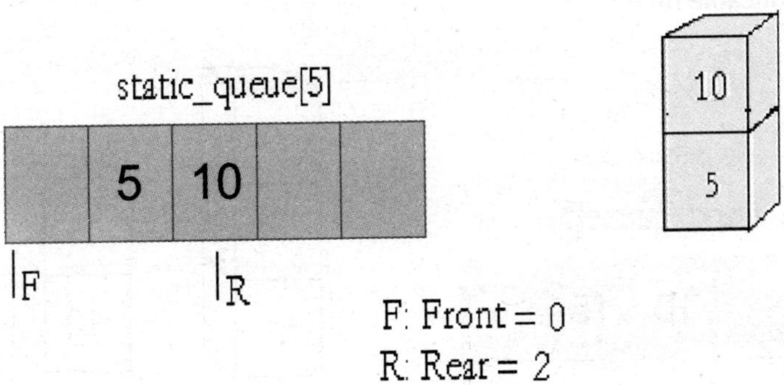

(a)

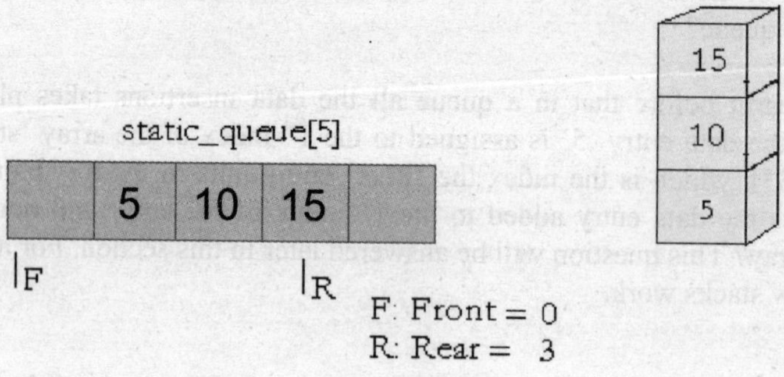

(b)

Figure 2.34: Enqueue operation

Now that we have a rough idea of about how the 'enqueue' operations work, let us now learn how the delete or the 'dequeue' operation is performed.

For explaining the working of this function, we will take the same queue we created in figure 2.34. If we recall queues are FIFO structures, so when this operation is executed the position 'Front' starts pointing to 1st index of the array and the data entry '5' is deleted (see figure 2.35). Similarly, if we apply this operation again then the position 'Front' starts directing to the 2nd data entry and then the data entry '10' is dequeued. How these operations exactly work and what role is played by the position variables 'front' and 'rear' during both operations 'queue' and 'dequeue' is explained in the program 2.5 given below, which declares and uses a dynamic circular queue with all the above operations applicable on it.

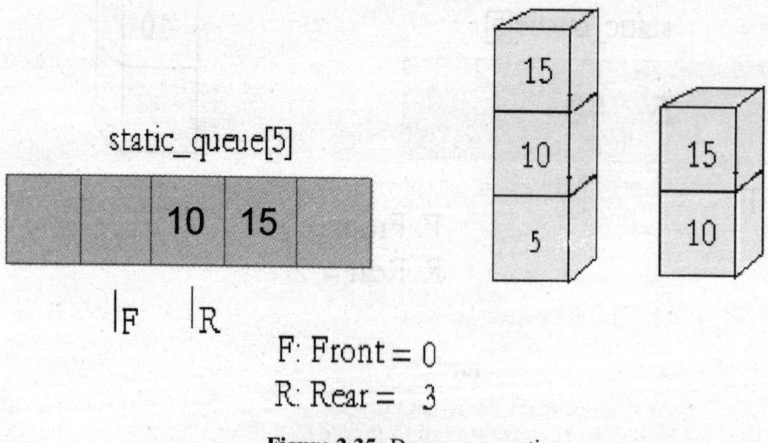

Figure 2.35: Dequeue operation

Program 2.5: Static circular queue

```
/***********************
Program 2.5
Static Circular Queue
***********************
/* Header Files */
# include <iostream.h>
# include <conio.h>

const int max=10;

/*******************
Name: qinsert
Return Type: void
Purpose: To enter data into the queue
*************************************/
void qinsert (int q[], int &r, int f)
{
 if ((r+1)%max != f);
  {
  r = (r+1)%max;
  cout<<"\n Data";
  cin>>q[r];
  cout<<"\n Data has been entered";
  }
}

/*******************
Name: qinsert

Return Type: void
Purpose: To delete data from the queue
*************************************/
void qdelete( int q[], int r, int &f)
{
 if (r!=f)
 {
  f=(f+1)%max;
  cout<<endl<<q[f]<<"has been Deleted\n";
 }
 else
 {
```

```
 cout<<" Queue is empty \n"<<endl;
 }
}


/*******************
Name: qdisplay
Return Type: void
Purpose: To display the contents of the queue
**********************************************/
void qdisplay(int q[], int r, int f)
{
 int cn=f;
 cout<<"\n Displaying the contents of the queue \n";
 while (cn!=r)
  {
  cn = (cn+1)%max;
  cout<< q[cn]<<endl;
  }
}

// Main Function
void main()
{
 clrscr();
 // Initialization steps
 int queue[max], rear=0, front=0;
 int ch;
 do
  {
  cout<<"\n === MENU ===";
  cout<<"\n 1: Insert\n";
  cout<<" 2: Delete\n";
  cout<<" 3: Show\n";
  cout<<" 4: Quit\n";
  cout<<" !: Enter choice";
  cin>>ch;
  switch(ch)
   {
   case 1: qinsert(queue,rear,front);
           break;

   case 2: qdelete(queue,rear,front);
           break;
```

```
case 3: qdisplay(queue,rear,front);
        break;
  }
}
while (ch != 4);
getch();
}
```

Let us closely observe this program. In this program, we have declared a one dimensional array 'queue' which can hold 10 integer data values represented by the constant variable 'max' in the program. We have also declared two integer variables 'rear' and 'front' which are position variables. The variable 'rear' is the position variable which directs to the index of the array from where all the data entries are inserted and the other position variable 'front' directs to the index of the array from where all the dequeue operation is executed. This program also consists of the following functions to insert, delete and display the contents of the queue:

Function 'qinsert'

```
void qinsert (int q[], int &r, int f)
{
if ((r+1)%max != f);
 {
 r = (r+1)%max;
 cout<<"\n Data";
 cin>>q[r];
 cout<<"\n Data has been entered";
 }
}
```

This function is used to insert data entries into the queue. The function receives the linear array 'queue', position variable 'front' as variable parameters and the position variable 'rear' as a reference parameter which are represented by 'q', 'f' and 'r' in the function. The function inserts the data entry at the index 'r' of the linear array provided the position variable 'r' and 'f' do not direct to the same index of the array or in other words it enters data in the queue until the queue is full. Let us take an example, say this function is called for the first time by the program to enter the first data entry then the expression '(r+1)%max' would yield the value '1' which is not equal to 'f' as 'f' was initialized to '0' and hence the program would enter the 'if' loop. In the 'if' loop the function would insert the data entered by the user at '(r+1)%max' index of the array, which happens to be the 1st index of the array.

Function 'qdelete'

```
void qdelete( int q[], int r, int &f)
{
if (r!=f)
{
f=(f+1)%max;
cout<<endl<<q[f]<<"has been Deleted\n";
}
else
{
cout<<" Queue is empty \n"<<endl;
}
}
```

This function is used to delete or pop data entries from the static queue. It receives the static array 'queue', the position variable 'rear' as variable parameters and the other position variable 'front' as a reference parameter. The entries are deleted or dequeued until the queue is not empty which is performed by the if condition 'r!=f'. To delete data entries the position variable 'front' represented by the formal parameter 'f' in the function is incremented by unity every time the program enters the if loop deleting the entry at this index of the array. Let us analyze figure 2.36.

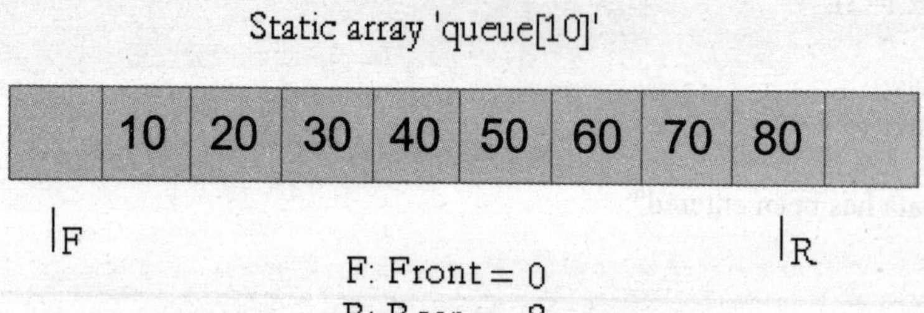

Figure 2.36: static array queue[]

Assume this is the state of the static array 'queue' when this function is called for the first time by the program. First, before entering the 'if' loop it will check for equality between position variables 'f' and 'r'. As 'f=0' is not equal to 'r=8' it will enter the 'if' conditional loop. After it enters the 'if' conditional loop, the position variable 'f' is assigned the value of ((f+1)%max, (0+1)%10=1) deleting the data entry '10' at this index of the static array.

Function 'qdisplay'

```
void qdisplay(int q[], int r, int f)
{
int cn=f;
```

```
cout<<"\n Displaying the contents of the queue \n";
while (cn!=r)
{
 cn = (cn+1)%max;
 cout<< q[cn]<<endl;
 }
}
```

All this function does is that it prints all the data entries present in the queue on the screen.

2.4.2 Dynamic Queue

The concept of dynamic queues is similar to that of dynamic stacks. As queues can be represented as arrays they can also be represented with the use of pointers by creating a link list. Dynamic queues overcome the limitations present with static circular queues as they can grow and shrink during program execution, thus, save memory. Program 2.6 implements a 'Dynamic Queue'.

Program 2.6: Dynamic Queue

```
/**************************
Program
Dynamic Queue
**************************/

/* Header Files */
# include <iostream.h>
# include <conio.h>

/**************************
Self referencial structure
Name: node
Members: 'data' of type integer
          : 'next' of type node
********************************/

struct node
{
 int data;
 node *next;
};

/*****************************
Name: queue
```

```
Members: Private members: Pointer 'rear' of type queue
                          Pointer 'front' of type queue
         Public members:  Constructor Function queue()
                          Function qinsert()
                          Function qdelete()
                          Function qdisplay()
                          Destructor Function queue
*********************************************************/
class queue
{
 node *rear, *front;
 public:
 queue() {
          rear = NULL;
          front = NULL;
         }
 void qinsert();
 void qdelete();
 void qdisplay();
 ~queue();
};

/**********************
Name: qinsert
Parameters: None
Return Type: void
Purpose: To enter data entries into the queue
**********************************************/
void queue::qinsert()
{
 node *temp;
 temp = new node;
 cout<<"\n Data:";
 cin>>temp->data;
 cout<<" Data has been entered \n\n";
 temp->next=NULL;
 if (rear == NULL)
 {
  rear = temp;
  front = temp;
 }
 else
 {
  rear->next = temp;
  rear = temp;
```

```
}
}

/**********************
Name: qdelete
Parameters: None
Return Type: void
Purpose: To delete data entries from the queue
**********************************************/
void queue::qdelete()
{
 if (front !=NULL)
 {
  node *temp=front;
  cout<<endl<<front->data<<" has been Deleted \n";
  front = front ->next;
  delete temp;
  if (front==NULL)
  {
   rear = NULL;
  }
 }
  else
  {
   cout<<" Queue is Empty \n";
  }

 }


/**********************
Name: qdisplay
Parameters: None
Return Type: void
Purpose: To display the data entries of the queue
***********************************************/
void queue::qdisplay()
{
 cout<<"\nDisplaying Queue............... \n";

 node *temp=front;
 while (temp != NULL)
 {
  cout<<temp->data<<endl;
  temp= temp ->next;
```

```
}
}

/*********************
Destructor Function
Name:queue
Parameters: None
Return Type: void
Purpose: To free the memory allocated to nodes of the queue
***********************************************************/
queue::~queue()
 {
 while (front != NULL)
 {
  node *temp = front;
  front = front ->next;
  }
 }

/* Main Function */
void main()
{
 clrscr();
 queue q1;
 int choice;
 do
 {
 cout<<"\n $$$ MENU $$$\n";
 cout<<"1. Push \n";
 cout<<"2. Pop \n";
 cout<<"3. Display \n";
 cout<<"4. Quit \n";
 cout<<"!  Enter Choice ";
 cin>>choice;
 switch(choice)
   {
   case 1:
          q1.qinsert();
          break;
   case 2:
          q1.qdelete();
          break;
   case 3:
          q1.qdisplay();
```

```
        break;
    }
}
while (choice != 4);
getch();
}
```

Let us commence from the beginning of this program. At first, we have declared a self referential structure 'node' which contains an integer variable 'data' and a pointer variable 'next' of type 'node'. Which means that this pointer can hold an address of a structure variable of type 'node'? It might become more obvious if we glance at figure 2.37.

```
struct node
{
 int data;
node *next;
};
```

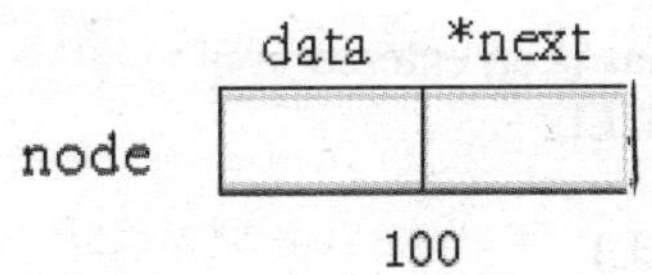

Figure 2.37: Self referential structure

After this we have declared a class 'queue'. Which consists of two pointer variables 'rear' and 'front' of type 'node' as its private members and contains 'qinsert', 'qdelete' and 'qdisplay' as its public member functions. We will take up these functions in the next section.

```
class queue
{
 node *rear, *front;
 public:
 queue(){
          rear = NULL;
          front = NULL;
          }
 void qinsert();
 void qdelete();
 void qdisplay();
 ~queue();
};
```

One may note that we have used a constructor to assign the pointer variables 'rear' and 'front' default values of 'NULL' to prevent errors from garbage values and a destructor to free up the memory assigned to the memory blocks created by the queue. The important thing to remember here is that whether one represents queues as arrays or queues as pointers, the operation of 'queues' remains same.

2.4.2.1 Functions of a dynamic queue

- **The 'qinsert' function**

```
void queue::qinsert()
{
node *temp;
temp = new node;

cout<<"\n Data:";
cin>>temp->data;
cout<<" Data has been entered \n\n";
temp->next=NULL;

if (rear == NULL)
        {
          rear = temp;
          front = temp;
        }
        else
          {
            rear->next = temp;
            rear = temp;
          }
}
```

When this function is called then a pointer variable 'temp' is declared pointing to type 'node'.

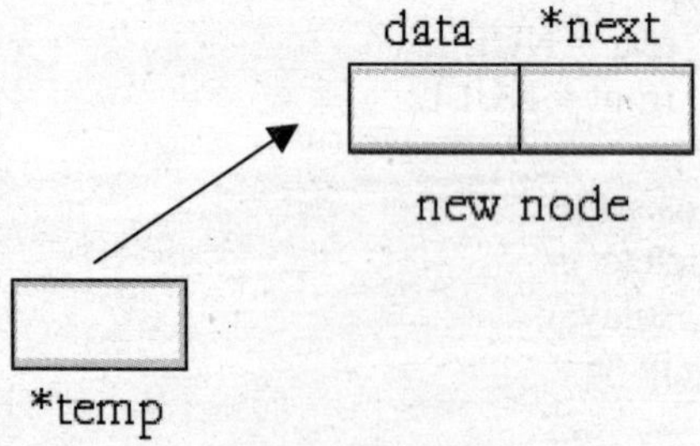

Figure 2.38: Self referential structure

For understanding the concept let us say we enter the data value '5' then how does this data entry get pushed on to the queue?

To understand how insertion of a data entry takes place in a dynamic queue look at the following statements.

```
cout<<"\n Data:";
cin>>temp->data;
```

'cin>>temp->data', this statement is used to enter data entries into the 'data' part of the new node. We can also understand this by looking at the figure 2.39 assuming that the user enters '5' into the dynamic queue.

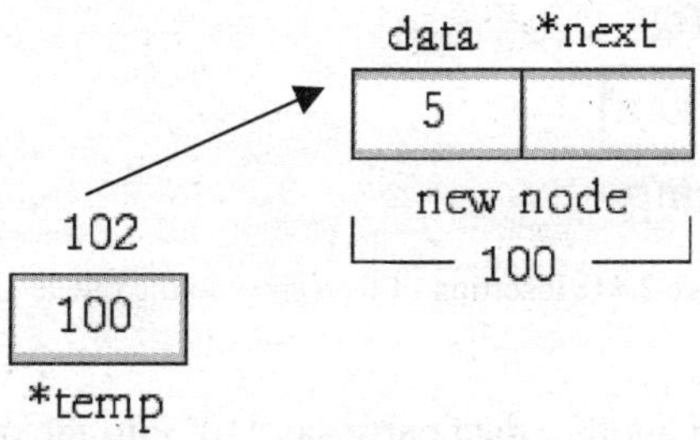

Figure 2.39: Insertion of data entry into the queue

In the subsequent statements, we have assigned the address 'NULL' to the pointer part of the new node (see figure 2.40).

```
cout<<" Data has been entered \n\n";
 temp->next=NULL;
```

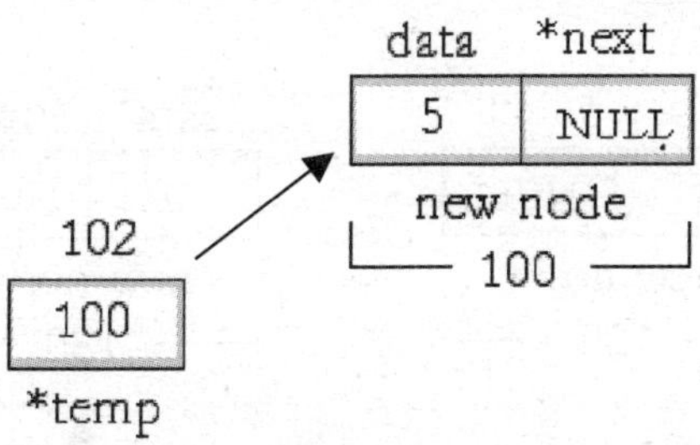

Figure 2.40: Insertion of data entry in the queue

Once this is done, we enter the if loop as 'rear' has been initialized to the NULL and in the if loop the pointer variables 'rear' and 'front' are also assigned the address stored in the pointer variable 'temp' as a result of which they too start pointing to the same memory location (see figure 2.41) as pointer variable 'temp'.

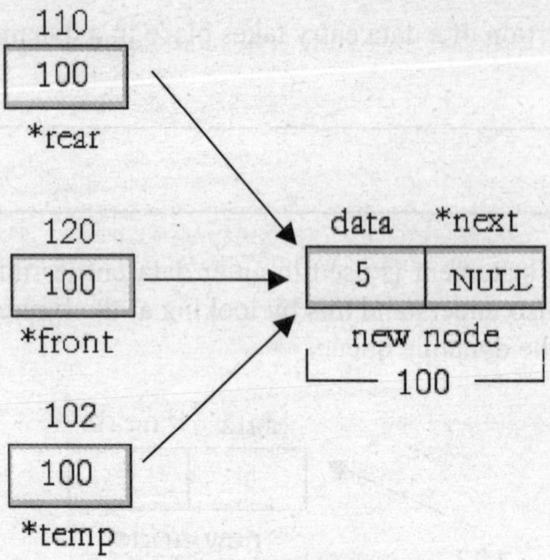

Figure 2.41: Insertion of data entry in the queue

Now what happens if we insert another data entry say '10' into the queue?

We will follow the same steps as we followed to enter our first data '5'. The pointer 'temp' is again initialized pointing to a new memory block of type node in which the new data entry '10' is entered into the data part of this node and the pointer part of the node is assigned a NULL value (see figure 2.42)

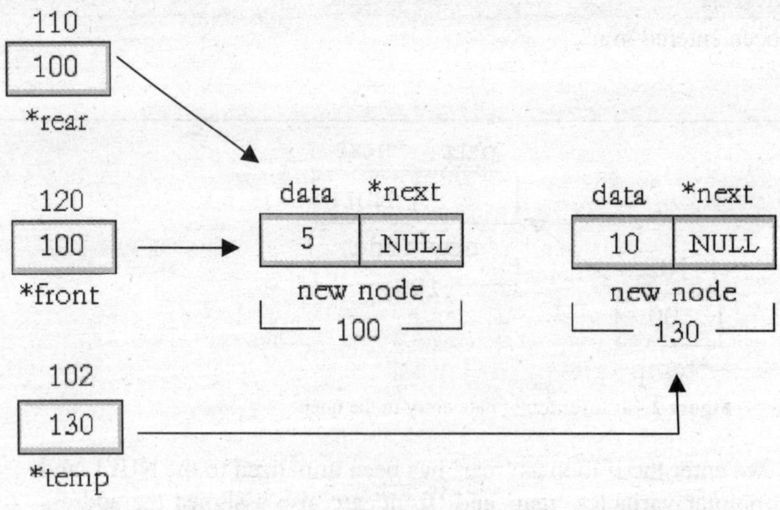

Figure 2.42: Insertion of data entries in the queue

The only difference is that the program would not enter the 'if' loop as the initial condition 'rear==NULL' will not be satisfied and instead the following statements will be executed resulting in assigning the pointer part of the node to the address of the new node we just created and then finally assigning the pointer variable 'rear' the address stored in the variable 'temp' (see figure 2.43).

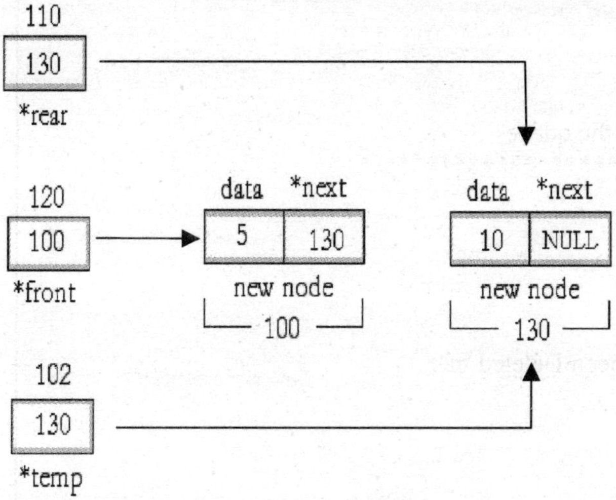

Figure 2.43: Insertion of data entry in the queue

Using the same concept function 'push' can be used again and again to enter many more data entries. Figure 2.4 shows the state of the queue once we have inserted the data entries '15'and '20' in the queue.

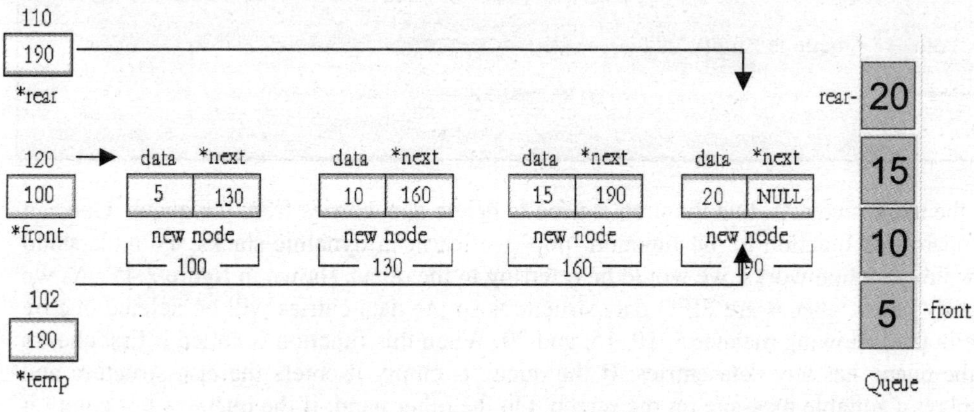

Figure 2.44: Insertion of data entries in the queue

- **The 'qdelete' function**

```
/**********************
Name: qdelete
Parameters: None
Return Type: void
Purpose: To delete data entries from the queue
*********************************************/
void queue::qdelete()
{
 if (front !=NULL)
 {
  node *temp=front;
  cout<<endl<<front->data<<" has been Deleted \n";

  front = front ->next;
  delete temp;

  if (front==NULL)
  {
    rear = NULL;
  }

 }

   else
   {
    cout<<" Queue is Empty \n";
   }
 }
```

As the name suggests, this function is used to delete data entries from the queue. One can compare this function to the function 'pop' we learnt in dynamic stacks. To understand how this function works, we would be referring to the queue shown in figure 2.45. As we already know, queues are FIFO data structures so the data entries will be deleted one by one in the following manner 5, 10, 15, and 20. When this function is called it first checks if the queue has any data entries. If the queue is empty it enters the else structure and displays a suitable message on the screen. On the other hand, if the queue is not empty it enters the 'if' control structure.

In this control structure we declare a pointer variable 'temp' and assign it the address stored in the pointer variable 'front'.

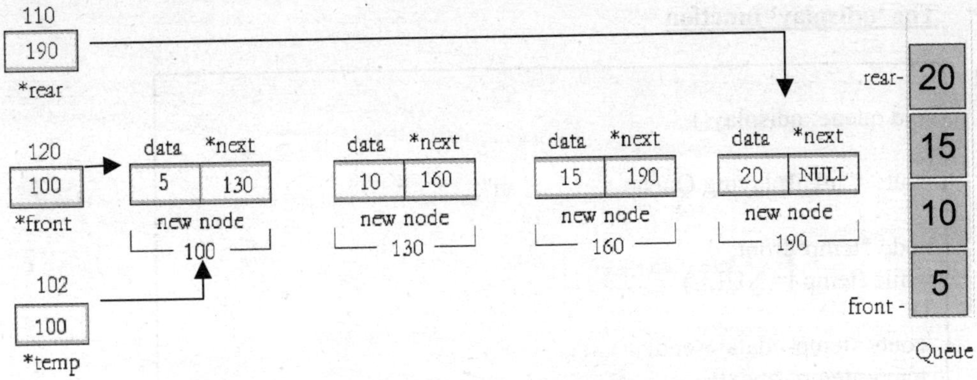

Figure 2.45: Deleting data entries from a queue

Using the next few statements, the function deletes the node to which both the pointer variables 'front' and 'temp' point to, but before deleting this node from the queue the pointer variable 'front' is assigned the value stored in the pointer part of the node to which it was pointing to as a result of which it starts pointing to the next adjacent node.

```
node *temp=front;
cout<<endl<<front->data<<" has been Deleted \n";
front = front ->next;
delete temp;
```

The important thing to remember is that in this entire process, we do not delete the 'new node' we just delete the link to this memory location by deleting the pointer variable 'temp' which we created in the 'if' structure. The outcome of these statements is also shown in the figure 2.46.

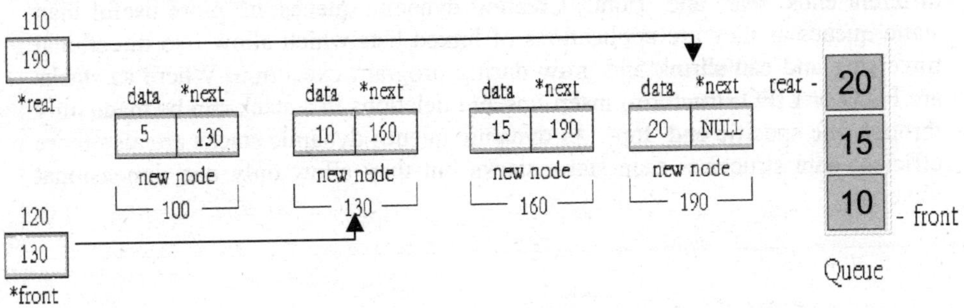

Figure 2.46: Deletion of data entries from the queue

- **The 'qdisplay' function**

```
void queue::qdisplay()
{
cout<<"\nDisplaying Queue............... \n";

node *temp=front;
while (temp != NULL)
 {
 cout<<temp->data<<endl;
 temp= temp ->next;
 }
}
```

This function is used to display the data entries present in the queue. It works on the logic that each node in the queue points to the next adjacent node. Using the address of the node to which the pointer variable 'front' points to, as the starting point, the while loop is repeated displaying the data entries in each node till the temporary pointer variable 'temp' reaches the node having a NULL address stored its pointer part, which happens to be the last node or the last entry in the queue. The exact working of this function though is left to the reader as an exercise.

PROGRAMMING TIPS

- The major difference between stacks and queues is the fact that queues are LILO or FIFO structures and there practical applications lie in creating job queues for job scheduling problems. Insertions and deletions in it are made from two different ends 'rear' and 'front'. Creating dynamic queues are more useful than static queues as they are applications of linked lists which allow two directional traversing and can shrink and grow during program execution. Where as stacks are FILO or LIFO structures, insertions and deletions in a stack can be made only through one specific end 'top'. As dynamic queues dynamic stacks are also more efficient data structures than static stacks but they allow only one dimensional traversing.

2.4.2.2 Solved examples

Example 2.4.2.2.1

Give the necessary declarations for a linked implementation queue containing float values. Write a function insert() to add an element to this queue?

Solution of 2.4.2.2.1

```
struct node
{
 float data;
 node *next;
};

class queue
{
 node *rear, *front;

 public:

          queue() {
                    rear = NULL;
                    front = NULL;
                  }

          void qinsert();
          ~queue();
};

void queue::qinsert()
{
 node *temp=new node;

 cout<<"Data:";

 cin>>temp->data;

 temp->next = NULL;

 if (rear == NULL)
 {
  rear = temp;
  front =temp;
 }
```

```
else
{
 rear->next=temp;
 rear=temp;
 }
}
```

Example 2.4.2.2.2

Write a function in C++ to perform insert operation on dynamically allocated queue containing names of students.

```
struct node
{
 char name[20];
 node *link;
};

class queue
{
 node *rear,*front;
 public:
 queue();
 void insert();
 void delete();
};
void queue::insert()
{
 node *temp;
 temp = new node;
 gets(temp->name);
 temp->link=NULL;
 if (front==NULL)
 {
  rear = temp;
  front =temp;
 }
 else
 {
  rear->link=temp;
  rear=temp;
 }
}
```

2.5 Solved Examples

Example 2.5.1

Evaluate the following postfix notation of expression:

True, False, AND, True, True, NOT, OR, AND

Solution of 2.5.1

Example 2.5.2
Evaluate the following postfix notation of expression:

20, 30, +, 50, 40, -, *

Solution of 2.5.2

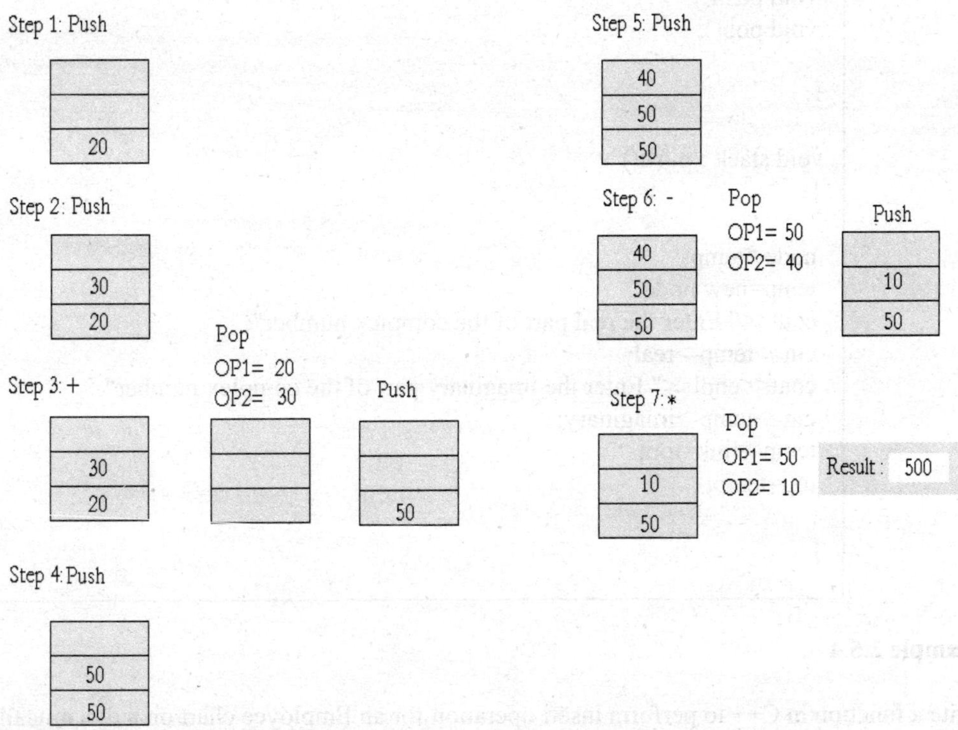

Example 2.5.3
Write a function in C++ to perform push operation on a dynamically allocated stack containing complex numbers?

Solution of 2.5.3

```
struct node
{
int real;
int imaginary;
node *link;
};

class stack
{

 node *top;
 public:
 stack();
 void push();
 void pop();

};

void stack ::push()
{

 node *temp;
 temp=new node;
 cout<<" Enter the real part of the complex number";
 cin>>temp->real;
 cout<<endl<<" Enter the imaginary part of the complex number";
 cin>>temp->imaginary;
 temp->link=top;
 top=temp;

}
```

Example 2.5.4

Write a function in C++ to perform insert operation for an Employee chart on a dynamically allocated queue using the following structure:

```
struct node
 {
   char Emp_name[20];
   int Emp_code;
   int Emp_basic;
   node *link;
 };
```

Solution of 2.5.4

```
# include<iostream.h>
# include<conio.h>
# include<stdio.h>

struct node
{
 char Emp_name[20];
 int Emp_code;
 int Emp_basic;
 node *link;
};

class queue
{
 node *rear,*front;

 public:
 queue();
 void insert();
 void delete();
};

void queue::insert()
{
 node *temp;
 temp = new node;
 cout<<" Enter Employee Name";
 gets(temp->Emp_name);
 cout<<endl<<" Enter Employee Code";
 cin>>temp->Emp_code;
 cout<<endl<<" Enter Basic Salary";
 cin>>temp->Emp_basic;
 temp->link=NULL;
 if (front==NULL)
```

```
{
rear = temp;
front =temp;
}
else
{
rear->link=temp;
rear=temp;
}
}
```

2.6 Review Exercise

1/2 Mark Questions

1 Mark/ 2 Mark

Q1) A self referential structure
  a) holds the address of a structure.
  b) references address of a structure.
  c) is an example of a pointer to a pointer.
  d) both a and b are correct.
  e) none of the above

Q2) A link list is
  a) a collection of self referential structures each representing a node.
  b) a collection of a list of pointers.
  c) an example of a primitive data structure.
  d) both a and c are correct
  e) none of the above

Q3) Stack is an example of
  a) FILO data structure
  b) LILO data structure
  c) LIFO data structure
  d) Both a and c are correct
  e) None of the above

Q4) The difference between a stack and a queue is
  a) Stack is a LIFO structure where as queue is an FILO structure
  b) Stack is a FILO structure where as queue is an LILO data structure
  c) Stacks are one directional data structures where as queues are multi directional
  d) Both a, b and c are correct
  e) None of the above

Q5) A circular link list is an example of a link list
  a) in which no node contains a NULL value in its pointer part.
  b) which are always one directional.
  c) having no head or tail.
  d) both a and b are correct.
  e) both c and b are correct.

Q6) What are the various advantages of using dynamic data structures over traditional static data structures?

Q7) Represent the following infix statements in postfix form:

(182+9) / 2
((10*7) * 2)/4
(3+4)/(3*2)
8 % (5 + 4)

Q8) What are the various differences between a linked list and a stack?

Q9) Evaluate the following postfix notation of expressions:
  a) False, True, And, False, False, Not, And, And
  b) True, False, False, Or, And, True, Not, Or
  c) 40,50,+, 60,90,-,*

Q10) Write a function in C++ to perform the display operation on a dynamically allocated stack containing real numbers.

3 Mark/ 4 Mark

Q11) Create a link list which inputs a set of 10 strings and copies them to another link list with all the strings reversed.

Q12) Write a function in C++ to perform the 'push' and the 'pop' function for creating a circular static stack?

Q13) Write a program to insert and delete nodes in an already existing link list using the following node.

```
struct node
nt data;
node &ptr;
} ;
```

Q14) Create a menu driven program to 'create' a link list using the structure given below. The program should also 'display' and 'sort' the link list in ascending order of the structure member 'Emp_Basic'.

```
struct node
{
    char Emp_Name[20];
    int Emp_No;
    int Emp_Basic;
    node *ptr;
};
```

Q15) Create two link lists storing integers say 'A' and B', once this is done write a function merge to which these link lists 'A' and 'B' are passed to it as parameters. This function should merge these two link lists 'A' and 'B' and produce a third linked 'C' sorted in ascending order of integers.

Q16) Write a function in C++ to perform insert and delete operation on a dynamically allocated queue using the following structure.

```
struct node
{
    char Book_Name[20];
    char Book_Author[20];
    int Book_Price;
    node Book_ptr;
};
```

Q17) Given the following structure of a node that represents a clinic in a dynamic stack.

```
struct clinic
{
    char bednumber[10];
    char patientname[20];
    char disease[30];
    char doc_attending[20];
    int patientno;
```

```
        clinic *nextclinic;
    };
```

Define a class 'clinicstack' that shall have functions to push a clinic into a stack of clinics, pop out a clinic from the stack of clinics and display the names of all the patients ('patientname') with there patient numbers ('patientno') on the screen.

5 Mark

Q18) Write a program to create a dynamic circular queue using the following structure.

```
struct node
    {
     int data;
     node *ptr;
    };
```

The queue should allow the user to enter data entries and also delete data entries. The program should also include functions to sort the nodes of the queue in ascending and descending order of integers ('data') entered into them.
Hint: The hint lies in figure 2.47 given below.

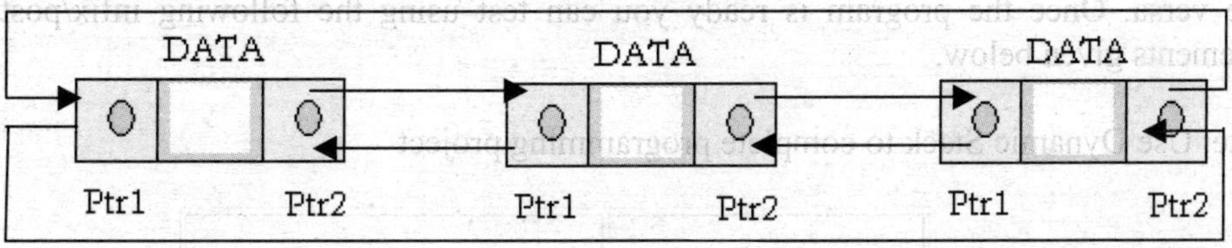

Figure 2.47: Dynamic circular stack

Q17) The following figure 2.48 depicts a link list, fill the missing ' ' memory addresses in each of them?

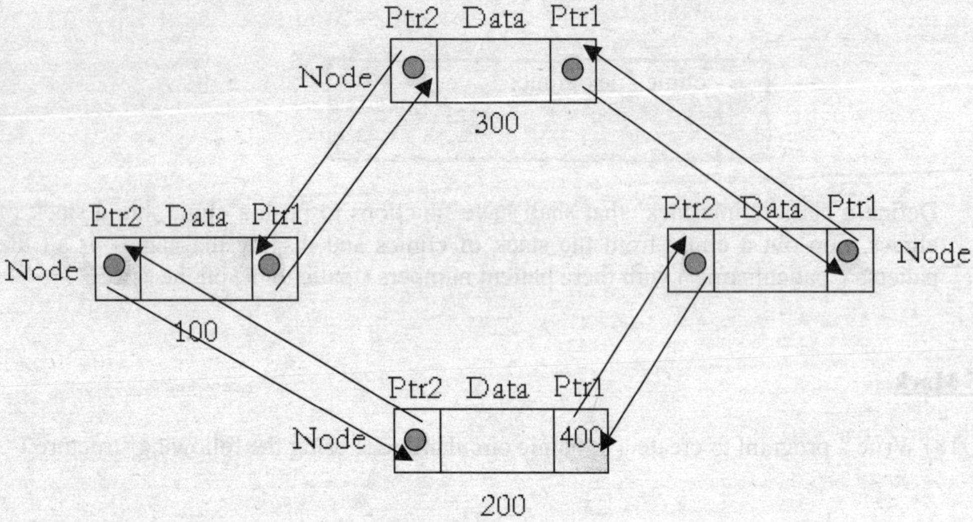

Figure 2.48: Link List

2.7 Programming Project

'Infix' and 'Postfix' expressions are two different but equivalent ways of writing an expression. 'Infix' notation is one in which operators are written in between their operands for example A+B. On the other hand postfix notation is one in which operators are written after their operands. For example, A B + is a postfix expression.Our programming project involves a creation of menu driven program using dynamic memory allocation, which prompts the user with the choice to enter a postfix expression or an infix expression. The program should then convert the postfix expression to infix and vice versa. Once the program is ready you can test using the following infix/postfix statements given below.

Note: Use Dynamic Stack to complete programming project

Infix	Postfix
A * B + C / D	A B * C D / +
A * (B + C) / D	A B C + * D /
A * (B + C / D)	A B C D / + *

2.8 Let us revise!

- Linked lists are dynamic data structures which can shrink and expand during program execution.
- Linked lists are a collection of a group of self referential structures grouped together logically.
- A link list can grow till the point memory is available to it.
- Linked lists are very similar to arrays. The difference in them though lies in the creation of their structures for storage in memory.
- Arrays are stored as a single block of memory storing huge amounts of data.
- Linked lists allocate different blocks of memory to each element called 'node' where each node consists of two fields. The 'data' field to store all data parameters and the 'next' field which could be a pointer to a node.
- Linked lists are generated by creating a series of self referential structures logically linked together.
- Linked lists can be traversed using the following algorithm:

  Algorithm

  Prerequisite: This algorithm works for a linked list in which each node stores the address of its preceding node.

  1. Declare a pointer, pointing to the last node.
  2. Assign the pointer variable declared in step 1, the address stored in the pointer part of the self referential structure.
  3. Repeat the process described in step 2 until the pointer is assigned a NULL value which marks the end of the link list.
- Singly linked lists in which traversing was one directional gave birth to 'multi-lists'.
- The nodes of such lists have more than one link and hence allow atleast two directional traversing.
- Stacks are non primitive linear data structures in which insertion and deletion of data takes place from only one end known as the 'TOP'.
- They are homogeneous collection of data of one type. Stacks are also an example of a LIFO structure that is 'Last in First out' data structure.
- Stacks can also be implemented as one dimensional arrays known as 'Static' stacks.
- Static stacks have a fixed amount of data that can be fed into them.
- Stacks are implemented using three basic functions. The function 'push' is used to enter data entries in the stack, 'pop' is used to delete data entries and function 'display' is used to display the contents of the stacks.
- Static stacks can cause wastage of significant amount of computer's memory hence using dynamic stacks is a more viable solution.

- Stacks represented as pointers by creating a linked list with the use of which one can create 'Dynamic stacks'.
- This can waste a significant amount of the computer's memory if the loop only recurs a few times during the execution of the program.
- Stacks are used for converting an infix expression to postfix and finding the value of an postfix expression.
- Any algebraic statement is termed as an infix expression. For example 4+5.
- A post fix expression places each operator after the two operands to which it applies as its name might suggest as 'post' means after. For example 4 5 +
- A queue is an example of an abstract data type structure.
- It is also termed as an FIFO (first in first out) or a LILO (last in last out structure).
- One of the major applications of queue is to create job queues for 'job scheduling'
- Queues can also be implemented as one dimensional arrays known as 'Static circular' Queues.
- Queues comprise of two basic operations:
  Enqueue: It is the process by which data entries are added in the queue.
  Dequeue: It is a process by which data entries are deleted from a queue.
- Link Lists are very efficient method of data storage and are far more advantageous over traditional static arrays and should be used where ever possible to improve program efficiency.

Part III

CHAPTER 3

STREAMS & FILES

AIM

- Introduce the concept of 'Streams and Files'.
- Understand how streams provide input/output capabilities.
- Able to create and use 'text' files for purposes of data storage.
- Create binary files and be able to read and write data on and from them

OUTLINE

3.1 Introduction
3.2 Streams
3.3 Text files
3.4 Binary files
3.5 Solved examples
3.6 Review exercise
3.7 Programming project
3.8 Let us revise!

3.1 Introduction

The chapter focuses on the streams and files present in C++. Streams provide an extensive set of input/output capabilities. They control the flow of data informs of sequence of bytes some of which, that we have already been using in our programs. Files on the other hand are collection of related data or program records stored as a unit with a single name. In simple terms, files are used for data storage. In computer terminology we divide files into two categories 'text' and 'binary' which will be dealt with later in this chapter. The chapter also explains us how to create our own files, read and write data on and from them.

3.2 Streams

In C++, input and output (I/O) occurs with the usage of streams. Stream is a general name given to any kind of flow of data say, in form of a sequence of bytes. Streams are represented by an object of a particular class. All of us have already used streams in programs that we have written through use of 'cin' and the 'cout' stream objects - to enter and display data using standard input and output devices. There exist many streams in C++ which determine the various kinds of data flow. For example, the 'ofstream' classes are used to write operations on a file. Figure 3.1 shows all the basic stream classes available in C++.

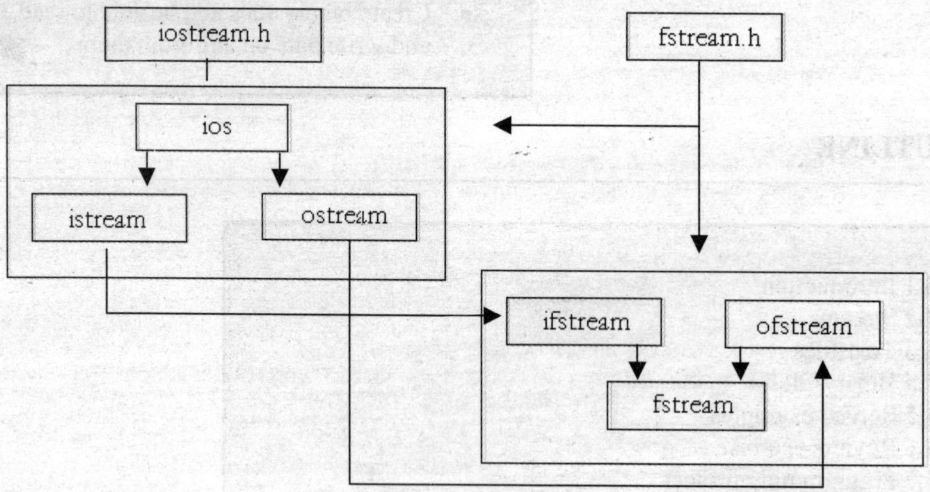

Figure 3.1: Stream classes in C++

Let us begin with the 'iostream' class. We have already used this class while declaring the 'iostream.h' header file in our previous programs. The 'iostream' class - also known as 'I/O stream' - is used to manage most of the input and the output operations through C++ statements, such as, 'cin' and 'cout'. The 'iostream' class is actually a derived class of the 'istream' and the 'ostream' classes. All the input or extraction operations, e.g., get(), getline() and read() are accessed through 'istream'. The 'ostream' class manages all the output or insertion operations for example, the functions put() and write(). These classes in turn are also derived from the base class 'ios' which also serves as a base class for many other streams. Figure 3.2 shows the complex hierarchy of these classes.

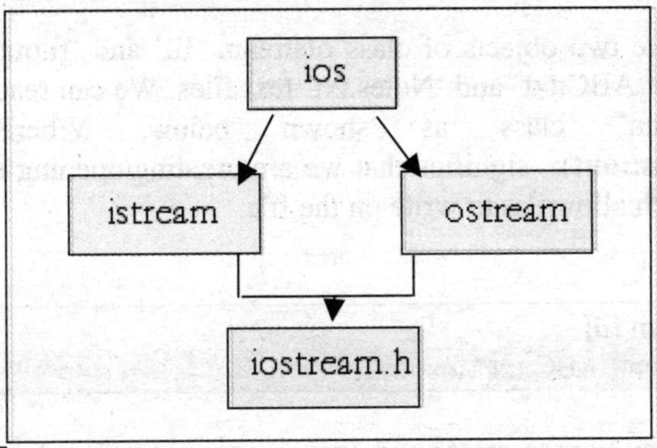

Figure 3.2: Stream class hierarchy

Let us now look at the other set of classes shown in figure 3.1. File processing in C++, is carried out using the 'fstream' class. The fstream class provides two distinct classes for file processing. The 'ofstream' class derived from the 'ostream' class and the 'ifstream' class derived from the 'istream' class. The 'ofstream' class is used to write on a file by using constructors available in the class where as the 'ifstream' class, is used to read data from a file. The 'fstream' class is derived from the 'iostream' class and it coalesces the functions defined in both the 'ifstream' and the 'ofstream' classes.

3.3 Text Files

Text files are files where bytes or a sequence of bytes represent ordinary textual characters such as digits and numbers which are represented by their ASCII codes. Text files are mainly used by computer programs for data storage. The Windows system regards a file to be a text file if the suffix of the name of the file is "txt". However, source code for computer programs are also text, but usually have file name suffixes indicating which programming language the source is written in.

3.3.1 Creating/Opening Text Files in OUTPUT mode

In this section we will learn how to create and open already existing text files. To create or open a text file we have to take help of the 'ofstream' class. For achieving this purpose we can either include the 'fstream.h' header file or the 'ostream.h' header file as both these header files include the definition of the 'ofstream' class. A text file can be

STREAMS & FILES

created/opened using the following statement. What these statements do is create objects of the 'ostream' or the 'fstream' class depending upon which set of statements are used and then the object is used to create or open an existing text file. For example,

```
ofstream fil("ABC.txt");
ofstream filout ("Notes.txt");
```

These statements create two objects of class ofstream 'fil' and 'filout'. These objects are then used to create the 'ABC.txt' and 'Notes.txt' text files. We can reach the same outcome using the 'fstream' class as shown below. Where the statement 'fil.open("ABC.txt",**ios::out**);' signifies that we are creating/opening a text file 'ABC.txt' in the 'out' mode which allows us to write on the file.

```
fstream fil;
fil.open("ABC.txt",ios::out);
```

Now that we have learnt how to create and open existing text files let us now learn how to write on a file. Program 3.1 given below creates a text file "ABC.txt" and allows the user to write or insert data into this file.

Program 3.1: Writing on a text file

```
/* Header Files */
# include <fstream.h>
# include <conio.h>
# include <stdio.h>

void main()
{
 clrscr();
 ofstream fil;
 fil.open("ABC.txt");
 char lin[80];
 char ch;
 do
 {
 cout<<"\n Enter lines of text in the text file";
 gets(lin);
 fil<<lin<<endl;
 cout<<" Do you want to enter more lines of text (y/n)";
```

```
 cin>>ch;
}
while (ch!='n');
fil.close();
getch();
}
```

As we already know that this program opens/creates a text file "ABC.txt" and allows the user to write on the text file, but how does this process take place?

What we have done in this program is that we have initialized a buffer string 'lin' which is used to input data from the user. This data is then fed into the file using the following statement. **'fil<<lin<<endl'**. This statement might look familiar to the statement 'cout' with ('<<') predefined operators, but the only thing we have to know is that all this statement does is insert the data stored in the variable 'lin' into the file. This process is repeated until the user wants, inserting data into the text file. The program ends with the statement 'fil.close()' which calls the member function 'close()' which closes the text file we opened/created. Once this function is called the stream object created becomes free and can be used to open another file.

3.3.2 Opening a text file in INPUT mode

In the previous section we learnt about how to create/open text files and then write on these files. In this section we will learn about how to read existing files and display their contents on the screen. A text file can be opened for reading using the 'ifstream' or the 'fstream' class. The process of opening a file for reading purposes is very similar to opening the file for writing purposes involving only minor changes. For opening a text file for reading purposes we use the following syntax.

Syntax:

```
ifstream <FileObject> (<FileName>);

or

fstream <FileObject>;
<FileObject>.open (<Filename>,ios::in);
```

What these statements do is create objects of the 'ifstream' or the 'fstream' class depending upon which set of statements are used and then the object is used to create or open an existing text file for reading purposes. For example,

```
ifstream fil("ABC.txt");

fstream fil;
fil.open("ABC.txt",ios::in);
```

When these statements are executed the file 'ABC.txt' is opened for reading purposes. Now that we know how to open text files for reading purposes let us learn how to display the contents stored in a text file. Program 3.2 given below opens the text file 'ABC.txt' for reading purposes and displays its contents on the screen.

Program 3.2: Reading a text file

```
/* Header Files */
# include <fstream.h>
# include <conio.h>
# include <stdio.h>

// Main Function
void main()
{
  clrscr();

  fstream fil; // Creates an object of class fstream

  fil.open("ABC.txt",ios::in); // Opens the file "ABC.txt" in Read Mode

  char lin[80]; // String buffer

  while (fil.getline(lin,80))
    {
      puts(lin);
    }

  getch();
}
```

In this program we have used the 'fstream' class and read the file from it one line at a time using the getline() function which is a member function of 'fstream' or the 'ifstream' class. This function reads characters, including blank spaces until it encounters the '\n' operator and places the resulting string in the buffer supplied to it as an argument. The maximum size of the buffer is passed as the second argument. This process is repeated until we reach the end of the file displaying the contents stored in the buffer each time the condition is checked for. In our program this process is carried out by the following statements.

```
while (fil.getline(lin,80))
  {
    puts(lin);
  }
```

Where the character array 'lin' acts as the buffer string having a maximum size of 80 characters. This is only one of the ways in which the contents of a file can be read and displayed program 3.4 illustrates another method of performing this function.

Programming Tips

- Always try to use the 'fstream' class to declare stream objects as one can then use the same class for opening the file in input/output modes and the syntax happens to be very similar to what we will use for binary files as well
- Whenever a file is opened for writing command using the 'ostream' class or the 'fstream' class using the 'out' specifier all the previous content of the file gets deleted. In order to keep our previous data intact we should use the 'app' specifier.

Program 3.3: The EOF function

```
/* Header Files */
# include <fstream.h>
# include <conio.h>
# include <stdio.h>

// Main Function
void main()
{
 clrscr();

 fstream fil; // Creates an object of class fstream

 fil.open("ABC.txt",ios::in); // Opens the file "ABC.txt" in Read Mode

 char lin[80]; // String buffer

 while (!fil.eof())
 {
  fil.getline(lin,80);
  puts(lin);
 }

getch();
}
```

If we notice carefully, this program is very similar to program 3.3. The only change in this program is that we have used the **'eof()'** function as the condition specifier in the while loop. The **'eof()'** function is a member function defined in the 'fstream' class which checks for the end of file. Hence when this function is used as a condition specifier in the while loop the loop continues until the end of file is reached allowing us to read through the entire file. The rest of the statements have already been dealt with in the previous programs.

3.3.3 Opening a file in append mode

When we are opening the file in output mode what was happening was that all the previous data stored in the file was being deleted. In simple terms we were left with a black file. The advantage of opening a file in append mode is that the earlier content if existing, is not over writer and the file write pointer moves to the end of the file for adding new lines at the bottom of the file. This can be done using the following syntax.

Syntax:

```
fstream <Fileobject>;
<Fileobject>.open(<Filename>,ios::app);
```

For example for opening the text file 'ABC.txt' in append mode we would use the following statements.

Example:

```
fstream fil;
fil.open("ABC.txt",ios::app);
```

Common Programming Errors

- When creating text files always remember to use the '.txt' extension.
- Remember to always close created file objects as this closes the input/output stream and the stream objects can be used to open other streams.
- Always try not to open a file for reading and writing at the same time using different stream objects as this might lead to unpredictable outcomes.

3.3.4 Solved Examples

Example 3.3.4.1

Write a function to transfer the content of a text file to another text file

Solution of 3.3.4.1

```
void transfer()
{
 char fn1[20],fn2[20];
 fstream fil1,fil2;
 fil1.open(fn1,ios::in);
 fil2.open(fn2,ios::out);
 char lin[80];
 while(fil1.getline(lin,80))
 {
  fil2<<lin<<endl;
 }
 fil1.close();
 fil2.close();
}
```

Example 3.3.4.2

Write a function to transfer the content of a text file to another text file after changing the cases to uppercase with each line reversed.

Solution of 3.3.4.2

```
void newchange()
{
 char fn1[20],fn2[20];
 fstream fil1,fil2;
 fil1.open(fn1,ios::in);
 fil2.open(fn2,ios::out);
 char lin[80];
 while (fil1.getline(lin,80))
 {
  for (int i=strlen(lin)-1;i>=0;i--)
  {
   lin[i]=toupper(lin[i])
  }
  fil2<<lin<<endl;
 }
```

```
fil1.close();
  fil2.close();
 }
```

Example 3.3.4.3

Write a menu driven program to create a text file 'Experiment.txt'. The program should also have an option to display the contents of the text file and also count the number of words starting from the letter's'.

Solution of 3.3.4.3

```
 /* Header Files */
# include<fstream.h>
# include<conio.h>
# include<stdio.h>
# include<string.h>

int counter=0;

/*************
Function Name: create
Purpose: creates a text file 'Experiment.txt'
*********************************************/
void create()
{
 fstream fil;
 fil.open("Experiment.txt",ios::out);
 char choice;
 char lin[80];
 do
  {
  cout<<"\n\n Enter the lines of text";
  gets(lin);
  fil<<lin<<endl;
  cout<<"\n Do you want to enter more lines of text (y/n)";
  cin>>choice;
  }
 while (choice!='n');
 fil.close();
}



/*************
Function Name: display
Purpose: displays the text file 'Experiment.txt'
```

```
*******************************************/
void display()
{
 fstream fil;
 fil.open("Experiment.txt",ios::in);
 char lin[80];
 while (fil.getline(lin,80))
 {
  puts(lin);
 }
 fil.close();
}

/*************
Function Name: count
Purpose: counts the number of words beginning with the letters 's'
*************************************************************
***/
void count()
{
 counter=0;
 fstream fil;
 fil.open("Experiment.txt",ios::in);
 char lin[80];
 int i=0;
 while (fil.getline(lin,80))
 {
  if (lin[0]=='s')
  {
  counter++;
  }

  for (i=0;i<strlen(lin);i++)
  {
   if (lin[i]==' ' & lin [i+1] =='s')
   {
    counter++;
   }
  }
 }
 cout<<"\n\n The number of words starting from letter 's' are "<<counter;

 fil.close();
}

// Main function
```

```
void main()
{
 clrscr();
 int choice;
 do
 {
 cout<<"\n\n------------- MENU -----------\n";
 cout<<"1. Create\n";
 cout<<"2. Display\n";
 cout<<"3. Count\n";
 cout<<"4. Quit\n";
 cout<<"! Enter Choice\n";
 cin>>choice;
 switch(choice)
  {
  case 1:
         create();
         break;

  case 2:
         display();
         break;

  case 3:
          count();
          break;
  }
 }
 while (choice !=4);
 getch();
 }
```

Example 3.3.4.4

Write a menu driven program to perform the following operations for each of the following

- Create a text file with a user defined name.
- Count the number of vowels in the text file created
- Display the text file created

Solution of 3.3.4.4

```
/* Header Files */
# include<fstream.h>
# include<conio.h>
# include<stdio.h>

# include<string.h>
```

```
int counter=0;

/*************
Function Name: create
Purpose: creates a text file with a user defined name
*********************************************************/
void create(char filename[])
{
 fstream fil;
 fil.open(filename,ios::out);
 char choice;
 char lin[80];
 do
 {
  cout<<"\n\n Enter the lines of text";
  gets(lin);
  fil<<lin<<endl;
  cout<<"\n Do you want to enter more lines of text (y/n)";
  cin>>choice;
 }
 while (choice!='n');
 fil.close();
}


/*************
Function Name: display
Purpose: displays the text file created
**********************************************/
void display(char filename[])
{
 fstream fil;
 fil.open(filename,ios::in);
 char lin[80];
 while (fil.getline(lin,80))
 {
  puts(lin);
 }
 fil.close();
}

/*************
Function Name: count_vowels
Purpose: counts the number of vowels in the text file
*********************************************************/
```

```
void count_vowels(char filename[])
{
 int vowels=0;
 fstream fil;
 fil.open(filename,ios::in);
 char lin[80];
 int i=0;
 while (fil.getline(lin,80))
 {
  for (i=0;i<strlen(lin);i++)
  {
   if (lin[i]=='a' || lin [i] =='e'|| lin [i] =='i'|| lin [i] =='o'|| lin [i] =='u')
   {
     vowels++;
   }
  }
 }
 cout<<"\n\n The number of vowels are "<<vowels;

 fil.close();
}

// Main function
void main()
{
 clrscr();
 int choice;
 char filename[15];
 cout<<"Enter the file name";
 gets(filename);
 do
 {
 clrscr();
 cout<<"\n\n------------- MENU -----------\n";
 cout<<"1. Create the text file\n";
 cout<<"2. Count the number of vowels \n";
 cout<<"3. Display the text file\n";
 cout<<"4. Quit\n";
 cout<<"!  Enter Choice\n";
 cin>>choice;
 switch(choice)
   {
  case 1:
          create(filename);
           break;
```

```
case 2:
        count_vowels(filename);
        getch();
        break;

case 3:
        display(filename);
        getch();
        break;
   }
}
while (choice !=4);
getch();
}
```

Example 3.3.4.5

Write a menu driven program using separate function to perform the following operations:

- Create a text file with a user defined name.
- Copy the contents of this text file into another text file 'Copy.txt' with all the blank spaces in the text file converted to '$'.
- Display both the text files.

Solution of 3.3.4.5

```
/***************
    Header Files
***************/
# include <fstream.h>
# include <conio.h>
# include <stdio.h>
# include <string.h>

/*****************
 Function Definitions
 ********************/

/*****************
Function: create
Parameters: filename[]
Return Type: void
Purpose: Creates a text file with a user defined name
*****************************************************/
void create(char filename[])
{
 fstream fil;
 fil.open(filename,ios::out);
```

STREAMS & FILES

```
 char lin[80];
 char ch;
 do
 {
  cout<<"\nEnter lines of text";
  gets(lin);
  fil<<lin<<endl;
  cout<<"\nDo you want to enter more lines of text (y/n)\n";
  cin>>ch;
 }
 while (ch!='n');
 fil.close();
 getch();
}

/*****************
Function: display
Parameters: filename[]
Return Type: void
Purpose: Displays the text file entered by the user
*****************************************************/
void display(char filename[])
{
 fstream fil;
 fil.open(filename, ios::in);
 char lin[80];
 while (fil.getline(lin,80))
 {
  puts(lin);
 }
 fil.close();
 getch();
}

/*****************
Function: copy
Parameters: filename[]
Return Type: void
Purpose: Creates the text file 'Copy.txt' with all the
            blank spaces converted to '$' sign.
*****************************************/
void copy(char filename[])
{
 fstream fil1,fil2;
 fil1.open(filename,ios::in);
 fil2.open("Copy.txt",ios::out);
```

```
 char lin[80];
 while(fil1.getline(lin,80))
 {
  for(int i=0;i<strlen(lin);i++)
  {
   if (lin[i]==' ')
   {
    lin[i]='$';
   }
  }
  fil2<<lin<<endl;
 }
 cout<<"\n The text file 'Copy.txt' has been created";
 fil1.close();
 fil2.close();
}

// Main Function
void main()
{
  clrscr();
  char filename[15];
  char file[15];
  int choice;
  do
  {
   cout<<"\n\n ----------- MENU ----------- \n";
   cout<<" 1. Creating the text file \n";
   cout<<" 2. Displaying the text file\n";
   cout<<" 3. Create the text file 'Copy.txt' \n";
   cout<<" 4. Exit\n";
   cin>>choice;
   switch(choice)
    {
    case 1:
           cout<<"\n\n Enter Filename:";
           gets(filename);
           create(filename);
           break;

    case 2:
          cout<<"Enter the name of the file to be displayed\n\n";
          gets(file);
          display(file);
          break;
```

```
case 3:
        copy(filename);
        break;
  }
}
while (choice!=4);
getch();
}
```

Programming Tips

- Be careful on the usage of brackets when using the following statement:

```
while (fil1.getline(lin,80))
```

3.4 Binary Files

A file stored in binary format is known as a binary file. A binary file is only computer readable and cannot be read by humans. Operating systems store the files in binary format as computers can only deal with binary numbers. Binary files in contrast to the text files can include any kind of data. The sound and image files we encounter in our daily use when using computers are also examples of binary files

3.4.1 Opening binary files in output mode (For writing)

In this section we will learn how to open already existing binary files. For opening a binary

file one has to use the 'fstream' class. The syntax for opening an existing an already existing binary file is given below.

```
Syntax:
        fstream<FileObject>;
        <FileObject>.open (<Filename>,ios::binary |ios::out);
```

For example,

```
Example:
        fstream fil;
        fil.open("Binary_File.DAT",ios::binary|ios::out);

         OR

        char fname[20];
        cout<<" Enter Filename:";
        gets(fname);
        fstream fil;
        fil.open(fname,ios::binary|ios::out);
```

The set of statements given above would create a binary file 'Binary_File'. The 'ios::binary' statement in the piece of code given above signifies that we are opening a binary file where as the proclamation 'ios::out' tells the compiler that we are opening the binary file for writing purposes. This syntax should seem similar to the one we learnt for opening text files as binary files are nothing but a more general form of text files.

3.4.2 Opening binary files in input mode (For reading from a file)

In the previous section we learnt about how to open binary files for writing purposes. Let us now learn how to open binary files for reading purposes. For opening binary files in input mode we again use the 'fstream'class using the following syntax.

```
Syntax:
        fstream<FileObject>;
        <FileObject>.open (<Filename>,ios::binary |ios::in);
```

The example given below opens the binary file 'Binary_File.DAT' in input mode.

```
Example:
        fstream fil;
        fil.open("Binary_File.DAT",ios::binary|ios::in);

         OR

        char fname[20];
        cout<<" Enter Filename:";
        gets(fname);
        fstream fil;
        fil.open(fname,ios::binary|ios::in);
```

The only change we observe from the previous section is in the statement 'fil.open("Binary_File.DAT",ios::binary|ios::in);'. Where we have changed the proclamation from 'ios::out' to 'ios::in' which signifies we are opening the binary file for reading purposes.

3.4.3 Opening binary files in APPEND mode (For writing on a file)

When we are opening the binary file in output mode what was happening was that all the previous data stored in the file was being deleted. In simple terms we were left with a black file. The advantage of opening a file in append mode is that the earlier content if existing, is not over writen and the file write pointer moves to the end of the file for adding new lines at the bottom of the file. This can be done using the following syntax.

Syntax:

```
fstream<Fileobject>;
<Fileobject>.open(<Filename>,ios::binary|ios::app);
```

For example for opening the text file 'ABC.txt' in append mode we would use the following statements.

Example:

```
fstream fil;
fil.open("Binary_File.DAT",ios::binary|ios::app);

OR

char fname[20];
cout<<" Enter Filename:";
gets(fname);
fstream fil;
fil.open(fname,ios::binary|ios::in);
```

3.4.4 Creation of binary files

When creating binary files inputting and outputting data using operators like << and >> and functions like 'getline' does not make too much sense although it is possible to use them. The file streams include two member functions which are specially designed for input and output of data sequentially. They are the 'write' and the 'read' functions. The 'write()'

function is a member function of the 'ostream' class and is inherited by 'ofstream' where as the function 'read()' is a member function of the 'istream' class and is inherited by ifstream. Both these functions can be accessed by creating objects of 'fstream' class. These functions have the following prototypes.

```
write ( char * buffer, streamsize size );

read ( char * buffer, streamsize size );
```

The function prototype takes two arguments. The first one being `'buffer'` which is the address of the memory block where the data is inserted by the user or the data to be written on the binary file is stored temporarily where as the second argument defines the maximum allowed size that can be fed into the buffer. Binary files can be created in C++ with the help of structure variables or objects of a class. Program 3.4 given below declares a function which creates a user defined binary file with a single record.

Program 3.4: Insertion of a record in a binary file using structures and classes

Using Structures

```
struct stock
 {
  int Ino;
  char Item[20];
  float qty;
 };

 void create(char fname[])
 {
  fstream fil;
  stock s;

 fil.open(fname,ios::binary|ios::out);
  cout<<"Item No. ";
  cin>>s.Ino;
  cout<<"Item Name";
  gets(s.Item);
  cout<<"Quantity";
  cin>>s.qty;
  fil.write((char *)&s,sizeof(s));
  fil.close();
 }
```

Using Classes

```
class stock
{
int Ino;
char Item[20];
float qty;
public:
void input()
{
cout<<"Item No.";
cin>>Ino;
cout<<"Item Name";
gets(Item);
cout<<"Quantity";
cin>>qty;
}

void output()
{

cout<<Ino<<":"<<Item<<":"<<qty;
}
 int Rino()
{
 return Ino;
}
};
/***********
Function: create
Parameters: fname
```

```
*****************/
void create( char fname[])
{
 fstream fil;
 stock s;
 fil.open(fname,ios::binary|ios::out);
 s.input();
 fil.write((char*)&s,sizeof(s));
 fil.close();
}
```

The entire structure of this program might seem very seimilar to the one we have already dealt in text files. The only difference one will observe is in the writing and the reading of binary files in this program we have used the following piece of code to write on the binary file.

```
fil.write((char*)&sizeof(s));
```

Let us see how this statement works. For this purpose let us look at it its general form.

```
stream_object.write((char*)&(structure_variable/class_object),sizeof(structure
_variable/class_object));
```

The first part of the statement '(char*)&(structure_variable/class_object)' typcasts the structure or the class to character type. Where as the second part of the statement 'sizeof(structure_variable/class_object)' allocates the number of bytes to be fed into the binary file. For example, in our statement given above. The first part of the statement '(char*)&s' typcasts the class 's' so that data from it can be inserted into the binary file and the second part of the statement 'sizeof(s)' allocates the amount of data interms of bytes to be fed into the file at one time. This is the procedure one has to follow in order to insert a single record into a binary file but what happens if we want to insert multiple records and not just a single record ?

Program 3.5 declares a function 'create' which proposes a solution to the given problem.

Program 3.5: Creation of a binary file with multiple records

struct stock	class stock

`{`
`int Ino;`
`char Item[20];`
`float qty;`
`};`
	`{`
	`int Ino;`
	`char Item[20];`
	`float qty;`
	`public:`

```
void create (char Fname[])
{
  fstream fil;
  stock S;
  fil.open
(Fname,ios::binary|ios::out);
  char choice;
  do
  {
    cout<<" Item No?";
    cin>>S.Ino;
    cout<<"Item Name";
    gets(S.Item);
    cout<<"Quantity";
    cin>>S.qty;
    fil.write((char
*)&S,sizeof(S));
    cout<<"More(Y/N) ?";
    cin>>choice;
  }
  while (choice=='y');
  fil.close();
}
```

```
void input()
{
  cout<<"Item No.";
  cin>>Ino;
  cout<<"Item Name";
  gets(Item);
  cout<<"Quantity";
  cin>>qty;
}
void output()
{
cout<<Ino<<":"<<Item<<":"<<qty;
}
 int Rino()
{
 return Ino;
}
};
void create(char Fname[])
{
 fstream fil;
 stock s;
fil.open(Fname,ios::binary|ios::out);
 char choice;
 do
 {
  s.input();
  fil.write((char*)&s,sizeof(s));
  cout<<" More(Y/N) ?";
  cin>>choice;
 }
 while (choice == 'y');
 fil.close();
}
```


3.4.5 Reading a binary file

In this section of the chapter we will learn how to dislay already created binary files. We have already learnt in the previous section that binary files can be displayed using the function 'read()' which is a member function of the 'istream' class' inherited by ifstream and the fstream classes. The process of reading data from binary files is very similar to the process of writing on them. Program 3.6 given below displays the piece of code required to display a single record.

Program 3.6:

Using Structures	Using Classes

Using Structures

```
struct stock
 {
   int Ino;
   char Item[20];
   float qty;
 };

void display (char Fname[])
{
 fstream fil;
 stock S;

fil.open(Fname,ios::binary|ios::in);
 fil.read((char*)&S,sizeof(S));
 cout<<"ItemNo:"<<S.Ino;
 cout<<"Item_Name:";
 gets(S.Item);
 cout<<"Item quantity";
 cin>>S.qty;
 fil.close();
}
```

Using Classes

```
class stock
 {
 int Ino;
 char Item[20];
 float qty;
 public:
 void input()
 {
  cout<<"Item No.";
  cin>>Ino;
  cout<<"Item Name";
  gets(Item);
  cout<<"Quantity";
  cin>>qty;
 }

void output()
{

cout<<Ino<<":"<<Item<<":"<<qty;
 }

 int Rino()
 {
  return Ino;
 }
};

void display(char Fname[])
{
  fstream fil;
  stock S;

fil.open(Fname,ios::binary|ios::in);
  fil.read((char*)&S,sizeof(S));
  S.output;
  fil.close();
}
```

As it is clear we have used the 'read' function to display records from the file. The function 'read' works in the same way as the function 'write()' we learnt in the last section the only difference being that this time data is being fed out of the file. Rest of the program should be easily understood as it follows the same logic as present in program 3.5. It is also possible to read various records from a binary file. Program 3.8 given below shows how this is done.

Program 3.7: Reading Records from a binary File

```
struct stock
{
  int Ino;
  char Item[20];
  float qty;
};

void display(char Fname[])
{
 fstream fil;
 stock S;

 fil.open(Fname,ios::binary|ios::in);

 while(fil.read((char*)&S,sizeof(S)))
 {
  cout<<"Item No:"<<S.Ino<<endl;
  cout<<"ItemName:"<<S.Item<<"Qty:"<<S.qty<<en
  dl;
 }
 fil.close();
}
```

```
class stock
{
int Ino;
char Item[20];
float qty;

public:
 void input()
 {
 cout<<"Item No.";
 cin>>Ino;
 cout<<"Item Name";
 gets(Item);
 cout<<"Quantity";
 cin>>qty;
 }

void output()
 {
cout<<Ino<<":"<<Item<<":"<<qty
 }

 int Rino()
 {
 return Ino;
 }

};

void display(char Fname[])
```

STREAMS & FILES

```
{
  fstream fil;
  stock S;

  fil.open(Fname,ios::binary|ios::in);

 while(fil.read((char*)&S,sizeof(S)))
  {
    S.output();
  }

 fil.close();
}
```

Programming Tips

- When declaring binary files make sure that one is using the '.dat' extension.
- Remember to use the 'ios::binary' specifier with the fstream class when opening/creating binary files for reading or writing purposes.
- The major difference between text and binary files is that text files are human readable where bytes or a sequence of bytes represent ordinary textual characters such as digits and numbers which are represented by their ASCII codes where as binary files are not human readable Binary files in contrast to the text files can include any kind of data not necessarily just numbers digits and characters

3.4.6 Solved Examples

Example 3.4.6.1

Using the following class write functions to do the following:

(i) Store the objects of clinic in a binary file
(ii) Read all the records from the binary file and display them on the screen

(iii) Accept a disease name from the user and display the details of all such patients who are suffering of that particular disease

```
// class definition of class 'clinic'
class clinic
{
 char bednumber[10];
 char patientname[20];
 char disease[30];
 char doc_attending[20];
 public:
 void getdetails()
 {
  gets(bednumber);
  gets(patientname);
  gets(disease);
  gets(doc_attending);
 }

 void showdetails()
 {
  cout<<"Bed Number"<<bednumber;
  cout<<"Patient Name"<<patientname;
  cout<<"Disease"<<disease;
  cout<<"Doctor Attending"<<doc_attending;
 }

 char*retdisease()
 {
  return disease;
 }
};
```


Solution of 3.4.6.1

(i)

```
void store()
{
 fstream fout;
 fout.open("clinic.dat",ios::out|ios::binary);
 clinic ob;
```

```
char ch;
do
{
 ob.getdetails();
 fout.write((char*)&ob,sizeof(ob));
 cout<<"More Records...(y/n)";
 cin>>ch;
}
while (toupper(ch)=='y');
fout.close();
}
```

(ii)

```
void readrecords()
{
 fstream fin;
 fin.open("clinic.dat",ios::in|ios::binary);
 clinic ob;
 while(fin.read((char*)&ob,sizeof(ob)))
 {
  ob.showdetails();
 }
 fin.close();
}
```

(iii)

```
void diseasedetails()
{
 char dis[30];
 cout<<"Enter Disease name";
 gets(dis);
 fstream fin;

 fin.open("clinic.dat",ios::in|ios::binary);
 clinic ob;
 while (fin.read((char*)&ob,sizeof(ob)))
 {
  if (!strcmp(ob.retdisease(),dis))
  {
    ob.showdetails();
  }
 }
```

```
fin.close();
}
```

Example 3.4.6.2

Write a function in C++ to add new objects at the bottom of a binary file "student.dat" assuming the binary file is containing the objects of the following class:

```
class stud
 {
 int rno;
 char name[20];

 public:

 void enter()
 {
  cin>>rno;
  gets(name);
 }

 void display()
 {
  cout<<rno<<name<<endl;
 }

 };
```

Solution of 3.4.6.2

```
void addnew()
 {
 fstream fil;


fil.open("student.dat",ios::binary|ios:
:app);

 stud s;

 char ch;

 do
```

```
{
 s.enter();

 fil.write((char*)&s,sizeof(s));

 cout<<"More(Y/N)?";

 cin>>ch;
}

while(ch!='y');

fil.close();
}
```

3.5 Solved Examples

Example 3.5.1

Write a program in C++ to create a text file with a user defined name. The program should also display the created text file and count the number of times the letters ''g''h''o''s''t'' appear together ?

Solution of 3.5.1

```
/**********
   Header Files
              **********/
# include <fstream.h>
# include <conio.h>
# include <stdio.h>
# include <string.h>

/********
 Function Definitions
                        ***********/
/*****************
Function: create
Parameters: filename[]
Return Type: void
 fstream fil;
 fil.open(filename,ios::out);
```

```
 char lin[80];
 char ch;
 do
 {
  cout<<"\nEnter lines of text";
  gets(lin);
  fil<<lin<<endl;
  cout<<"\nDo you want to enter more lines of text (y/n)\n";
  cin>>ch;
 }
 while (ch!='n');
 fil.close();
 getch();
}

/*****************
Function: display
Parameters: filename[]
Return Type: void
Purpose: Displays the text file
******************************/
void display(char filename[])
{
 fstream fil;
 fil.open(filename, ios::in);
 char lin[80];
 while (fil.getline(lin,80))
 {
   puts(lin);
 }
 fil.close();
 getch();
}


/*****************
Function: count
Parameters: filename[]
Return Type: void
Purpose: counts the number of times the letters 'g''h''o''s''t' encountered
*****************************************************/
```

```
void count(char filename[])
{
 fstream fil;
 fil.open(filename, ios::in);
 char lin[80];
 int count=0;
 while (fil.getline(lin,80))
 {
   for (int i=0;i<strlen(lin);i++)
   {
    if (lin[i]=='g'&lin[i+1]=='h'&lin[i+2]=='o'&lin[i+3]=='s'&lin[i+4]=='t')
    count++;
   }
 }
 cout<<" No. of times "<<count;
 fil.close();
 getch();
}

// Main Function
void main()
{
 clrscr();
 char filename[15];
 int choice;
 do
 {
  cout<<"\n\n ---------------------- MENU ---------------------- \n";
  cout<<" 1. Creating the text file \n";
  cout<<" 2. Displaying the text file\n";
  cout<<" 3. Number of times the letters 'g''h''o''s''t' are encountered together";
  cout<<"\n 4. Exit\n";
  cin>>choice;
  switch(choice)
   {
   case 1:
   cout<<"\n\n Enter Filename:";
              gets(filename);
              create(filename);
              break;
```

```
case 2:
        display(filename);
        break;

case 3:
        count(filename);
        break;
 }
}
while (choice!=4);
getch();
}
```

Example 3.5.2
Write a program to create a user defined text file and display alternate lines of the file?

Solution of 3.5.2

```
/**********
   Header Files
            **********/
# include <fstream.h>
# include <conio.h>
# include <stdio.h>
# include <string.h>

/********
 Function Definitions
                ***********/

/*****************
Function: create
Parameters: filename[]
Return Type: void
Purpose: Creates a text file with a user defined name
*****************************************************/
void create(char filename[])
{
```

```
 fstream fil;
 fil.open(filename,ios::out);
 char lin[80];
 char ch;
 do
 {
  cout<<"\nEnter lines of text";
  gets(lin);
  fil<<lin<<endl;
  cout<<"\nDo you want to enter more lines of text (y/n)\n";
  cin>>ch;
 }
 while (ch!='n');
 fil.close();
 getch();
}

/*****************
Function: display
Parameters: filename[]
Return Type: void
Purpose: Displays alternate lines of the text file entered by the user
**********************************************************************/
void display(char filename[])
{
 fstream fil;
 fil.open(filename, ios::in);
 char lin[80];
 int even=0;
 while (fil.getline(lin,80))
 {
  if (even%2==0)
  {
   puts(lin);
  }
  even++;
 }
 fil.close();
 getch();
}
// Main Function
void main()
```

```
{
 clrscr();
 char filename[15];
 int choice;
 do
 {
  cout<<"\n\n ---------------------- MENU ---------------------- \n";
  cout<<" 1. Creating the text file \n";
  cout<<" 2. Displaying the text file\n";
  cout<<" 3. Exit\n";
  cin>>choice;
  switch(choice)
   {
   case 1:
               cout<<"\n\n Enter Filename:";
               gets(filename);
               create(filename);
               break;

   case 2:
               display(filename);
               break;

   default:
               cout<<"Enter Valid Choice";
   }

 }

  while (choice!=3);
  getch();
}
```

Example 3.5.3

Write a program in C++ to create a text file called 'notes.txt'. Once this is done write separate functions to achieve the following.

(a) No. of lines in each file.
(b) No of words in each line.
(c) No of uppercase vowels

Solution of 3.5.3

```
/*****************
Function: display
Parameters: filename[]
Return Type: void
Purpose: Displays the text file entered by the user
**************************************************************************/
void display(char filename[])
{
 fstream fil;
 fil.open(filename, ios::in);
 char lin[80];
 while (fil.getline(lin,80))
 {
   puts(lin);
 }
 fil.close();
 getch();
}


/*****************
Function: count
Parameters: filename[]
Return Type: void
Purpose: counts the number of lines, vowels and words in each line
**********************************************************************
*****/
void count(char filename[])
{
 fstream fil;
 fil.open(filename, ios::in);
 char lin[80];
 int words=1;
 int lowercount=0,uppercount=0;
 while (fil.getline(lin,80))
 {
   words=1;
   for (int i=0;i<strlen(lin);i++)
   {
    if (islower(lin[i]))
    {
    if (lin[i]=='a'|| lin[i]=='e'|| lin[i]=='o' || lin[i]=='i'|| lin[i]=='u')
    lowercount++;
```

```
   }
   else
    if (isupper(lin[i]))
   {
   if (lin[i]=='A'|| lin[i]=='E'|| lin[i]=='O' || lin[i]=='I'|| lin[i]=='U')
   uppercount++;
   }

   if (lin[i]==' '&lin[i+1]!= ' ')
   {
       words++;
   }
  }
   cout<<"\n Words in the line are "<<words;

 }
 cout<<"\n No. of lines in the file "<<lines;
 cout<<"\n No. of lower case vowels "<<lowercount;
 cout<<"\n No. of upper case vowels "<<uppercount;
 fil.close();
 getch();
}

// Main Function
void main()
{
 clrscr();
 char filename[15];
 int choice;
 do
{
  cout<<"\n\n ---------------------- MENU ---------------------- \n";
  cout<<" 1. Creating the text file \n";
  cout<<" 2. Displaying the text file\n";
  cout<<" 3. No of lines, words, vowels in the file";
  cout<<"\n 4. Exit\n";
  cin>>choice;
  switch(choice)
   {
   case 1:
           cout<<"\n\n Enter Filename:";
           gets(filename);
           create(filename);
           break;
```

```
  case 2:
          display(filename);
          break;

  case 3:
          count(filename);
          break;
    }
 }
 while (choice!=4);
 getch();
}
```

Example 3.5.4

Write a function in C++ to search for a book number from a binary file "book.dat" assuming the binary file is containing the objects of the following class.

```
class book
{
 int bno;
 char title[20];

 public:

 int rbno()
 {
  return bno;
 }

 void enter()
 {
  cin>>bno;
  gets(title);
 }

 void display()
 {
  cout<<bno<<title<<endl;
 }
};
```

Solution of 3.5.4

```
void booksearch()
{
 fstream fil;
 fil.open("book.dat",ios::binary|ios::in);

 book b;
 int bn,found=0;

 while (fil.read((char*)&b,sizeof(b)))
 {
  if (b.rbno()==bn)
   {
   b.display();
   found++;
   }
 }

 if (found==0)
 {
  cout<<"Sorry! Book not found";
 }
 fil.close();
}
```

3.6 Review Exercise

1 Mark questions

For questions 1-6 choose the most appropriate answer:

Q1) A stream is defined as
a) flow of data from one place to another
b) a sequence of bytes
c) a special function which takes control of program
d) an example of header files
e) none of the above

Q2) The 'fstream' class is derived from
a) 'iostream' class.
b) 'istream' class
c) 'ios' class
d) a and c are correct

e) None of the above

Q3) The function 'getline()' can be accessed through the
a) 'ios' class
b) 'istream' class
c) 'iostream' class
d) 'ostream' class
e) None of the above

Q4) Text files usually have the following extension:
a) '.dat'
b) '.txt'
c) '.doc'
d) '.jpeg'
e) none of the above

Q5) Text files are:
a) human readable.
b) represent bytes as ASCII codes.
c) used for data storage.
d) a and b are correct.
e) all of the above.

Q6) The statement 'fil.read((char*)&b,sizeof(b))'
a) writes the member functions of 'b' to 'fil'
b) writes the data of 'b' to 'fil'
c) writes the member functions and data of 'b' on 'fil'
d) writes the address of 'b' on 'fil'
e) none of the above

Q7) What are the major differences between text and binary files?

Q8) Why is it necessary to close a file object after it has been used?

Q9) What is the function of the 'eof' operator?

Q10) By using which feature in files, text be added to a binary file without deleting its previous content?

2/3 Marks

Q11) Write a function which takes in the name of a text file as a parameter and copies the alternate lines of the file to another text file "creation.txt".

Q12) Write a function in C++ which takes in the names of two text files as parameters and creates a third text file 'merge.txt' by merging the two text files whose names are passed to it as parameters.

Q13) Write a function in C++ which takes in the name of a text file as a parameter and checks for the following line "How do I do this" in the text file.

Q14) Assuming the class 'sanctuary' given below, write functions in C++ to perform the following:

```
class sanctuary
{
 char location[20];
 int no_of_animals;

 public:

  void readdata()
  {
   gets(location);
   cin>>no_of_animals;
  }

  void writedata()
  {
   cout<<location<<" "<<no_of_animals;
  }

 int check(char loc[])
 {
   return strcmp(location,loc);
  }
};
```

(i) Read the objects of 'sanctuary' from the file and display them on the screen.
(ii) Ask the user to enter a location, search it from the file and display the details (location and number of animals) for that location.

4/5 Mark questions

Q16) Write function definitions for the following and use them in a menu driven program:
(i) To create a text file
(ii) To display the contents of the file

(iii) To transfer the contents from one file to another such that the new file contains the upper case equivalent of each line of the first file.

Q17) Write a program in C++ to create a text file with a user defined file name. The program should contain seprate functions to perform the following operations:
(i) Count the number of words starting with 'a'.
(ii) Count the number of words in each line
(iii) Convert the 1st letter of every word to uppercase and rest of the letters in lower case.
(iv) Display the original contents as well as converted contents of the file.

Q18) Write a program in C++ to create a file with a user defined name store each line of the reversed in another file called "ultra.txt". Display the original file as well as "ultra.txt". Then display alternate lines from the original file.

Q19) Write a program in C++ to create a text file with a user defined name. Reverse each word of the file and display its contents.

Q20) Write a function in C++ to search for a file number from a binary file "file.dat" assuming the binary file is containing the objects of the following class.

```
class file
{
 int fileno;
 char file_title[20];
public:
 int file_no()
 {
  return fileno;
 }
 void enter()
 {
  cin>>fileno;
  gets(file_title);
 }
 void display()
 {
  cout<<fileno<<file_title<<endl;
 }
};
```

3.7 Programming Project

A dictionary is a reference book containing an alphabetical list of words, with information given for each word, usually including meaning, pronunciation, and etymology. Our programming project for this chapter is to create a dictionary which includes the meaning of each word entered into the dictionary. This should be done using text files. The user should be prompted to enter any word and the dictionary should come up with its meaning of the word. You can use the following words to start with your dictionary.

Word	Meaning
Splendid	Brilliant with light or color; radiant: *a splendid field of poppies.*
Hospitable	Disposed to treat guests with warmth and generosity.
Crucible	A vessel made of a refractory substance such as graphite or porcelain, used for melting and calcining materials at high temperatures.
Immortal	Not subject to death: *immortal deities; the immortal soul.*
Prudent	**Wise in handling practical matters; exercising good judgment or common sense.**

3.8 Let us revise!

- ✓ Stream is a general name given to any kind of flow of data say, in form of a sequence of bytes.
- ✓ The 'iostream' class - also known as 'I/O stream' - is used to manage most of the input and the output operations
- ✓ All the input or extraction operations, e.g., get(), getline() and read() are accessed through 'istream' class.
- ✓ The 'ostream' class manages all the output or insertion operations for example, the functions put() and write().
- ✓ File processing in C++, is carried out using the 'fstream' class.
- ✓ The fstream class consists of two classes the 'ofstream' and the 'ifstream' class.
- ✓ The 'ofstream' class is derived from the 'ostream' class and it is used to write on a file by using constructors available in the class.
- ✓ The 'ifstream' class is derived from the 'istream' class and is used to read data from a file.
- ✓ Text files are files where bytes or a sequence of bytes represent ordinary textual characters such as digits and numbers which are represented by their ASCII codes.
- ✓ Text files are mainly used by computer programs for data storage and used in human readable format.\

- ✓ Text files usually have '.txt' extension.
- ✓ The text files are opened in output mode with the use of the 'ofstream' or the 'fstream' class using the following syntax.

Syntax:

ifstream <FileObject> (<FileName>);
or
fstream <FileObject>;
<FileObject>.open (<Filename>,ios::out);

- ✓ The text files are opened in input mode with the use of the 'ofstream' or the 'fstream' class using the following syntax.

Syntax:

ifstream <FileObject> (<FileName>);
or
fstream <FileObject>;
<FileObject>.open (<Filename>,ios::in);

- ✓ Data is read from a text file using the getline() function.
- ✓ Files can be opened in append mode so that the earlier content if existing, is not over written and the file write pointer moves to the end of the file for adding new lines at the bottom of the file.

- ✓ The following syntax is used to open the file in append mode.

Syntax:

fstream <Fileobject>;
<Fileobject>.open(<Filename>,ios::app);

- ✓ A file stored in binary format is known as a binary file. A binary file is only computer readable and cannot be read by humans.
- ✓ Operating systems store the files in binary format as computers can only deal with binary numbers.
- ✓ The 'ios::binary' statement in the piece of code given above signifies that we are opening a binary file where as the proclamation 'ios::out' tells the compiler that we are opening the binary file for writing purposes.
- ✓ Binary files have the '.dat' extension.
- ✓ For opening binary files in input mode we again use the 'fstream'class using the following syntax.

Syntax:

fstream<FileObject>;
<FileObject>.open (<Filename>,ios::binary |ios::in);

- ✓ To open the binary files in output mode one has to use the following syntax:

Syntax:

fstream<FileObject>;
<FileObject>.open (<Filename>,ios::binary |ios::in);

✓ The write() function is used to write on the binary file.

fil.write((char*)&sizeof(s));

Where the first part of the statement '(char*)&(structure_variable/class_object)' typecasts the structure or the class to character type. Where as the second part of the statement 'sizeof(structure_variable/class_object)' allocates the number of bytes to be fed into the binary file.

Binary files are read using the 'read()' function.

fil.read((char*)&sizeof(s));

The first part of the statement '(char*)&(structure_variable/class_object)' typecasts the structure or the class to character type. Where as the second part of the statement 'sizeof(structure_variable/class_object)' allocates the number of bytes to be fed into the binary file.

Notes

PART IV

DATA BASES & C++

Part IV

Chapter 1

DATABASE CONCEPTS

AIM

- To introduce database and its usage
- To learn about database Models and Relational Algebra
- To know what is normalization
- To understand use of databases through examples

OUTLINE

1.1 Introduction
1.2 Databases
1.3 Database Management System
1.4 Purpose of Databases
1.5 DBMS Models
1.6 Relational Database Terminology
1.7 Relational Algebra
1.8 Normalization
1.9 Review Examples
1.10 Let us revise

1.1 Introduction

Computers are used in business and industry for diverse purposes. For example, an industry might be using computers for storing sales data, inventory control, and production scheduling and similar activities. An educational institute might be using computers for storing the information about the performance of students, school fees, scholarships granted or other forms of financial assistance. Software for such a system uses customized data files and reports specifically designed for the application. If these applications have been designed for the same organization then the same data may be used in each of the application for a different purpose. For example, the name, address and roll no of a student may be stored in both the result file as well as the payment file (which stores information about the payments made by a student as school fees). This leads to some duplication and redundancy of data.

It would have been better had all the relevant information about an organization been centralized and accessible without the need for creating separate files for different purposes. The concept of database attempts to achieve this objective. This part of the appendix briefly discusses the concept of databases and its applications.

1.2 Databases

A database is a collection of related files. Database is a collection of interrelated files containing collection of records, where each record of the file is a collection of logically related data items. It is required for keeping the information of different applications of an organization to enable manipulation of the data and generate reports for its operation as well as the management. Database should be made in the following way that

- It can accept the required changes and grow in the future.
- It can be used by more than one independent application.

Organizations seeking computer assistance prefer to store their data in the form of an integrated database. A person of the organization is assigned the responsibility to maintain the database. He is usually designated as the database administrator (DBA). Any group of the organization can be granted access to the centralized database for a specific purpose.

1.3 Database Management System

A **database management system** (DBMS), or simply a **database system** (DBS), consists of the following:

- A collection of interrelated and persistent data (usually referred to as the database (DB)).
- A set of application programs used to access, update and manage that data (which form the data management system (MS)).

The goal of a DBMS is to provide an environment that is both **convenient** and **efficient** to use in.

1.4 Purpose of Databases

To see why database management systems are necessary, let's look at a typical ``file-processing system'' supported by a conventional operating system.

1. The application is a savings bank:
    - Savings account and customer records are kept in permanent system files.
    - Application programs are written to manipulate files to perform the following tasks:
        - Debit or credit an account.
        - Add a new account.
        - Find an account balance.
        - Generate monthly statements.

2. Development of the system proceeds as follows:
    - New application programs must be written as the need arises.
    - New permanent files are created as required.
    - Over a long period of time files may be in different formats, and application programs may be in different languages.

3. So we can see there are problems with the straight file-processing approach:
    - Data redundancy and inconsistency
        - Same information may be duplicated in several places.
        - All copies may not be updated properly. ..
    - Data isolation
        - Data in different files.
        - Data in different formats.
        - Difficult to write new application programs.
    - Multiple users
        - Want concurrency for faster response time.
        - Need protection for concurrent updates.

        For example, two customers withdrawing funds from a common account at the same time - account has $500 in it, and they withdraw $100 and $50. The result could be $350, $400 or $450 if no protection is provided.

    - Security problems
        - Every user of the system should be able to access only the data they are permitted to see.

          For example, payroll people only handle employee records, and cannot see customer accounts; tellers only access account data and cannot see payroll data.

- Difficult to enforce this with application programs.

- Integrity problems
  - Data may be required to satisfy constraints.
  - For example, minimum account balance allowed $25.00.

These problems and others led to the development of **database management systems**.

1.5 DBMS Models

A DBMS is divided into 4 models given below:

1. Hierarchical data model
2. Network data model
3. Relational data model
4. Object based logical models

A brief description of relational\object based data models is given in the following section.

1.5.1 Relational data model

Relational database is a collection of related tables (relations) where each table is a collection of rows (tuples) and columns (attribute). A relation among set of values (in each column) is represented by a row of a table, hence the term relational database. A relation in a database has the following characteristics:

1. Every value in a relation is atomic which means that it can not be further divided
2. The rows in the relation are not ordered.
3. Names of columns are distinct and order of columns is immaterial

"Since relation is a set, and sets are not ordered hence no ordering is defined on tuples of relation"

1.5.2 Object based logical model

Object based logical models describe data at the conceptual and view levels. It provides fairly flexible structuring capabilities. It allows one to specify data constraints explicitly. Over 30 such models, including the few given below:

- Entity-relationship model.
- Object-oriented model.
- Binary model.
- Semantic data model.
- Info logical model.
- Functional data model.

1.6 Relational Database Terminology

Relational database terminology consists of the following parameters:

Entity

An entity is an object which can be uniquely identified. For example, Chris a student with 'R.NO' 101(table 1.1) is an entity

Attribute

An entity can be presented with a set of attributes. Thus, a row in a table represents an entity and a particular column of this entity is an attribute. So, we can say that a set of attributes define characteristics of an entity. In the 'student table' (table 1.1) NAME, R.NO, CITY are all attributes.

Domain

Domain is a collection of possible values that an attribute can have. An atomic domain is that containing values representing individual units. Thus, values of NAME of the student entity are drawn from all valid names. Similarly the domain of attribute R.NO can be considered to be only a valid integer number. The percentage can never be more then 100. The domain of this attribute is a valid number in the range of 0 to 100.

Relation

A relation is most conveniently represented by a table. A row of the table is known as a **tuple**. Number of rows or records is defined as 'cardinality' of the relation. Consider the relation shown in table 1.1.

Table 1.1: TABLE STUDENT

NAME	R.NO	CITY
Ankit	1000	Delhi
Deepti	1100	Delhi
Karan	1107	Patna
Lucky	1111	Chennai
Raghav	1007	Mathura

The relation is named 'STUDENT'. The cardinality of this relation is 5.

A tuple consisting of 'n' number of attributes is called a n-tuple. In term of tuple definition, we can say that the number of tuples in a relation is known as 'cardinality' and the number of attributes in a tuple is known as 'degree' of a relation.

Key

Within a given relation there is one attribute or collection of attributes with values that are unique within the relation and thus can be used to identify a tuple from a relation, such attribute or collection of attributes of the relation is known as key. In a relation, we may have more than one key identifying a tuple uniquely. All such keys are known as **candidate keys**. From the candidate keys, one can be used as **primary key** and others will become **alternate keys.**

In the relation, CONSUMABLE (table 1.2), **Ccode** and **Item** are candidate keys. If **Ccode** is taken to be the primary key then **Item** will become the alternate key 'else if' **Item** is taken as primary key than **Ccode** will become an alternate key.

Table 1.2 CONSUMABLE

Ccode	Item	Qty Stock
C01	CD-ROM	50
C02	DISK 1.44	120
C03	DISK 1.20	50
C04	ST.80 COL.	30
C05	ST.132 COL.	120

1.7 Relational Algebra

In relational algebra we study about the various operations that can be carried out on a relation. Some of the major operations are given below:-

- **Selection (Unary Operator)**

  By using selection operation one selects the horizontal subset of a relation.

- **Projection (Unary Operator)**

  By using projection operation one selects the vertical subset of a relation.

- **Cartesian product(Binary Operator)**

  It operates on two relations and is denoted by **X.** For example Cartesian product of two relations **R1** and **R2** is represented by **R=R1*R2.** The **degree** of **R** is equal to the sum of the degrees of R1 and R2. Similarly the cardinality of R is obtained by the product of cardinality of **R1** and cardinality of **R2**.

For Example,

Relation: R1

Roll no	Student Name	Class
1	Varun	XII
4	Ankit	X
10	Deepti	X I

Relation: R2

Teacher Code	Teacher Name
107	Mr Malik
109	Mr Chopra

Resultant Relation: R= R1 * R2

Col1	Col2	Col3	Col4	Col5
1	Varun	XII	107	Mr Malik
1	Varun	XII	109	Mr Chopra
4	Ankit	X	107	Mr Malik
4	Ankit	X	109	Mr Chopra
10	Deepti	XI	107	Mr Malik
10	Deepti	XI	109	Mr Chopra

- **Union (Binary Operator)**

  The union operation operates on two relations. The operation is indicated by the alphabet capital 'U'.
  For example, **R=R1** U **R2** represents **sum** of cardinality of **R1** and of **R2** but before the union operation can be used the following have to be considered for the operation **R1** U **R2.**

  - **Degree** of R1 = Degree of R2
  - j^{th} attribute of R1 and j^{th} attribute of R2 must have a common domain.

  For Example,

Relation: R1

Student_Code	Student_Name
S101	Raghav
S102	Anisha

Relation: R2

Student_ID	Name
R101	Anshuman
R103	Gaurav
R107	Kartik

Resultant Relation: R = R1 U R2

Column 1	Column 2
S101	Raghav
S102	Anisha
R101	Anshuman
R103	Gaurav
R107	kartik

1.8 Normalization

As we have observed earlier the main goal of relational database design is to generate a set of relational structures (schemes) that allow us to store information without necessary redundancy, yet allow easy retrieval of information, effective updating and manipulation of data at the same time. If the database design is not proper then it may have some undesirable characteristics like:-

1. Redundancy/ Duplicity of information
2. Inability to map certain information
3. Loss pf information

A design is said to be good if one fact is stored at one place. Theory of normalization is a design aid which tries to approach the concept of one fact at one place. Thus, we can say that 'normalization is the process of analyzing data for grouping entries and data elements into set of harmonious relations'.

There are many forms of normalization the ones to learn are given as follows:-

- **First Normal form**

  A database is said to be in the first normal form if each of its attributes contains atomic values and has no repeated values or no two rows are identical.

Table 1.3 Raw Data

ICode	IName	I_type	S_Code1	Suplier1	Scity1	S_Code2	Supplier2	Scity2	S_code3	Supplier3	Scity3
8102	Saree	L_wear	S101	Krishna	Delhi	S201	Yuvraj	Mumbai			
7945	Belt	Accs	S102	Kriti	Mumbai	S201	Yuvraj	Mumbai	S113	Parekh	Mumbai
6789	Bag	Accs	S103	Gupta	Kolkata						
1060	Tie	M.wear	S104	Sinha	Delhi	S102	Kriti				

Table 1.3 in First Normal Form

ICode	IName	Item_type	Supplier_Code	Supplier_Name	Supplier_city
8102	Saree	L_wear	S101	Mr. Krishna	Mumbai
8102	Saree	L_wear	S201	Mr.Yuvraj	Delhi
7945	Belt	Accs	S102	Mr. Kriti	Madras
7945	Belt	Accs	S201	Mr. Yuvraj	Delhi
7945	Belt	Accs	S113	Mr. Parekh	Mumbai
6789	Bag	Accs	S103	Mr. Gupta	Kolkata
1060	Tie	M.wear	S104	Mr. Sinha	Delhi
1060	Tie	M.wear	S201	Mr. Kriti	Madras

- **Second Normal Form**

A database is in the second normal form (2NF) if it is already in first normal form(1NF) and each table in the database contains data about one and only one entity (this can be optionally checked by looking at the primary key) and that all non key attributes of the table are dependent on the key value(s).If we convert the above relation into 2NF, table 1.4 'Item' consists of complete details of 'Item' whereas table 1.5 'Supplier' contains details of the supplier and the items he is supplying:

Second Normal Form

Table 1.4 Item Table

ICode	IName	Item_type
8102	Saree	L_wear
7945	Belt	Accs
6789	Bag	Accs
1060	Tie	M.wear

Table 1.5 Supplier Table

ICode	Supplier_Code	Supplier_Name	Supplier_city
8102	S101	Mr. Krishna	Mumbai
8102	S201	Mr. Yuvraj	Delhi
7945	S102	Mr. Kriti	Madras
7945	S201	Mr. Yuvraj	Delhi
7945	S113	Mr. Parekh	Mumbai
6789	S103	Mr. Gupta	Kolkata
1060	S104	Mr. Sinha	Delhi
1060	S201	Mr. Kriti	Madras

- **Third Normal Form**

A database is said to be in the third normal form if it is already in the second normal form and none of the non key attributes are dependent on any other non key attributes. In other words, all the non key attributes directly depend only on the primary key.

So for bringing a table in the third normal form all attributes not dependent on the primary key attribute should be separated out to another table or removed. For converting the database that we converted into third normal form the table 'Item' will undergo no changes, where as the 'Supplier' table will be divided into two tables 'Item_supply' which consists of who the supplier is (Supplier_code) and what he is supplying (ICode) and the 'Supplier' table which has the details of the 'Supplier'.

Third Normal Form

Table Item

ICode	IName	Item_type
8102	Saree	L_wear
7945	Belt	Accs
6789	Bag	Accs
1060	Tie	M.wear

Table Item_supply

ICode	Supplier_code
8102	S101
8102	S201
7945	S102
7945	S201
7945	S113
6789	S103
1060	S104
1060	S201

Table Supplier

Supplier_Code	Supplier_Name	Supplier_city
S101	Mr. Krishna	Mumbai
S201	Mr. Yuvraj	Delhi
S102	Mr. Kriti	Madras
S201	Mr. Yuvraj	Delhi
S113	Mr. Parekh	Mumbai
S103	Mr. Gupta	Kolkata
S104	Mr. Sinha	Delhi
S201	Mr. Kriti	Madras

1.9 Review Examples

Example 1.9.1
What is data redundancy and how does redundancy of data lead to data inconsistency? Explain with an example?

Solution of 1.9.1
Data redundancy is the storage of same data in more than one file. This leads to data inconsistency. This is because the same data might have been entered by different users at different times or it might have been updated by different users at different times. For example, the address of students in an educational institution may be stored in the students section of the institution. Some of these students might be residing in the hostel of the institution. Their addresses may be available in the hostel as well. Suppose the address of a student is changed. It is possible that the change in address is entered in the file maintained in the hostel. But the same may not be updated in the file of the student section. Thus duplication may lead to data inconsistency.

Example 1.9.2
What is a relation? What is the difference between a tuple and an attribute?

Solution of 1.9.2
A relation is like a table in which data are arranged in the form of rows and columns. The rows of the table are known as the tuples and the columns of the table are known as the attributes.

Example 1.9.3
What is data security?

Solution of 1.9.3
Data security is the protection given to the data against modification or destruction, intentional or inadvertent, by authorized users.

Example 1.9.4
What is the degree and cardinality of the table products? Also check if the 2 tables given below are union compatible or not?

Table 'PRODUCTS'

VEDOR	PRODUCT	QTY.	PRICE
V1	P1	5	500
V1	P2	7	700
V2	P3	7	750
V3	P4	10	720
V4	P5	8	780

Table 'CUSTOMER'

ORDER NO.	CUSTOMER
1	C1
2	C2
3	C3

Solution of 1.9.4
The degree of table product is 4 and the cardinality is 5 and the two tables specified are not compatible union.

Example 1.9.5
Define the following terms:-
- Tuple
- Attribute
- Domain
- Degree
- Cardinality

Solution of 1.9.5
- Tuple: The rows of the table are known as tuples.
- Attribute: The columns of the table are knows as the attributes.
- Domain: It is a set to which each entry in the column of a relation belongs.
- Degree: The number of columns (attributes) is a relation known as the degree of the relation.
- Cardinality: The number of rows (tuples) in a relation are known as the cardinality of the relation.

Example 1.9.6
Find the cartesian product of the two relations 'R1' and 'R2' given below:-

Relation R1

T1	T2	T3
R	1	25
J	2	24
P	3	23

Relation R2

T4	T5
A	X
B	Y
C	Z

Solution of 1.9.6

The Cartesian product is relation R3 = R1 * R2 given below:-

T1	T2	T3	T4	T5
R	1	25	A	X
R	1	25	B	Y
R	1	25	B	Z
J	2	24	A	X
J	2	24	B	Y
J	2	24	C	Z
P	3	23	A	X
P	3	23	B	Y
P	3	23	C	Z

1.10 Let us revise!

- A database is a collection of related files.
- A database is required for keeping the information of different applications of an organization
- Relational database is a collection of related tables (relations) where each table is a collection of rows **(tuples)** and columns **(attribute)**.
- An entity is an object which can be uniquely identified.
- Attributes define characteristics of an entity.
- Domain is a collection of possible values that an attribute can have.
- By using selection operation one selects the horizontal subset of a relation.
- By using projection operation one selects the vertical subset of a relation.
- In Cartesian product of two relations R1 and R2 the resultant relation R3 will be equal to the product of R1 and R2 that is **R3= R1* R2**
- 'Normalization is the process of analyzing data for grouping entries and data elements into set of harmonious relations'.

Part IV

Chapter 2

STRUCTURED QUERY LANGUAGE (SQL)

AIM

- To introduce SQL Commands
- To study the built-in functions
- To learn use of the SQL commands and functions through lot of solved examples

OUTLINE

2.1 Introduction
2.2 Capabilities of SQL
2.3 SQL Data types
2.4 SQL Commands and Functions
2.5 Review Examples
2.6 Review Exercise
2.7 Let us revise

2.1 Introduction

SQL is the base language of all 'Relational database management systems (RDBMS)'. SQL allows users to access data in relational database management systems, such as Oracle, Sybase, Informix, Microsoft SQL Server, Access, and others, by allowing users to perform operations, such as, create database tables, insert, delete, sort, and manipulate data. In this appendix, we will discuss elementary SQL commands. It may be noted that limited SQL commands are also available in recent versions of Dbase, Foxbase, Foxpro etc.

2.2 Capabilities of SQL

- DDL(Data Definition Language)

  A database schema (The overall design of the database) is specified by a set of definition that is expressed by a data definition language. The SQL DDL provides commands for defining relation schemes, creating indices, and modifying relation schemes.

- DML(Data Manipulation language)

  The SQL-DML includes those commands, which are based on both the relational algebra and the tuple relational calculus. DML is a language that enables users to access or manipulate data. By Data manipulation, we mean:
  - The retrieval of information stored in the database
  - The insertion of new information into the database
  - The deletion of information from the database
  - The modification of information stored in the database

2.3 SQL Datatypes

SQL supports following data types for specification of attributes of a relation:

1. **'char(n)' datatype**: An attribute can be declared of type char(n) which specifies that the attribute will store a string of n characters to a maximum of 240 characters.
2. **Small 'int'**: An integer having a value between -99,999 to 99,999.
3. **Date**: A date value that is displayed is in accordance with the
   SET DATE BRITISH/AMERICAN and SET CENTURY ON/ OFF commands in the format {dd/mm/yy}, {mm/dd/yy, {dd/mm/yyyy} or {mm/dd/yyyy}

2.4 SQL Commands and Functions

- The **SELECT** Statement

In a relational database, data is stored in tables. For example look at table 2.1 'EmployeeAddressTable' which relates Social Insurance number (SIN), Name (FirstName, LastName) and Address (Address, city, state) of an employee.

2.1 EmployeeAddressTable					
SIN	**FirstName**	**LastName**	**Address**	**City**	**State**
512687458	Ankit	Asthana	29 Sirifort Road	Kanpur	U.P.
758420012	Deepti	Asthana	H-43 Anand Lok	New Delhi	Delhi
102254896	Varun	Beri	E-39 Susant Lok	Bhopal	M.P.

Now let's say, we want to see the address of each employee. For doing so, one will have to use the SELECT statement. The command for using the SELECT clause to view the addresses of all the employees is given below.

```
SELECT FirstName, LastName, Address, City, State
FROM EmployeeAddressTable;
```

The following is the results of the *query* given above on the database:

FirstName	**LastName**	**Address**	**City**	**State**
Ankit	Asthana	29 Sirifort Road	Kanpur	U.P.
Deepti	Asthana	H-43 Anand Lok	New Delhi	Delhi
Varun	Beri	E-39 Susant Lok	Bhopal	M.P.

All we have done by executing this query is that we have asked for the entire data in the EmployeeAddressTable, Z which includes *columns* called 'FirstName', 'LastName', 'Address', 'City', and 'State'. Note that column names and table names do not have spaces...they must be typed as one word; and that the statement ends with a semicolon (;). The general form for a SELECT statement, retrieving all of the *rows* in the table is given below:

```
SELECT ColumnName, ColumnName, ...
FROM TableName;
```

To view all the columns of a table without typing all column names, we can also use the following statement:

```
SELECT * FROM TableName;
```

- **Conditional SELECT statement**

To further discuss the SELECT statement, let's look at a new example table ('EmployeeStatisticsTable):

EmployeeStatisticsTable			
EmployeeIDNo	**Salary**	**Benefits**	**Position**
010	75000	15000	Manager
105	65000	15000	Manager
152	60000	15000	Manager
215	60000	12500	Manager
244	50000	12000	Staff
300	45000	10000	Staff
335	40000	10000	Staff
400	32000	7500	Entry-Level
441	28000	7500	Entry-Level

Relational Operators

There are six Relational Operators in SQL as given in table below:

=	Equal
<> or != (see manual)	Not Equal
<	Less Than
>	Greater Than
<=	Less Than or Equal To
>=	Greater Than or Equal To

We can also use the 'WHERE' clause with the select statement. The 'WHERE' is used to specify that only certain rows of the table are to be displayed based on the criteria or conditions described in the WHERE *clause*. Let us take an example to learn how do we use the 'WHERE' clause. Suppose that from 'EmployeeStatisticsTable' we want to view the EmployeeIdNo's of all the employees making over $0000, we would use the following query.

```
SELECT EMPLOYEEIDNO
FROM EMPLOYEESTATISTICSTABLE
WHERE SALARY >= 50000;
```

Notice that the >= (greater than or equal to) sign is used, as we wanted to view Ids of those employees who earn greater than or equal to $50,000. The result of this query is given below:

EMPLOYEEIDNO
010
105
152
215
244

The *WHERE clause* SALARY >= 50000, is known as a *condition* (an operation which evaluates to True or False). Let us take another example, suppose we want to display the Id numbers of all the emplyoee(s) having position 'Manager' assigned to them. This can be done using the following query:

```
SELECT EMPLOYEEIDNO
FROM EMPLOYEESTATISTICSTABLE
WHERE POSITION = 'Manager';
```

This query displays the ID Numbers of all Managers. Generally, with text columns, stick to equal to or not equal to, and make sure that any text that appears in the statement is surrounded by single quotes (').

- **More Complex Conditions: Compound Conditions / Logical Operators**

  - **The 'And' Operator**

The *AND* operator joins two or more conditions, and displays a row only if that row's data satisfies **ALL** conditions listed in the query it is used in. For example, to display all the staff employees making over $ 40,000 the following query shall be used:

STRUCTURED QUERY LANGUAGE (SQL)

```
SELECT EMPLOYEEIDNO
FROM EMPLOYEESTATISTICSTABLE
WHERE SALARY > 40000 AND POSITION = 'Staff';
```

- **The 'OR' Operator**

The *OR* operator joins two or more conditions, but returns a row if **ANY** of the conditions listed hold true. To see all those who make less than $.40, 000 or have less than $10,000 in benefits, listed together, one would use the following query:

```
SELECT EMPLOYEEIDNO
FROM EMPLOYEESTATISTICSTABLE
WHERE SALARY < 40000 OR BENEFITS < 10000;
```

One can also combine the 'AND' & the 'OR' and use them to create queries. For example,

```
SELECT EMPLOYEEIDNO
FROM EMPLOYEESTATISTICSTABLE
WHERE POSITION = 'Manager' AND SALARY > 60000 OR BENEFITS > 12000;
```

When this query is accessed what SQL does is that it displays the ID numbers of those employees who are assigned the position 'Manager' and earning salary greater than $6000 or earning benefits greater than $12000. The important thing to note though is that the AND operation is done first. To generalize this process, SQL performs the AND operation(s) to determine the rows where the AND operation(s) hold true (remember: all of the conditions are true), then these results are used to compare with the OR conditions, and only display those remaining rows where any of the conditions joined by the OR operator hold true (where a condition or result from an AND is paired with another condition or AND result to use to evaluate the OR, which evaluates to true if either value is true). Mathematically, SQL evaluates all of the conditions, then evaluates the AND "pairs", and then evaluates the OR's (where both operators evaluate left to right).

> True AND False OR True AND True OR False AND False
>
> **Step 1**: Simplify the AND pairs:
>
> **Result** : False OR True OR False
>
> **Step 2:** Simplify the OR's from left to right in the statement
>
> **Result**: True OR False
> True

The result of this query hence comes out to be 'True', and the row passes the query conditions. The logical operations in SQL follow the precedence shown in table 2.2.

Table 2.2: SQL Order of Logical Operations (each operates from left to right)

1. NOT
2. AND
3. OR

- **DISTINCT clause with SELECT statement**

Before understanding how does the DISTINCT clause work with the SELECT statement, let us first look at the following table:

Table 2.3: ANTIQUES

OwnerID	OwnerLastName	OwnerFirstName	Ownercity
01	Jacob	Sam	New Delhi
02	Pathan	Ram	Kanpur
15	Dravid	Dinesh	Mumbai
21	Leander	Ramesh	Jhansi
50	Marley	Lucas	Kolkata

```
SELECT DISTINCT Ownercity from ANTIQUES
```

In this example, since everyone lives in a different city hence all of them will be displayed.

- **Aggregate Functions in SQL**

There are five important *aggregate functions*: SUM, AVG, MAX, MIN, and COUNT which are used in SQL. They are known as aggregate functions because they summarize the results of a query, rather than listing all of the rows.

• SUM ()	gives the total of all the rows, satisfying any conditions, of the given column, where the given column is numeric.
• AVG ()	gives the average of the given column.
• MAX ()	gives the largest figure in the given column.
• MIN ()	gives the smallest figure in the given column.
• COUNT(*)	gives the number of rows satisfying the conditions.

Let us take up a few examples using the 'EmployeeStatisticsTable' to understand how aggregate functions are used in SQL.

EmployeeStatisticsTable			
EmployeeIDNo	**Salary**	**Benefits**	**Position**
010	75000	15000	Manager
105	65000	15000	Manager
152	60000	15000	Manager
215	60000	12500	Manager
244	50000	12000	Staff
300	45000	10000	Staff
335	40000	10000	Staff
400	32000	7500	Entry-Level
441	28000	7500	Entry-Level

```
SELECT SUM(SALARY), AVG(SALARY)
FROM EMPLOYEESTATISTICSTABLE;
```

This query shows the total of all salaries in the table, and the average salary of all of the Employees in the table.

```
SELECT MIN(BENEFITS)
FROM EMPLOYEESTATISTICSTABLE
WHERE POSITION = 'Manager';
```

This query gives the smallest figure of the Benefits column, of the employees who are Managers, the result is '12500'.

```
SELECT COUNT(*)
FROM EMPLOYEESTATISTICSTABLE
WHERE POSITION = 'Staff';
```

This query tells us how many employees have Staff status (3).

▪ Views

In SQL, you might (check your DBA) have access to create views for yourself. A view allows you to assign the results of a query to a new, personal table, that you can use in other queries, where this new table is given the view name in the FROM clause. When you access a view, the query that is defined in your view creation statement is performed (generally), and the results of that query look just like another table in the query that you wrote invoking the view. To create a view we use the following syntax:

Syntax:

```
CREATE VIEW view_name as SELECT col1, col2 from table_name where
condition;
```

Example,

```
CREATE VIEW temp as SELECT salary, benefits, position
from  EmployeeStatisticsTable
```

Modification of database through views is possible (updates, deletion, insertion) since they are physically stored in the database, though this may have potentially disadvantageous consequences.

Note: To delete a view from the database one can use the drop view command.

Syntax: DROP VIEW View_Name;

▪ Creating New Tables

All tables within a database must be created at some point in time...let's see how we would create the ORDERS table:

Syntax:

```
Create table table_name(col1 datatype(size), col2 datatype(Size,……… .);
```

For Example,

```
CREATE TABLE ORDERS
(OWNERID INTEGER NOT NULL, ITEMDESIRED CHAR(40) NOT      NULL);
```

This statement gives the table name and tells the DBMS about each column in the table. ***Please note*** that this statement uses generic data types, and that the data types might be different, depending on what DBMS you are using. Some common generic data types are:

- **Char(x)** - A column of characters, where x is a number designating the maximum number of characters allowed (maximum length) in the column.
- **Integer** - A column of whole numbers, positive or negative.
- **Decimal(x, y)** - A column of decimal numbers, where x is the maximum length in digits of the decimal numbers in this column, and y is the maximum number of digits allowed after the decimal point. The maximum (4,2) number would be 99.99.
- **Date** - A date column in a DBMS-specific format.
- **Logical** - A column that can hold only two values: TRUE or FALSE.

NOT NULL means that the column must have a value in each row. If NULL was used, that column may be left empty in a given row.

▪ Altering Tables

Let's add a column to the Antiques table to allow the entry of the price of a given Item:

Syntax:

```
ALTER TABLE Table_Name ADD(col1datatype(size), col2 datatype(size) …… .);

ALTER TABLE ANTIQUES ADD (PRICE DECIMAL(8,2) NULL);
```

The data for this new column can be updated or inserted using the 'INSERT INTO' clause explained in the following section.

▪ Adding Data

To insert rows into a table, do the following:

Syntax,

```
INSERT INTO Table_Name (col1,col2,….) VALUES ( value 1, value 2…);

INSERT INTO ANTIQUES VALUES (21, 01, 'Ottoman', 200.00);
```

This query inserts the data into the table, as a new row, column-by-column, in the pre-defined order. Instead, let's change the order and leave Price blank:

```
INSERT INTO ANTIQUES (BUYERID, SELLERID, ITEM)
VALUES (01, 21, 'Ottoman');
```

- ## Deleting Data

Syntax:

```
DELETE FROM Table_Name where condition;
```

For Example,

```
DELETE FROM ANTIQUES WHERE ITEM = 'Ottoman';
```

For deleting entries from the data base the 'delete' clause is used. The statement given above deletes all rows where ITEM is 'Ottoman'. In order to delete the row we added in the previous section, we have to be more specific in our query. The following statement deletes the row; we created in the previous section.

```
DELETE FROM ANTIQUES
WHERE ITEM = 'Ottoman' AND BUYERID = 01 AND SELLERID = 21;
```

- ## Updating Data

Let's update a Price into a row that doesn't have a price listed yet:

Syntax:

```
UPDATE Table_Name SET COL1 = expression 1, COL2= expression 2, where condition;
```

Example,

```
UPDATE ANTIQUES SET PRICE = 500.00 WHERE ITEM = 'Chair';
```

This sets all the Chair's Prices to 500.00. As shown above, more WHERE conditionals, using AND, must be used to limit the updating to more specific rows. Also, additional columns may be set by separating equal statements with commas.

- **GROUP BY & HAVING**

Antiques

SellerID	BuyerID	Item
01	50	Bed
02	15	Table
15	02	Chair
21	50	Mirror
50	01	Desk
01	21	Cabinet
02	21	Coffee Table
15	50	Chair
01	15	Jewelry Box
02	21	Pottery
21	02	Bookcase
50	01	Plant Stand

One special use of GROUP BY is to associate an aggregate function (especially COUNT; counting the number of rows in each group) with groups of rows. First, assume that the Antiques table has the Price column, and each row has a value for that column. We want to see the price of the most expensive item bought by each owner. We have to tell SQL to *group* each owner's purchases, and tell us the maximum purchase price:

```
SELECT BUYERID, MAX(PRICE)
FROM ANTIQUES
GROUP BY BUYERID;
```

Now, say we only want to see the maximum purchase price if the purchase is over $ 1000, so we use the HAVING clause:

```
SELECT BUYERID, MAX(PRICE)
FROM ANTIQUES
GROUP BY BUYERID
HAVING PRICE > 1000;
```

2.5 Review Examples

Example 2.5.1

What is difference between terms DDL and DML?

Solution of 2.5.1

DDL stands for data definition language. It is used for creation of tables where as DML stands for Data Manipulation Language and is used for updating tables.

Example 2.5.2

Observe the following table given below. It gives Id Number, Name, Quantity and price of the enlisted products. The table is named products.

Idno	Name	Quantity	Price
101	Oil filter	335	45.00
102	Spark Plug	224	57.00
103	Tie Rod	136	245.00
104	Head Light	45	125.00
105	Shocker	86	225.00
106	Coolant	120	100.00

Write the SQL queries for the following:-

(a) Name of the products along with the price of each.
(b) Name and Quantity of all the products for which qty<150.
(c) Name and Quantity of all products , excluding shocker for which qty.<150
(d) Count the number of products in the list.
(e) Find the name of the product with the maximum quantity in the stock.

Solution of 2.5.2

(a) SELECT name, price FROM products;
(b) SELECT name, qty FROM products where qty<150;
(c) SELECT name, Quantity FROM products where qty<150 AND name <> 'shocker';
(d) SELECT products, count(*) FROM products;
(e) SELECT name, MAX(Quantity) FROM products;

Example 2.5.3

Write SQL commands for (a) to (g) and write the outputs for (h) on the basis of table HOSPITAL.

Table: HOSPITAL

NO.	Name	Age	Department	Dateofadm	Charges	Sex
1	Arpit	62	Surgery	21/01/98	300	M
2	Zarina	22	ENT	12/12/97	250	F
3	Kareem	32	Orthopedic	19/02/98	200	M
4	Arun	12	Surgery	11/01/98	300	M
5	Zublin	30	ENT	12/01/98	250	M

STRUCTURED QUERY LANGUAGE (SQL)

6	Ketaki	16	ENT	24/02/98	250	F
7	Ankita	29	Cardiology	20/02/98	800	F
8	Zareen	45	Gynecology	22/02/98	300	F
9	Kush	19	Cardiology	13/01/98	800	M
10	Shilpa	23	Nuclear Medicine	21/02/98	400	F

a) To select all the information of patients of the cardiology department.
b) To list the names of female patients who are in the ENT department.
c) To list names of all patients with their date of admission in ascending order.
d) To display patients name, charges, Age for only the female patients.
e) To count the number of patients with age<30.
f) To insert a new row in the HOSPITAL table with the following data:
11,"Aftab", 24,"Surgery",{25/02/98},300,"M"
g) Give the output of following SQL statements:
   i. Select COUNT(DISTINCT charges) from HOSPITAL;
   ii. Select MIN(Age) from HOSPITAL where sex = "f";
   iii. Select sum(charges) from HOSPITAL where department = "ENT";
   iv. Select AVG(charges) from HOSPITAL where Dateofadm<{12/02/98}.

Solution of 2.5.3

a) SELECT * FROM hospital where department = "Cardiology";
b) SELECT Name FROM hospital where Department = "ENT" AND Sex="F";
c) SELECT Name, Dateofadm FROM hospital ORDER BY Dateofadm;
d) SELECT Name, Dateofadm FROM hospital WHERE Sex="f";
e) SELECT COUNT(*) FROM hospital where Age<30;
f) INSERT INTO hospital values (11,"Aftab",24,"Surgery",{24/02/98},300,"M"};
g) i) 5
   ii) 16
   iii) 500
   iv) 380.00

Example 2.5.4

Write SQL statement to create a table EMP with the under mentioned structure:-

EmpNo	NUMBER(4)
DeptNo	NUMBER(2)
EmpName	CHAR(20)
Job	CHAR(10)
Manager	NUMBER(4)
Hiredate	DATE
Salary	NUMBER(7,2)
Commission	NUMBER(7,2)

Solution of 2.5.4

```
Create table EMP
(EmpNO       NUMBER(4) NOT NULL PRIMARY KEY,
 DeptNo       NUMBER(2),
 EmpName      CHAR(20),
 Job      CHAR(10),
 Manager          NUMBER(4),
 Hiredate         DATE,
 Salary          NUMBER(7,2),
 Commission  NUMBER(7,2));
```

Example 2.5.5
Discuss about the various types of datatypes in SQL?

Solution of 2.5.5

- Char(x) - A column of characters, where x is a number designating the maximum number of characters allowed (maximum length) in the column.
- Integer - A column of whole numbers, positive or negative.
- Decimal(x, y) - A column of decimal numbers, where x is the maximum length in digits of the decimal numbers in this column, and y is the maximum number of digits allowed after the decimal point. The maximum (4,2) number would be 99.99.
- Date - A date column in a DBMS-specific format.

Example 2.5.6
What is a view? What are the advantages of this clause?

Solution of 2.5.6
A view allows you to assign the results of a query to a new, personal table, that you can use in other queries, where this new table is given the view name in your FROM clause. When you access a view, the query that is defined in your view creation statement is performed (generally), and the results of that query look just like another table in the query that you wrote invoking the view. For example, to create a view:

Syntax:

```
create view view_name as select col1, col2 from table_name where condition;
```

Example:

```
CREATE VIEW temp as SELECT salary, benefits, position from
EmployeeStatisticsTable
```

Modification of database through views is possible (updates, deletion, insertion) since they are physically stored in the database, though this may have potentially disadvantageous consequences.

2.6 Review Exercise

Q1) What do you understand by primary key and candidate key?

{**HINT:** An attribute or set of attributes which are used to identify a tuple is known as primary key. If a table has more than one such attributes which identify a tuple uniquely than all such attributes are known as Candidate Keys.}

Q2) Consider the following tables Activity and Coach. Write SQL commands for the statements (i) to (vi) and give outputs for SQL queries (vii) to (x)?

Table: ACTIVITY

ACODE	ActivityName	Number	PrizeMoney	ScheduleDate
1001	Relay 100*4	16	10000	23/01/2004
1002	High Jump	10	12000	12/01/2004
1003	Shot Put	12	8000	14/02/2004
1005	Long Jump	12	9000	01/01/2004
1008	Discuss Throw	10	15000	19/03/2004

Table: COACH

PCode	Name	ACode
1	Ahmad Husain	1001
2	Ravinder	1008
3	Janila	1001
4	Naaz	1003

(i) To display the name of all activities with their ACode in descending order.

(ii) To display details of those activities which are having PrizeMoney less than 10000

(**HINT:** SELECT * FROM ACTIVITY where prize money < 10000;)

(iii) To display the content of the activity table whose ScheduleDate earlier than 01/01/2004 in ascending order of Number.

(iv) To display the coach's name and ACode in ascending order of ACode from the table COACH.

(v) SELECT COUNT(DISTINCT Number) from ACTIVITY;

(vi) SELECT MAX(ScheduleDate),MIN(ScheduleDate)FROM ACTIVITY;

(vii)SELECT SUM (PrizeMoney) FROM ACTIVITY;

2.7 Let us revise!

Here are the general forms of the statements discussed in this chapter, plus some extra important ones (explanations given). **REMEMBER** that all of these statements may or may not be available on your system, so check documentation regarding availability: **ALTER TABLE** <TABLE NAME> ADD|DROP|MODIFY (COLUMN SPECIFICATION[S]...see Create Table); --allows you to add or delete a column or columns from a table, or change the specification (data type, etc.) on an existing column; this statement is also used to change the physical specifications of a table (how a table is stored, etc.), but these definitions are DBMS-specific, so read the documentation. Also, these physical specifications are used with the Create Table statement, when a table is first created. In addition, only one option can be performed per Alter Table statement--either add, drop, **OR** modify in a single statement.

CREATE [UNIQUE] INDEX <INDEX NAME>
ON <TABLE NAME> (<COLUMN LIST>); --UNIQUE is optional; within brackets.

CREATE TABLE <TABLE NAME>
(<COLUMN NAME> <DATA TYPE> [(<SIZE>)] <COLUMN CONSTRAINT>,
...other columns); (also valid with ALTER TABLE)
--where SIZE is only used on certain data types (see above), and constraints include the following possibilities (automatically enforced by the DBMS; failure causes an error to be generated):

1. NULL or NOT NULL (see above)
2. UNIQUE enforces that no two rows will have the same value for this column
3. PRIMARY KEY tells the database that this column is the primary key column (only used if the key is a one column key, otherwise a PRIMARY KEY (column, column, ...) statement appears after the last column definition.
4. CHECK allows a condition to be checked for when data in that column is updated or inserted; for example, CHECK (PRICE > 0) causes the system to check that the Price column is greater than zero before accepting the value...sometimes implemented as the CONSTRAINT statement.
5. DEFAULT inserts the default value into the database if a row is inserted without that column's data being inserted; for example, BENEFITS INTEGER DEFAULT = 10000
6. FOREIGN KEY works the same as Primary Key, but is followed by: REFERENCES <TABLE NAME> (<COLUMN NAME>), which refers to the referential primary key.

CREATE VIEW <TABLE NAME> AS <QUERY>;

DELETE FROM <TABLE NAME> WHERE <CONDITION>;

INSERT INTO <TABLE NAME> [(<COLUMN LIST>)]
VALUES (<VALUE LIST>);

SELECT [DISTINCT|ALL] <LIST OF COLUMNS, FUNCTIONS, CONSTANTS, ETC.>
FROM <LIST OF TABLES OR VIEWS>
[WHERE <CONDITION(S)>]
[GROUP BY <GROUPING COLUMN(S)>]
[HAVING <CONDITION>]
[ORDER BY <ORDERING COLUMN(S)> [ASC|DESC]]; --where ASC|DESC allows the ordering to be done in ASCending or DESCending order

UPDATE <TABLE NAME>
SET <COLUMN NAME> = <VALUE>
[WHERE <CONDITION>]; --if the Where clause is left out, all rows will be updated according to the Set statement

Notes

Part IV

Chapter 3

CONNECTING DATABASES WITH C++

AIM

- Introduce the technique of connecting C++ programs to Databases
- To learn steps of connecting Borland C++ with databases
- To know how to connect Microsoft's 'Visual C++' to databases

OUTLINE

3.1 Open Database Connectivity (ODBC)
3.2 Setting up ODBC data source
3.3 Connecting from Delphi or C++ Builder using the ODBC data source
3.4 Connecting MS Visual C++ 5.0 to Databases
3.5 Code to Connect C/C++ to the ODBC data source

3.1 Open Database Connectivity (ODBC)

ODBC is a standard or open application programming interface (API) for accessing to database management systems (DBMS). This API is independent of any one programming language, database system or operating system. ODBC is based on the Call Level Interface (CLI) specifications from SQL, X/Open (now part of The Open Group), and the ISO/IEC. ODBC was created by the SQL Access Group and first released in September, 1992.

By using ODBC statements in a C++ program, you can access files in a number of different databases, such as, MS Access, MS SQL, Oracle, DB2 and My SQL. In addition to the ODBC software, a separate module or driver is needed for each database to be accessed.

3.2 Setting up ODBC data source

In order to make a connection from 3rd party products using ODBC, an ODBC data source is needed. A data source stores connection information such as user name, password, and location of database.

Steps for setting up a data source:

Step 1:

ODBC Administrator can be started by going to Control Panel and double clicking on 32 bit ODBC or Starting the utility called "32bit ODBC Administrator" if you have the ODBC SDK installed.

Step 2:

Stay at the User Data Source tab and click on Add. This will bring up another window titled "Create New Data Source".

Step 3:

Pick the ODBC driver that to be used. Pick the InterBase driver which is called "InterBase 5.x driver by Visigenic (*.gdb)" and then click on Finish. This will bring up a new window with the title "InterBase ODBC Configuration".

Step 4:

Fill in the blank fields in this window
Data Source Name: Make up a name for your data source.
Description: This is the description of the data source. It's not required.
Network Protocol: Choose the protocol from the drop down list.

Database: Fill in the physical full path to the database including the database name to server.
Server: Fill in the server name. If you choose the protocol "local", this will default to the local server.
Username: Fill in the database user name.
Password: Fill in the password corresponding to the above user name.

Go to the Advanced tab and fill in the CharacterSet and Roles.

Step 5:

Clicking the OK button will bring back to the main form. You should see the newly added user data source there.

Note: A user data source is a data source visible to the user whereas a system data source is visible to the system.

3.3 Connecting from Delphi or C++ Builder using the ODBC data source

ODBC connection from Delphi is very similar to connecting using Borland Development Environment from Delphi. Here is an example of connecting using the Tquery component. This example will also display the results of a sql statement.

Step 1:
Drop a Tquery, a Tdatasource, and a Tdbgrid component on a Delphi form.

Step 2:
Set the following properties for the Tquery component:

DatabaseName: Pick from the list the data source name you just created in ODBC Administrator.

SQL: Input the SQL statement to be executed. For example: "select * from table1".

Active: Set to True to connect. And supply user name and password on connection.

Step 3:
Set the following properties for the Tdatasource component:
Data Set: Set to the name of the Tquery component, or "query1" in this case.

Step 4:
Set the following properties for the TDBGrid component:
Data Source: Set to the name of the Tdatasource component, or "data source1" in this case.

Step 5:
Now you can see the returned results from select statement in the dbgrid area.

3.4 Connecting MS Visual C++ 5.0 to Databases

Now we have to create an ODBC data-source, which points to your database.
Step 1: Start up ODBC Administrator.
Double click the "32bit ODBC" icon in Control Panel to start the ODBC administrator.

Step 2: Click the "Add" button to create a new data-source, select the driver you wish to use (if your database is say, MS SQL select the "Microsoft SQL Driver" and so on) and click the "finish" button.

Step 3:
Enter a name for the data source in the "Data Source Name" field. "Description" field is optional.

Step 4: Click on the "Select" button from the "Database" field. A browser box appears where you select the location of your MS SQL database file. When done click the "OK" button to return back to the previous screen and "OK" again to complete the creation of the data source. Now click the "OK" button to quit the ODBC administrator.

Step 5: Now, we can start writing a C++ program that will open a connection to the database and perform an SQL query. The SQL query can be any SQL statement to search, insert, update or delete data in the database. This program will not do any validation of whether or not a record with the same value already exists in the database table and the SQL string is a legal SQL statement.

A set of C/C++ functions are supplied with ODBC and are found in the two header files sql.h and sqlext.h. We would need to include both the header files in the program using the "#include" operation.

3.5 Code to Connect C/C++ to the ODBC data source

The code for connecting C/C++ to OBDC data source ("ABC") and performing SQL query is given in program 3.1. The code does not include error handling considered desirable when modifying the table or establishing and closing the connection to the database. You will need to change the name of the data source if you wish to use this code. The database may also require a user ID and password.

Program 3.1

```
// ODBC data source is called "ABC". It then executes a SQL statement "SELECT
Model
// FROM Makes WHERE Make = ' Suzuki';" should pull out all models made by Suzuki
stored in the database
```

```
#include <windows.h>
#include <sqlext.h>
#include <stdio.h>
#include <iostream.h>
void main()
{
        HENV  hEnv = NULL;                              // Handle from SQLAllocEnv()
        HDBC  hDBC = NULL;                              // Handle for Connection
        HSTMT   hStmt = NULL;                 // Statement handle
        UCHAR    szDSN[SQL_MAX_DSN_LENGTH] = "ABC"; // Data Source Name
UCHAR*  szUID = NULL;              // User ID buffer
        UCHAR*  szPasswd = NULL;          // Password buffer
        UCHAR    szModel[128];                 // Model buffer
        SDWORD       cbModel;                  // Model buffer bytes received
        UCHAR          szSqlStr[] = "Select Model From Makes Where Make="Suzuki";
        // SQL string
        RETCODE      retcode;                  // Return code

        // allocate memory for ODBC Environment handle
        SQLAllocEnv (&hEnv);        // Allocate memory for the connection handle
        SQLAllocConnect (hEnv, &hDBC);
        // connect to the data source "ABC" using userid and password.
        retcode = SQLConnect (hDBC, szDSN, SQL_NTS, szUID, SQL_NTS, szPasswd,
SQL_NTS);
        if (retcode == SQL_SUCCESS || retcode == SQL_SUCCESS_WITH_INFO)
        {
         // allocate memory for the statement handle
         retcode = SQLAllocStmt (hDBC, &hStmt);
         // prepare the SQL statement by assigning it to the statement handle
         retcode = SQLPrepare (hStmt, szSqlStr, sizeof (szSqlStr));
         // execute SQL statement handle
         retcode = SQLExecute (hStmt);

         // Project only column 1 which is the models
         SQLBindCol (hStmt, 1, SQL_C_CHAR, szModel, sizeof(szModel), &cbModel);
         // Get row of data from the result set defined above in the statement
         retcode = SQLFetch (hStmt);
         while (retcode == SQL_SUCCESS || retcode == SQL_SUCCESS_WITH_INFO)
         {
                      cout ("\t%s\n", szModel);        // Print row (model)
                      retcode = SQLFetch (hStmt);  // Fetch next row from result set
         }
         // Free the allocated statement handle
         SQLFreeStmt (hStmt, SQL_DROP);
         // Disconnect from datasource
         SQLDisconnect (hDBC);
```

```
    }
    // Free the allocated connection handle
    SQLFreeConnect (hDBC);
    // Free the allocated ODBC environment handle
    SQLFreeEnv (hEnv);
}
```

APPENDICES

APPENDIX A

ASCII TABLE

The **A**merican **S**tandard **C**ode for **I**nformation **I**nterchange is a standard seven-bit code that was finalized by ANSI in 1968. ASCII is a standard code used for information interchange and communication between data processing systems (including Internet). ASCII which is pronounced as 'ask key' represents 'English' characters like alphabets, decimal numbers, control and graphic characters as unique numbers from 0 to 127.

A.1 CONTROL CHARACTERS

The 7 bit ASCII table is given in table A.1 and A.2. The first part of the table includes descriptions of the first 32 non-printing also referred to as control characters. ASCII was designed for use with teletypes as a result control characters are not as frequently used as intended.

Table A.1 ASCII TABLE

Name/Meaning	Ctrl char	Dec	Hex	Char
Null	ctrl-@	0	00	NUL
start of heading	ctrl-A	1	01	SOH
start of text	ctrl-B	2	02	STX
end of text	ctrl-C	3	03	ETX
end of xmit	ctrl-D	4	04	EOT
Enquiry	ctrl-E	5	05	ENQ
acknowledge	ctrl-F	6	06	ACK
Bell	ctrl-G	7	07	BEL
Backspace	ctrl-H	8	08	BS
horizontal tab	ctrl-I	9	09	HT
Line feed	ctrl-J	10	0A	LF
vertical tab	ctrl-K	11	0B	VT
Form feed	ctrl-L	12	0C	FF
carriage feed	ctrl-M	13	0D	CR
shift out	ctrl-N	14	0E	SO

shift in	ctrl-O	15	0F	SI
data line escape	ctrl-P	16	10	DLE
device control 1	ctrl-Q	17	11	DC1
device control 2	ctrl-R	18	12	DC2
device control 3	ctrl-S	19	13	DC3
device control 4	ctrl-T	20	14	DC4
Neg acknowledge	ctrl-U	21	15	NAK
synchronous idel	ctrl-V	22	16	SYN
End of xmit block	ctrl-W	23	17	ETB
Cancel	ctrl-X	24	18	CAN
end of medium	ctrl-Y	25	19	EM
Substitute	ctrl-Z	26	1A	SUB
Escape	ctrl-[	27	1B	ESC
file separator	ctrl-\	28	1C	FS
group separator	ctrl-]	29	1D	GS
record separator	ctrl-^	30	1E	RS
unit separator	ctrl-_	31	1F	US

A.2 PRINTABLE CHARACTERS

The ASCII table also includes of 96 printable characters which are given in table A.2. For example, the capital letter 'A' is always represented by the order number '65',

Table A.2: ASCII TABLE

Dec	Hex	Char	Dec	Hex	Char	Dec	Hex	Char
32	20	Space	64	40	@	96	60	`
33	21	!	65	41	A	97	61	a
34	22	"	66	42	B	98	62	b
35	23	#	67	43	C	99	63	c
36	24	$	68	44	D	100	64	d
37	25	%	69	45	E	101	65	e
38	26	&	70	46	F	102	66	f
39	27	'	71	47	G	103	67	g
40	28	(	72	48	H	104	68	h

41	29	)	73	49	I	105	69	i
42	2A	*	74	4A	J	106	6A	j
43	2B	+	75	4B	K	107	6B	k
44	2C	,	76	4C	L	108	6C	l
45	2D	-	77	4D	M	109	6D	m
46	2E	.	78	4E	N	110	6E	n
47	2F	/	79	4F	O	111	6F	o
48	30	0	80	50	P	112	70	p
49	31	1	81	51	Q	113	71	q
50	32	2	82	52	R	114	72	r
51	33	3	83	53	S	115	73	s
52	34	4	84	54	T	116	74	t
53	35	5	85	55	U	117	75	u
54	36	6	86	56	V	118	76	v
55	37	7	87	57	W	119	77	w
56	38	8	88	58	X	120	78	x
57	39	9	89	59	Y	121	79	y
58	3A	:	90	5A	Z	122	7A	z
59	3B	;	91	5B	[	123	7B	{
60	3C	<	92	5C	\	124	7C	|
61	3D	=	93	5D	]	125	7D	}
62	3E	>	94	5E	^	126	7E	~
63	3F	?	95	5F	_	127	7F	DEL

A.3 EXTENDED CHARACTER SET

The Extended ASCII Character Set (table A.3) also consists of 128 decimal numbers and ranges from 128 through 255 (using the full 8-bits of the byte) representing additional special, mathematical, graphic, and foreign characters.

Table A.3: ASCII table

136	0x88	ˆ	179	0xB3	³	222	0xDE	Þ
137	0x89	‰	180	0xB4	´	223	0xDF	ß
138	0x8A	Š	181	0xB5	µ	224	0xE0	à
139	0x8B	‹	182	0xB6	¶	225	0xE1	á
140	0x8C	Œ	183	0xB7	·	226	0xE2	â
141	0x8D		184	0xB8	¸	227	0xE3	ã
142	0x8E	Ž	185	0xB9	¹	228	0xE4	ä
143	0x8F		186	0xBA	º	229	0xE5	å
144	0x90		187	0xBB	»	230	0xE6	æ
145	0x91	‘	188	0xBC	¼	231	0xE7	ç
146	0x92	’	189	0xBD	½	232	0xE8	è
147	0x93	“	190	0xBE	¾	233	0xE9	é
148	0x94	”	191	0xBF	¿	234	0xEA	ê
149	0x95	•	192	0xC0	À	235	0xEB	ë
150	0x96	–	193	0xC1	Á	236	0xEC	ì
151	0x97	—	194	0xC2	Â	237	0xED	í
152	0x98	˜	195	0xC3	Ã	238	0xEE	î
153	0x99	™	196	0xC4	Ä	239	0xEF	ï
154	0x9A	š	197	0xC5	Å	240	0xF0	ð
155	0x9B	›	198	0xC6	Æ	241	0xF1	ñ
156	0x9C	œ	199	0xC7	Ç	242	0xF2	ò
157	0x9D		200	0xC8	È	243	0xF3	ó
158	0x9E	ž	201	0xC9	É	244	0xF4	ô
159	0x9F	Ÿ	202	0xCA	Ê	245	0xF5	õ
160	0xA0		203	0xCB	Ë	246	0xF6	ö
161	0xA1	¡	204	0xCC	Ì	247	0xF7	÷
162	0xA2	¢	205	0xCD	Í	248	0xF8	ø
163	0xA3	£	206	0xCE	Î	249	0xF9	ù
164	0xA4	¤	207	0xCF	Ï	250	0xFA	ú
165	0xA5	¥	208	0xD0	Ð	251	0xFB	û
166	0xA6	¦	209	0xD1	Ñ	252	0xFC	ü
167	0xA7	§	210	0xD2	Ò	253	0xFD	ý
168	0xA8	¨	211	0xD3	Ó	254	0xFE	þ
169	0xA9	©	212	0xD4	Ô	255	0xFF	ÿ
170	0xAA	ª	213	0xD5	Õ			

APPENDIX B

Standard Template Library (STL)

B.1 Introduction

The Standard Template Library (STL) is a general-purpose C++ library of algorithms and data structures, container classes, and iterators. The STL has derived its name "template library as it is implemented by deploying template mechanism of C++. The STL is a generic library, meaning that its components are heavily parameterized. Almost every component in the STL is a template.

You must know how templates work in C++ as some aspects of the library are complex; however, it is straightforward to use most of its features. STL use facilitates reuse of the sophisticated data structures and algorithms it contains.

Although not part of the STL, the `string` class provides a commonly needed facility (character string handling) and is also part of the ANSI C++ standard library.

The STL documentation classifies components in two ways.

1. *Categories* are a classification by functionality. The categories are:
    - Container
    - Iterator
    - Algorithm
    - Function Object
    - Utility
    - Adaptor
    - Allocator
2. *Component types* are a structural classification: one based on what kind of C++ entity (if any) a component is. The component types are:
    - Type (*i.e.* a `struct` or `class`)
    - Function
    - Concept

B.2 Containers and Algorithms

The main purpose of container classes in STL is to contain other objects. The STL includes classes, viz., vector, list, deque, set, multiset, map, multimap, hash_set, hash_multiset, hash map, and hash_multimap. Each class in STL is a template, and can be instantiated to contain any type of object. For example, you can use a vector<int> in the same way as you would use an ordinary C array, except that if you use vector you don't need to manage dynamic memory allocation by hand.

```
vector <int> v(3);          // Declare a vector of 3 elements.
v[0] = 1;
v[1] = v[0] + 2;
v[2] = v[0] + v[1];         // v[0] == 1, v[1] == 3, v[2] == 4
```

The data stored in containers is manipulated through a large collection of algorithms included in STL, e.g. to reverse the order of elements in a vector, **reverse algorithm** described below can be used:

```
reverse(v.begin(), v.end()); //result will now be that  v[0] == 4, v[1] == 3, v[2] == 1
```

You need to observe two important points in reverse algorithm: 1) it is a global function, not a member function and 2) it takes two arguments which define a range of elements. Range can be a few selected elements or the entire container v.

STL algorithms are decoupled from the STL container classes. This means that reverse can be used not only to reverse elements in vectors, but also to reverse elements in lists, and even elements in arrays defined in the C++. The following program shows how reverse algorithm works equally well on a array:

```
double A[4] = { 1.0, 2.4, 3.6, 1.5};
reverse(A, A + 6);          //range is denoted [A, A + 6);
for (int i = 0; i < 4; ++i)
  cout << "A[" << i << "] = " << A[i];
```

B.3 Iterators

Iterators are the mechanism that makes it possible to decouple algorithms from containers. Algorithms are templates, and are parameterized by the type of iterator, so they are not restricted to a single type of container. Let us revisit the reverse algorithm in section D 1.2. You may note that arguments to reverse are iterators, which are a generalization of pointers. Pointers themselves are iterators, which is why it is possible to reverse the elements of an array using the same reverse algorithm. In the example above, the type returned by v.begin() and v.end() is vector<int>::iterator. There are also some iterators, such as istream_iterator and ostream_iterator, that aren't associated with containers.

Consider, for example, how to write an algorithm that performs linear search through a range (see Table B.1).

Table B.1: Algorithm for linear search

STL Find Algorithm	Equivalent Function in C++	Comments
template <class InputIterator, class T>	type int,	
InputIterator find(InputIterator first, InputIterator last, const T& value) {	int* find(int* first, int* last, const int& value) {	Find has three arguments: two iterators that define a range, and a value to search for in that range.
while (first != last && *first != value) ++first;	while (first != last && *first != value) ++first;	
return first; }	return first; }	

Variables 'First' and 'last' are of type InputIterator which is a template parameter. As you know, there isn't actually any type called InputIterator: when you call find, the compiler substitutes the actual type of the arguments for the formal type parameters InputIterator and T. See C++ function in Table B. 1.1.

Algorithms in the STL, in many cases, come in two versions, a plain and one that uses a predicate. Let's take an example of the algorithm *find*. In its plain version, it looks for a given element in a container:

```
it = find(first, last, elem);
```

Here, *first* and *last* are iterators defining a sequence, possibly stored in a container, and *elem* is an object of the same type as the elements of the sequence. The algorithm returns an iterator to the first position in the sequence between *first* and *last* — including *first* but not *last* — where the element of the sequence equals *elem*. If no such element exists, the function returns *last*.

If the elements of the sequence are complex structures, such as a customer-information structure as given below:

```
typedef struct _customer_info_tag {
  std::string str_name;
  long l_id;
  double order_value;
} CUSTOMER_INFO, *LPCUSTOMER_INFO ;
```

It is obvious that you will ever be searching for a CUSTOMER_INFO element as you know it beforehand. Most probably, you will be searching for an element whose *str_name* member or whose *l_id* member you know. This operation with the plain algorithm *find* is not possible and you will need to use the related algorithm *find_if*.

To this end, you write a suitable predicate in the form of a "functional" — a simple class that may be applied to a CUSTOMER_INFO object (via its defined operator()) and that returns true if the *str_name* member equals a specified name. Figure B.1 shows how to write such a predicate. Now you can search the container for an element whose *str_name* member equals a given customer name:

it = find_if(first, last, pred("Ankit"));

Figure B.1: Tests a CUSTOMER_INFO object for a match to a given name

```
#include<functional>

class name_pred : public std::unary_function<CUSTOMER_INFO, bool>
{
pubic:
  name_pred(string str_name) : m_str_name(str_name){}
  bool operator() (CUSTOMER_INFO arg) const
    { return m str name == arg.m str name; }
private:
  string m_str_name;
};
/* End of File */
```

B.4 Concepts and Modeling

Concepts are, in fact, not a part of the C++ language. Nevertheless, concepts are an extremely important part of the STL. Using concepts, it is possible to write programs that separate interface from implementation: for example, if you want to implement find function then you only have to consider the interface specified by the concept InputIterator.

Similarly, if you want to use find, you need only to ensure that the arguments you pass to it are compatible to the models of InputIterator. This is the reason why find and reverse can be used with lists, vectors, C arrays, and many other types: programming in terms of concepts, rather than in terms of specific types, makes it possible to reuse software components and to combine components together.

It is interesting to note that find implicitly defines a set of requirements on types, and that it may be instantiated with any type that satisfies those requirements. Whatever type is substituted for InputIterator must provide operations, such as, 1) compare two objects of that type for equality; 2) increment an object of that type and 3) dereference an object of that type to obtain the object that it points to, and so on.

Each STL algorithm has a set of requirements like find algorithm, e.g., the arguments to for_each and count, and other algorithms, must satisfy the same requirements. These requirements are sufficiently important that we give them a name: we call such a set of type requirements a concept, and we call this particular concept Input Iterator. We say that a type conforms to a concept, or that it is a model of a concept, if it satisfies all of those requirements. We say that int* is a model of Input Iterator because int* provides all of the operations that are specified by the InputIterator requirements.

B.5 Refinement

An InputIterator needs to perform not all but only a subset of pointer arithmetic. For example, to implement find algorithm it will suffice if an Input Iterator supports increment operation using prefix and postfix operator ++). In case of Reverse algorithm, you need both decrement and increment operation for its arguments as it uses the prefix operator in the expression '- -last'. In terms of concepts, reverse algorithm's arguments must be models of BidirectionalIterator rather than InputIterator. Therefore, the types that are models of BidirectionalIterator are a subset of the types that are models of InputIterator. Int*, e.g., is both a model of BidirectionalIterator and a model of InputIterator, but istream_iterator, is only a model of InputIterator as it does not conform to the more stringent BidirectionalIterator requirements.

One may, therefore, interpret that BidirectionalIterator is a refinement of InputIterator. Refinement of concepts is in some way identical to inheritance of C++ classes; but a different word is used instead of calling it "inheritance", is to emphasize that refinement applies to concepts rather than to actual types.

There are five iterator concepts, viz., Output Iterator, Input Iterator, Forward Iterator, Bidirectional Iterator, and Random Access Iterator. Forward Iterator is a refinement of Input Iterator, Bidirectional Iterator is a refinement of Forward Iterator, and Random Access Iterator is a refinement of Bidirectional Iterator.

Container classes, like iterators, are organized into a hierarchy of concepts. All containers are models of the concept Container; more refined concepts, such as Sequence and Associative Container, describe specific types of containers.

B.6 Other parts of the STL

The STL does, however, include several other types of components:

1. utilities: very basic concepts and functions that are used in many different parts of the library;
2. some low-level mechanisms for allocating and deallocating memory, and

3. Finally, the STL includes a large collection of function objects, also known as functors. Just as iterators are a generalization of pointers, function objects are a generalization of functions.

There are several different concepts relating to function objects, including Unary Function say, F(x) and Binary Function requiring two arguments, i.e. f(x, y). Function objects are an important part of generic programming because they allow abstraction not only over the types of objects, but also over the operations that are being performed.

TableB.2: Describes STL Categories and Classes

Categories	Sub-categories	Classes
Containers Concepts	Container	Forward, Reversible and Random Access Container
	Sequences	Front Insertion and Back Insertion
	Associative Containers	Simple, Pair, Sorted, Hashed, Unique, Multiple, Unique Sorted, Multiple Sorted, Unique Hashed, Multiple Hashed Associative Container and Hash Function
Container classes	Sequences	vector, deque, list, slist and bit_vector
	Associative Containers	set, map, multiset, multimap, hash_set, hash_map, hash_multiset, hash_multimap and hash
	String package	Character Traits, char_traits and basic_string
	Rope	
	Container adaptors	stack, queue and priority_queue
	Bitset	
Iterators	Concepts	Trivial, Input, Output, Forward, Bidirectional and Random

		Access Iterator
	Iterator Tags	iterator_traits, iterator_category, distance_type, value_type
	Iterator tag classes	Input, Output, Forward, Bidirectional and random access
	Iterator base classes	Input, output, forward, bidirectional and random access iterator
	Iterator functions	Distance and advance
	Iterator classes	istream_iterator ostream_iterator front_insert_iterator back_insert_iterator insert_iterator reverse_iterator reverse_bidirectional_iterator raw_storage_iterator sequence_buffer
Algorithm	Non-mutating algorithms	for_each, find, find_if , adjacent_find, find_first_of, count, count_if, mismatch, equal, search, search_n and find_end
Mutating algorithms	Copy Swap transform Replace fill, fill_n, generate, generate_n, Remove unique unique_copy reverse reverse_copy rotate rotate_copy random_shuffle random_sample	Copy, copy_n, copy_backward Swap, iter_swap, swap_ranges, replace, replace_if, eplace_copy, and replace_copy_if, remove, remove_if, remove_copy, and remove_copy_if

	random_sample_n partition stable_partition	
	Sorting	sort, stable_sort, partial_sort, partial_sort_copy, is_sorted and
	nth_element	
	Binary search	lower_bound, upper_bound, equal_range and binary_search
	merge	
	inplace_merge	
	Set operations on sorted ranges	includes, set_union, set_intersection, set_difference and symmetric_difference
	Heap operations	push_heap, pop_heap, make_heap, sort_heap and is_heap
	Minimum and maximum	min, max, min_element and max_element
	lexicographical_compare	lexicographical_compare_3way, next_permutation, and prev_permutation
	Generalized numeric algorithms	iota, accumulate, inner_product, partial_sum, adjacent_difference and power
Function Objects Concepts	Concepts	Generator Unary Function Binary Function Adaptable Generator Adaptable Unary Function Adaptable Binary Function
	Concepts - Predicates	Predicate, Binary, Adaptable, Adaptable Binary, and StrictWeakOrdering

	Concepts - Monoid Operation	
	Concepts - Random Number Generator	
Predefined function objects	Arithmetic operations	plus minus multiplies (formerly called "times") divides modulus negate
	Comparisons	equal_to, not_equal_to, less greater less_equal greater_equal
	Logical operations	logical_and logical_or logical_not
	Generalized identity operations	identity project1st project2nd select1st select2nd
	subtractive_rng	
Function object adaptors		binder1st, binder2nd, ptr_fun, pointer_to_unary_function, pointer_to_binary_function, unary_negate, binary_negate, unary_compose, and binary_compose
	Member function adaptors	mem_fun mem_fun_ref mem_fun1 mem_fun1_ref
Utilities	Concepts	Assignable, Default Constructible, Equality Comparable and LessThan

		Comparable and LessThan Comparable
	Functions	Relational Operators
	Classes	pair
Memory Allocation	Classes	Allocators and raw_storage_iterator
	Functions	Construct, destroy, uninitialized_copy, uninitialized_copy_n, uninitialized_fill, uninitialized_fill_n, temporary_buffer, get_temporary_buffer, and return_temporary_buffer

B.7 Links to other resources

For more information on the STL, try the following links:

- Reference and tutorial information
    - Title: C++ Programmer's Guide to the Standard Template Library
      Author: Mark Nelson
      Publisher: IDG Books Worldwide, 1995.
      Pages: 875, ISBN: 1-56884-314-3
    - Title: STL Tutorial and Reference Guide; C++ Programming With the Standard Template Library
      Authors: David R. Musser and Atul Saini
      Publisher: Addison-Wesley Publishing Company, Inc., 1996.
      Pages: 400, ISBN: 0-201-63398-1

APPENDIX C

Setting Up the C++ Development Environment

C.1 Introduction

To get started with setting up the C++ programming environment one needs to download a C/C++ compiler. A compiler is a computer program that translates a computer program written in a computer language (called the source language) into an equivalent program written in another computer language (called the output or the target language). Source files written in C++ have '.cpp' extension. When these files are compiled they turn into object files with '.obj' extension which when linked with necessary library routines and header files become executable files ('.exe' extension). It is these executable files, we access when we are running our programs. There are various compilers present today in the programming world. In this appendix, we will take up the most commonly used compilers which are efficient for both beginners and sophomores.

C.2 Borland's C++ Builder

Borland C++ builder is built on Borland's proven C++ compiler technology and shares Delphi's award winning Visual component Library giving you great interoperability with both Borland C++ and Delphi. Code generated on C++ builder is a visual front end to Borland C++ and code written with Borland C++ can be ported to other platforms. Borland has recently released their C++ Compiler (version 5.5) as a freeware.

The freeware includes the command line compiler, incremental linker, resource compiler and binder, C++ Win32 preprocessor, import library utility, librarian, obj/lib/exe dump utility, etc. The C/C++ runtime library and ANSI/ISO Standard Template Library (STL) are also included with this compiler. The CD provided with the book includes this compiler consists of all the instructions and help - you might need to get started. The compiler can also be downloaded by accessing the link given below.

http://www.borland.com/downloads/download_cbuilder.html

On accessing the link the following page should appear. Access the compiler link ↓ and traverse the corresponding links to download the compiler.

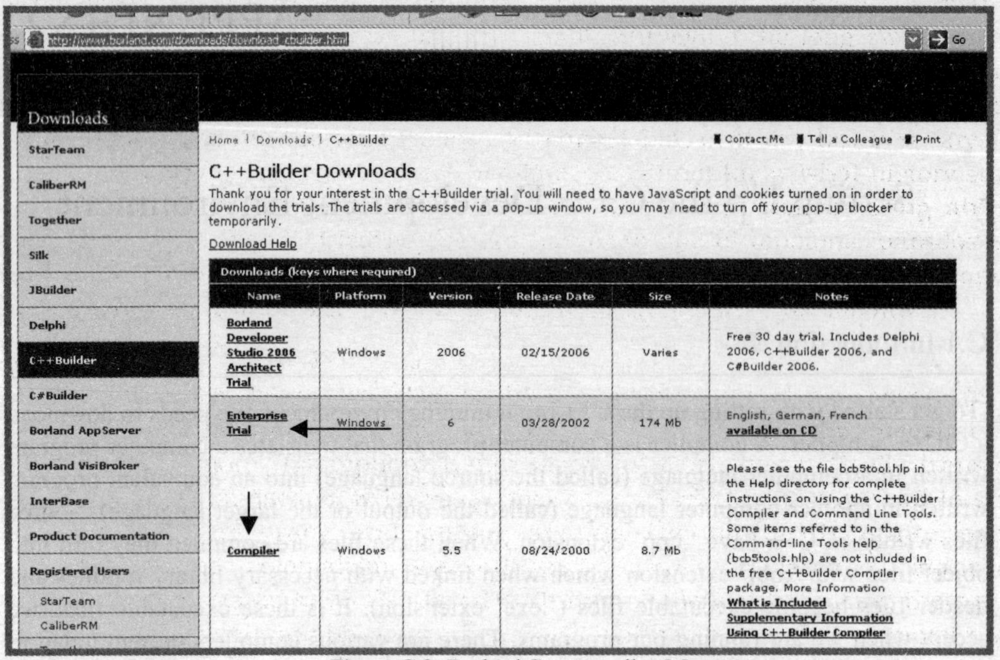

Figure C.2: Borland C++ compiler 5.5

With the Borland C++ builder one also requires a programming notepad. This can be easily found on the net. The CD also provides with a few downloading sties for these notepads on the internet.

C.3 Microsoft Visual C++

Microsoft Visual C++ has for long been an industry standard for C++ development on Windows and its applications. Earlier versions of Microsoft Visual C++ technology preview enabled us to start on developing for internet explorer by accessing the power and flexibility of Dynamic HTML and the new Common Controls. The Standard Editions (Visual C++ 6.0) present today are a complete integrated development environment including debugging support with a look and feel that should be familiar to users of other Microsoft products. Microsoft Visual C++ Toolkit 2003 launched earlier included the command line versions of the optimizing C++ compiler, linker, and static libraries (including the Standard C++ Library and STL) that ships with the commercial Visual Studio .NET Professional 2003 for about a hundred dollars. Recently Microsoft Visual C/C++ command line compiler, along with C#, VB.NET and JScript.NET, appears to be available from Microsoft for download for free. Accompanying the compiler one also needs to download the Microsoft Platform SDK which contains the Windows headers and libraries for the compilers. The latest version of Visual C++ compiler is the 'Visual C++ Express Edition Beta 2' launched in 2005. The edition is accompanied with professional-grade compiler, code editor, debugger and a project system. The system requirements necessary for the express edition are enlisted in 'http://lab.msdn.micros oft.com/express/readme/'. This edition can be downloaded using the following link.

http://lab.msdn.microsoft.com/express/visualc/default.aspx

The following page should appear on accessing the above mentioned link.

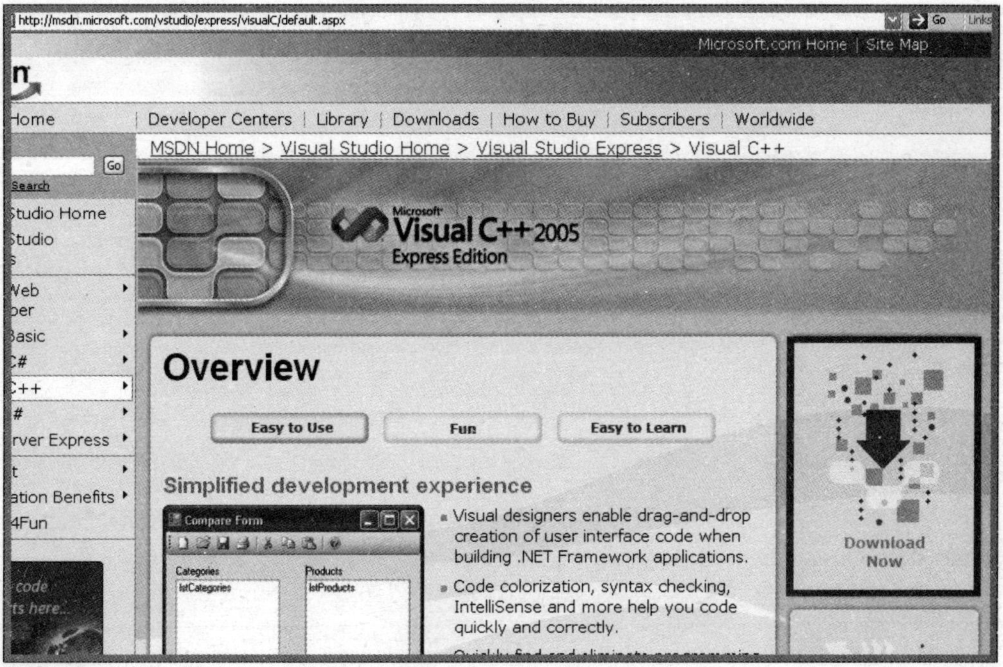

When the link is accessed it leads to downloading a file 'vcsetup.exe' (2.66 Mb) which acts as a setup for the entire installation process.To conclude Visual C++ Standard Edition is an excellent choice for beginners looking to learn C++ on Windows systems as it contains all one needs to begin to compile and test programs.

Notes

APPENDIX D

Graphics Programming in C++

D.1 Introduction

The Windows operating system provides a multitasking graphical environment that runs multiple applications simultaneously. Each application displays output in a rectangular area of computer screen called a window. If an application decides to write on the screen, it calls a function contained in API (Application Programming Interface) within Windows. Internally Windows decides the function calls and translates it to the hardware commands. If Windows was installed specifying VGA video system, VGA hardware commands are sent out. DOS does disk file access best, therefore, Windows designers used DOS disk file commands in Windows. Windows is also a DOS program so DOS is already running before Windows is run. All the disk support functions are available to Windows as they are available to DOS. A comparison of Windows and DOS programs is given in table D.1.

Table D.1- Comparison of Windows and DOS Programs

Feature	Windows	DOS
Resource Sharing	Each application shares the resources of the system through the API.	A DOS program captures all the resources of the system.
Graphical User Interface (GUI)	It has a GUI which is intuitive in nature. Each application is given access to the graphical display through a window.	A DOS application typically has a character oriented user interface.
Standardization	Every program has the same look and feel due to the use of menus, dialog boxes, push buttons, combo boxes, etc.	Programs can be different and a user may take lot of time to get used to their environments.
Input facilities	An application is structured to accept input whenever it is produced by the user.	Input is demanded from the user when needed by the application.

Device Independent Graphics	An application is not allowed to interact directly with hardware. The same program can produce graphics on display as well as printer or any other Windows supported device.	An application interacts directly with the hardware. Therefore, it becomes device dependent.
Memory management	Memory blocks are dynamic, and can pre-load or load on call. They can be fixed, moveable, discardable, or non-discardable.	Memory blocks are static.

The integrated Windows environment provided by C and Pascal compilers from Microsoft, Borland & many other vendors enables a programmer to carry out individual steps in compilation and linking (see figure D.1) automatically through the use of development tools. Windows programs have separate resource file that contain static data such as menu and bitmaps. Resourcedata is supplied by a separate compiler called resource compiler.

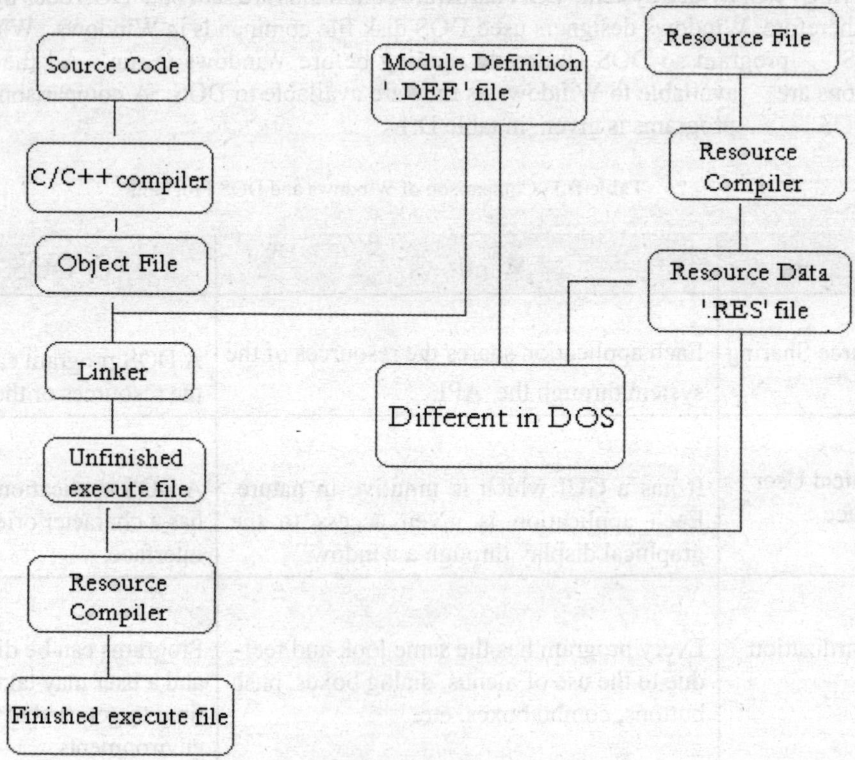

Figure D.1: Steps in compilation and linking

Section D.3 in this chapter describes graphics programming under DOS. This section will be useful to those users who still prefer to operate under DOS.

D.2 Windows Graphics Programming

Functions from the Windows Graphics Device Interface (GDI) are used for displaying graphics in an application's window. These can be accessed through the *TGdiBase* class hierarchy in *OWL in* Borland *C*. We briefly review some of the important concepts applicable to programming in Windows. Many uppercase identifiers are used. Several of these identifiers contain a two-letter or three-letter prefix followed by an underscore, e.g., *WM_PAINT, DT_SINGLELINE, CS_VREDRAW, IDC_ARROW* etc. These are simply numeric constants and indicate a general category to which the constant belongs, as indicated in table D.2. Handles are used quite frequently in Windows. A handle is a 16-bit number that refers to an object. The handles for icon, cursor, and brush are called *HICON, HCURSOR*, and *HBRUSH, respectively*. The actual value of the handle is unimportant to a program, since the Windows module that gives the program the handle knows how to use it to reference the object. One also encounters uppercase identifiers for various types of handles, such as *HANDLE, HWND*, and *HDC* for general handle, handle to a window and handle to a device context, respectively.

Table D.2: Prefix and category

Prefix	Category
CS	Class style
IDI	ID for an icon
IDC	ID for a cursor
WS	Window style
CW	Create Window
WM	Window message
DT	Draw text

We will use the ObjectWindows application framework for graphics programming. ObjectWindows supports the following classes of Window:

- **Windows**
  TWindow is the base class for all windows. It represents the functionality of all windows e.g. dialog boxes, controls, Multiple Document Interface (*MDI*) windows and so on.

- **Frame windows**
  TFrameWindow is derived from *Window* class. Frame windows manage application-wide tasks,like menus and tool bar,and support a client window which can be specialized to do a single task. Changes (i.e. adding tool or status bars) introduced in a frame window do not affect client windows.

- ***MDI* windows**
  MDI manages multiple documents or windows in a single application.

- **Decorated windows**
  Several classes, such as *TLayoutWindow* and *TLayoutMetrics* provide support for decoration controls like tool bars, status bars, and message bars.

- **Dialog Box Classes**
  TDialog is a derived class of *TWindow*. It is used to create dialog boxes that handle a variety of user interactions, such as choosing files, fonts, colors, and printing options as well as searching and replacing text, inputting text, and aborting printing jobs.

- **Control Classes**
  TControl is a class derived from *TWindow* for supporting behaviour common to all controls. *ObjectWindows* supports standard controls from Windows, such as widgets, gadgets band decorations.

- **Graphics Classes**
  Windows supports a graphics library called Graphics Device Interface (GDI). *ObjectWindows* encapsulates GDI to make it easier to use device context (DC) classes (*TDC)* and GDI objects (*TGDIObject*).

- **Printing classes**
  TPrinter and *TPrintout* encapsulate the communications with printer devices and the task of printing a document respectively.

- **Module and Application Classes**
  TApplication is responsible for initializing the windows and directing messages received from Windows to the proper window. Application objects are used for deriving an application object from the *TApplication* class, creating an application object, overriding base class function to customize the application behavior, using Borland custom control and Microsoft control 3D libraries. To create and use *TApplication* object one must include the correct header files create an application object, and call the application's call function. The following example shows a small program representing an application of *ObjectWindows*.

Program D.1

```
// p3_1.cpp - An application creating a main window with the caption "trial". It can
//resize, move, minmize, maximize, and close the generated window.

#include <owl\applicat.h>
// This header file has definition of Tapplication which is //derived from TModule
and includes owl\module.h.

        int OwlMain(int /*argc*/, char* /*argv*/ [])
{
                return  TApplication("trial").Run();
}
```


It is necessary to derive a new class from *TApplication* to introduce more functionality in the application. Initializing an *ObjectWindows* application requires the following steps:

i. **Constructing the application object**
Member functions are *InitApplication, InitInstance*, and *InitMainWindow*. One can override any of these members to customize initialization of one's application. The constructor for the *TrialApp* class derived from *TApplication* shown in the following example takes application name as only argument. The default value is zero indicating no name. The application name is referenced by a char far* member of the *TModule* base class called Name.

Program D.2

```
// p3_2.cpp -  Creates and shows a window entitled, " Trial".

#include <owl\applicat.h>

class TrialApp: public Tapplication
{
public:
TrialApp(const char far* name = 0): TApplication(name) {}
};
int
OwlMain(int /*argc*/, char* /*argv*/ [])
{
return TrialApp("trial").Run();
}
```

ii. **Initializing the application**
There are three initialization functions - *InitApplication* initializes the first instance of the application; *InitInstance* initializes the each instance of the application; and *InitMainWindow* initializes the application's main window.

iii. **Initializing each new instance**
One can run multiple instances (copies) of an application simultaneously.

iv. **Initializing the main window**
Tapplication::InitMainWindow creates a frame window with the same name as the application object. This window is not very useful as it can't receive or process any user input. It is therefore essential to override *InitMainWindow* to create a window object that does process user input. The following example creates a *TFrameWindow* object and makes it the main window.**Program D.3:** Creates and shows a maximized window entitled, "First MainWindow"

```
#include <owl\applicat.h>
#include <owl\framewin.h>

class TrialApp: public TApplication
{
  public:
  TrialApp(char far *name): TApplication() {}
  void InitMainWindow();
};

// override InitMainWindow
void TrialApp::InitMainWindow()
{

/* SetMainWindow takes a pointer to the TframeWindow object and returns a pointer to
the old main window. The return value is zero for a new application that has not set a
main window as yet. */

              SetMainWindow(new TFrameWindow(0, "First Main Window"));
/* value of nCmdShow controls the parameters of the window, e.g. when set to
SW_SHOWMAXIMIZED will show a maximized window whenever you run this
application.
*/
       nCmdShow = SW_SHOWMAXIMIZED;
}
```

```
int OwlMain(int /*argc*/, char* /*argv*/ [])
{
  return TrialApp("trial").Run();
/* The application name given in the TApplication constructor is used only if you do not
provide a main window. As this program has used SetMainWindow function -- the
caption bar is titled "First Main Window" and not "trial". */
}
```

- **Doc/View Classes**
  In Doc/View model data is contained in and accessed through a document object and displayed and manipulated through a view object. It comprises of *TDocManager, TDocument* and *TView* classes.

- **Miscellaneous Classes**
  ObjectWindows miscellaneous classes include menus and clipboard classes.

Once an application is initialized, the application object's *MessageLoop* starts running. All incoming messages from Windows are processed by the *MessageLoop*. One can override the default message handling functions and introduce additional message processing capability in the application. *TAppliaction* includes functions, such as *MessageLoop*, *IdleAction*, *PreProcessMenu,* and *ProcessAppMsg* which provide message handling functionality for any *ObjectWindows* application. *TAppliaction* also includes functions that enable one to load the Borland Custom Control Library (*BWCC.DLL* for 16- and 32- bit applications) and Microsoft 3-D Control Library (*CTL3DV2.DLL* and *CTL3D32.DLL* for16- and 32- bit applications, respectively. Function *TApplication::EnableBWCC* is used to open and close the Borland Custom Control Library. When one passes *True* to *EnableBWCC*, the function loads the *DLL* if it is not already loaded. Similarly, if one passes *False* to *EnableBWCC* it unloads the *DLL*. *EnableCTL3D* function works in the same way as *EnableBWCC* for loading and unloading Microsoft 3-D Control Library.

Response tables are used to handle all events in an ObjectWindows application. These tables are used in the following way:

- **Define the response table**
  ObjectWindows provides DEFINE_RESPONSE_TABLEX macro to help a user to define response tables.

```
DEFINE_RESPONSE_TABLE1( TrialFrame, TframeWindow)

EV_WM_LBUTTONDOWN,
EV_WM_LBUTTONUP,
EV_WM_MOUSEMOVE,
EV_WM_RBUTTONDOWN,

END_RESPONSE_TABLE;
```

- **Define the response table entries**
  When a window or control receives a message, it checks the response table to see if there is entry for that message. If an entry is found, it is passed to the corresponding function else the message is passed to its parent. If parent is the main window, message is passed to the application object. If application object also does not have a response entry , the message is processed by the ObjectWindows default processing mechanism.

- **Declare and define the response member functions**
  ObjectWindows provides a large number of macros, called *command message macros,* that let a user assign command messages to any function. The different types of command message macros and the corresponding function are given Table D.D.

Table D.3: Command Message Macros

Macro	Description
EV_COMMAND (CMD, UserName)	Calls function *UserName* when the CMD message is received.
EV_COMMAND_AND-ID (CMD, UserName)	Calls function *UserName* when the CMD message is received. Passes the command's ID(WPARAM parameter) to *UserName.*
EV_COMMAND_ENABLE(CMD, UserName)	Used to automatically enable and disable command controls such as menu items, tool bar buttons and so on.
EV_MESSAGE(MSG, UserName)	Calls *UserName* when the user- defined message MSG is received, MSG is passed to *UserName* without modification.
EV_REGISTERED(MSG, UserName)	Calls *UserName* when the registered message MSG is received. MSG is passed to *UserName* without modifications.

Program D.4

It illustrates use of a response table to capture events such as pressing of the left and right buttons of the mouse. A message box with the caption "Message Sent" and message "Left mouse button pressed" appears when the left button of the mouse is pressed. Similar message will appear when the right button of the mouse is pressed. The program also shows how to override the CanClose member function of *TWindow* to ensure that everything has been cleaned up before saving.

```
/*-----------------------------------------------------------------------------------------------
Program D.4
-----------------------------------------------------------------------------------------------*/
```

```
#include <owl/framewin.h>
#include <owl/owlpch.h>
#include <owl/applicat.h>
class TrialWindow : public TWindow
{
 public:
  TrialWindow(TWindow* parent = 0);
 protected:
  /* Override member function of TWindow - provide user an opportunity to ensure that
  everything has been cleaned up before saving. */
  bool CanClose();
  // Message response functions
  void EvLButtonDown(uint, TPoint&);
  void EvRButtonDown(uint, TPoint&);
 DECLARE_RESPONSE_TABLE(TrialWindow);
// Must be the last macro in its class
};

 DEFINE_RESPONSE_TABLE1(TrialWindow, TWindow)
 EV_WM_LBUTTONDOWN,
 EV_WM_RBUTTONDOWN,
 END_RESPONSE_TABLE;

TrialWindow::TrialWindow(TWindow* parent)
{
 Init(parent, 0, 0);
}
bool TrialWindow::CanClose()
{
// A message box is popped to get user feedback
       switch(MessageBox("Do you want to save?", "Not Implemented",
                                        MB_YESNOCANCEL | MB_ICONQUESTION))
 // One can add desired functionality here like saving data on a file.

       return true;
 }

void TrialWindow::EvLButtonDown(uint, TPoint&)
{
/* whenever one presses left button of the mouse, a message box with caption "Message Sent"
```

```
and message "Left mouse button pressed" appears. Attribute MB_OK will put an "OK" button.*/

 MessageBox(" Left mouse button pressed", "Message Sent", MB_OK);
}

void TrialWindow::EvRButtonDown(uint, TPoint&)
{
 MessageBox(" Right mouse button pressed",  "Message Dispatched", MB_OK);
}

class TrialApp : public TApplication
{
 public:
  TrialApp() : TApplication() {}
  void InitMainWindow()
  {
   SetMainWindow(new TFrameWindow(0, " Trial program", new TrialWindow));
  }
};

int  OwlMain(int /*argc*/, char* /*argv*/ [])
{
  return TrialApp().Run();
}
```

D.2.1 Graphics Device Interface

It refers to the graphics output function of Windows and isolates a Windows program from the physical output device such as display or printer. In addition to producing output on the physical devices it also supports output on two pseudo devices bitmaps and metafiles. Bitmaps refer to a rectangular array of pixels and metafiles. Most of the PC output devices like video display adapters, dot-matrix printers and laser printers are raster devices and represent images as a pattern of dots, i.e., bitmaps. The important *GDI* functions can be grouped in following categories:

- Vector drawing functions to draw graphical objects such as lines, circles and rectangles; bitmap manipulation functions.
- Text output functions
- Palette management functions to display colors supported by a display adapter. Palette management in systems with super VGA & other enhanced graphics adapters, supporting more than 16 colors, is useful.

D.2.2 Device Context (DC)

DC can be considered as a generalized model of a graphics output device and is key to the *GDI*'s support for device independent graphics in Windows. To perforn any sort of graphical operation in Windows, one needs a DC for the window or the area one wants to work with. DC, in fact, is a data structure which includes drawing objects , such as brush, pen and bitmap and graphics attributes, such as background color, text color, fill style, and fonts which control the appearance of the graphics and text. To generate graphics output using DC, one must call an appropriate *GDI* graphics function to access the DC, use this DC to draw and then release the DC. Windows permits only upto 5 DCs to be open at any given time for the entire Windows system.

The handle to the DC (*HDC*) is a protected member variable of the *TDC* class. TDC is the root class for encapasulation of *ObjectWindows GDI* device contexts and is used for drawing in a variety of devices and screen areas, including the *TClientDC* for drawing in the client area of a window, *TmemoryDC* for drawing on to an in-memory bitmap and *TPrintDC* for output to a printer. All GDI functions are member functions of the *TDC* class. The names of the member functions are the same as the GDI functions but the member functions do not need *HDC* as an argument. Table D.2 gives an example below of the call pattern of functions to draw a line from **(xleft, ytop)** to **(xright, ybottom)** using *GDI* functions, *OWL* classes and *TDC* Class in *OWL* 2.0 with *TPoint* objects as argument, respectively.

D.2.3 Contents of a DC

A DC has the following graphics objects:

- A pen which controls the appearance of lines and borders of rectangles, ellipses, and polygons. Drawing mode specifies how to combine pen's color with the color that already exists on the drawing surface.
- A brush which defines a fill pattern.
- Font specifies the shape and size of textual output.
- Palette is an array of colors. Palette facilitates to pick the current selection of available colors out of the millions of colors that can be shown on the display.
- Bitmap is used to draw images.
- Region is defined by a combination of rectangles, ellipses and polygons used for drawing or for clipping.

Table D.4: Call Pattern of Functions

GDI Functions	ObjectWindows Library (OWL) Classes	TDC class with TPoint obj-ects (represents a point in the x-y plane) as arguments
HDC hdc; // Assume that handle to DC is // properly set up	**TclientDC dc(HWindow);** // Assume that TclientDC // is a member of the //	**TclientDC dc(HWindow);** **TPoint start, end;**

	TWindow class	// Assume that the //TPoint objects are //initialized
MoveTo(hdc, xleft, ytop); LineTo(hdc, xright, ybottom);	dc.MoveTo(xleft, ytop); dc.LineTo(xright,ybottom);	dc.MoveTo(start); dc.LineTo(end);

D.2.4 Acquiring a DC

In order to draw on a graphics output device, it is necessory to first obtain a handle to a DC. Windows provides several methods for acquiring a DC handle. A DC can be acquired in response to the *WM_PAINT* message because this event causes redrawing of an application's window. Using*OWL* classes and deriving application's main window from the TWindow class, one can generate all graphics output in a member function named Paint. The prototype of the Paint function is

```
void Paint (   TDC& dc,       // Device context for the display
               Boolerase,     // TRUE = erase the background
               Trect&rect     // Rectangle to be redrawn - defines area
           );
```

The Paint function is called by OWL whenever Windows sends a message to the window. To avoid waiting for the *WM_PAINT* message to update the window, one can either call the *updateWindow* function or create an instance of the *TClientDC* class to get a *DC*. When the *TClientDC* is destroyed, the DC is automatically released.

Changes made the attributes from the handle to a DC are lost when the DC is released. One may also create a private DC for a window so that changes carried out in the attributes of the DC persist until the window is destroyed. The following example shows the procedure to create a persistent DC:

- A window class TrialWindow is derived from the OWL class *TWindow*
- override the *GetWindowClass* function
- add the CS_OWNDC flag to the class style as given below:

```
// TrialWindow:public TWindow
void TrialWindow :: GetWindowClass(WNDCLASS&  wclass);
{
        TWindow::GetWindowClass(wclass);
        wclass.style   |= CS_OWNDC;
}
```

Now each window created using the window class will have its own private DC that exists until the window is destroyed. While using the *CS_OWNDC* style, the DC attributes need initialization only once and continue to be valid until they are changed. The *CS_OWNDC* style affects only the DC retrieved from *GetDC* and BeginPaint and not the DC obtained from other functions, such as *GetWindowDC*. One needs 800 bytes of storage for the DC for each window with the *CS_OWNDC* style. Thus, the window associated with each instance of TrialWindow class has its own private DC. One must still release the DC before exiting from the window function. *SaveDC* and *RestoreDC* functions let a user save the current DC, make temporary changes in the attributes and revert back to the original attributes.

D.2.5 Graphics output using a DC

A typical procedure to generate graphics output using DC is given below:

Create the TDC object. For example, to draw in the client area of the window, one needs to create a *TClientDC* object.

- Define the graphics attributes.
- Invoke appropriate GDI drawing functions.
- If the new operator is used to create the *TDC* object, it must be destroyed by invoking the delete operator.

DC can also be used to determine the capabilities of a device, such as number of color planes in a graphics display by calling the GetDeviceCaps function.

Program D.5

This program makes it possible to create a freehand line drawing while keeping the left button of the mouse pressed. One can release the left button and move the mouse to a new position. Pressing the left button would let one draw freehand from the new position of the mouse. Pressing the right button of the mouse clears the entire client area of the window.

```
/*--------------------------------------------------------------------------------------------
  Program 5.5: Draws freehand line drawing
*/--------------------------------------------------------------------------------------------
#include <owl/owlpch.h>
#include <owl/applicat.h>
#include <owl/framewin.h>
#include <owl/dc.h>
/* Definition of the TrialWindow class -- data member CommonDC, a pointer to the TClientDC
object, is not destroyed automatically when  TrialWindow object is destroyed.  It is necessory to
add  a destructor to TrialWindow to ensure proper cleanup.*/

class  TrialWindow : public TWindow
{
 public:
  TrialWindow(TWindow* parent = 0);
 ~ TrialWindow() // Delete CommonDC
  {
   delete CommonDC;
  }
 protected:
        // Provides a valid device context across functions  EvLButtonDown,
        // EvMouseMove, and EvLButtonUp.
        TDC* CommonDC;
  // Override member function of TWindow
  bool CanClose();
  // Message response functions
        void EvLButtonDown(uint, TPoint&);
        void EvRButtonDown(uint, TPoint&);
        void EvMouseMove(uint, TPoint&);
        void EvLButtonUp(uint, TPoint&);
 DECLARE_RESPONSE_TABLE( TrialWindow);
};
DEFINE_RESPONSE_TABLE1( TrialWindow, TWindow)
 EV_WM_LBUTTONDOWN,
 EV_WM_RBUTTONDOWN,
 EV_WM_MOUSEMOVE,
 EV_WM_LBUTTONUP,
END_RESPONSE_TABLE;
 TrialWindow:: TrialWindow(TWindow* parent)
{
 Init(parent, 0, 0);       // Initialize TrialWindow base class
```

```
 CommonDC = 0;     //Initialize CommonDC-- a pointer to the TClientDC--to zero.
}
bool  TrialWindow::CanClose()
{
 return MessageBox("Do you want to save?", " Not Implemented",
            MB_YESNO | MB_ICONQUESTION) == IDNO;
}
void  TrialWindow::EvLButtonDown(uint, TPoint& point)
{
 if (!CommonDC)
 {
       SetCapture();
       CommonDC = new TClientDC(*this);
       CommonDC->MoveTo(point);
 }
}
void  TrialWindow::EvRButtonDown(uint, TPoint&)
{
 Invalidate();              // clears the entire client area of the window
}
void  TrialWindow::EvMouseMove(uint, TPoint& point)
{
 if (CommonDC)
        CommonDC->LineTo(point);
}
void  TrialWindow::EvLButtonUp(uint, TPoint&)
{
 if ( CommonDC)
 {
  ReleaseCapture();
        delete CommonDC;
        CommonDC = 0;
 }
}
class TDrawApp : public Tapplication
 {
 public:
  TDrawApp() : TApplication() {}
  void InitMainWindow()
  {
   SetMainWindow(new TFrameWindow(0, "Freehand Draw", new  TrialWindow));
  }
};
```

```
int OwlMain(int /*argc*/, char* /*argv*/ [])
{
  return TDrawApp().Run();
}
```

D.2.6 GDI Coordinate System

The GDI supports two coordinate systems referred to as physical(or device) and logicalcoordinates. The physical coordinate system is fixed for a device, e.g., for a window on the screen the origin is at the upper left corner of a window's client area, the positive x-axis extends to the right, and the positve y-axis extends downwards. In all device coordinate systems, units are in erms of pixels. Windows supports several logical coordinates systems and maps each one of them to the physical systems before displaying any graphics output.

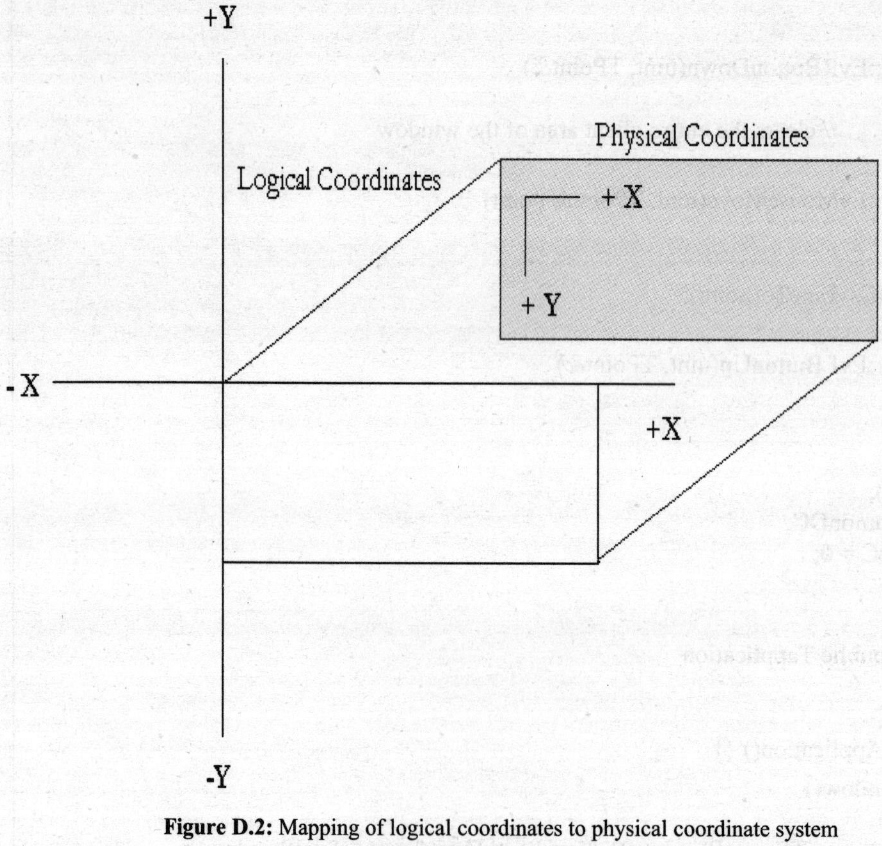

Figure D.2: Mapping of logical coordinates to physical coordinate system

Windows supports eight mapping mode identifiers specifying logical units as 0.001 inch, 0.01 inch, 0.01 millimeter, or 0.1 millimeter and the positive y-axis extending downward or upwards. One can use the *SetMapMode* function to set a mapping mode, such as *MM_ANISOTROPIC* so that logical units along x- and y- axes can be set independently, or MM_TEXT in which logical coordinate is the same as the physical one. The *GetMapMode* function is available to determine the current mapping mode. The mapping modes are listed in table D.5.

Table D.5: Mapping Modes

Mapping Mode	Logical Unit	X-axis	Y-axis
MM_TEXT	Pixel	Right	Down
MM_LOMETRIC	0.1 mm	Right	Up
MM_HIMETRIC	0.01 mm	Right	Up
MM_LOENGLISH	0.01 in.	Right	Up
MM_HIENGLISH	0.001 in.	Right	Up
MM_TWIPS	1/1440 in.	Right	Up
MM_ISOTROPIC	Arbitrary(x=y)	Selectable	Selectable
MM_ANISOTROPIC	Arbitrary(x!=y)	Selectable	Selectable

One can convert client area coordinates to screen coordinates or vice versa using the functions *ClientToScreen* and *ScreenToClient*. The position and the size of the whole window in terms of screen coordinates can be obtained using the *GetWindowRect* function

D.2.7 Drawing with GDI Functions

The GDI contains functions to draw individual pixels, lines, rectangles, polygons and ellipses. A summary of some important functions supported by the GDI is presented in the following sections.

D.2.7.1 Drawing Points

There are two ways of depicting a point on the screen. The main difference is in the way color is specified. One can specify the color either with a 32 bit value whose least significant three bytes represent the red (R), green (G), and blue (B) components of a color or using the RGB macro. The values of the red, green and blue components are between 0 and 255.

```
dc.SetPixel(x, y, color);  // Paints the point at the logical coordinates (x, y) with the
                           // specified color.
dc.SetPixel(x, y, RGB(r, g, b));    // Color is specified using a RGB macro.
```

Table D.6: Functions to Draw Closed Figures

Function	Figure
Rectangle(int xleft, int ytop, int xright, int ybottom);	Draws a rectangle whose upper left corner is **(xleft, ytop)** and lower right corner is **(xright, ybottom)**.
RoundRect(int xleft, int ytop, int xright, int ybottom, int x_ellipse, int y_ellipse);	Draws a rectangle with rounded corner. Each corner is rounded by a small ellipse whose width and height are **x_ellipse** and **y_ellipse**.
Ellipse(int xleft, int ytop, int xright, int ybottom);	Draws an ellipse bounded by rectangle whose opposite corners are given by two points.
Pie(int xleft,int ytop,int xright, int ybottom, int xbegin, int ybegin, int xend, int yend);	Draws a pie shaped wedge. Bounding rectangle is defined by the point **(xleft, ytop)** & point **(xright, ybottom)**. The two straight edges of the pie are defined by the line joining the center of the ellipse and the points **(xbegin, ybegin)**, and **(xend, yend)**.
Chord(int xleft, int ytop, int xright, int ybottom, int xbegin, int ybegin, int xend, int yend);	Draws a segment of ellipse similar to the Pie but unlike Piejoins the end points by a straight line.
Polygon(TPoint* pt, int numpt);	Draws a polygon by joining the points in the array **pt** by straight lines. The first and last points in the array **pt** are joined by a line segment to give a closed figure.

GDI provides a number of function to manipulate rectangles. OWL provides the RECT structure of Windows API, which is defined in the header file <windows.h) as follows:

```
typedef        struct   tagRECT
{
        int     left;    //     upper left corner of the rectangle
        int     top;
        int     right;   //     lower left corner of the rectangle
        int     bottom;
}       RECT;
```

The functions included in GDI that manipulate rectangles are

CopyRect Copyrect(&dest_rect, &src_rect); copy one rectangle structure to another

EqualRect	EqualRect(&rect1, &rect2);	returns TRUE if two rectangle structures are equal
Fill Rect	dc.FillRect(rect, hbrush);	fills the rectangle with the specified brush
FrameRect	dc.FrameRect(rect, brush);	uses the brush to draw a rectangular frame
InvertRect	dc.InvertRect(rect);	inverts all the pixels in the rectangles
OffsetRect	OffsetRect(&rect, x, y);	move a rectangle a number of units along the x- and y-axes
InflateRect	InflateRect(dx,dy);	increase or decrease the size of a rectangle
SetRect	SetRect(&rect, left, right, top, bottom);	sets the fields of a RECT structure
IntersectRect	IntersectRect(&destrect, &srcrect1, &srcrect2);	Obtains the intersection of two rectangles,
UnionRect	Un ionRect(&result_rect, &rect1, &rect2);	Sets the fields of a RECT structure to be union of two other rectangles
SetRectEmpty	SetRectEmpty(&rect);	Sets the fields of a RECT structure to empty
PtInRect	PtInRect(&rect, point);	Returns TRUE if a point is in a rectangle

D.2.7.5 Creating and Painting Regions A region is a description of an area of the display that is a combination of rectangles, polygons, and ellipses. Regions are GDI objects like pens brushes and bitmaps. Regions are also useful in clipping by selecting the region in device context. When one creates a region, Windows returns a handle to the region of type HRGN. Two ways of creating rectangular regions are given below:

```
hRgn = CreateRectRgn (xleft, ytop, xright, ybottom);
```

or

```
hRgn = CreateRectRgnIndirect(&rect);
```

One can use the *TRegion* class to define a region in the device context and perform a number of operations, such as painting, filling, inverting and so on. Table D.7 describes the GDI functions available for manipulating regions.

Table D.7:GDI functions that manipulate regions

FUNCTION	DESCRIPTION
CreateRectRgn (xleft, ytop, xright, ybottom);	Creates a rectangular region using specified coordinates for the opposite corners of the rectangle.
CreateRoundRectRgn	Creates a rectangular region wih rounded corners - similar to *RoundRect* function.
CreateEllipticRgn (xleft, ytop, xright, ybottom);	Creates an elliptic region.

APPENDIX D

CreateEllipticRgnIndirect (& rect)	Creates an elliptic region using the fields in a RECT structure
CreatePolygonRgn (points, npoints, fill_mode);	Creates a polygon region. Parameter fill_mode is *ALTERNATE* to *WINDING*
CreatePolyPolygonRgn	Creates a region out of multiple polygons.
CombineRgn(hresult_rgn, hrgn1, hrgn2, combine_flag);	Combines two regions into one according to a specified combining mode.
EqualRgn (hrgn1, hrgn2);	Returns *TRUE* if two regions are equal.
dc.FillRgn (rgn, brush);	It belongs to the *TDC* class that fills a region with the specified brush.
FrameRgn (rgn, brush, pt); //pt is a TPoint with width and height of the frame	It belongs to the *TDC* class and draws a frame around a region with the specified brush.
rgn.GetRgnBox (rect);	It belongs to the *TRegion* class that returns the bounding box of the region.
InvalidateRgn (hrgn, erase_flag);	It belongs to the *TWindow* class that marks the specified region for repainting.
dc.InvertRgn (rgn);	A member function of the TDC class that inverts the pixels in a region.
OffsetRgn (hrgn, x, y);	Moves a region by a specified x-and y-offset
dc.PaintRgn (rgn);	Fills the region with the current brush:
PtInRegion(hrgn, x, y);	Returns *TRUE* if the specified point is in the given region.
RectInRegion(hrgn, & rectangle);	Returns *TRUE* if any part of the specified rectangle is in the region.
rgn.SetRectRgn (rect);	It belongs to the *TRegion* class that changes the region to a rectangular shape specified by the TRect argument.
ValidateRgn (hrgn);	A member function of the *TWindow* class that removes the region from the area to be repainted:

D.2.8 Drawing Mode

GDI consists of number of line modes which can be used for combining the pen color with the existing color and draw lines and filled figures. The mode name starts with R2_ prefix. The default mode is R2_COPYPEN which overwrites whatever exists on the drawing surface. The drawing mode is also referred to as raster operation (ROP).

The following statement can be used to set a new drawing mode and to save the previous mode:

```
int old_ROP = dc.setROP2 (R2_BLACK);
```

Table D.8 lists the drawing modes supported in GDI.

Table D.8: Drawing modes in Windows GDI

Mode Name	Boolean Operation	Comments
R2_BLACK	all bits zero	Draws in black irrespective of pen color and existing color
R2_COPYPEN	pen	Draws with the pen color
R2_MASKNOTPEN	(NOT pen) AND dest	Inverts bits in the pen color, performs a bitwise-*AND* with existing color
R2_MASKPEN	pen AND dest	Performs bitwise-*AND* of pen color and existing color
R2_MASKPENNOT	pen AND (NOT dest)	Inverts existing color and does bitwise-*AND* with pen color
R2_MERGENOTPEN	(NOT pen) OR dest	Inverts pen color and does bitwise-*OR* with existing color
R2_MERGEPEN	pen OR dest	Performs bitwise-*OR* of pen color and existing color
R2_MERGEPENNOT	pen OR (NOT dest)	Inverts existing color and does bitwise-*OR* with pen color
R2_NOP	dest	Leaves existing color unchanged (hence the name *NOP* for ``no operation")
R2_NOT	NOT dest	Inverts existing color
R2_NOTCOPYPEN	NOT pen	Draws with inverted pen color

APPENDIX D

R2_NOTMASKPEN	NOT (pen AND dest)	Performs bitwise-*AND* of pen and existing color and inverts the result
R2_NOTMERGEPEN	NOT (pen OR dest)	Does bitwise-*OR* of pen and existing color and inverts the result
R2_NOTXORPEN	NOT (pen XOR dest)	Performs bitwise exclusive-*OR* of pen and existing color and inverts the result
R2_WHITE	all bits 1	Draws in white color
R2_XORPEN	pen XOR dest	Does bitwise exclusive-*OR* of pen color and existing color

D.2.9 Colors, Palettes and Bitmaps

D.2.9.1 Colors

Windows *API* defines a 32- bit integer called *COLORREF*. The low order bytes contain the intensities of the red, green and blue colors and the most significant byte contains the type which indicates whether to interpret the value as a color or a palette entry.

The *RGB* macro represents the *RGB* color, e.g. RGB(0, 0, 255) denotes a full intensity blue color.Each color is represented by 8-bits, i.e. by intensities between 0 to 255. *TColor* class in *OWL* 2.0 maintains color as *COLORREF* value. Windows uses dithering (described in chapter 2) only when filling areas to display neighbouring pixels in different colors to create unique shades. It cannot use dithering when drawing points lines and text.

D.2.9.2 Palettes The number of colors that can be displayed at a time is determined by the number of bits of storage allocated for each pixel. In standard VGA, there is 4-bits storage to represent each color pixel, therefore, this adapter can display only 2^4, i.e., 16 simultaneous colors. A super VGA card can have memory to support upto 8-bits per pixel and hence can display 2^8 (or 256) simultaneous colors. Display adapter represents each color by the RGB intensities. Given below is the number of distinct colors supported and number of simultaneous colors shown by a display adapter:

Adapter	Bits/pixel Components	Intensities R G B			Distinct Colors available	Bits/Pixel Supported	Simultaneous Colours
VGA	6	2^6	2^6	2^6	$2^6 \times 2^6 \times 2^6 = 262,144$	4	$2^4 = 16$
SVGA	8	2^8	2^8	2^8	$2^8 \times 2^8 \times 2^8 = 16,777,216$	8	$2^8 = 256$

The display adapter converts each pixel's contents into a color by interpreting the pixel's value as an index into a table called color palette. The entries in this table are the RGB values. Windows defines a system palette which has 16 predefined colors for EGA and VGA. System palette has 20 predefined colors for display adapters which support more than 256 colors.

The concept of logical palette in Windows enables a user to take advantage of the large number of colors available in the system. Windows supports an extended system palette that is the mirror image of the hardware palette. Windows assigns 20 values corresponding to the default colors in the extended pallete. Windows maps each color in the logical palette to the extended system palette as follows:

- If color in logical palette already exists in the system palette, that color is mapped to the matching color index in the system palette.
- If color in logical palette does not exist in the system palette, it is added in the system palette if there is space.
- In case the system palette is full, a color in the logical palette is mapped to the closest matching color in the system palette.

Windows supports only 20 default colors in the system palette. One needs to use a logical palette to develop applications with all 256 colors in the Super VGA mode. Table D.9 gives a brief description of the Windows functions to manipulate palette.

Table D.9: Functions to manipulate palettes

Function	Description
pal.AnimatePalette (start_indx, count, pal_entries);	Belongs to the *TPalette* class - changes entries in a logical palette resulting in instant changes to colors on the display.
CreatePalette	Creates a logical palette and returns a handle (that can be used to create a *TPalette*) to the palette
pal.GetNearestPaletteIndex (color);	Belongs to the *TPalette* class - returns the index of the palette entry that most closely matches a specified TColor
pal.GetPaletteEntries (start_indx, count, pal_entries);	Belongs to the *TPalette* class - retrieves the color values for a specified number of entries in a logical palette
dc.GetSystemPaletteEntries (start, num, pal_entries);	Belongs to the *TDC* class - retrieves the color values for a specified number of entries in the system palette
GetSystemPaletteUse ();	Belongs to *TDC* class - returns a flag indicating whether an application can change the system palette
dc.RealizePalette ();	Belongs to the *TDC* class - maps the entries of the currently selected logical palette into the system palette
dc.ResizePalette();	Belongs to the *TPalette* class - enlarges or reduces the size of a logical palette after it has been created
pal.SetPaletteEntries (start, count, pal_entries);	Belong to the *TPalette* class - changes the color values of a specified number of entries in the logical palette
SetSysColors	Sets one or more colors in the system palette, identified by constants such as *COLOR_ACTIVEBORDER*, *COLOR_MENU* and *COLOR_WINDOW*
dc.SetSystemPaletteUse (flag);	Belongs to the TDC class - allows the active application to change the entries in the system palette and flag is one of *SYSPAL_NOSTATIC* or *SYSPAL_STATIC*
dc.UpdateColors ();	Belongs to the class - updates the color of the pixels in the client area of a window to reflect the current entries in the system palette

In case an application uses a logical palette, it should handle the following three palette specific Windows messages:

- Whenever the application's window becomes active, Windows sends a

WM_QUERYNEWPALETTE message. This is the time when one can load the desired set of colors using RealizePalette function which maps logical palette to the system palette.

- Windows sends a *WM_PALETTECHANGING* message to the top level windows of all applications when the system palette is about to change.

- *WM_PALETTECHANGED* message is sent to the top level windows of all applications when the system palette has changed.

D.2.9.3 Bitmaps

Bitmap is a digital representation of the picture. Each pixel in the picture represents one or more bits in the bitmap. Monochrome bitmaps require only one bit per pixel but color bitmaps require additional number of bits to indicate the color of each pixel.

Device Independent Bitmap (*DIB*) format is called device indepedent because it consists of the color table. The color table gives the pixel values corresponding to the *RGB* color values. The *DIB* format is an extension of bitmap format of *OS/2* presentation manager. The *WINDOWS.H* header file contains a few structures that support *OS/2* bitmaps. The *GDI* bitmap objects are called device dependent bitmap (*DDB*) objects because they must be compatible with a specific graphics output device. The *DIB* is represented by the *TDib* class and has no *GDI* handle like a regular bitmap as it is not a *GDI* object. The *DIB* is, therefore, kept outside *GDI* either as files or in the memory. One can convert a *DIB* into a *GDI* object but in such case the device independent color information in the *DIB* is lost.

The *DIB* format is useful for storing images in a file. One can create a *DIB* using Microsoft Image Editor, Paintbrush, or Borland Resource Workshop. The files, thus, created have extension *.BMP* or in some cases extension *.DIB*. The internal representation of data, i.e., number of bits per pixel is : i) 1 for monochrome bitmaps; ii) 4 for 16- color bitmaps; iii) 16 for 256- color bitmaps and iv) 24 for 16,777,216 - color bitmaps. Given below is a constructor for creating a *TDib* object:

```
Tdib( int width, int height, int ncolors, uint 16 mode=DIB_RGB_COLORS);
```

'width' and 'height' parameters give width and the height of the *DIB* in pixels; ncolors & mode refer to number of colors and RGB or PAL palette respectively.

Program D.6

```
/*-----------------------------------------------------------------------------------------------------------
Program D.6:
This program shows how to

a) Create a menu and use of SetMainWindow and GetMainWindow functions to activate the
   menu "COMMANDS" to set Pen Width & color
```

```
b) Declare and define response table
c) Process events caused by pressing and releasing of mouse buttons.
d) Create a freehand line drawing while keeping the left button of the mouse pressed
   The left button can be released to move the mouse to a new position.  Pressing the left button
   would allow freehand drawing from the new position.)
e) Clear the entire client area of the window when the cleanup option is selected from the setup
   menu
f) Output text (in the chosen color) on the window
g) Show current mouse position by pressing the right button of the mouse
h) Terminate a running program through use of menu Exit/Close option
i) Select color  using TChooseColorDialog
j) Take value of a parameter using TInputDialog
k) Use message box (MessageBox)
-------------------------------------------------------------------------------------------------------*/

#include <owl/owlpch.h>
#include <owl/applicat.h>
#include <owl/framewin.h>
#include <owl/dc.h>
#include <owl/inputdia.h>
#include <stdlib.h>
#include <string.h>
#include "p3_6.rc"

/* Definition of the TrialWindow class -- data member CommonDC, a pointer to the TClientDC
object, is not destroyed automatically when  TrialWindow object is destroyed.  It is necessory to
 add  a destructor to TrialWindow to ensure proper cleanup. */

class  TrialWindow : public TWindow
{
 public:
   TrialWindow(TWindow* parent = 0);
  ~ TrialWindow() // Delete CommonDC
   {
                  delete CommonDC;
                  delete Pen;
        }

        void GetPenSize();
        void SetPenSize(int newSize);
        void SetPen(TColor& newColor, int penSize = 0);

 protected:
        // Provides a valid device context across functions  EvLButtonDown,
```

```
        // EvMouseMove, and EvLButtonUp.
        TDC* CommonDC;
        TPen*  Pen;
         int PenSize;
        TColor Color;

        // Override member function of TWindow
        bool CanClose();

        // Message response functions
        void EvLButtonDown(uint, TPoint&);
        void EvRButtonDown(uint, TPoint&);
        void EvMouseMove(uint, TPoint&);
        void EvLButtonUp(uint, TPoint&);

       //Menu processing functions
        void CmPenSize();
        void CmPenColor();
        void CmAbout();
        void CmClearWindow();
        void CmClose();

 DECLARE_RESPONSE_TABLE( TrialWindow);
};

 DEFINE_RESPONSE_TABLE1( TrialWindow, TWindow)
  EV_WM_LBUTTONDOWN,  //Mouse left button down
  EV_WM_RBUTTONDOWN,  //Mouse right button down
  EV_WM_MOUSEMOVE,
  EV_WM_LBUTTONUP,    //Mouse left button  up
  EV_COMMAND(CM_PENSIZE, CmPenSize),
  EV_COMMAND(CM_PENCOLOR, CmPenColor),
  EV_COMMAND(CM_ABOUT, CmAbout),
  EV_COMMAND(CM_CLEARWINDOW, CmClearWindow ),
  EV_COMMAND(CM_CLOSE,CmClose ),
END_RESPONSE_TABLE;

 TrialWindow:: TrialWindow(TWindow* parent)
{
  Init(parent, 0, 0);           // Initialize TrialWindow base class
  CommonDC = 0;                 // Initialize CommonDC-- a pointer to the TClientDC--to zero.
  PenSize  = 1;                 // Initialize pen size
  Color = TColor::Black;        // Initialize color
```

APPENDIX D

```
 Pen = new TPen(Color, PenSize);    //TColor::Black defined in owl\color.h
}

void  TrialWindow::SetPen(TColor& newColor, int penSize)
{
 // If penSize isn't the default (0), set PenSize to the new size.
 if (penSize)
        PenSize = penSize;
 Color = newColor;
 delete Pen;
 Pen = new TPen( Color, PenSize);   // pickup a pen of new color
}

bool  TrialWindow::CanClose()        // file save feature not implemented
{
 return MessageBox("Do you want to save?", "Not implemented",
                                        MB_YESNO | MB_ICONQUESTION) == IDNO;
 // insert logic for saving the file
}

void  TrialWindow::EvLButtonDown(uint, TPoint& point)
{

 if (!CommonDC)
 {
        SetCapture();
        CommonDC = new TClientDC(*this); //'this' is a local variable avialable
         // in the body of a nonstatic function
        CommonDC->SelectObject(*Pen); //select pen in device context
        CommonDC->MoveTo(point);
 }
}

/* Let us learn to output text on the window.  Output mouse position when right button of mouse
is pressed. */
void  TrialWindow::EvRButtonDown(uint, TPoint& point)
{
char str[40];
 short posx = point.x;
 short posy = point.y;
 TClientDC  CommonDC(*this);
 wsprintf(str, "Mouse Position (%d,%d)        ", posx, posy);
 CommonDC.SetTextColor(RGB(255,0,0));           // set text color to red
 CommonDC.SetTextAlign(TA_BOTTOM | TA_LEFT);   //Text Alignment
```

```
 CommonDC.TextOut(20, 20, str, strlen(str));
}

void  TrialWindow::EvMouseMove(uint, TPoint& point)
{
 if (CommonDC)
 CommonDC->LineTo(point);
}

void  TrialWindow::EvLButtonUp(uint, TPoint&)
{
 if ( CommonDC)
 {
        ReleaseCapture();
        delete CommonDC;
        CommonDC = 0;
 }
}

void TrialWindow::CmPenSize() //Processes menu command Pen Size
{
 GetPenSize();
}

void TrialWindow::CmPenColor()
{
 TChooseColorDialog::TData colors;  //Processes menu command Pen Color
 static TColor custColors[16] =
 {
  0x010101L, 0x101010L, 0x202020L, 0x303030L,
  0x404040L, 0x505050L, 0x606060L, 0x707070L,
  0x808080L, 0x909090L, 0xA0A0A0L, 0xB0B0B0L,
  0xC0C0C0L, 0xD0D0D0L, 0xE0E0E0L, 0xF0F0F0L
 };

 colors.Flags = CC_RGBINIT;
 colors.Color = TColor::Black;
 colors.CustColors = custColors;
 if (TChooseColorDialog(this, colors).Execute() == IDOK)
         SetPen(colors.Color);
}

void TrialWindow::GetPenSize()
```

```
{
 char inputText[6];

 wsprintf(inputText, "%d", PenSize);
 if ((TInputDialog(this, "Line Thickness","Input a new thickness:",
inputText,sizeof(inputText))).Execute() == IDOK)
 {
        int newPenSize = atoi(inputText);
        if (newPenSize < 0)
        newPenSize=1;
        SetPenSize(newPenSize);
 }
}

void TrialWindow::SetPenSize(int newSize)
{
 delete Pen;
 PenSize = newSize;
 Pen     = new TPen(Color, PenSize);
}

void TrialWindow::CmClearWindow()
{
 Invalidate(); // clears the entire client area of the window
}

void TrialWindow::CmAbout()
{
 TDialog(this, IDD_ABOUT).Execute();
}

void TrialWindow::CmClose()        // terminate the program
{
        EvClose();     // shuts down the main window and ends the application
}

class TDrawApp : public TApplication
{
 public:
   TDrawApp() : TApplication() {}

   void InitMainWindow();
};
```

```
void TDrawApp::InitMainWindow()
{
  SetMainWindow(new TFrameWindow(0, "Freehand Drawing", new TrialWindow));
  GetMainWindow()->AssignMenu("COMMANDS");
}
int OwlMain(int /*argc*/, char* /*argv*/ [])
{
 return TDrawApp().Run();
}
```

Resource file for Program D.6

```
//--------------------------------------------------------------------------
// Resource file for program D.6
//--------------------------------------------------------------------------
#include <owl/inputdia.rc>
#include <owl/except.rc>

#define CM_ABOUT      205
#define CM_PENSIZE    206
#define CM_PENCOLOR   207
#define CM_CLEARWINDOW 208
#define IDD_ABOUT     211
#define CM_CLOSE      212
#ifdef RC_INVOKED
#ifndef WORKSHOP_INVOKED
# include <windows.h>
#endif

COMMANDS MENU
{
 POPUP "&Setup"
 {
  MENUITEM "Pen &Size",   CM_PENSIZE
  MENUITEM "Pen &Color", CM_PENCOLOR
  MENUITEM "&CleanUp",   CM_CLEARWINDOW
 }
 POPUP "&Help"
 {
  MENUITEM "&About",     CM_ABOUT
 }
  POPUP "&Exit"
  {
```

```
 MENUITEM "&Close",     CM_CLOSE
 }
}
STRINGTABLE
{
 CM_PENSIZE,            "Change the pen width"
 CM_PENCOLOR,           "Change the pen color"
 CM_ABOUT,              "show an information dialog box"
 CM_CLEARWINDOW, "Clear window"
 CM_CLOSE,              "Terminate the Program"
}
IDD_ABOUT DIALOG 37, 25, 170, 95
STYLE DS_MODALFRAME | WS_POPUP | WS_VISIBLE | WS_CAPTION | WS_SYSMENU
CAPTION "About Freehand Drawing"
FONT 8, "MS Sans Serif"
{
 DEFPUSHBUTTON "Ok", IDOK, 60, 70, 50, 14
 CTEXT "ObjectWindows 2.5 Program", -1, 23, 46, 127, 10
 CTEXT "Freehand Drawing", -1, 23, 24, 126, 8
}
#endif // RC_INVOKED
```

D.2.10 Tool Bar and Status Bar

A tool bar generally appears at the top of main window of application and consists of collection of push buttons. It enables the user to quickly initiate action as compared to the pull down menu. For example, in Word Perfect, the tool bar comprises of buttons, such as New Blank Document, Open, Save, Print, Cut, Copy, Paste, Undo, Redo, Bold, Italic, Underline, and Quick Format. Most packages provide buttons for special functions, like File open and Edit dialog box.

A status bar is another common decoration that is included in many Windows applications. This is an area at the bottom of the main window where an application displays help messages as well as the status of some keys (Caps lock, Num lock and Insert).

To insert status and control bars one has to change the main window from a *TFrameWindow* to a *TDecoratedFrame* and modify the function InitMainWindow() as follows:

```
// Create the decorated frame window
TDecoratedFrame* frame = new TDecoratedFrame(Name, "Caption of window", new
                                    TdrawWindow, true);
//Create a status bar
TStatusBar* sb = new TStatusBar(frame, Tgadget::Recessed,
                                    TstatusBar::CapsLock|
                                    TstatusBar::NumLock|
                                    TStatusBar::OverType);
// Create a control bar
```

```
TControlBar* cb = new TcontrolBar(frame);
// Insert button gadgets into the TControlBar. Each button gadget has an associated bitmap
// resource ID and a control ID that tie together a message response function to that button.
  cb->Insert(*new TButtonGadget(CM_FILENEW, CM_FILENEW, TButtonGadget::
  Command));
  cb->Insert(*new TButtonGadget(CM_FILEOPEN, CM_FILEOPEN, TButtonGadget::
  Command));
  cb->Insert(*new TButtonGadget(CM_FILESAVE, CM_FILESAVE, TButtonGadget::
  Command));
  cb->Insert(*new TButtonGadget(CM_FILESAVEAS, CM_FILESAVEAS, TbuttonGadget::
  Command));
// Insert the status bar and control bar into the frame
frame->Insert(*sb, TDecoratedFrame::Bottom);
frame->Insert(*cb, TDecoratedFrame::Top);
```

Source: Chapter 3 of the book 'Computer Graphics for Engineers and Scientists' by R.G.S. Asthana and N.K. Sinha, New Age International Publishers Pages 539, First Edition 1996, Second Edition: 1998, Reprint 2005.

APPENDIX E

NUMBER SYSTEM

Any use of numbers implies the use of a base value for the numbers. The simplest base value in a numbering scheme is '1'. In this scheme the number '2' is two things, or two groups of ones. The number '9' is nine things or nine groups of ones. The basic rules for a base numbering system entail ordering items, grouping ordered items and then expressing the groups and items in a consistent way. The way it represents the different groups gives the numbering system an order of magnitude. This can be expressed in several ways.

A special symbol is used to represents a specified grouping value. For example, a picture of a hand may represent numeral 5. The Roman numerals and the Egyptian numbering represent each order of magnitude with a special symbol. This approach, however, limits how high a numbering system may count because a new symbol needs to be devised for each successive grouping. For example, the number 1,295,468 is represented in the Egyptian numbering system as follows:

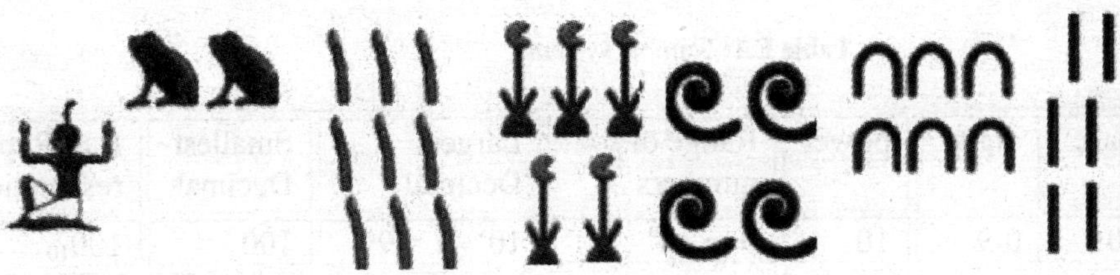

Each of the magnitudes of 10 was represented in the above number, for example the 4 frogs represent 4 hundred thousands and the 5 lotus flowers represent 5 thousands, etc. In this numbering system, only the magnitudes of 10 that are used are expressed in the written number. The number 6,060 is thus represented as:

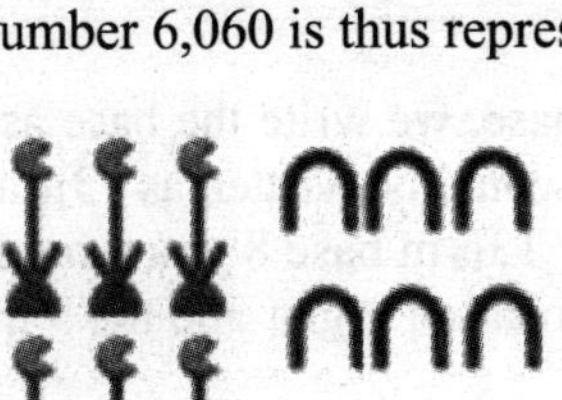

Grouping values can be represented by the place they hold in the representation of the number. Our Hindu/Arabic numbering system uses this method, as we have a place value for 1's, 10's, 100's, etc. Since no new symbols are used (0-9), the numbering system can continue to incredibly large values. From the use of this method a representation of 0 emerges so that there is a way to represent 0 of a group.

The orders of magnitude may represent a consistent gradation of value where each successive order of magnitude will be 'n' times the last order of magnitude. In the decimal system, each successive place value is 10 times the last place value.

Some examples of number base systems are: Binary (base 2), Hand (base 5), Octal (base 8), Decimal (base 10), Base 12 (duodecimal), Hexadecimal (base 16), Mayan (base 20) (Vigesimal), and Time and Ancient Sumerian (base 60) Base 60 (Sexagesimal).

One can imagine that we would have evolved a strategy of using the letter A to represent ten; or we might have used IIIIIIIII to represent that idea. The Romans used X. The Arabic system, which we use, makes use of position in conjunction with numerals to represent values. The first (right-most) column is used for "ones," and the next column is used for tens. Thus, the number fifteen is represented as 15 (read "one, five"); that is, 1 ten and 5 ones.

Certain rules emerge, from which some generalizations can be made as given in Table E.1.

Table E.1: Number systems

Number System	Base	digits	power	Range of numbers	Largest Decimal	Smallest Decimal	BaseRep-resentation
Decimal	10	0-9	10	0 to $10^n - 1$	$10^2 - 1 = 99$	100	100_{10}
Octal	8	0-7	8	0 to $8^n - 1$	$8^2 - 1 = 63$	64	100_8
Binary	2	0 & 1	2	0 to $2^n - 1$	$2^2 - 1 = 3$	4	100_2
Hexa-Decimal	16	0-9 & A-F	16	0 to $16^n - 1$	$16^2 - 1 = 255$	256	100_{16}

To distinguish numbers written in each base, we write the base as a subscript next to the number. The number thirteen in base 10 would be written as 13_{10} and read as "One, three, base ten." Thus, to represent the number 13_{10} in base 8 you would write 15_8. This is read "one, five, base eight." Why 15? The 1 means 1 eight, and the 5 means 5 ones. One eight plus five ones equals fifteen.

Around the Bases

How do you generalize the process? To convert a base ten number to base 8, think about the columns: in base 8 they are ones, eight, sixty four, five-hundred-ten-two, and so on. Why these columns? They represent 1, 8, 64, 512 and so forth.

To understand the procedure to convert from a decimal value to base 8, we take 202 as a decimal number and give below a step by step procedure:

Step 1:

Examine the number and decide which column to use first. The number is 202 so you know that column 4 (202/512) is **0** and you don't have to worry about it.

Step 2:

To find out how many 64s there are, divide 202 by 64. The answer is 3, so put **3** in column 3.

Step 3:

Examine the remainder of step 2 which is 10 so divide remainder by 8 and u get 1, so put a **one** in the second column.

Step 4:

The remainder is now two. There are 2 ones in 2 so put a **2** in the1s column.

Result:

The resultant octal number is **0312**.

Let us take up another example. Say we want to convert 202 to a binary number.

To convert the number to base 2, you follow the same procedure: There are no 256s, so column 8 is **0**.

There is one 128 in 202, so column 7 is **1** and 74 is the remainder. There is one 64s in 78 so column 6 is **1** and remainder is 10. There is no 16 in 10 so column 5 is **0**. There is one 8 in 8, and so column 4 is **1** and remainder is 2. There is no 4 in remainder 2 so column 3 is **0** and the remainder remains 2. There is one 2 in 2, and so column 1 is **1** and remainder is zero. There is no remainder, so the column 1 is **0**.

The binary number, therefore, is **01101010**.

Why Base 2?

Once you make this great leap of intuition, the power of binary becomes clear: With 1s and 0s you can represent the fundamental truth of every circuit (there is power or there isn't). All a computer ever knows is, "Is you is, or is you ain't?" Is you is = 1; is you ain't = 0.

Bits, Bytes, and Nibbles

Once the decision is made to represent true and false with 1s and 0s, binary digits (or bits) become very important. Since early computers could send 8 bits at a time, it was natural to start writing code using 8-bit numbers--called bytes. Half a byte (4 bits) is referred to as nibble.

With 8 binary digits you can represent up to 256 different values.

What's a KB?

It turns out that 1,024 is roughly equal to 1,000. This coincidence was too good to miss, so computer scientists started referring to 1024 bytes as 1KB or 1 kilobyte, based on the scientific prefix of kilo for thousand.

Similarly, 1024 * 1024 (1,048,576) is close enough to one million to receive the designation 1MB or 1 megabyte, and 1,024 megabytes is called 1 gigabyte (giga implies thousand-million or billion).

Hexadecimal

Because binary numbers are difficult to read, a simpler way to represent the same values is sought. Translating from binary to base 10 involves a fair bit of manipulation of numbers; but it turns out that translating from base 2 to base 16 is very simple, because there is a very good shortcut.

To understand this, you must first understand base 16, which is known as hexadecimal. In base 16 there are sixteen numerals: 0, 1, 2, 3, 4, 5, 6, 7, 8, 9, A, B, C, D, E, and F. The last six are arbitrary; the letters A-F were chosen because they are easy to represent on a keyboard.

To translate from hexadecimal to decimal, you can multiply. Thus, the number C8C represents:

Hexadecimal	C8C	Result
Step 1	C*256	12*256 = 3072
Step 2	8*16	= 128
Step 3	C*1	12*1 = 12
Decimal	Sum of Step 1-3	3212

Translating the number AB to binary is done by translating first to base 10, and then to binary:

Conversion to base 10			
Hexadecimal	AB		Result
Step 1	A*16		10*16 = 160
Step 2	B*1		11* 1 = 11
Decimal	171	Sum of Step 1-2	**171**
Conversion to binary			
Step 1	There is 1 128	Remainder 43	1
Step 2	There is 0 64		0
Step 3	There is 1 32	11	1
Step 4	There is 0 16		0
Step 5	There is 1 8	3	1
Step 6	There is 0 4		0
Step 7	There is 1 2	1	1
Step 8	There is 1 1		1
Binary			10101011

Thus, the answer in binary is **1010** 1011.

Let us look at this binary number as two sets of 4 digits and you are set to do a magical transformation.

The right set is 1011, i.e., 11 decimal or in hexadecimal it is 'B'. The left set is 1010, i.e., 10 in Decimal or 'A' in Hexadecimal. We replace each set with its equivalent hexadecimal digit and we have:

Number System	**Left Set**	Right Set
Binary	**1010**	1011
Hexadecimal	**A**	B

Putting the two hex numbers together we get the hex number 'AB' which is the real value of binary number '1010 1011'. This method always works irrespective of binary number of any length. To repeat the process, first reduce the given binary number in to sets of 4, translate each set of four to hex, and put the hex numbers together to get the result in hex. Similarly, you can easily convert any hex to binary.

Notes

APPENDIX F

Recursion

F.1 Introduction

In computer science, *recursion* specifies (or constructs) a class of objects or methods (or an object from a certain class) by defining a few very simple base cases or methods (often just one), and then defining rules to break down complex cases into simpler cases.

F.2 Recursive Functions

A useful way to think of recursive functions is to imagine them as a process being performed where one of the instructions is to "repeat the process". This makes it sound very similar to a loop because it repeats the same code, and in some ways it *is* similar to looping. On the other hand, recursion makes it easier to express ideas in which the result of the recursive call is necessary to complete the task. Of course, it must be possible for the "process" to sometimes be completed without the recursive call. One simple example is the idea of building a wall that is ten feet high; if one wants to build a ten foot high wall, and then one may first build one foot high wall, and then add an extra foot of bricks repeatedly till the height become 10 feet. Conceptually, this is like saying the "build wall" function builds wall of one feet height and repeats itself till the height is equal to 10 feet..

Each recursive function should have the following properties.

- **Base case**: Must have at least one case which can be solved without recursion.
- **Making progress**: At each step there must be some progress toward the base case so that the base case condition is eventually met.
- **Design rule**: during the design of the recursive algorithm, assume that all simpler recursive calls work.

Let us look at an example to further understand the concept of recursion.

```
/*
Example F.1: Factorial function
n! = n · (n − 1) · (n − 2) · · · 3 · 2 · 1
n! = n · (n − 1)!
n! = n · (n − 1) · (n − 2)!

A recursive algorithm to calculate a factorial of a function */
```

```
#include <iostream.h>

int factorial(int n)
  {
     if (n > 1)
        {
            return n * factorial(n - 1); //'Line R' 'Recursive call to the function factorial
        }
     else {
              return 1; // 'Line B' Base Case
           }
  }

int main()
  {
     int n;
     int fact;

     cout << "Enter an integer for which the factorial is to be calculated: ";
     cin >> n;

     fact = factorial(n); // Line 'C'
     cout << n << "! = " << fact << endl;

     return 0;
  }
```

Example F.1 illustrates a recursive algorithm to calculate the factorial of an integer entered by the user. So lets suppose the user enters the integer 'n' as the input to the program.

The statement 'fact = **factorial (n);**' marks the first call to the factorial function. Once this function is called as it might already be evident from the function structure that the function does indeed have two decision cases. The first being if the value of the inputted integer 'n' is greater than '1' in which case the function calls itself again (recursive call). Where as in the second case if the value of 'n' is lesser than or equal to '1' in which case it returns the value '1'.

In order to really understand this example, let us trace it say with value of n = 4. The program execution reaches 'Line C' in the main function, as a result of which the factorial function is called with 'n = 4'. As '4 > 1' so the 'Line R' in the factorial function is called with 'n = 3' (factorial (n - 1)). Again as '3' is greater than '1' the 'Line R' is executed in the factorial function and it is called again with 'n = 2'. Similarly, factorial (2) results in calling the factorial function again with 'n = 1'. When this happens the 'Line B' gets executed and the integer value of '1' is returned. As a result of which factorial (2) returns (2 * factorial (1)) = 2 ('return n * **factorial(n - 1)' Line C).** Similarly factorial (3) returns (3 * factorial (2)) = 6 and finally returning factorial (4) as 24 (4 * factorial(3)).

The calling sequence of the factorial function is also illustrated in figure F.1 given below.

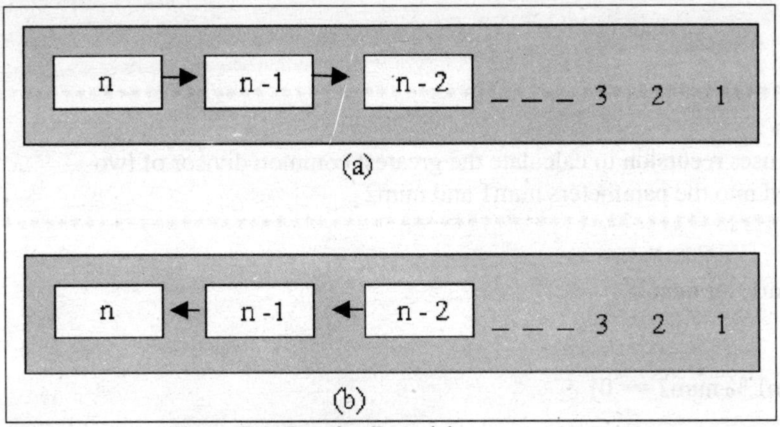

Figure F.1: Function Factorial
a) Calling Sequence
b) Returning Sequence

You should now be able to understand better how a recursive function solves a problem by representing it as an instance of the same problem with a smaller input size in each iteration of the function.

Let us look at another example which demonstrates a recursive function to calculate the greatest common divisor (GCD) of two numbers.

```
// GCD recursive function
# include <iostream>
using namespace std;

//Function prototype
int gcd(int, int);


int main()
  {
     int number1, number2;

     cout<<" Enter the two integers ";

     cin>>number1>>number2;
```

```
cout<<" Enter the greatest common divisor of " << number1;

cout << " and " << number2 << " is:"<<gcd(number1, number2)<<endl; // Line R

return 0;

}

/************************************************************************
GCD function
This function uses recursion to calculate the greatest common divisor of two
integers passed into the parameters num1 and num2
************************************************************************/

int gcd(int num1, int num2)
{

    if (num1 % num2 == 0)

        return num2;

    else
        return gcd(num2, num1 % num2);
}
```

To understand this program let us again trace it for a simple example say 'number1 = 4' and 'number2 = 14'. When the program execution reaches 'Line R' in the main function the 'GCD' function is called with 'num1 = 4' and 'num2 = 14'. As (4%14) is not equal to zero the flow of the program enters the else structure and the function is recursively called with 'num1 = 14' and 'num2 = 4'. As again in this iteration (14%4) is not equal to zero the flow of program enters the else structure and the function is recursively called with 'num2 = 4' and 'num1=2' and then with 'num1 = 4' and 'num2 = 2'. During this last iteration of the function as the condition specifies the base case (4%2 == 0). The integer 'num2=2' is returned as the GCD for the two integers.

F.3 Practical Applications of Recursion

In this section we will look at some of the practical applications of recursion.

F.3.1 Tower of Hanoi

The Tower of Hanoi puzzle was invented by the French mathematician Eduard Lucas in 1883. We are given a tower of eight disks (initially four in the applet below), initially stacked in increasing size on one of three pegs. The objective is to transfer the entire tower to one of the other pegs exercising the following set of rules (fig F.2):

- Move the disks from pile 1 to pile 3 using pile 2 as a temporary holding location.
- Move one disc at a time.
- A disk may not be replaced by a smaller disks

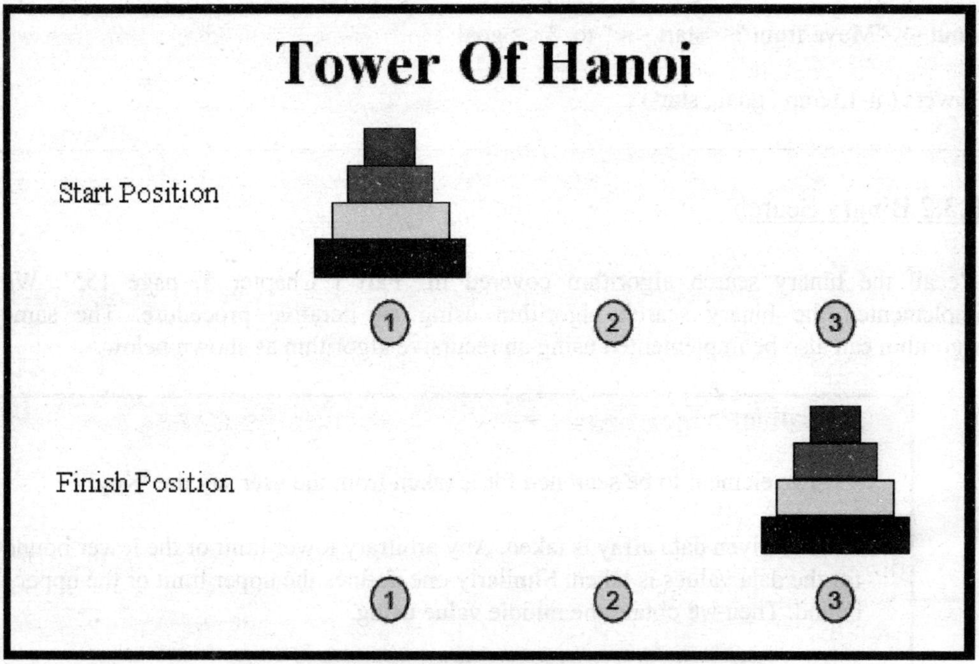

Figure F.2: Tower of Hanoi

The recursive algorithm for solving this puzzle is given below:

<u>Algorithm: Tower Of Hanoi</u>

1. Move n − 1 disks from pile 1 to pile 2, using pile 3 are temporary holding location.
2. Move 1 disk from pile 1 to pile 3.
3. Move n − 1 disks from pile 2 to pile 3, using pile 1 as temporary holding location.

Exercising this algorithm we can now develop the recursive function for doing so. The recursive function implementing this algorithm is given in program F.1.

Program F.1: Tower Of Hanoi

```
int towers (int n, int start, int goal, int temp)
{
 if ( n==0)
 return 0 ; // Base Case

 towers ( n-1, start, temp, goal );

 cout << "Move from "<<start << " to  " << goal  ;

 towers ( n-1,temp , goal , start) ;
}
```

F.3.2 Binary Search

Recall the binary search algorithm covered in 'Part I Chapter 5, page 155'. We implemented the binary search algorithm using an iterative procedure. The same algorithm can also be implemented using an recursive algorithm as shown below.

Algorithm:

- The element to be searched for is taken from the user say the 'Key'.

- The given data array is taken. Any arbitrary lower limit or the lower bound for the data values is taken. Similarly one defines the upper limit or the upper bound. Then we obtain the middle value using.

  Middle = (lower bound + upper bound)/2;

- The search 'key' is compared to the Middle value if 'Key=Middle' then the search is complete. If Key<Middle, the program continues and the search is confined to the first half only. On the other hand if Key>Middle then also the program continues and the search is confined to the latter half. This process is continued till the time 'Key = Middle'.

Program F.2 implements the algorithm given above using an recursive function.

Program F.2: Binary Search

```
int binsrch(list x[],int srch ,int left ,int right)
 {
 int mid = (left + right)/2 ;
```

```
if (x [ mid]== srch)
        return (mid) ;

         else if(x(mid)>srch && mid>left)

return binsrch (x , srch , left ,mid-1);

else if (x(mid)<srch && right>mid)

return binsrch (x , srch , mid+1 , r i g h t )

else
return UNSUCCESSFUL;
}
```


F.4 Recursion Vs Iteration

It is a popular computer science belief that any algorithm that can be coded with recursion can also be coded with an iterative control structures. Both approaches achieve the same goal, but the question arises which one is the best to use among them?

Although a recursive algorithm might be easier to understand but there are several reasons why use of recursion in curbed. Recursive algorithms are certainly less efficient than corresponding iterative algorithms. Each time a function is called, the system incurs an overhead that is not necessary with a loop. Also, in some cases it is possible the algorithm design for an iterative procedure might be simpler.

The speed and amount of memory available to modern computer today however decreases the impact of recursion so much that its inefficiency is no longer a strong argument against it. Today the choice for a recursive or an iterative algorithm is just a matter of design.

Notes

APPENDIX G

XML & C++

G.1 Overview of XML

Extended Markup Language (XML) is a subset of the Standard Generalized Markup Language (SGML), a complex standard for describing document structure and content. XML is a language for organizing - not merely presenting – data. XML is intended to be a metalanguage, i.e., a language in which you can describe another language. XML, therefore, empowers you to design your own markup.
Hyper Text Markup Language (HTML) most popular in making web pages has following limitations:

- It's only a presentation format and does not describe contents.
- HTML search engines can carry out key word searches and yield high number of irrelevant results as they do not have capacity to search based on context.
- Links are hard coded into a document when it is created.
- HTML does not permit link to an element or to multiple locations; XML does.

XML defines structure of data in an open and self describing manner facilitating transfer over a network and consistence processing by the receiver.

G.1.1 Data, Information and Knowledge

XML has potential to tag data so that it can be interchanged among applications, such as business-to-business e-commerce, directory services, financial transactions and wireless devices. The tags are context related and instantly turn data into information. Here context refers to the identity of, and relationships between a data set's entities. A set of numbers [B 75 120 R] alone may not make any sense but if we associate it with say, type, passenger capacity, maximum permissible speed and color respectively of a railway coach – it becomes information. Information, in fact is union of data and context whereas knowledge is union of information with specific issues. XML has potential to play a key role in knowledge management as it is designed to do just this, i.e., to make information self-describing.

G.1.2 XML – Syntax and Organization

XML defines both document syntax and organization. This aspect is exploited to create data markup tags, schemas (Collection of tags and data structuring rules), and document type definitions (DTDs).

Schemas and DTDs are transmitted with XML documents to identify how receiving application should interpret the tags, and developers may create style sheets to customize output.

XML uses markup tags as well, but, unlike HTML (Hyper-text markup language), XML tags describe the content, rather than the presentation of that content. By avoiding formatting tags in the data, but marking the meaning of the data itself with custom user definable tags, it is easier to search various documents for a tag and view documents tailored to the preferences of the user. The XML processor can exist on the server, the client, or both. XML is the would-be de-facto standard of the web. While HTML has been around for some time without actually giving the users any great flexibility, the advent of XML threatens to dwarf its existence. XML, as the name implies, gives you the freedom to name and define your own tags. If you have ever had a look at any HTML file, you would have seen tags like <title> </title> spread around. That's the way to write a tag, then input whatever you want to write in it and then close (using /) the tag.

For example: <title> My Home Page </title>

In HTML, you thus had a fixed number of tags like title, table, body that could be used to generate web pages. It severely undermined the potential of the World Wide Web. The entry of XML changes all that. In this new paradigm, you can define your own tags and then use them, as you want them to be used. Thus the number of tags that can be used becomes unlimited.

For example: <my_anniversary> 05/20/77 </my_anniversary>

Of course, there are several restrictions on how they have to be written and named and all that. For instance, your element name can't start with an underscore; you can't have spaces in the name, etc. Thus XML not only allows you to define your own tags, but also allows you to describe what they are. This approach is markedly different from HTML where you can only display your data but can't describe it in a nice way.

For example, if you had seen a date in an HTML document, you wouldn't have known if it were someone's birthday or someone's anniversary or whatever. You would have to go to the document and actually read the text to know anything about it. To illustrate the advantages of XML, we are presenting below a code segment in HTML and XML..

Example – G.1: A code segment in HTML and XML

HTML	XML
<Table>	<Employee>
<TR>	<EmployeeID> 1001 </EmployeeID>
<TD> Name </TD> <TD> Ankit </TD>	<DOB> 25/12/1986 </DOB>
</TR>	<Name> Ankit </Name>
<TR>	</Employee>
<TD> DOB </TD> <TD> 25/12/1986 </TD>	
</TR>	
<TR>	
<TD> EmployeeID </TD> <TD> 1001 </TD>	
</TR>	
</Table>	

G.1.3 Terminology associated with any XML document

Element: Basically the names of the tags you use.

Attribute: As the name implies, properties of the elements that you want to use. For instance, if <person> is an element in your file, his nationality can be an attribute. You state this in the following way. <person nationality="Any country"> pretty vague</person>.

DTD: This is the Document Type Definition. This is a set of rules that you specify for your elements in the XML file. Living in a practical world, you would not want your elements to go astray and accommodate everything possible. You would want to write some rules that they adhere to. All this is done in a DTD.

CSS: This is the Cascading Style Sheet. In order to display your XML file the way you want you would like to write some styles for the elements of the XML file. CSS is the file where you can specify the stylistic rules for your elements.

Well-formed document: Unlike HTML, XML is strict about nesting the tags and writing the end tag. For example, if you had a tag like <body> in your HTML document and forgot to end the content with a </body>, it is still fine. But you can't do the same thing with XML. Any tag that starts has to end. Also the nesting has to make sense.
For instance to use <city> Delhi City <state-province> Delhi </city> </state-province> would be wrong. As you can see, the nesting is not appropriate.
To say <city> Delhi City <state-province> Delhi</state-province> </city> makes more sense and is correct.
Any XML document that adheres to these rules is a well-formed document.

Valid Document: In addition to the well-formed ness, if an XML document also adheres to the rules specified in a DTD, it is supposed to be valid.

G.1.4 XML Repositories

Repositories would provide XML documents templates based on schemas for domain specific data, such as say within the financial industry. Two such repositories, which offer public access or pointers to XML schemas for application development and processing of XML data, are Microsoft's BizTalk.org and Oasis' XML.org.

G.1.5 XML Summary

Humans have successfully done business for long by exchanging standardized documents, such as, purchase orders, invoices, manifests, receipts and so on. XML was designed for document exchange, and it is becoming evident that electronic commerce will heavily rely on flow of agreements, expressed in millions of XML documents pulsing around the Internet. Thus, for its users, the XML-powered Web will be faster, friendlier and a better place to do business.

G.2 C++ and XML

C++ is a popular programming language for which many XML related efforts already exist. Several toolkits and libraries have been produced for C++ based manipulation. Those toolkits mainly fall into two categories: event-driven processors and object model construction processors.

G.2.1 Event-driven approaches

In an event-driven approach, a parser reads the XML data and notifies *specialized handlers* to carry out desired actions. In fact, an event-driven process calls specific handlers when the contents of a XML document are encountered. For instance, calling endDocument() when the end of the XML document is found.

XML parser implementations differ in their application program interfaces, e.g.,

- A parser could report to a handler of the start of an element, passing it only the name of the element and then attribute information in another call or
- A parser reports to a handler when it encounters the same start-element tag and passes it name of the element along with a list of the attributes and values of that element.
- A parser could use an STL list of strings, while another could use a specially made class to hold attributes and values.

```
virtual void HypotheticalHandler::startElementHandler
(const String name,const list<String> attributes) = 0;
//  IBM's xml4c2 parser.
virtual void DocumentHandler::startElement
(const XMLCh* const name,    AttributeList& attrs) = 0;
```

As you can see, the way processors notify applications about elements, attributes, character data, processing instructions and entities is parser-specific and can greatly influence the programming style behind the XML-related modules of your system.
SAX (the Simple API for XML) is a standard event-driven XML processing API. Microsoft C++ provides support for SAX.

G.2.2 Non SAX event-driven approaches

Expat is an XML 1.0 parser written in C by James Clark. It is event-driven, in the sense that it calls handlers as parts of the document are encountered by the parser. User-defined functions can be registered as handlers. C++ wrappers for expat Parser are available. C++ wrapper will encapsulate the C details and provide you with a clean list of methods that you can override to suit your particular needs.

G.2.3 'expatpp' Interface

The expatpp interface defines wrappers for all the methods in expat and includes the following members:

```
virtual void startElement (const XML_Char* name, const XML_Char** atts);
virtual void endElement(const XML_Char* name);
virtual void charData(const XML_Char *s, int len);
virtual void processingInstruction(const XML_Char* target, const  XML_Char* data);
virtual void defaultHandler(const XML_Char *s, int len);
```

```
virtual void unparsedEntityDecl(const XML_Char *entityName, const XML_Char*
base, const XML_Char* systemId, const XML_Char* publicId, const XML_Char*
notationName);
virtual void notationDecl(const XML_Char* notationName, const XML_Char* base,
const XML_Char* systemId, const XML_Char* publicId);
 // XML interfaces
 int XMLPARSEAPI XML_Parse
 (const char *s, int len, int isFinal);
 XML_Error XMLPARSEAPI XML_GetErrorCode();
 int XMLPARSEAPI XML_GetCurrentLineNumber();
```

This interface defines a handler base for expatpp.

Expat is under the GPL (General Public License), is very fast and very portable. But it is just plain C, so you need to find a way to integrate it with your OO C++ project.

A good option would be to wrap expat using a C++ class that will encapsulate the C details and provide you with a clean list of methods that you can override to suit your particular needs. This is how wrappers like *expatpp* work.

Expatpp is a C++ wrapper for expat. It was developed by Andy Dent with this basic idea: the constructor of expatpp creates an instance of an expat parser, and registers dummy functions as handlers that call the corresponding expatpp override-able methods.

G.2.4 DOM

The Document Object Model is a language- and platform-independent interface that allows programs and scripts to dynamically access and update the content structure and style of documents. There is a core set of interfaces that every DOM 1.0-compliant implementation must provide. Expressing a document as a structure and making it available to the application is not new: all major browsers have done so for years in their own proprietary way. The important idea behind the XML DOM is that it *standardizes* the model to use when representing any XML document in memory. DOM-based C++ parsers produce a DOM representation of the document instead of informing the application when they encounter elements, attributes etc.

The DOM, as the name implies, is an *object model* as opposed to a data model. The object-oriented interfaces define the semantics of a structural model, independently of the implementation chosen for it. That means that DOM parser implementations are free to choose whatever internal representation they like, as long as they comply with the DOM interfaces.

G.2.5 DOM Interfaces

The DOM level 1 core defines a basic set of interfaces that allow the manipulation of XML documents. It provides methods for the access and population of the document. These methods are encapsulated in two sets of interfaces: the fundamental core interfaces and the extended interfaces. For a complete description and all the methods, you will need to download a DOM library. Again, xml4c2 is a good choice because of its excellent documentation.

G.2.6 XSD

'XSD', is a cross-platform, open source W3C XML Schema to C++ translator. Given an XML instance description (XML Schema), it generates C++ classes that represent the given vocabulary as well as parsing and serialization code (collectively called a mapping or binding).

Compared to APIs such as DOM and SAX, the generated code allows you to access the information in XML instance documents using your domain vocabulary instead of generic elements, attributes, and text. Static typing helps catch errors at compile-time rather than at run-time. Automatic code generation frees you for more interesting tasks while minimizing the effort needed to adopt your applications to changes in the document structure.

XSD supports two C++ mappings: in-memory C++/Tree and event-driven C++/Parser. The C++/Tree mapping consists of C++ classes that represent data types defined in XML Schema, a set of parsing functions that convert XML instance documents to a tree-like in-memory data structure, and a set of serialization functions that convert the in-memory representation back to XML.

The C++/Parser mapping provides parser templates for data types defined in XML Schema. Using these parser templates you can build your own in-memory representations or perform immediate processing of XML instance documents. XSD features C++ standard library-based language mappings, configurable base character type (char/wchar_t), platform-independent generated code, comprehensive documentation, and more.

XSD runs on a range of platforms, including GNU/Linux, Windows, Mac OS X, and Solaris. Supported C++ compilers include GNU g++ (3.3, 3.4, 4.0), Intel C++ 8.1, Sun C++ 5.7 (Studio 10) and 5.8 (Studio 11), Microsoft Visual C++ 7.1 (Visual Studio .NET 2003) and 8 (Visual Studio 2005).

APPENDIX H

Exceptions and Exception Handling

H.1 Exceptions

Exceptions provide a way of handling "less than ideal" situations, such as

- Action your program should take if it runs out of memory when trying to dynamically allocate storage
- what should your program do if the file you're trying to open is locked or does not exist

When writing reusable code, there are times when your classes will encounter situations where they don't know what to do, and can't continue.

One trivial solution is to just terminate the program. However, if the program is controlling a chemical process in real time then this can not be a desirable solution. The ideal situation will be that your program informs that it could not continue execution for whatever reason and the application code has necessary provision to resolve this condition suitably.

Exceptions are a brilliant programmatic concept, but implementation of them in C++ language leaves lot to be done. Even ANSI C code is also somewhat lax in how programmers deal with exceptions and exception handling.

H.2 Conventional Error Handling Methods

Methods of handling errors usually involve returning an error code from every function, either through a return value, an extra reference parameter, or a global variable such as 'errno'. These methods of error reporting, however, have several limitations:

- Checking for an error condition after *every* function call practically doubles the amount of code you have to write.
- Programmer may forget to check for an error condition, or otherwise choose to ignore them.
- Propagating errors upward from function to function can become untidy because of the constraint of returning one type of error condition from a function.

H.3 Exceptions in C++

C++ provides a way to minimize these problems through the use of exceptions. You need not deal with exceptions on each function call. If you call a series of functions dealing with one aspect of a program, you need to look for the error conditions only in one location.

Suppose you have three functions A, B and C. You call a function A which calls function B which in turn calls function C, and C reports an error. If you handle the exception in A then instead of reporting error, C will return control to A if B does not handle that error type. If you do not handle an exception and ignore it, your program will terminate. You can also report different types of exceptions from a single function.

H.4 Types of Exception

You can define a separate exception handler for each of exception types. The type of an exception can be any type in C++, e.g., it can be a built-in type, such as an int or a char *, or it can be a user-defined type.

You may define a class which encapsulates the information relevant to the exception, e.g., if you had an out-of-range exception when subscripting an instance of an 'IntArray', you may want to have an exception class which encapsulates the valid range of the array as well as the index requested.

H.5 Throwing Exceptions

Reporting an exception in C++ is called 'throwing' an exception. You do this by using the throw keyword along with an object or variable you want to throw. You can throw an exception of any type. The code below can be used to throw a string exception,

```
int IntArray::operator[](int index) const
{
if (index < 0 || index >= numElements)
throw "Out of Bounds";
return this->elements[index];
}
```

Further you can also create a special 'IndexOutOfBounds' class and throw a temporary instance of it. The advantage is that you have a type specific to the nature of the exception in this case.

```
int IntArray::operator[](int index) const
{
if (index < 0 || index >= numElements) {
throw IndexOutOfBounds(index, numElements);
}
return this->elements[index];
}
```

H.6 Catching Exceptions

Catching exceptions is the C++ lingo for handling exceptions. If you don't catch an exception that has been thrown, your program will terminate. The basic control structure for exception handling in C++ is the try/catch block. A 'try/catch' block that handles 'IndexOutOfBounds' exceptions might look like this:

```
try {
// code that might throw an IndexOutOfBounds exception
} catch (IndexOutOfBounds iobe) {
// code designed to handle any exception of type IndexOutOfBounds
}
```

Any exceptions thrown within the 'try' block will be handled by a matching exception handler in the 'catch' block. You can catch different types of exceptions within one 'try/catch' block, and you can catch exceptions of any type by using an ellipsis (...) as the exception type. This is also called a catch-all handler, and is demonstrated below:

```
try {
// Call some code here...
} catch (char* str) {
// Handle character string exceptions here...
} catch (IndexOutOfBounds& boundsError) {
// Handle IndexOutOfBounds exceptions here...
} catch (...) {
// Handle all other exceptions here...
}
```

The order in which catch blocks are placed is important. The first matching Exception handler will be invoked, so if you placed the catch-all exception handler first, no other exception handler would be called.

One should never throw and catch an actual object— always use a reference, a pointer, or a built-in as the exception type. You can choose to filter out some exceptions by handling them in a particular 'try/catch' block and allowing an outer 'try/catch' block to handle the ones you don't want to handle. This can be done by re-'throw'ing the exceptions you don't want to handle from the 'catch' block.

H.7 Resource Management

Between the point where an exception is thrown and an exception is caught, all fully initialized direct objects that are local variables or parameters to functions are destroyed while the stack is unwound to the point where the exception is caught. For instance, consider the following code:

```
bool TrainList::contains(Train *f) const throw(char*)
{
Train Train;
Station *a = new Station("SFO", "San Francisco");
...
throw "Out of Bounds";
...
}
try {
if (TrainList->contains(Station))
...
} catch(char* str) {
// Handle the error
}
```

In this case, the destructor for the 'Train' object is called. However, the destructor for the 'Station' object is not, because it is not a direct object. Because of this, it is often wise to declare objects directly in the presence of exceptions.

H.8 Exception Specifications

C++ allows you to specify which exception types a function will throw, or to specify that a function will throw no exceptions at all. This specification is provided as part of a function interface. For example, we might have a function 'ReadStationsFromFile' that might throw a 'FileNotFoundException' exception. The prototype for this function would then need to be:

```
void ReadStationFromFile(const char *filename) throw (FileNotFoundException);
```

Exception specifications can have any number of exception types, or even no exception types. If we select no exception types in an exception specifier then the function will not throw any exceptions. Class methods can have exception specifications:

```
class Stack {
...
Stack(); // can throw any exception type
~Stack() throw (); // can't throw any types whatsoever
```

```
int pop(void) throw(EmptyStackException);
int peek(void) const throw (EmptyStackException);
void push(int value) throw (FullStackException, bad_alloc);
...
};
```

The exception specification must be duplicated word for word when implementing a function or method or there will be a compile-time error according to the C++ standard. The compiler won't check the transitivity of exception specifications.

For instance, the 'pop' method above can call a function that throws exceptions other than those of type 'EmptyStackException'. If you provide no exception specification, it means that the function can throw any type of exception. The compiler can't always check to see that a function doesn't throw an exception type that isn't specified, but it can catch many cases of this.

H.9 Efficiency Concerns

Throwing exceptions is costly in terms of performance. It takes minimal overhead to use 'try/catch' blocks, but the actual throwing of exceptions is very expensive. Because of this, you should only be throwing exceptions in situations where an unexpected event is occurring. Unexpected events are presumably rare enough that the performance penalty isn't what's important.

H.10 Exceptions in Constructors

It is recommended that exceptions should be thrown within constructors. This way it is known that the constructor could not do its job. However, as a constructor has no explicit return type, there is no easy way to report error conditions except using an exception.

A lot of care should be taken to make sure that a constructor never leaves an object in a half constructed state. It is generally unsafe to throw exceptions from within a copy constructor. This is because copy constructors often acquire and release resources. If an exception is thrown in the middle of the copy constructor, it could leave the copied object in an unpredictable state.

H.11 Throwing Exceptions in Destructors

Destructors should be exception-safe. This is because a destructor will be automatically called when an exception is thrown to de-allocate all objects that are on the stack between the exception throw and catch. If a destructor ends up throwing an exception, either directly or indirectly, the program will terminate. To avoid this problem, your destructor really needs to catch any exceptions that might be thrown by calls to helper methods and functions.

The lesson is that never allow an exception of any sort to be thrown from a destructor, the alternative opens up the possibility that a program with bugs simply terminates without presenting any easily identifiable source for the bug.

APPENDIX I

C++ Namespaces

I.1 Introduction

As a programmer you often face the problem that global names of some functions, variables, types, and enumerators--declared in one library clash with names found in another library or in your own application. Namespaces are a recent addition to C++, accepted in July 1993 at the Munich meeting of X3J16. Namespace is a named declarative region and resolves such problems in C++.

For example, a function name in a graphics library from a source say 'x' and a math library from other source say, 'y' can both have a method called *Circle::draw(int radius, a, b).* You are writing a program that needs to integrate classes from Library 'x' as well as library 'y', but the compiler generates an error because the two class objects have the same name. You cannot modify the class libraries because the software vendor does not provide the source code. What you have is only library of object code.

The solution to such problem is that the software vendor places each set of classes in its own namespace with its own name, which must be used to qualify the name of its members. For instance, the Circle object that is part of the graphics library might exist in a namespace entitled 'x', while the object that is part of the Maths library might exist in a namespace say, 'y'. Thus, circle function from source 'x' and 'y' can be invoked by *x_graphics::Circle::draw*, and *y_math::Circle::draw* respectively.

Even if you are using a library that predates namespaces, you can use namespaces to encapsulate names in your own code that clash with those of the library. A namespace definition is syntactically a declaration, but it may only appear at the global scope or within another namespace definition. See the declarations given below:

- Namespace definition

```
namespace identifier {
        ... List of zero or more declarations
        }
```

- Extending a namespace

```
namespace x {        // Declare 'x' as a namespace.
    int f() { ... }
    typedef int T;
    }
```

```
...
namespace y {            // Add more to namespace 'x'.
int g();
}
```

If the *namespace* identifier is not declared in the current scope, it is declared as a namespace. If it has already been declared, the definition "continues" the namespace. In this way, a namespace can be extended to allow a single large namespace to be defined over different header files.

- Use of long names for namespaces to minimize potential clashes

```
namespace Distributed_System_Object_Model_Library {
    ...
    }
```

- using a shorthand name or alias

```
namespace DSOML = Distributed_System_Object_Model_Library;
```

A namespace-aliasing definition allows you to use a shorthand name 'DSOML' instead of long name as shown above.

I.2 Using the Names

The names declared in a namespace can be denoted explicitly using the existing qualified name syntax for classes. For instance, *Colors::invert* denotes a member *invert* of namespace *Colors*.

```
namespace Colors {
        enum color {red, green, blue};
        typedef int color;
        color invert(color);
        extern color c;
        };
...
func()
        {
        Colors::color C = ...;
        Colors::invert(C);
        }
```

A *using* declaration declares a name N from a namespace as a current declaration in the scope in which the *using* declaration appears. The declaration of N is an alias of its

declaration in the namespace. For example, a *using* declaration uses a qualified name to refer to the used name.

```
func() {
        using Colors::red, Colors::green, Colors::blue;
        Colors::color a = red;
        using Colors::invert;
        a = invert(a);
        }
```

A *using* declaration can introduce a function that overloads other functions in the same scope. And just as with normal declarations, a *using* declaration can cause a duplicate declaration if a nonfunction of the same name has already been declared;

```
func() {
 extern int invert(int);
 using Colors::invert;       // invert is overloaded.
 using Other_namespace::invert;// OK if invert is a function.
 Colors::color C =...;
 invert(C);                  //1 Selects from 3 inverts.
 typedef int T;
 using Other_namespace::T;   // Error.
 }
```

Unlike normal declarations, *using* declarations can overload functions with the same argument types. The ambiguity is detected at the point of use, rather than the point of declaration. Suppose *Other_namespace::invert* had the same signature as *Colors::invert*; then for *//1 invert(C)*, an error message would result.

If ambiguity exists between two functions with identical argument types, where one function was introduced by a *using* declaration and the other by a non-*using* declaration, the non-*using* declaration is preferred over the *using* declaration.

```
extern int invert(Colors::color);
        using Colors::invert;          // invert is now overloaded.
        Colors::color C = ...;
        invert(C);
```

Comments

Function invert (C) calls the *extern int* function rather than the function introduced by // the *using* declaration and no warning is generated.

I.3 The *using* Directive

Namespace can be defined by placing a *using namespace* statement in the source file that references the namespace's member object. For example, the following statement instructs the compiler that the file uses members of the '**x**' namespace.

using namespace x;

A *using* directive is quite different from a *using* declaration. The directive imports an entire namespace at once, but not as declarations in the scope containing the directive.

A *using* directive begins with *using namespace* followed by the name denoting the namespace, e.g.

```
func() {
  using namespace Colors;
  color C = red;
 invert(C);
}
```

The names are treated as though they were declared globally, so local declarations of the same name, hide the global declarations. The local declaration *//1* hides the global; *//2* invokes *//1Other_namespace::invert*.

```
func() {
  using namespace Colors;
  using Other_namespace::invert;  //1 local declaration
  color C = red;
  invert(C);          //2 gets //1.
  }
```

Case 3: Code below introduces two Global namespace members (see //1 and //2). At *//3* there is the choice of two globally declared *invert* functions. As stated above, ambiguity between two functions with identical argument types is resolved in favor of a function that was not introduced by a *using* directive. Similarly, ambiguity that cannot be resolved via overload resolution is reported at the use of a name, not at the occurrence of the *using* directive.

```
func() {
  using namespace Colors;          //1 invert declared globally
  using namespace Other_namespace;//2 another global invert
  color C = red;
  invert(C);                      //3 chooses between 1 and 2
  }
```

Case 4: Names introduced by *using* directives are ignored when an expression uses explicit qualification. Thus, even though the names are treated as being declared globally,

a reference *::global_name*, as in code given below, does *not* refer to any names introduced by *using* directives.

```
namespace A { int g; }
using namespace A;
int g;            // OK, now we have two of them globally.
func() {
 g++;             // Ambiguous: A::glob or ::glob.
 ::g++;           // Refers to global, non-namespace glob.
 A::g++;          // Refers to namespace A's glob.
 }
```

ANSI C++ and Namespace std

All the identifiers in the ANSI standard header files are part of the \ namespace. In ANSI C++, cin and cout are written as std::cin and std::cout . If you do not wish to specify std:: with cin or cout (or any of the ANSI standard identifiers), you must write the following statement in your program:

using namespace std;

Use "using namespace std" at the top of each file, outside of any function - this will make the standard library facilities available throughout the program. However, it does make globally visible a lot of function and variable names that you're probably not going to use. For example, we use a graphics include file that defines a value RED. Unfortunately RED is also defined in the std namespace, thus causing a potential name-clash when a global "using namespace std" is used.

Program I.1

```
#include <iostream>
using namespace std;
namespace x
{
int a, b, c;
}
int main()
{
 x::a = 1;
 x::b = 2;
 x::c = 3;
cout << "The values are:\n";
cout << x::a << " " << x::b
<< " " << x::c << endl;
return 0;
}
```

Program Output

The values are:
1 2 3

Comments
In Program 1, the variables a, b, and c are defined in the scope of 'x' namespace. Each time the program accesses one of these variables, x:: must precede the variable name. Otherwise, a compiler error will occur.

I.4 Example of Name clashes

If you have a local integer with the same name as a global integer, then the local variable simply masks the global one - it's not an error. Neither is it an error to have 2 sufficiently different types of things with the same name - you can't have a string and an integer with the same name in the same function, but the following (which uses i for 2 different purposes) is legal, neither usage interfering with the other.

```
int main()
{
  class i {int j;};
  enum letter {i, j};
  letter l=i;

  return 0;
}
```

There are cases where the compiler gives an error message when it can't resolve the situation. The following program is written to illustrate some potential sources of conflict. Though it uses many i symbols it compiles on our system without error. The comments show some conflicts which would cause trouble. It might be worth trying to compile the code with and without the changes to see what your compiler says.

```
#include <iostream>
using namespace std;

namespace extra {
  int i;
}

void i(){
  // Compilation would fail were the next line "using extra::i"
  using namespace extra;

  int i; // this i masks the i in the 'extra' namespace
  i=9;
  cout << i << endl;
}
```

```
int main()
{
  enum letter { i, j};

  // Compilation would fail were the next line "class i { letter i; };"
  class i { letter j; };

  // Can you create an object called 'j' of type i by doing "i j;" ?

  // Compilation would fail were the next line "i();"
  ::i();
  return 0;
}
```

I.5 Friend and extern Declarations

Friends first declared in a class are declared in the smallest enclosing nonclass, nonfunction - prototype scope. With the addition of namespaces, this means a *friend* declaration like that in code given below can be introduced into the namespace. The same holds for an *extern* declaration first declared within a function in a namespace. Rather than being a global *extern*, the declaration is owned by the namespace.

```
namespace x {
class C {
// This is x::func.
friend func();
};
}
int x::func() { ... }
```


I.6 Unnamed Namespaces

Identifier in a namespace definition can be omitted, in which case you are then referring to that "unnamed" namespace that exists for every compilation unit e.g. 'std' in C++. The unnamed namespace is unique for that compilation unit, and a *using* directive for it is automatically assumed. The resultant effect is that you can enclose your local data in the unnamed namespace without fear of it clashing with local data in other compilation units. Code segment (i) below is equivalent to having written to (ii), as in C++ 'std' is a compiler-chosen name unique to each compilation unit.

(i)
```
namespace {
    int a, b, c;
    void f() { ... }
    }
```

(ii)
```
namespace std {
    int a, b, c;
    void f() { ... }
    }; using namespace std;
```

INDEX

SYMBOLS

-A-

-B-

-C-

-F-

-G-

H-K

O-Q

R-S

T-Z

CD's with the Book

This book contains following CD's:

1. Microsoft Visual C++ 2005 Express Edition and
2. CD entitled, 'CD accompanying Book', containing write-up on Borland C++ 5.5 and MS Visual C++ 2005, Data Structure Tutorial, source code from book and additional resources on the web.

Visual C++ 2005 Express Edition

This write-up has two aims — guide you step at a time in the installation process of Microsoft Visual C++ 2005 Express Edition and show you how to build your first program in it.

Installation of Visual C++ 2005 Express Edition

1. When you insert the CD into the drive, the installation program should run automatically. If it does not run, open 'My Computer' or 'Windows Explorer', go to the CD and double click the 'setup.exe' file to start the installation.
2. Click 'Next' button to begin the installation.
3. On the next screen you should accept the License agreement and click 'Next' button to proceed with the installation.
4. The next screen will show you the installation options.
    a. It is recommended that you install the MSDN Express Library because that will provide you the help files for the Visual C++ Express compiler.
    b. SQL Server 2005 Express Edition is a basic version of Microsoft SQL Server Database. Install it if you are going to write programs that require a database system.
5. The next screen will show you the folder where Visual C++ 2005 Express Edition will be installed. Click on 'next' button to continue. The installation will now begin and you shall see a progress indicator on the screen.

6. After the installation is finished the screen will inform you about completion of installation. Now click the 'Exit' button to come out of the setup program.

Writing your first program in Visual C++ 2005 Express Edition

Writing your first C or C++ program with Visual C++ 2005 Express Edition is very simple. This program will write Hello World on the screen using 'cout'. Here are the steps that you need to follow:

1. Start Visual C++ 2005 Express Edition by clicking on Start -> Programs -> Visual C++ 2005 Express Edition -> Microsoft Visual C++ 2005 Express Edition.
2. Click on File -> New Project. On the left hand under 'Project Types' choose 'Win32'. On the right hand choose 'Win32 Console Application'. At the bottom you should give a name to your project so type it in the 'Name' box. Click on OK.
3. The Win32 Application Wizard will come up. Click on 'Next'. Make sure you click on 'Empty Project' in the next screen and then click on 'Finish'.
4. Now Visual C++ Express is ready with your project settings and you can add programming code to it. Right click on 'Source Files' in the 'Solution Explorer' that is showing on the left and click on 'Add -> New Item'.
5. In the next screen, under 'Categories' on the left choose 'Code' and choose 'C++ File (.cpp)' on the right.
6. You need to give a name to the C++ file that you are adding to your project. So type it in the 'Name' box at the bottom and click on 'Add'. The name can be the same as the name for your project.
7. Now your C++ file will be open in the code window and you can start writing your program. Type the following code into the C++ file.

```
#include <iostream>
#include <conio.h>
using namespace std ;
void main ()
{
   cout << "Hello World\n";
    getch ();
}
```

8. Press 'F5' to compile, link and run the program. You should see the output 'Hello World' in a console screen.

It should be noted that Visual C++ Express cannot compile single .C or .CPP files. Source code files must be contained within a project. So there are 2 steps to create a program.

1. Create a project
2. Create your .C or .CPP file "inside" the project.

More information available at http://msdn.microsoft.com/vstudio/express/visualc/

Please do register your installation of Visual C++ 2005 Express Edition. Registration can be done online and it is free. To register, start Visual C++ 2005 Express Edition and click on 'Help -> Register Product'.

There are a number of benefits for a registered user and they can be seen at http://msdn.microsoft.com/vstudio/express/register/